P9-BAT-568

iPad® and iPhone®
Tips and Tricks

FIFTH EDITION

Jason R. Rich

800 East 96th Street,
Indianapolis, Indiana 46240 USA

IPAD® AND IPHONE® TIPS AND TRICKS, FIFTH EDITION

COPYRIGHT © 2016 BY PEARSON EDUCATION, INC.

All rights reserved. No part of this book shall be reproduced, stored in a retrieval system, or transmitted by any means, electronic, mechanical, photocopying, recording, or otherwise, without written permission from the publisher. No patent liability is assumed with respect to the use of the information contained herein. Although every precaution has been taken in the preparation of this book, the publisher and author assume no responsibility for errors or omissions. Nor is any liability assumed for damages resulting from the use of the information contained herein.

ISBN-13: 978-0-7897-5535-3
ISBN-10: 0-7897-5535-1

Library of Congress Control Number: 2015955046

Printed in the United States of America

First Printing: November 2015

TRADEMARKS

All terms mentioned in this book that are known to be trademarks or service marks have been appropriately capitalized. Que Publishing cannot attest to the accuracy of this information. Use of a term in this book should not be regarded as affecting the validity of any trademark or service mark.

iPad and iPhone are registered trademarks of Apple, Inc.

WARNING AND DISCLAIMER

Every effort has been made to make this book as complete and as accurate as possible, but no warranty or fitness is implied. The information provided is on an "as is" basis. The author and the publisher shall have neither liability nor responsibility to any person or entity with respect to any loss or damages arising from the information contained in this book.

SPECIAL SALES

For information about buying this title in bulk quantities, or for special sales opportunities (which may include electronic versions; custom cover designs; and content particular to your business, training goals, marketing focus, or branding interests), please contact our corporate sales department at corpsales@pearsoned.com or (800) 382-3419.

For government sales inquiries, please contact governmentsales@pearsoned.com.

For questions about sales outside the U.S., please contact international@pearsoned.com.

EDITOR-IN-CHIEF
Greg Wiegand

SENIOR ACQUISITIONS EDITOR
Laura Norman

DEVELOPMENT EDITOR
Jennifer Ackerman-Kettell

MANAGING EDITOR
Sandra Schroeder

SENIOR PROJECT EDITOR
Tonya Simpson

COPY EDITOR
Geneil Breeze

INDEXER
Valerie Perry

PROOFREADER
Nancy Davis

TECHNICAL EDITOR
Greg Kettell

EDITORIAL ASSISTANT
Cindy Teeters

COVER DESIGNER
Mark Shirar

COMPOSITOR
Jeff Lytle, Happenstance Type-O-Rama

CONTENTS AT A GLANCE

Introduction 1

1   Tips and Tricks for Customizing Settings 33

2   Using Siri, Dictation, and CarPlay to Interact with Your Mobile Device 69

3   Strategies for Finding, Buying and Using Third-Party Apps 91

4   Sync, Share, and Print Files Using AirDrop, AirPlay, AirPrint, and Handoff 113

5   Use iCloud and the iCloud Drive App from Your iPhone or iPad ... 121

6   Navigating with the Maps App 145

7   Make the Most of Online Social Networking Apps 167

8   Shoot, Edit, and Share Photos and Videos 185

9   Make and Receive Calls with an iPhone 221

10   Improve Your Health and Manage Your Wealth Using Your iPhone 247

11   Send and Receive Emails, Texts, and Instant Messages with the Mail and Messages Apps 263

12   Surf the Web More Efficiently Using Safari 303

13   Tips for Using Calendar, Contacts, Reminders, and Notes 327

14   Get Acquainted with the Music, Videos, and iTunes Store Apps ... 367

15   Customize Your Reading Experience with iBooks and the News App 401

Index 425

TABLE OF CONTENTS

Introduction 1
    How to Upgrade from iOS 8 to iOS 9 4
    Interacting with Your iPhone or iPad 6
        Touchscreen Techniques You'll Need to Master 6
        How to Make the Best Use of the Virtual Keyboard 12
        Take Advantage of the iPad's New Display Options 14
        Sometimes an Optional External Keyboard or Stylus Works Better 17
    How to Turn the iPhone or iPad on or Off, Versus Placing It
        Into Sleep Mode 18
    Discover What's New In iOS 9 20
        Apple Pay Offers a New Way to Pay for Things 25
        Securing Your iOS Mobile Device with a Passcode 27
        Find Your Lost or Stolen Device Using the
            Find My iPhone/iPad Feature 28
        Maintain a Backup of Your Device 29
    What This Book Offers 31
    Attention, Please… 32

1 Tips and Tricks for Customizing Settings 33
    Using the Settings App 35
        Main Options Available from the Settings App 36
    Control Center Gives You Quick Access to Popular
        Features and Functions 60
    Organize Apps on Your Home Screen with Folders 62
        Moving App Icons Around on the Home Screen 64
    Discover What's Possible from the Lock Screen 65
    Manage Your Customized Notification Center Screen 66

2 Using Siri, Dictation, and Carplay to Interact with
    Your Mobile Device 69
    What You Should Know Before Using Siri 70
    Customizing Siri 71
    Ways to Activate Siri 73
    Discover How Siri Can Help You 74
        Find, Display, or Use Information Related to Your Contacts ... 76
        Initiate a Call 77
        Set Up Reminders and To-Do Items 78
        Read or Send Text Messages 79

Check the Weather or Your Investments..79

Find Information on the Web or Get Answers to Questions 80

Schedule and Manage Meetings and Events....................................81

Send Email and Access New (Incoming) Email................................82

Set an Alarm or Timer..82

Get Directions Using the Maps App...82

Control the Music App..83

Forget Sticky Notes—Dictate Notes to Yourself.............................84

Siri Knows All About Sports, Movies, Entertainment,
    and Restaurants, Too 84

Practice (with Siri) Makes Perfect...87

Use Dictation Mode Instead of the Virtual Keyboard...........................88

Connect or Link Your iPhone to Your Car to Use the Carplay Feature.....89

3   Strategies for Finding, Buying, and Using Third-Party Apps 91

App Store Basics..92

How New Apps Install themselves...92

Restoring or Reinstalling Apps You've Already Downloaded...........93

Where to Find Apps, Music, and More...94

Everything You Need to Know About Apps...95

Compatibility: Does the App Run on Multiple Devices?...................95

Quick Guide to App Pricing...97

How to Shop with the App Store App 101

Quick Tips for Finding Apps Relevant to You.......................................108

Keep Your Apps Up to Date with the Latest Versions 109

Manage Your Kids' App Acquisitions 110

**4   Sync, Share, and Print Files Using Airdrop, Airplay,
    Airprint, and Handoff...113**

Stream Content from Your iPhone or iPad to Other
    Compatible Devices Using Airplay..116

Print Files Wirelessly Using an AirPrint-Compatible Printer 117

Continue a Task on One Device Exactly Where You
    Left Off on Another Using Handoff...118

5   Use iCloud and the iCloud Drive App from Your iPhone or iPad....121

Content Saved to iCloud Is Available Anywhere....................................124

Access Your Purchased Itunes Store Content from Any Device..........126

Use iCloud to Sync Your App-Specific Data, Documents, and Files....128

Customizing iCloud to Work with Your Apps...................................130

Access Your App-Specific Data Online from iCloud.com 132

Automatically Transfer Documents Using iCloud 134

Create a Photo Library Using iCloud 134

Using a Unique Apple ID for iCloud 136

Backing Up with iCloud 136

Family Sharing Allows for the Sharing of Purchased Content 138

Using the New iCloud Drive App on Your Mobile Device 140

iCloud: Many Uses, One Storage Space 144

6 Navigating with the Maps App 145

Get the Most from Using the Maps App's Features 147

Overview of the Maps App's Screen 149

View a Map from Multiple Perspectives 152

The Maps App's Info Screen 152

Obtain Turn-By-Turn Directions Between Two Locations 155

Look Up Contact Entries, Businesses, Restaurants, Landmarks, and Points
of Interest 159

Use the Interactive Location Screens to Find More Information 161

The Maps App's Flyover View 163

Navigate a City's Public Transportation System 163

7 Make the Most of Online Social Networking Apps 167

Facebook, Twitter, Flickr, and Vimeo Integration Is Built In to iOS 9 ... 169

Manage Your Facebook Account Using the Official Facebook App 171

Participate In Chats Using the Facebook Messenger App 175

Read Your News Feed Using the Facebook App 177

Manage Your Twitter Account(s) Using the Official Twitter App 178

Discover the Official Apps for Other Popular
Online Social Networking Services 180

The YouTube App 180

The Instagram App 182

8 Shoot, Edit, and Share Photos and Videos 185

Some Camera App Features Are Available Only on
Certain iPhone and iPad Models 186

The Camera and Photos Apps Are Chock Full of Features 186

Methods for Loading Digital Images into Your iPhone or iPad 187

Use the Camera App to Take Photos or Shoot Video 189
   Ways to Launch the Camera App 189
   How to Shoot Photos or Video with the Camera App 190
   Take Advantage of the Autofocus and Exposure Control Options 197
How to Snap a Photo 197
How to Shoot a Panoramic Photo 200
How to Shoot HD Video 201
Using the Photos App to View, Edit, Enhance, Print, and
   Share Photos and Videos 204
View an Image in Full-Screen Mode 204
Editing Videos 206
Tools for Editing Photos 208
   Enhance 208
   Crop 208
   Filters 209
   Adjust 209
Printing Photos 212
Third-Party Apps for Ordering Prints from Your Images 213
Sharing Photos and Videos 213
   Deleting Photos Stored on Your iOS Device 218
Take Advantage of iCloud Photo Library 218
   The Photos App Supports iCloud's Family Sharing 219
Move Images Between Albums 219

9 Make and Receive Calls with an iPhone 221
Answering an Incoming Call 223
Use the Handoff Feature to Answer Incoming iPhone
   Calls on Your iPad or Mac 227
Managing the Do Not Disturb Feature 228
Manage Calls in Progress from the Call in Progress Screen 230
Respond to a Call Waiting Signal While on the Phone 233
Making Calls from Your iPhone 234
   Manual Dialing 235
Dialing from a Contacts Entry in the Phone App 236
Reestablish Contact from the Spotlight Search Screen's Recents Listing 236
Use the Call Over Wi-Fi Calling Feature 236

Managing Your Voicemail 237
    Record Your Outgoing Message 237
    How to Play and Delete Voicemail Messages 238
Create and Use a Favorites List 240
Accessing Your Recents Call Log 241
Do You Talk Too Much? Keeping Track of Usage 242
Customizing Ringtones 243
    Custom Ringtones for Specific Contacts 243
More Information about Bluetooth Wireless Headsets 245

10 Improve Your Health and Manage Your Wealth
    Using Your iPhone 247
Discover the iPhone-Specific Health App 248
    Start Using the Health App Right Away 249
    Every iPhone User Should Utilize the Health App's
      Medical ID Feature 251
Manage Apple Pay and More Using the Wallet App 252
    Set Up and Use Apple Pay from Your iPhone 253
    Adding Debit/Credit Card Details to the Wallet App 255
    Use the Wallet App to Manage Reward Cards,
      Membership Cards, and More 260

11 Send and Receive Emails, Texts, and Instant Messages
    with the Mail and Messages Apps 263
How to Add Email Accounts to the Mail App 264
How to Customize Mail Options from Settings 267
Tips for Viewing Your Incoming Email 272
Composing an Email Message 273
    Insert a Photo or Video Into Your Outgoing Email 278
    Insert an Attachment within an Email 278
Using Select, Select All, Cut, Copy, and Paste 279
How to Save an Unsent Draft of an Email Message 280
Tips for Reading Email 281
    The Mail App's Inbox 283
Communicate Effectively with the Messages App 289
Get Started Using the Messages App with Apple's iMessage Service ...291
    Set Up a Free iMessage Account 291
    Some Benefits to Using iMessage 292

Tips and Tricks for Using the Messages App..293
    Create and Send a Text Message..293
    Record and Send an Audio Message..294
    Record and Send a Video Message..296
    Participating in a Text-Message Conversation................................297
    Responding to an Incoming Message..299
    Relaunch or Review Past Conversations..299
    Participating in a Group Conversation..300
    Share More Information from the Details Screen
        During a Conversation Via the Messages App................................300
    Customize the Messages App..301

12 Surf the Web More Efficiently Using Safari..303
    Customize Your Web Surfing Experience..305
    How to Use Tabbed Browsing with Safari..310
        Switching Between Web Pages on an iPhone................................310
        Tabbed Browsing on the iPad..312
    Remove Screen Clutter with Safari's Reader Option................................314
    Create and Manage Reading Lists..316
        Working with Bookmarks..318
    Options for Sharing Web Content in Safari..318
    Create, Manage, and Sync Safari Bookmarks..324
        Sync Usernames and Passwords Using iCloud Keychain................324
    Launch Your Favorite Websites Quickly with Home Screen Icons................326

13 Tips for Using Calendar, Contacts, Reminders, and Notes................327
    Sync App-Specific Data with Online-Based Apps................................328
    Sync App-Specific Data with iCloud..329
    Get Acquainted with the Calendar App..329
        Controlling the Calendar View..330
        How to Enter a New Event into the Calendar App................335
        Use Siri to Enter New Events into the Calendar App................338
        Viewing Individual Appointment Details................................339
        How to Delete an Event from the Calendar App................340
        Quickly Find Appointment or Event Details................................340
        Customizing the Calendar App..340
    Use the Contacts App to Keep Track of People You Know................341
        You Determine What Information You Add to Each Contact Entry................342
        The Contacts App Works Seamlessly with Other Apps................343
        How to View Your Contacts..344

How to Create a New Contacts Entry..................346
How to Add a Photo to a Contacts Entry..................348
Editing or Deleting a Contact..................349
Sharing Contact Entries..................349

Create and Manage Lists with the Reminders App..................350
Stay Up to Date with Reminders..................352
How to Delete an Entire To-Do List..................355

Take Notes or Gather Information Using the Newly Redesigned
Notes App..................355
Create and Manage Notes App Folders..................357
How to Create Individual Notes..................359
Moving Notes Between Folders..................361
Create Interactive Checklists within Notes..................362
Using the Drawing Tools in the Notes App..................362

Sharing Notes..................365

14 Get Acquainted with the Music, Videos, and iTunes Store Apps..................367
Get Started Using the Music App..................369
Discover the New Apple Music Service..................370
Using the Music App: A Quick Tutorial..................370
Managing Your Music Via the Music App..................376
How to Create Custom Playlists Using the Music App..................380
Control the Music App from Control Center..................385

Streaming Music Via the Internet..................387

Use the Videos App to Watch TV Shows, Movies, and More..................388

Use the iTunes Store App to Acquire New Music, TV Shows,
Movies, and More..................395
Quickly Find TV Episodes You Want to Purchase on iTunes..................398

Stream Video Content Instead of Purchasing and Downloading It..................399

15 Customize Your Reading Experience with
iBooks and the News App..................401
Customize Your eBook Reading Experience..................402

Customize iBooks Settings..................403

Organize Your Personal eBook Library..................404

Navigating Around the iBooks App..................406

Learn More About Specific eBooks While Visiting iBook Store..................410
How to Find a Specific eBook—Fast..................410
Learn About an eBook from Its Description..................411
Purchasing an eBook..................412

Customize Your eBook Reading Experience Using iBooks 412
    Tools You Can Use While Reading 415
Alternative Methods for Reading Your eBooks 416
Discover the New News App 417
    Get Started By Customizing the News App 418
    Navigating Around the News App 418
    Read Articles that Cater to Your Interests 420
    How to Expand Your Personalized Collection of
    Sources and Content Providers 421
Some Final Thoughts 423

Index 425

ABOUT THE AUTHOR

Jason R. Rich (www.JasonRich.com) is the best-selling author of more than 55 books, as well as a frequent contributor to a handful of major daily newspapers, national magazines, and popular websites. He also is an accomplished photographer and avid Apple iPhone, iPad, Apple TV, Apple Watch, and Mac user.

Jason R. Rich is the author of the books *Your iPad at Work*, Fourth Edition; *Apple Watch and iPhone Fitness Tips and Tricks*; *My Digital Photography for Seniors*; *My GoPro Hero Camera*; *and My Digital Entertainment for Seniors*, all published by Que Publishing.

An ongoing series of feature-length how-to articles by Jason R. Rich, covering the Apple iPhone and iPad, can be read for free online at the Que Publishing website. Visit www.iOSArticles.com and click on the Articles tab. Additionally, more than 40 free how-to videos by Jason R. Rich can be found on Que's YouTube channel (www.youtube.com/QuePublishing).

Please follow Jason on Twitter and Instagram (@JasonRich7).

DEDICATION

I am honored to dedicate this book to Steve Jobs (1955–2011), a true visionary, entrepreneur, and pioneer who forever changed the world, and to Tim Cook, who is now expertly reigning over the Apple empire. This book is also dedicated to my wonderful niece, Natalie, and my nephew Parker Graham Riley Skehan.

ACKNOWLEDGMENTS

Thanks once again to Laura Norman at Que Publishing for inviting me to work on all five editions of this book, and for all of her guidance as I've worked on this project. My gratitude also goes out to Greg Wiegand, Todd Brakke, Kristen Watterson, Tonya Simpson, Cindy Teeters, Jennifer Ackerman-Kettell, Greg Kettell, and Paul Boger, as well as everyone else at Que Publishing/Pearson who contributed their expertise, hard work, and creativity to the creation of this all-new edition of *iPad and iPhone Tips and Tricks*.

Finally, thanks to you, the reader. I hope this book helps you fully utilize your iOS mobile device in every aspect of your life and take full advantage of the power and functionality your iPhone and/or iPad offers.

WE WANT TO HEAR FROM YOU!

As the reader of this book, *you* are our most important critic and commentator. We value your opinion and want to know what we're doing right, what we could do better, what areas you'd like to see us publish in, and any other words of wisdom you're willing to pass our way.

We welcome your comments. You can email or write to let us know what you did or didn't like about this book—as well as what we can do to make our books better.

Please note that we cannot help you with technical problems related to the topic of this book.

When you write, please be sure to include this book's title and author as well as your name and email address. We will carefully review your comments and share them with the author and editors who worked on the book.

Email: feedback@quepublishing.com

Mail: Que Publishing
              ATTN: Reader Feedback
              800 East 96th Street
              Indianapolis, IN 46240 USA

READER SERVICES

Visit our website and register this book at quepublishing.com/register for convenient access to any updates, downloads, or errata that might be available for this book.

Introduction

Late 2015 and 2016 is an exciting time for Apple mobile device users! Not only does iOS 9 provide some really useful new features, functions, and bundled apps, as well as improved integration with iCloud, but from a technological standpoint, the newest iPhone and iPad models are extraordinary in terms of their capabilities.

This all-new, fifth edition of *iPad and iPhone Tips and Tricks* quickly gets you up to speed on using iOS 9, as you discover all that this operating system has to offer, while at the same time acclimating you to the newest functions of your iPhone 6s, iPhone 6s Plus, iPad mini 4, iPad Air 2, or iPad Pro.

However, if you haven't yet upgraded to one of these new devices, you can still take full advantage of what iOS 9 has to offer, as long as you're using a compatible iPhone or iPad model released within the past few years.

> **NOTE** The iOS 9 operating system is compatible with the iPhone 4s, iPhone 5, iPhone 5c, iPhone 5s, iPhone 6, iPhone 6 Plus, iPhone 6s, iPhone 6s Plus, as well as the iPad 2, iPad 3rd Generation, iPad 4th Generation, iPad Air, iPad Air 2, iPad Pro, iPad mini, iPad mini 2, iPad mini 3, and iPad mini 4, plus the iPod touch (5th and 6th generations).
>
> Keep in mind that although iOS 9 runs on these devices, not all of the new features and functions are compatible with all iPhone and iPad models.

> **TIP** If you purchased a new iPhone, iPad, or iPod touch after September 2015, iOS 9 came preinstalled on your mobile device, but you might still need to upgrade to a more recent version of iOS 9 (such as iOS 9.1 or later).

For those who are new to using an iPhone or iPad and have recently migrated from another smartphone or tablet (such as an Android device), this edition of *iPad and iPhone Tips and Tricks* teaches you what you need to know to become proficient using iOS 9 on your new iPhone or iPad. One example is Apple's new Move to iOS app for Android, which helps you easily transfer all your important data from your old Android smartphone or tablet to your new iOS mobile device.

Once again, with the introduction of iOS 9, Apple has implemented hundreds of new features and functions. For example, if you're an iPad user, the new Slide Over, Split View, and Picture in Picture features enable you to simultaneously display two apps and do two things at once on your compatible tablet, such as the iPad Air 2, iPad mini 4, or iPad Pro.

Meanwhile, among many other things, iOS 9 provides iPhones and iPads with better multitasking and an improved Spotlight Search feature. Plus, for iPhone 6s and iPhone 6s Plus users, there's 3D Touch—a touchscreen technology that introduces the new Peek and Pop gestures—offering more efficient ways to interact with your smartphone or tablet.

Not only has iOS 9 introduced awesome improvements to the operating system itself, but many of the core apps that come preinstalled with iOS 9—like Contacts, Calendar, Reminders, Notes, Safari, Mail, Messages, Maps, and so on—have some impressive and useful new features. Plus, you'll discover how to use the new apps that come bundled with iOS 9, like News, Wallet (iPhone), and iCloud Drive.

Of course, features introduced last year with iOS 8 continue to be improved upon. For example, using the Continuity and Handoff features, you can begin using one application on your iPhone and then pick up exactly where you left off on your iPad or Mac (or vice versa). In addition, it's possible to answer incoming calls made to your iPhone from your iPad, Apple Watch, or Mac, as long as your smartphone is nearby and wirelessly linked with your other computers and devices.

NOTE Throughout this book, an "iOS mobile device" refers to any Apple iPhone, iPad, or Apple mobile device that's running the iOS 9 operating system. If you plan to continue using iOS 8 with your iOS mobile device, pick up a copy of *iPad and iPhone Tips and Tricks*, Fourth Edition, which focuses on the older version of Apple's mobile device operating system.

If you're a veteran iPhone or iPad user, when you upgrade from iOS 8 to iOS 9, you'll discover that the graphical interface is pretty similar to what you're already accustomed to, although improvements have been made.

As for you first-time iPhone or iPad users, congratulations! Now is the perfect time to introduce yourself to these mobile devices, or switch from another smartphone or tablet to what Apple has to offer. Not only can you expect an exciting experience as you begin using your new iPhone or iPad hardware that's running the iOS 9 operating system, but you have the opportunity to access the App Store to utilize any of the more than 1.5 million third-party apps that can greatly expand the capabilities of these mobile devices.

WHAT'S NEW Thanks to the new Wallet app for the iPhone, it's even easier, faster, and more secure to utilize Apple Pay to pay for purchases at participating retail stores and restaurants, as well as online from within apps.

This past year, not only have hundreds of new banks and credit unions begun supporting Apple Pay, but thousands of additional merchants now accept it. In fact, you probably have seen the Apple Pay logo displayed near the checkout counter at many of your favorite retail stores, and these sightings will become even more frequent in 2016 and beyond.

To view a list of Apple Pay participating banks in the United States and United Kingdom, visit https://support.apple.com/en-us/HT204916.

In addition, Apple Pay now supports the Discover credit card, as well as store credit cards from participating merchants, and the new Wallet app can also be used to manage retail store reward cards, so when you adopt the Wallet app into your life, you can dramatically slim down your traditional wallet.

In a nutshell, iOS 9 is now really good at combining the technological capabilities of the iPhone or iPad with apps and the Internet to put a vast amount of personalized information at your fingertips, exactly when and where you need it. This includes content such as breaking news stories, your personal schedule, important emails, incoming text/instant messages, as well as your personal financial information from your bank(s) and credit card issuers.

Plus, these mobile devices make it more efficient to stay in contact with people via phone calls, video calls, emails, text/instant messages, and/or social media.

HOW TO UPGRADE FROM iOS 8 TO iOS 9

Anyone who purchased an iPhone, iPad, or iPod touch before September 16, 2015, needs to upgrade to iOS 9. The easiest way to do this is to use your mobile device to access any Wi-Fi hotspot or wireless home network to establish a high-speed Internet connection. Then, from the device's Home screen, launch Settings.

> **TIP** Before upgrading your iOS mobile device from iOS 7 or iOS 8 to iOS 9, be sure to create a backup of your iPhone or iPad using the iTunes Sync Backup feature or the iCloud Backup feature. After you install the iOS 9 operating system, all your apps, data, and personalized device settings will automatically be fully restored.

Next, tap on the General option from the main Settings menu, and then tap on the Software Update option (shown in Figure I.1). If your device is running iOS 8, for example, a message appears indicating that an operating system upgrade is available (shown in Figure I.2). Follow the onscreen prompts to download and install iOS 9 (or later) for free.

The upgrade process takes between 20 and 30 minutes, depending on which iPhone or iPad model you're using, its internal storage capacity, the Internet connection speed, and how much information is currently stored on your device.

> **TIP** Every few months, Apple updates the iOS to add new features to your iPhone or iPad. When a free iOS update is available, a message appears on your device's screen, and a Badge icon appears in the Settings app icon on your Home screen. iOS updates typically add new features and functions, fix bugs, and improve device performance. Thus, it's a good strategy to ensure your devices are running the most current version of iOS, and if you use both an iPhone and iPad, that they both have the same version of iOS installed.

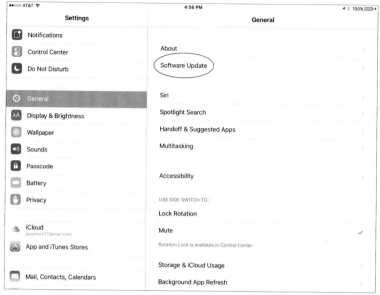

Figure I.1

The easiest way to upgrade your iPhone or iPad from iOS 8 to iOS 9 is to use Wi-Fi and access the Software Update option from within Settings.

Figure I.2

If an operating system update is available, a message like this one is displayed.

INTERACTING WITH YOUR iPHONE OR iPAD

If you're a veteran iPhone or iPad user, you already know that Apple's iOS mobile operating system enables you to interact with your mobile device using its touchscreen. Data entry, for example, is typically done using the virtual keyboard that is displayed on screen when it's needed. Based on the type of information you're entering and the app you're using, the keyboard's layout adapts automatically.

WHAT'S NEW In addition to interacting with your iOS mobile device using the touchscreen, the capabilities of Siri have been improved with iOS 9, allowing you to better control your iPhone or iPad, and your favorite apps, using voice commands.

Plus, as you'll soon discover, the Spotlight Search feature built in to iOS 9 has been dramatically improved, so it's now faster and easier to find information stored in your mobile device and simultaneously retrieve information from the Internet, when applicable.

When not using the virtual keyboard, much of your interaction with the iPhone or iPad is done using a series of taps, swipes, and other finger gestures on the Multi-Touch display. iPhone 6s, iPhone 6s Plus, as well as iPad Air 2, iPad mini 4, and iPad Pro users need to learn a few new gestures to take advantage of new features, such as 3D Touch (iPhone) and Split-Screen (iPad), which are explained shortly.

WHAT'S NEW iPad Pro users have the opportunity to interact with their tablet using an optional pen-shaped stylus device, called Apple Pencil, which enables users to write or draw directly on the tablet's screen with extreme accuracy.

TOUCHSCREEN TECHNIQUES YOU'LL NEED TO MASTER

To navigate your way around iOS 9 on your iPhone or iPad, you need to learn a series of basic taps and finger gestures.

iOS 9 **WHAT'S NEW** The iPhone 6s and iPhone 6s Plus offer the new 3D Touch feature, which introduces two new touchscreen gestures called Peek and Pop.

When using certain apps, if you press and hold your finger firmly on an item, you can get a quick glimpse of what tapping or holding down your finger would reveal. Then, if you want to access that content, press a bit harder on the screen to "pop" into it.

For example, if you're using the Mail app and looking at your Inbox, which displays a listing of incoming messages, you can gently hold your finger on a message to preview it ("peek"), and then if you want to open the message and work with it, press your finger down a bit harder to "pop" it open.

This also works on the Home screen. Many apps offer quick access to the most common features of the app by pressing firmly on its icon. For example, if you hold your finger on the Camera app icon, a menu that enables you to quickly take a selfie, record a video, record a slow-mo video, or take a photo (shown in Figure I.3) is displayed.

Figure I.3

The new Peek feature on the iPhone 6s. This new menu appears when you press and hold your finger on the Home screen's Camera app icon.

As you learn more about iOS 9's new features throughout this book, you'll also discover how to best utilize them by executing the necessary taps, swipes, pinches, and other finger gestures.

As in previous editions of the iOS, when you turn on the device or wake it up from Sleep mode, virtually all of your interaction with the smartphone or tablet is done though the following finger movements and taps on the device's highly sensitive multitouch display:

- **Tap**—Tapping an icon, button, or link that's displayed on your device's screen serves the same purpose as clicking the mouse when you use your main computer.

- **Hold**—Instead of a quick tap, in some cases it is necessary to press and hold your finger on an icon or onscreen command option. When a hold action is required, place your finger on the appropriate icon or command option, and hold it there with a slight pressure. There's never a need to press down hard on the smartphone or tablet's screen. (Hold works with all iOS mobile devices running iOS 9, and is different from the Peek and Pop gestures that are exclusive to the iPhone 6s and iPhone 6s Plus.)

- **Swipe**—A swipe refers to quickly moving your finger along the screen from right to left, left to right, top to bottom, or bottom to top, in order to scroll left, right, up, or down, depending on which app you're using.

- **Pinch**—Using your thumb and index finger, perform a pinch motion on the touchscreen to zoom out when using certain apps. Or "unpinch" (by moving your fingers apart quickly) to zoom in on what you're viewing on screen when using many apps.

> **TIP** Another way to zoom in or out when looking at the device's screen is to double-tap the area of the screen on which you want to zoom in. This works when you're surfing the Web in Safari or looking at photos using the Photos app, as well as in most other apps that support the zoom in/out feature. To zoom out again, double-tap the screen a second time.

- **Pull-down**—Using your finger, swipe it from the very top of the iPhone or iPad's screen quickly in a downward direction. This causes the Notification Center window to appear. You can hold the device in portrait or landscape mode for this to work. As you'll discover in Chapter 1, "Tips and Tricks for Customizing Settings," the functionality of Notification Center and the information you can access from it has been enhanced in iOS 9 and is more customizable than before.

☑ **TIP** The pull-down gesture is also used to access iOS 9's enhanced Spotlight Search feature. Use a pull-down gesture that starts in the *middle* of the iPhone or iPad's Home screen to access the improved Spotlight Search feature.

One use of Spotlight Search is to quickly find any information that's stored in your mobile device, such as a Contacts entry, Calendar event, or content in an email message. Enter a keyword or search phrase into the Search field that appears, tap on the Search key on the virtual keyword, and then tap on one of the search result listings to access the related data or content by automatically launching which- ever app it relates to.

On the iPhone, the Spotlight Search screen also showcases icons representing the last few apps you've used, or apps it thinks you might want to use next.

When your iPhone or iPad has Internet access, Spotlight Search utilizes online- based resources automatically to give you access to additional information, includ- ing relevant suggested websites, movie show times, local restaurants, and other content based on what you're searching for (shown in Figure I.4).

To view a more detailed Spotlight Search screen, from the Home screen, swipe your finger horizontally from left to right. Doing this displays the Search field, plus icons representing the last few people you've communicated with; icons repre- senting the last few apps you've used; icons that allow you to seek out nearby businesses, restaurants, and services; as well as a listing of breaking news head- lines. Any of these icons or listings are interactive, so you can tap them.

- **Swipe up**—From the bottom of the iPhone or iPad's screen at any time, swipe your finger in an upward direction to make the Control Center appear. From here, you can access a handful of functions, such as Airplane Mode, Wi-Fi, Bluetooth, the Do Not Disturb feature, and the Screen Rotation Lock, as well as screen brightness controls and Music app controls. You can also utilize AirDrop and AirPlay/Bluetooth functions, and access commonly used core apps, such as Clock, Calculator, and Camera. On the iPhone, you can quickly turn on/off the Flashlight function. How to use Control Center is also covered in Chapter 2, "Using Siri, Dictation, and CarPlay to Interact with Your Mobile Device."

- **Five-finger pinch (iPad only)**—To exit out of any app and return to the Home screen, place all five fingers of one hand on the screen so that they're spread out, and then draw your fingers together, as if you're grabbing some- thing. Be sure, however, that the Multitasking Gestures are turned on in the Settings app (found under the General heading).

Figure I.4
From Spotlight Search, you can look up local dining options. Here, "Mexican Food" was entered into the Search field.

What's New For iPad users, iOS 9 introduces a new two-finger gesture. It allows you to more accurately move the cursor around on the screen (in some apps), which is useful when editing text or highlighting text to select, copy, cut, and then paste, for example.

To move the cursor on the screen, place two fingers next to each other over the cursor or text you want to highlight, and drag your fingers slowly around on the screen. The onscreen cursor follows your movement.

TIP Return to the Home screen anytime by pressing the Home button once, regardless of which app is being used. The Home button is the circular button located on the front (bottom center) of the device (below the screen) on the iPhone or iPad.

■ **Multi-finger horizontal swipe (iPad only)**—When multiple apps are simultaneously running, swipe several fingers from left to right or from right to left on the screen to switch between the active app and the other apps that are currently running in the background (using the app switcher). Alternatively, iPad and iPhone users alike can access the app switcher to quickly switch between apps by quickly pressing the Home button twice.

> **TIP** Apple continues to make navigating around your favorite apps with taps, finger gestures, and swipes easy. For example, on any screen where you're scrolling downward, such as when you're surfing the Web with Safari, you can simply tap on the time that's displayed at the top center of the screen to quickly return to the top of the page or screen.
>
> Meanwhile, if you're in the process of typing something on your iPhone and don't like what you typed, instead of pressing and holding the Delete key to delete your text, simply shake the smartphone in your hand for a second or two to "undo" your typing. Be sure to turn on this Shake to Undo feature by launching Settings and tapping Accessibility.

> **TIP** You can also easily interact with the iPhone using just one hand.
>
> When using the iPhone 6/6s/6 Plus/6s Plus, double touch (use a gentle tap, as opposed to pressing) the Home button, and everything that's displayed on the screen shifts downward, so you can more easily reach it with your thumb. Plus, as you're reading emails, you can use your thumb (on the hand you're holding the iPhone with) to swipe left or right across an Inbox message listing to manage that incoming message.

HOME BUTTON QUICK TIPS

Here's how to use some of the Home button's main functions when using iOS 9:

■ **Activate Siri**—Press down and hold the Home button for 2 seconds from the Home screen or when using any app.

■ **Access the app switcher**—From any app (or from the Home screen), quickly press the Home button twice. Press the Home button again (or select an app) to exit the app switcher.

■ **Exit an app and return to the Home screen**—When using any app, press the Home button once to exit it and return to the Home screen. Keep in mind, in most cases this does not shut down the app; it will continue running in the background.

- **Reboot the device (without deleting any of your apps or data)**—Press and hold the Home button simultaneously with the Sleep/Wake button for about 5 seconds, until the Apple logo appears on the screen. The Sleep/Wake button is located on the right side (near the top) of newer iPhones, and on the top-right corner of older iPhones and all iPads.

- **Return to the main Home screen**—When viewing any of the Home screens on your mobile device, press the Home button once to return to the main Home screen.

- **Wake up the device from Sleep mode**—Press the Home button once when your iPhone or iPad is in Sleep mode. If the device is powered down, press and hold the Sleep/Wake button for several seconds instead.

Use the Touch ID that's built in to the Home button (available in the more recently released iOS mobile devices) to unlock the device or confirm a payment using Apple Pay, or when making a content purchase from the App Store, iTunes Store, iBook Store, or within a participating app. Touch ID can also be used to grant you access to certain apps that otherwise require a password, such as a banking or credit card app.

HOW TO MAKE THE BEST USE OF THE VIRTUAL KEYBOARD

Whenever you need to enter data into your iPhone or iPad, you almost always use the virtual keyboard that pops up on the bottom portion of the screen when it's needed. The virtual keyboard typically resembles a typewriter or computer keyboard; however, certain onscreen keys have different purposes, depending on which app you're using.

For example, when you access the Spotlight Search screen (refer to Figure I.4), you will notice the large Search key on the right side of the keyboard. However, when you use the Microsoft Word app, the Search key becomes the Return key. When you surf the Web using Safari, the Search key becomes the Go key in certain situations, and other keys along the bottom row of the virtual keyboard change as well.

When you're using an app that involves numeric data entry, such as Numbers or Excel, the layout and design of the virtual keyboard can change dramatically.

VIRTUAL KEYBOARD QUICK TIPS

Use these tips to more easily work with the virtual keyboard on your iPhone or iPad:

- **Divide the virtual keyboard in half (iPad, iPad Pro, and iPad mini only)**—Make it easier to type on the virtual keyboard with your two thumbs while holding the device. To split the keyboard, hold down the Hide Keyboard key, located in the lower-right corner of the virtual keyboard, and select the Split option. Alternatively, use the index fingers on your right and left hand simultaneously, place them in the center of the virtual keyboard when it's visible, and then move them apart.

- **Unlock and move the virtual keyboard upward (iPad, iPad Pro, and iPad mini only)**—Hold down the Hide Keyboard key (displayed in the lower-right corner of the keyboard). You'll be given the opportunity to split or merge the keyboard, as well as unlock the keyboard.

- **Turn on/off the keyboard's key click sound**—Launch Settings, tap on the Sounds option, and then from the Sounds menu, scroll down and turn on or off the virtual switch associated with Keyboard Clicks.

- **Adjust auto-capitalization, autocorrection, check spelling, enable caps lock, predictive, split keyboard (iPad only), and the keyboard shortcuts options**—Launch Settings, tap on the General option, and then tap on the Keyboard option to access the Keyboard menu. Turn on or off the virtual switch associated with each option.

- **Access alternative keys within the virtual keyboard**—When you press and hold down certain keys, it's possible to access alternative letters, characters or symbols. For example, this works when you press and hold down the A, C, E, I, N, O, U, S, Y, or Z keys. When using Safari, press and hold down the period (".") for a second or two to access the .us, .org, .edu, .net, and .com extensions.

> **TIP** When using the virtual keyboard, to turn on Caps Lock, quickly double tap the Shift key (it displays an upward-pointing arrow). Tap the key again to turn off Caps Lock as you're typing or doing data entry.

- **Make the virtual keyboard disappear**—You can often tap anywhere on the screen except on the virtual keyboard itself, or you can tap on the Hide Keyboard key (iPad, iPad Pro, and iPad mini only), which is always located in the lower-right corner of the keyboard.

- **Make the virtual keyboard appear**—If you need to enter data into your iPhone or iPad but the virtual keyboard doesn't appear automatically, simply tap on an empty data field. An appropriately formatted virtual keyboard will appear.

- **Make the keys on the virtual keyboard larger**—For some people, this makes it easier to type. Simply rotate the iPhone or iPad from portrait to landscape mode. Keep in mind that not all apps enable you to rotate the screen.

▪ **Access Emoji/Symbols Keyboards**—Tap on the smiley face key, located between the 123 and microphone key, to access alternative virtual keyboards that enable you to incorporate hundreds of different graphical emojis into your messages and documents.

▪ **Create keyboard shortcuts**—If there's a sentence, paragraph, or phrase you need to enter repeatedly when using an app, it's possible to enter that text just once and save it as a keyboard shortcut. Then, instead of typing a whole sentence, you can simply type a three-letter code that you assign to that shortcut, and the virtual keyboard will insert the complete sentence. To create your own keyboard shortcuts, follow these steps:

1. Launch Settings and tap the General option followed by the Keyboard option.

2. From the Keyboard menu, tap the Shortcuts option. (On iPhones, tap Text Replacement.)

3. When the Shortcut window appears, press the "+" icon to add a new shortcut.

4. Fill in the Phrase field with the complete sentence (or any text) you want to include, such as, "I am in a meeting and will call you back later."

5. In the Shortcut field, enter a three-letter combination to use as the keyboard shortcut, such as "IAM" (representing In A Meeting).

6. Now, anytime the virtual keyboard is displayed (when using any app), simply type IAM to input the sentence, "I am in a meeting and will call you back later."

TAKE ADVANTAGE OF THE iPAD'S NEW DISPLAY OPTIONS

When you're using one of the newer iPad models (such as the iPad Air 2, iPad mini 4, or iPad Pro), you can view multiple items at once on the screen. This is done using the Slide Over, Split View, and Picture in Picture features.

▪ **Slide Over**—On many iPad models (including the iPad Air, iPad Air 2, iPad mini 2/3/4, and iPad Pro), when using any app, place your finger on the extreme right side of the tablet's screen and drag to the left. This activates the Slide Over feature. You can now launch and access a second app within the right margin of the screen (shown in Figure I.5). To view a menu of compatible apps, swipe down on the bar icon displayed in the top center of the right margin window if a second app is already running. This feature enables you to do two things at once or quickly copy and paste (or in some cases, drag and drop) content between apps.

Figure I.5

Use the Slide Over option to access a second app while still using the first.

■ **Split View**—When using the iPad Air 2, iPad mini 4, or iPad Pro, after you've opened a second app using the Slide Over option, place your finger on the horizontal app divider bar and drag it to the left to launch Split View mode. This enables both apps to run in equal-sized windows on the tablet's screen. Split View works better if you hold your iPad sideways in landscape mode (shown in Figure I.6). By swiping the app divider bar left or right, it's possible to readjust the size of the two app windows.

■ **Picture in Picture**—When using compatible apps on your iPad that enable you to watch video, it's possible to display a small video window on your screen, while using the majority of the screen to work with another app altogether (shown in Figure I.7). This feature is currently supported by the iPad Air, iPad Air 2, iPad mini 2/3/4, and iPad Pro.

Figure I.6

Run two apps at once, in equal-sized windows, on your iPad using the Split View mode. Here, the Photos app (left) and Maps app (right) are running simultaneously on an iPad Air 2.

Figure I.7

Watch a video or participate in a FaceTime call while working with another app (such as Safari) on your iPad's screen using the Picture in Picture feature.

TIP Initially, the Picture in Picture feature worked with the Videos and FaceTime app preinstalled with iOS 9; however, it's now compatible with a grow-ing lineup of third-party apps used to display video.

To use this feature, start watching your video on a compatible app using the Slide Over or Split View feature. Tap on the video window, and then tap on the Picture in Picture icon displayed in the lower-left corner of the video window.

When the tiny video window appears on your screen, place and hold your finger on the window to drag it around the screen and place it where you want. Tap on the video window again to make menu icons appear that allow you close the video window, or pause the playback of the video.

SOMETIMES AN OPTIONAL EXTERNAL KEYBOARD OR STYLUS WORKS BETTER

If you expect to do a lot of data entry or word processing on your iOS mobile device, instead of using the virtual keyboard, you can purchase an optional exter-nal keyboard that connects to the smartphone or tablet using a wireless Bluetooth connection or the device's Lightning port.

What's New Apple's optional Smart Keyboard ($169) is available exclusively for the iPad Pro. It connects to the tablet using a proprietary Smart Connector that's built in to the new iPad Pro and its keyboard accessory. When not in use, this keyboard serves as a cover for the tablet.

The Apple Pencil stylus for the iPad Pro ($99.00) enables you to handwrite or draw directly on the tablet's screen with extreme accuracy when using compatible apps, like Notes or Adobe Photoshop Sketch.

MORE INFO For other iPad and iPhone models, Apple (http://store.apple.com), Brookstone (www.brookstone.com), Logitech (www.logitech.com), and Zagg (www.zagg.com) are just a sampling of companies that offer compatible external keyboards. Some of these keyboards are built in to phone or tablet cases that also double as stands.

☑ TIP   The Siri and Dictation features in iOS 9 have also been enhanced.
Discover tips and strategies that focus on how to "communicate" with your iPhone
or iPad using your voice in Chapter 2.

HOW TO TURN THE iPHONE OR iPAD ON OR OFF, VERSUS PLACING IT INTO SLEEP MODE

Your iOS mobile device can be turned on, turned off, placed into Sleep mode, or placed into Airplane mode.

- **Turned on**—When your phone or tablet is turned on, it can run apps and perform all the tasks it was designed to do. The touchscreen is active, as is its capability to communicate. To turn on the iPhone or iPad when it is powered off, press and hold the Sleep/Wake button for about 5 seconds, until the Apple logo appears on the screen. Release the Sleep/Wake button, and then wait a few additional seconds while the device boots up. When the Lock screen appears, you're ready to begin using the iPhone or iPad.

- **Turned off**—When your iPhone or iPad is turned off and powered down, it is not capable of any form of communication, and all apps that were running are shut down. The device is dormant. To turn off your phone or tablet, press down and hold the Sleep/Wake button for about 5 seconds, until the Slide To Power Off banner appears on the screen. Swipe your finger along this red-and-white banner from left to right. The device will shut down.

- **Sleep mode**—To place your iPhone or iPad into Sleep mode, press and release the Sleep/Wake button once. To wake up the device, press the Sleep/ Wake button or the Home button. In Sleep mode, your device's screen is turned off but the phone or tablet can still connect to the Internet, receive incoming calls (iPhone) or text messages, retrieve emails, and run apps in the background. Notification Center also remains fully operational, so you can be alerted of preset alarms, for example. Sleep mode offers a way to conserve battery life when you're not actively using your phone or tablet.

✐ NOTE   By default, your iPhone or iPad will go into Sleep mode and Auto-Lock after 5 minutes. To adjust this time interval or turn off the Auto-Lock feature, launch Settings, tap on the General option, and then tap on the Auto-Lock feature. Options then include activating Auto-Lock after 2, 5, 10, or 15 minutes, or never.

> ☑ **TIP** Another way to place an iPad into Sleep mode is to place an Apple Smart Cover (or compatible cover) over the screen, assuming the iPad Cover Lock/Unlock option is turned on from the General menu within Settings. When in Sleep mode, an iPad will "wake up" for an incoming call (when used with iOS 9's Continuity feature), a FaceTime call, or an incoming text message.

- **Airplane mode**—This mode enables your device to remain fully functional, except it can't communicate in any way using a cellular (3G/4G/LTE) connection. The iPhone cannot make or receive calls, and neither the iPhone nor iPad can send or receive text/instant messages via a cellular network. Apps that do not require Internet access continue to function normally. So, if you're aboard an airplane, you can switch to Airplane mode and continue reading an eBook, playing a game, word processing, watching a movie that you've downloaded from the iTunes Store, or working with a wide range of other apps. After switching into Airplane mode, it is possible to turn Wi-Fi Internet access back on, yet keep the cellular connection turned off. This is useful if you're traveling abroad, for example, and don't want to incur international cellular roaming charges, or if you're aboard an airplane that offers Wi-Fi service.

> ☑ **TIP** To turn on/off Airplane mode, launch Settings, and from the main Settings menu, tap on the virtual switch that's associated with Airplane mode. Alternatively, launch Control Center (by placing your finger at the bottom of the screen and swiping upward), and then tap on the Airplane mode icon.
>
> Once in Airplane mode, keep in mind that from Control Center, it's possible to quickly reenable Wi-Fi, if needed, by tapping on the Wi-Fi icon.

It's also possible to place an iPhone or iPad into Do Not Disturb mode. This automatically routes incoming calls directly to voice mail. As you'll discover, you can customize the Do Not Disturb feature to allow certain people that you preselect to reach you, when you otherwise want to be left alone.

> ☑ **TIP** To activate and customize the Do Not Disturb feature, launch Settings and tap on the Do Not Disturb option. From the Do Not Disturb menu, turn on the Manual or Scheduled virtual switch, based on how you have this feature set up.
>
> To later turn on or off the feature, access the Control Center and tap on the crescent moon-shaped icon.

When turned on, a moon icon is displayed on the iPhone or iPad's Status Bar, and all calls and alerts are silenced. This feature can be turned on or off at anytime, or you can preschedule specific times you want Do Not Disturb to be activated, such as between 11:00 p.m. and 7:00 a.m. on weekdays. From the Do Not Disturb menu within Settings, you can also determine whether certain callers are allowed to reach you when the phone is in Do Not Disturb mode.

If you set the Alarm Clock feature in your iPhone or iPad via the Clock app or using Siri, this feature continues to work, even with Do Not Disturb turned on.

Keep in mind that when your iPhone is turned off, all incoming calls are forwarded directly to voicemail, and it is not possible to initiate an outgoing call. Likewise, incoming text messages, FaceTime calls, and other communications from the outside world cannot be accepted when an iPhone or iPad is turned off. Instead, when you turn on the device, notifications for these missed messages are displayed in Notification Center, within their respective apps, and potentially on the Lock screen, depending on how you set up Notification Center.

DISCOVER WHAT'S NEW IN iOS 9

Let's take a quick look at some of the major new features and enhancements made to iOS 9. You'll learn strategies for best utilizing the majority of these features later in the book. But first, here's a rundown of what's new and noteworthy about iOS 9:

- **Camera**—When used on an iPhone 6s or iPhone 6s Plus, there are a handful of useful new features built in to this app. For example, the new Selfie shooting mode allows you to use the front-facing, 5 megapixel resolution camera to take a photo of yourself and use the screen as a flash to help ensure ideal lighting when needed. Using the Peek and Pop gestures, this new mode can be launched from the Home screen as well as from within the Camera app itself. Plus, the new Live Photos shooting mode transforms still photos into several-second animated images that can be viewed on any Apple mobile device or computer. Chapter 8, "Shoot, Edit, and Share Photos and Videos," focuses on using the Camera app to take awesome photos.

- **News**—Get the latest news and read articles that specifically cater to your areas of interest using this new app that comes preinstalled with iOS 9. Apple has teamed up with hundreds of newspapers, magazines, and other content providers to provide up-to-the-minute news and highly customized content directly to your smartphone or tablet's screen in an interactive format that's easier to read than a typical newspaper or magazine.

■ **Notes**—This app (shown in Figure I.8) has been redesigned, giving it a plethora of new note-taking and information gathering features that make it easy to create lists, type text into the app, add photos, and gather content in one place that you collect from the Internet or other apps. Tap on the new Draw icon that appears in the top-right corner of the virtual keyboard, and a brand new set of onscreen writing and drawing tools becomes available, allowing you to handwrite, draw, or sketch content on your iPhone or iPad's screen using your finger or a stylus. You can also use these tools to annotate typed text. As always, all your Notes sync with your other iOS mobile devices and Macs via iCloud, and when you tap the Share icon, it's possible to share specific notes with other people via text message, email, or certain social networks if you have the apps for them installed.

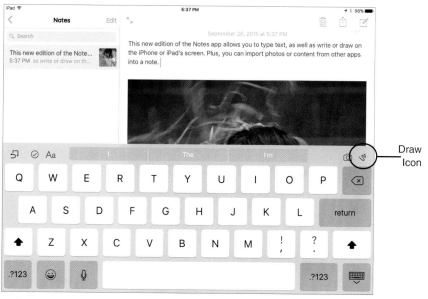

Figure I.8

The redesigned Notes app is now a full-featured note-taking tool that enables you to type content, import photos, and/or handwrite/draw on your mobile device's screen.

■ **Maps**—In addition to being more accurate than ever before, the newly enhanced Maps app now includes public transit information for many major U.S. cities, as well as cities abroad. The new Nearby feature enables you to quickly locate businesses and points of interest simply by tapping on a category icon, such as Food, Drinks, Shopping, Travel, Services, Fun, Health, or Transport. As always, you can also enter a business name (or point of interest) directly into the app's Search field.

- **Wallet**—Manage your credit and debit cards, participating store credit cards, and reward cards digitally and securely within your iPhone, and then use Apple Pay to make in-store or in-app purchases with ease by tapping on the Touch ID sensor built in to the compatible iPhone's Home button.

- **iCloud Drive**—Using your iPhone or iPad's Internet connectivity, you can now directly access files and data stored online within the iCloud Drive portion of your iCloud account. Preview documents and files from the iCloud Drive app, and then launch the appropriate app to work with that content on your mobile device.

- **"Hey Siri"**—Veteran iPhone and iPad users know that Siri is a powerful and continuously evolving tool that allows people to interact with their mobile device using their voice. Thanks to iOS 9, Siri is now "smarter" than ever and can provide information or respond to a broader range of requests. But when the "Hey Siri" feature is active, you no longer need to press and hold down the Home button to activate Siri. You simply need to be in close proximity to your mobile device and say "Hey Siri," followed by your question or command. Much more on how to use Siri and the "Hey Siri" feature can be found in Chapter 2.

- **Spotlight Search**—Like so many other features built in to iOS 9, your ability to quickly locate information stored in your iPhone or iPad has been greatly enhanced thanks to the improved Spotlight Search feature. Based on your recent activity and with whom you've been in contact, the Spotlight Search screen offers icons representing people you've recently communicated with as well as apps you've recently used and allows you to quickly find nearby places and access news headlines. Plus, with the actual Search field, it's possible to find content stored on your device or accessible via the Internet.

- **Enhanced Notification Center**—Notification Center offers a centralized place where your iPhone or iPad keeps track of alerts, alarms, and notifications related to the apps you're running and device's functions you're using. Thanks to iOS 9, additional information, such as the current weather forecast and/or local traffic conditions, can now be displayed as part of Notification Center's Today screen. Plus, app-specific widgets can be used, allowing you to quickly access content or utilize specific app features without actually having to launch the app. In Chapter 1, you discover strategies for managing Notification Center and learn how to customize the information it tracks and displays.

TIP To access the Notification Center window, regardless of which app you're working with or what you're doing on your iOS mobile device, simply swipe your finger from the top of the screen in a downward direction. To begin customizing how Notification Center functions on your device, launch Settings, and then tap on the Notifications option listed in the main Settings menu.

Additional customization options can be accessed by launching Notification Center, tapping on the Today tab, and then scrolling down to the bottom of the screen. Tap on the Edit button to determine what information should appear within this screen and rearrange the order in which information is displayed.

■ **Enhanced multitasking**—Your iPhone or iPad has the capability to run multiple apps simultaneously, although on the iPhone screen, you can be working with only one app at a time. The rest continue running in the background. To quickly switch between apps that are running, or shut down one or more apps, enter the improved and redesigned app switcher on your device. To do this, press the Home button twice quickly.

The app switcher displays icons for all the apps currently running on your device along the top of the screen, and in the main area of the screen are images representing the apps that are currently running.

Scroll from right to left, or from left to right (using a swipe motion with your finger), to see all the apps that are running. To switch to a different app and make it active, tap on its thumbnail or app icon.

To shut down an app while in the app switcher, swipe your finger in an upward direction along the thumbnail image for the app you want to close.

While using any app, if you open the app switcher to change apps, the last app you used (not the current one) is centered with the app switcher's listing. After switching to a new app, the original app continues running in the background. To switch back to it, you'll find a new "Back to…" option displayed in the top-left corner of the screen. This is also a new iOS 9 feature.

NOTE After you launch most apps, they continue running in the background if you simply press the Home button to exit out of them to return to the Home screen. You can shut down an app from the app switcher. If an app was running before you turned off your device, however, it automatically reopens in the background when you restart the device.

iOS 9 WHAT'S NEW When using most iPad models, you can run two apps at once using the Slide Over feature. However, if you're using the iPad Air 2, iPad mini 4, or iPad Pro, it's possible to utilize the Split View mode and run two apps side by side. Now, you can be word processing and managing email at the same time, for example, and quickly copy and paste content between apps, should the issue arise.

- **QuickType Keyboards**—With iOS 8, Apple introduced QuickType keyboards, which included a handful of new features for faster and more accurate typing. Added to iOS 9 is the virtual keyboard's Shortcut Bar. This makes it easier to select, copy, and paste text. Another new iPad-only feature allows you to reposition the cursor anywhere on the screen by placing two fingers on the screen simultaneously and dragging them around on the screen to move the cursor.

- **New Music App and Apple Music**—A few months before iOS 9's release, Apple released a revamped version of the Music app (shown in Figure I.9) and at the same time launched the Apple Music service and the Beats One global Internet-based radio station. Now, between the Music app and this fee-based service, more than 43 million songs from well-known and up-and-coming artists are readily available without having to purchase the music.

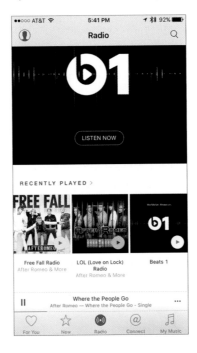

Figure I.9

The new Music app allows you to manage your own digital music library, access the Apple Music services, and stream music in ways never before possible.

NOTE As you'll learn in Chapter 14, "Get Acquainted with the Music, Videos, and iTunes Store Apps," the Apple Music service requires a monthly subscription fee of $9.99 for a personal account or $14.99 for a family account, but a free, three-month trial subscription is offered to everyone. This is an online-based service, so your mobile device requires cellular or Wi-Fi Internet access to use it.

■ **Better integration with iCloud**—In addition to serving as an online-based file sharing and data backup service, iCloud works seamlessly with many core iPhone and iPad functions built in to iOS 9, as well as many of the apps that come bundled with the operating system. You'll also discover more third-party apps now sync data with iCloud, allowing you to share information more seamlessly between your Macs and iOS devices.

NOTE Some iCloud-related functions can be utilized from your iPhone or iPad using a 3G or 4G (LTE) cellular data connection. However, to use some of iCloud's other features, such as iCloud Backup, a Wi-Fi connection is required.

■ **More Powerful Third-Party Apps**—Simply having a powerful and feature-packed smartphone and/or tablet isn't enough. To really get the most use out of your mobile device, you'll want to use third-party apps. Many of the latest versions of these apps are more powerful than ever.

APPLE PAY OFFERS A NEW WAY TO PAY FOR THINGS

Built in to iOS 9, Apple Pay is available when using the iPhone 6, iPhone 6 Plus, iPhone 6s, iPhone 6s Plus, and Apple Watch. Introduced with iOS 8, Apple Pay is a more secure way to pay for purchases in retail stores throughout the United States, as well as when shopping online via enabled apps.

With Apple Pay (shown in Figure I.10), your iPhone is used to scan each of your credit or debit cards just once. This information is then securely stored in a special chip built in to your smartphone.

When you're visiting a participating retail store, simply hold your iPhone up to a special scanner connected to a cash register, place your thumb or finger on the Touch ID sensor built in to the iPhone, and within seconds, your credit or debit card purchase is initiated, in a secure fashion.

The merchant doesn't actually gain access to your credit card number or your name, and Apple does not collect any personal details related to the purchase transaction.

During 2015, thousands of new merchants throughout the United States and the United Kingdom began accepting Apple Pay, and hundreds of banks and financial institutions, including American Express and Discover, now support this payment service.

Figure I.10
Using Apple Pay, initiate a debit card, credit card, or store credit card purchase without having to physically present or swipe your credit card.

Note If your iOS mobile device gets lost or stolen, simply use the Find My iPhone feature to lock down the device. Your stored credit/debit card details can't be used by an iPhone thief, because their fingerprint will not be recognized by the Touch ID sensor, and because Apple Pay does not retain your actual credit/debit card numbers, there's no need to contact your bank to cancel the cards and have them reissued.

Apple Pay works with the Wallet app that comes preinstalled on the iPhone with iOS 9 and makes shopping and paying for purchases at your favorite retail stores, supermarkets, and other businesses a fast and secure process.

SECURING YOUR iOS MOBILE DEVICE WITH A PASSCODE

If you're worried about other people being able to pick up your iPhone or iPad and access your confidential information or use it to access your favorite websites by signing in using your username, it continues to be possible to password protect your iOS mobile device. When the Passcode Lock feature is turned on, you must manually enter a four- or six-digit passcode (or a longer password) that you prese-lect to get past the device's Lock screen.

> **NOTE** Older iOS mobile devices still use a four-digit passcode, but newer iPhones and iPads require users to create a six-digit passcode. If you're using an older device and want to utilize a six-digit passcode, or you're using a newer device and want to utilize a four-digit passcode, this setting can be adjusted in the Touch ID & Passcode submenu within Settings. Tap on the Change Passcode option, enter your current passcode, and then tap on the Passcode Options option prior to entering a new passcode.

To turn on the Passcode Lock feature, launch Settings and tap on the Touch ID & Passcode option. From the expanded Touch ID & Passcode submenu, adjust the various virtual switches to turn on/off the passcode and/or Touch ID feature related to locking/unlocking the iPhone or iPad itself, as well as utilizing Apple Pay and/or App and iTunes Store purchases.

When you activate the Passcode Lock or Touch ID feature, you are promoted to create and enter a passcode.

> **! CAUTION** When creating a passcode, do not use something obvious, like 123456, 654321, 111111, or your birthdate.

Also from the Touch ID & Passcode menu screen, it's possible to customize Passcode Lock functionality. For example, you can restrict certain iPhone/iPad features from being accessible from the Lock screen. Plus, by turning on the Erase Data option, you can set up the device to automatically delete its contents if some-one enters the wrong passcode 10 times in a row.

> **Note** The following devices currently have a Touch ID sensor built in to the Home button: iPhone 5s, iPhone 6, iPhone 6 Plus, iPhone 6s, iPhone 6s Plus, iPad Air 2, iPad mini 3, iPad mini 4, and iPad Pro. This sensor enables the device to be unlocked using a fingerprint scan, as opposed to a passcode. This same Touch ID can be used to authorize purchases.

FIND YOUR LOST OR STOLEN DEVICE USING THE FIND MY iPHONE/iPAD FEATURE

The Find My iPhone/iPad feature enables you to quickly pinpoint the exact location of your device if it gets lost or stolen, and then offers tools to help you lock down, erase, or retrieve your device. At the same time, if the device does get stolen, you can render the device absolutely useless unless someone knows your Apple ID and password.

For the Find My iPhone/iPad feature to work, however, it must be turned on and activated once. Then, to pinpoint the location of your phone or tablet, it will need to be turned on, plus be able to connect to the Internet (that is, not be in Airplane mode).

To activate Find My iPhone/iPad, as soon as you install iOS 9, or anytime thereafter, access Settings and tap on the iCloud option from the main Settings menu. Then, from the iCloud menu, tap on the Find My iPhone/iPad option. When the Find My iPhone/iPad submenu screen is displayed, make sure the virtual switch associated with Find My iPhone/iPad feature is turned on.

(iOS 9) WHAT'S NEW Be sure to turn on the virtual switch associated with the Send Last Location option. To access this option, launch Settings, tap on the iCloud option, select the Find My iPhone/iPad option, and then turn on the virtual switch associated with Send Last Location.

When you do this, anytime your smartphone or tablet's battery gets extremely low, the last thing it does before going dead is send the location of the device to Apple, so you can locate it via the iCloud.com website or the Find My iPhone app on another iOS mobile device or Mac.

Now, if you ever need to locate your iPhone or iPad, you have several options. Using a different iOS mobile device, you can use the free Find My iPhone app that's available from the App Store. Launch the app and sign in using your Apple ID and password. The location of your device will then be displayed on a detailed map.

Tap on the virtual pushpin on the map, or any of the command buttons displayed at the bottom of the app's screen, to then use online-based tools to help you locate, lock down, or erase your mobile device remotely.

Another way to locate your iOS mobile device is to use any computer's web browser and visit www.icloud.com/#find.

Sign in to the iCloud.com website using your Apple ID and password. The same tools for locating and protecting your iOS mobile device are then made available to you online—from anywhere. The Find My feature can also be set up to work with iCloud's Family Sharing function, so you can use a family member's Apple equipment to pinpoint the location of your iPhone or iPad.

> **✓ TIP** Be sure you turn on Find My iPhone/iPad on your mobile device imme-
> diately. If this feature is not active, you will not be able to use the tools Apple offers
> to locate, lock down, or remotely erase your device if it later gets lost or stolen.
>
> Even if the device is not turned on or connected to the Internet when it's initially
> lost or stolen, the Find My iPhone/iPad feature can alert you the moment someone
> finds or tries to turn on your device.

MAINTAIN A BACKUP OF YOUR DEVICE

Using Apple's iCloud service, it is possible to set up your iPhone or iPad to automatically back itself up once per day, as long as you turn on the auto backup
feature. For this feature to work, the device needs access to a Wi-Fi Internet connection. It also must be locked and plugged in to an external power source to
auto-initiate the backup process.

To set up the iCloud Backup feature, which needs to be done only once, follow
these steps:

1. Launch Settings and tap on the iCloud option.

2. Make sure Wi-Fi is turned on and your device can link to the wireless network
   in your home or office.

3. From the iCloud menu screen, tap on the Backup option.

4. From the Backup menu screen, turn on the virtual switch that's associated
   with the iCloud Backup option (shown in Figure I.11).

> **✓ TIP** At any time, you can initiate a manual backup of your device. Access
> the Backup menu screen within Settings, and then tap on the Back Up Now
> option. You'll notice that the time and date of the last successful backup is dis-
> played on this screen.

Later, if you need to reset your iPhone or iPad and erase its contents, or you need
to replace your phone or tablet, you can easily restore your data using the last
successful iCloud backup. When using this backup method, the backup files associated with your mobile device are stored "in the cloud" within your iCloud account.
These backup files utilize some of your allocated iCloud online storage space.

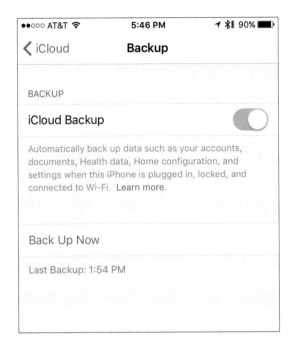

Figure I.11

After turning on the virtual switch associated with the iCloud Backup option in Settings, it's possible to manually initiate a backup by tapping on the Back Up Now option.

iTUNES SYNC IS ALSO A VIABLE BACKUP OPTION

When it comes to syncing data between your primary computer(s) and other iOS mobile device(s), as well as maintaining a backup of your iPhone or iPad, this can be done by connecting your iOS mobile device(s) directly to your primary computer via the supplied USB cable, and then by using the iTunes Sync process.

Because iOS 9 is fully integrated with iCloud, maintaining a backup of your device and syncing app-specific data, as well as transferring data, files, photos and content between your Mac(s), PC(s), and other iOS mobile device(s), can now much more easily be done using iCloud.

When you use iCloud Backup, for example, your iPhone or iPad's backup files are stored online "in the cloud," and not on your primary computer's hard drive. Because this is the more popular way to back up and sync data, it's the approach we'll focus on in this book.

> ### ⌕ MORE INFO
> To use the iTunes Sync process between your iPhone or iPad and a Mac or Windows-based PC, download and install the latest version of the iTunes software onto your computer. To do this, visit www.apple.com/itunes.
>
> To learn more about using the iTunes Sync process to transfer, sync, and back up apps, data, content, and photos, visit www.apple.com/support/itunes.

WHAT THIS BOOK OFFERS

This all-new fifth edition of *iPad and iPhone Tips and Tricks* will help you quickly discover all the important new features and functions of iOS 9 and show you how to begin fully utilizing this operating system and its bundled apps so that you can transform your iPhone, iPad, iPad mini, iPad Pro, or iPod touch into the most versatile, useful, and fun-to-use tool possible.

Each chapter of this book focuses on using various aspects of iOS 9 or the apps that come preinstalled with it. You'll also discover strategies for finding and installing optional third-party apps from the App Store, plus learn all about how to experience various other types of content—from music, TV shows, and movies, to eBooks and audiobooks, plus learn how to best organize, view, and share your own digital photos.

In terms of using your iPhone or iPad as a powerful communications tool, you'll discover strategies for efficiently making and receiving calls, sending and receiving text messages, participating in FaceTime calls (video calling), and participating on the online social networking services (like Facebook, Twitter, and Instagram), while simultaneously making full use of iOS 9's latest features. The book also explores how to take full control of and customize your phone or tablet using the tools and features available from Settings, Control Center, and Notification Center.

In *iPad and iPhone Tips and Tricks*, Fifth Edition, you'll also discover tricks for utilizing iCloud with your iOS mobile device, plus learn all about how to use the most popular apps that come bundled with the iOS 9 operating system (including Contacts, Calendar, Reminders, Notes, Mail, Messages, Safari, Camera, Photos, Maps, Music, Videos, Wallet, iCloud Drive, News, FaceTime, and iTunes Store), as well as popular apps released by Apple and third parties that enhance the capabilities of your device, including Find My iPhone, YouTube, Facebook, and Twitter.

You'll also read about how to manage your health using the iPhone's Health app. For this, see Chapter 10, "Improve Your Health and Manage Your Wealth Using Your iPhone."

> **⌁ NOTE** Now that the iPhones and iPads come with a variety of differ-
> ent screen sizes, based on the model you choose, iOS 9 automatically adjusts all
> apps to best utilize available screen space. Thus, as you're looking at screenshots
> throughout this book, keep in mind that what you see on your device's screen
> may vary slightly if you're using a different model iPhone or iPad than what was
> used to create the screenshot.

ATTENTION, PLEASE...

Throughout the book, look for What's New, Tip, Note, Caution, and More Info boxes
that convey useful tidbits of information relevant to the chapter you're reading. In
some chapters, you'll also discover Quick Tips sections, which quickly outline how
to perform a series of common tasks related to the iOS 9 features, functions, or
app(s) that are being discussed.

The What's New boxes, for example, highlight new features or functionality introduced in iOS 9, while the More Info boxes provide website URLs or list additional
resources that you can use to obtain more information about a particular topic.

IN THIS CHAPTER

- Personalize your iPhone or iPad by adjusting the options available from within Settings
- Customize the Lock screen and Home screen
- Learn to use Control Center
- Discover what's possible from the Lock screen

TIPS AND TRICKS FOR CUSTOMIZING SETTINGS

Thanks to iOS 9, the functionality of your iPhone or iPad is more customizable than ever. You can adjust many device and app-related options from within Settings, plus use Notification Center to help you manage alerts, alarms, notifications, and other informative content in one centralized location. Meanwhile, iOS 9's Control Center gives you quick access to a handful of commonly used features and functions.

This chapter focuses on personalizing and customizing your iOS mobile device and gets you acquainted with Settings, Control Center, Notification Center, and Spotlight Search.

> **TIP** To access Settings, simply tap on the Settings app icon from the Home screen (shown in Figure 1.1).

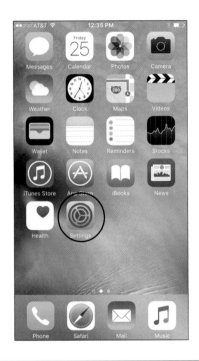

Figure 1.1

To launch Settings, tap on the Settings icon from the iPhone or iPad's Home screen.

In Settings, it's possible to personalize and customize many different options that give you more control than ever over how your iPhone or iPad responds to you, while managing your apps, files, content, and data.

After iOS 9 is installed onto your iPhone or iPad, you'll definitely want to manually adjust some of the options in Settings, as opposed to relying entirely on their default settings.

> **TIP** As you install additional apps onto your iPhone or iPad, if those apps enable you to customize specific features within the app, those customization options are often available to you from within Settings.

NOTE To customize iCloud-related functions, including Family Sharing and iCloud Drive, launch Settings and tap on the iCloud menu option. More about using iCloud with your iOS mobile device is covered in Chapter 5, "Use iCloud and the iCloud Drive App from Your iPhone or iPad."

USING THE SETTINGS APP

After you launch Settings, the menus and submenus are displayed in a hierarchical structure. Under the main Settings heading are a handful of menu options relating to various apps and functions offered by your iPhone or iPad (shown in Figure 1.2). When you tap on many of these options, a submenu displays with additional related options.

Figure 1.2

On the iPad, the left side of the screen shows the main Settings menu. To the right are available submenu options.

NOTE Added to the iOS 9 edition of Settings is a new Search field. Use it to quickly find which feature/function you want to adjust, simply by typing a keyword associated with that feature/function.

☑ TIP   When you access Settings (shown in Figure 1.3), you'll immediately discover some new menu options that were not available in iOS 8. Keep in mind that when an option's virtual switch is positioned to the right and you see green, that option is turned on. When the switch is positioned to the left, it's turned off.

Virtual Switch
Turned On

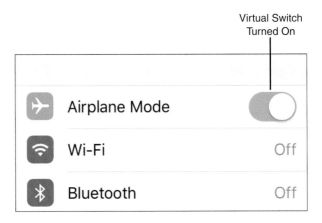

Figure 1.3

To turn on a feature, the switch should be positioned to the right and green should be showing.

For example, if you tap on the Wallpaper option, the submenus associated with customizing your device's Lock and Home screens appear. By tapping on the wallpaper thumbnails displayed under the Wallpaper heading, additional submenu options are displayed.

As you work your way deeper into each submenu, a left-pointing arrow icon appears near the upper-left corner of each submenu screen. It enables you to exit out of each Settings submenu and move a step back toward the main Settings menu. At any time, tap on this left-pointing arrow icon to exit out of the submenu you're in (before or after you've made adjustments to the various option settings). If you opt to make adjustments, those changes are automatically saved when you exit out of the menu or submenu within Settings. If you exit out of a menu or submenu without making any changes, nothing is altered.

MAIN OPTIONS AVAILABLE FROM THE SETTINGS APP

The following is a list of the most commonly used main options available from the Settings app. These vary slightly, based on whether you're using an iPhone, an iPad, or another iOS device and how that device is configured.

AIRPLANE MODE (iPHONE/iPAD CELLULAR + WI-FI MODELS)

The Airplane mode option has no submenu; it simply offers one virtual on/off switch. When Airplane mode is turned on, a small airplane icon appears in the upper-left corner of the iPhone or iPad's screen, as shown in Figure 1.4.

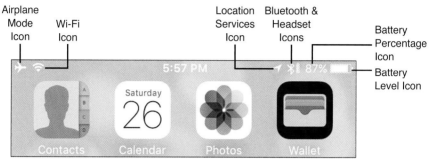

Figure 1.4

In Airplane mode, a small airplane icon appears in the upper-left corner of your iPhone or iPad's screen.

Even while your device is in Airplane mode, you can still turn on Wi-Fi and/or Bluetooth, enabling the iOS device to access the Web via a Wi-Fi hotspot (to utilize the wireless web access available on some commercial aircrafts, for example), and also communicate with a Bluetooth-enabled wireless keyboard, external speaker(s), and/or headset.

> **TIP** When you turn on Airplane mode, the Wi-Fi and Bluetooth features of your iPhone or iPad get turned off automatically. You can, however, turn them back on manually while still in Airplane mode. This can be done from within Settings or the Control Center.

In Figure 1.4, the iPhone is in Airplane mode (the airplane icon is displayed in the upper-left corner of the screen). However, the smartphone is also connected to a Wi-Fi network. You can see the Wi-Fi signal strength icon displayed in the upper-left corner of the screen, near the Airplane Mode icon. In addition, this iPhone has Bluetooth turned on and a Bluetooth headset is linked to the phone. You can tell this from the Bluetooth icons displayed in the upper-right corner of the screen, next to the battery indicator icon and percentage meter.

The tiny arrow icon displayed to the left of the Bluetooth icon is the Location Services icon. When it's visible, this means the main Location Services feature of your iPhone or iPad is turned on, and one or more apps are utilizing the feature to automatically determine the current location of your mobile device.

> **TIP** Turn on Airplane mode on your iPhone or iPad when plugging it in to speed up the charging process. Keep in mind, however, that this prohibits the device from receiving calls (they go straight to voice mail), and the iPhone or iPad does not receive incoming text messages, emails, or FaceTime calls until Airplane mode is turned off.

WI-FI (iPHONE/iPAD)

Located directly below the Airplane Mode option is the Wi-Fi option. When you tap this option, a submenu containing a virtual on/off switch is displayed. When it's turned on, a listing of available Wi-Fi networks (hotspots) is displayed directly below the Choose a Network heading.

> **TIP** When you're reviewing a list of available Wi-Fi networks, look to the right side of each listing for a lock icon. This indicates that the Wi-Fi hotspot is password protected. Tap on a hotspot that does not display a lock icon unless you possess the password for that network.
>
> Also on the right side of each listing is the signal strength of each Wi-Fi hotspot in your immediate area.

To choose any Wi-Fi hotspot listed, simply tap on it. In a few seconds, a check mark appears to the left of your selected Wi-Fi hotspot, and a Wi-Fi signal indicator appears in the upper-left corner of your device's screen, indicating that a Wi-Fi connection has been established.

If you select a Wi-Fi network that is password protected, when you tap on it, an Enter Password window appears on your screen. Using the device's virtual keyboard, enter the correct password to connect to the Wi-Fi network you selected. You will often have to do this when connecting to a Wi-Fi hotspot offered in a hotel, for example.

> **NOTE** If you attempt to access a public Wi-Fi hotspot—in an airport, library, or school, for example—you might be required to accept terms of a user agreement before Internet access is granted. In this case, your iOS device will say it's connected to a Wi-Fi hotspot, but until you launch Safari and accept the user agreement terms, your apps will not be able to access the Internet.

BENEFITS OF CONNECTING TO A WI-FI HOTSPOT TO ACCESS THE WEB

There are several benefits to connecting to the Internet using a Wi-Fi connection, as opposed to a cellular-based 3G/4G (LTE) connection (if you're using an iPhone or iPad Cellular + Wi-Fi model), including the following:

- A Wi-Fi connection is typically faster than a 3G/4G (LTE) connection. (Although if you're within a 4G LTE coverage area, you might experience faster connectivity using it as opposed to Wi-Fi.)

- When connected to the Internet via Wi-Fi, you can send and receive as much data as you'd like without worrying about using up the monthly wireless data allocation for your cellular data plan. This is the best option when streaming content from the Internet, such as music or video programming.

- Using a Wi-Fi connection, you can download large files, such as movies and TV show episodes, from the iTunes Store directly onto your device. Use the iCloud Backup feature to create wireless backups of your iPhone or iPad that get stored within iCloud.

NOTE The main drawback to using a Wi-Fi connection is that a Wi-Fi hotspot must be present, and you must stay within the radius of that hotspot to remain connected to the Internet. The signal of most Wi-Fi hotspots extends for only several hundred feet from the wireless access point (the Internet router). When you go beyond this signal radius, your Internet connection will be lost.

If you leave the Wi-Fi option turned on, your iPhone or iPad can automatically find and connect to an available Wi-Fi hotspot based on whether you have the Ask to Join Networks option turned on or off. When the Ask To Join Networks feature is turned off, your iPhone or iPad reconnects automatically to wireless networks and Wi-Fi hotspots that you have connected to previously, such as each time you return to your home or office.

TIP By turning off the Ask To Join Networks option found in the Wi-Fi submenu of Settings, your iOS mobile device automatically joins known Wi-Fi networks without first asking you for permission.

BLUETOOTH (iPHONE/iPAD)

Turn on Bluetooth functionality to use compatible Bluetooth devices, such as a wireless headset, external keyboard, or wireless speakers, with your iOS mobile device. Bluetooth is also needed to use AirDrop and certain iOS 9 Continuity features (including Handoff) that enable your iPhone or iPad to communicate with other iOS mobile devices and/or Macs.

In Settings, tap Bluetooth and then turn on the virtual switch in the submenu. The first time you use a particular Bluetooth device with your iOS mobile device, you will probably need to pair it. Follow the directions that came with the device or accessory for performing this initial setup task. Some Bluetooth 4.0 devices automatically pair with your iOS device. The pairing process should take only about a minute or two. Multiple Bluetooth devices can be used simultaneously with your iPhone or iPad.

Keep in mind that after an optional device has been paired once, as long as it's turned on and in close proximity to your iOS device, and the iOS device has the Bluetooth feature turned on, the two devices will automatically establish a wireless connection and work together.

> **TIP** If you're using your iPhone or iPad without having a Bluetooth device connected, and you do not want to use the Handoff feature built in to iOS 9, turn off the Bluetooth feature altogether. This helps extend the battery life of your iOS device.

> **NOTE** Handoff allows your iPhone to forward calls to your iPad, so you can answer them on your tablet. You can also initiate outgoing calls on your iPad that are ultimately routed through your iPhone when the Handoff feature is active on both your iPhone and iPad.

CELLULAR (iPHONE) OR CELLULAR DATA (iPAD WITH CELLULAR + WI-FI)

When the Cellular Data option is turned on, your iOS mobile device can access the wireless data network from the wireless service provider to which you're subscribed. When this option is turned off, your device can access the Internet only via a Wi-Fi connection, assuming that a Wi-Fi hotspot is present.

The Data Roaming option appears on the Cellular submenu. When turned on, Data Roaming enables your iPhone or iPad to connect to a cellular network outside the one you subscribe to through your wireless service provider. The capability to tap into another wireless data network might be useful if you must connect to the Internet, there's no Wi-Fi hotspot present, and you're outside your own service provider's coverage area (such as when traveling abroad).

! CAUTION When your iPhone or iPad is permitted to roam (the Data Roaming option is turned on), you will incur hefty roaming charges, often as high as $20 per megabyte (MB). Refrain from using this feature unless you've prepurchased a cellular data roaming plan through your service provider, or be prepared to pay a fortune to access the Web.

From the Cellular menu within Settings, you can determine which apps and iPhone or iPad features can use your phone or tablet's cellular data network in order to connect to the Internet. Scroll down and set the virtual switch that's associated with each app or device feature to turn it on or off. When turned on, Internet access via a cellular data network and/or Wi-Fi is granted. When turned off, only Wi-Fi Internet access is granted.

Depending on your service provider, you might be able to transform your iOS device into a personal hotspot so other devices can connect wirelessly to the Internet via Wi-Fi using your iPhone or iPad's cellular data connection. If your provider allows, this option is available from the main Settings menu or within the Cellular submenu.

NOTE To use iOS 9's Continuity and Handoff functions, your iPhone can establish a private wireless hotspot that can be utilized by your own iPad and Mac that are located within Bluetooth range. This enables you to answer incoming calls to your iPhone from your iPad or Mac, for example. This feature is covered in Chapter 4, "Sync, Share, and Print Files Using AirDrop, AirPlay, AirPrint, and Handoff."

The Cellular menu also enables you to track call time (on the iPhone) and cellular data usage.

NOTIFICATIONS (iPHONE/iPAD)

This Settings option (shown in Figure 1.5) enables you to determine which apps and app widgets function with Notification Center, plus it enables you to determine the other ways in which apps that generate alerts, alarms, or notifications notify you.

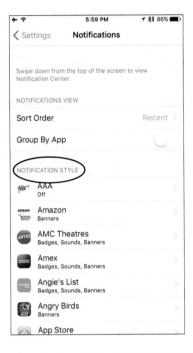

Figure 1.5

All apps that are capable of exchanging data with Notification Center are listed under the heading Notification Style.

> **TIP** It's possible to customize additional content that's displayed in the Notification Center window, beyond just how alerts, alarms, and notifications are presented. For example, you can toggle between and personalize the appearance of the Today and Notifications screens, which are part of the Notification Center feature.
>
> On the iPhone, displayed near the top of the Notification Center window are two tabs. The Today tab displays a summary of the day's weather forecast, along with an overview of your appointments and tasks for the day that are stored in the Calendar and Reminders apps. Below this information are options related to the app-specific widgets you've turned on. The Notifications tab reveals a list of alerts and notifications generated by all the apps that Notification Center is monitoring. This includes notification of missed calls and text messages, for example.

On the iPad (in landscape mode), the left side of the Notification Center screen displays the date, weather, and details about your upcoming schedule. Tap on the Edit tab to access the app-specific widgets you can set up. On the right side of the screen are your Notifications, which include missed alerts, alarms, and notifications generated by your tablet and the apps running on it.

When the iPad is in portrait mode, displayed near the top-center of the screen are the Today and Notifications tabs.

NOTE Widgets are associated with certain specific apps that get displayed within Notification Center. When you use an app's widget, you can quickly manage or handle tasks associated with that app without manually launching the app. Tap on the Edit button at the bottom of the Notification Center to set up and configure available widgets. Not all apps have widgets associated with them.

When you tap on the Notifications option within Settings and scroll down, a section of the submenu under the Notification Style heading lists all apps currently installed on your iPhone or iPad that are compatible with Notification Center, and that you can set up to automatically share data with Notification Center. Tap on an app listing to customize how that app interacts with Notification Center.

TIP When you tap on an app in the Notification Style list, the first option is labeled Allow Notifications. When turned on, this app shares information with Notification Center. When turned off, no alerts, alarms, or notifications will be generated by that app.

When the Show in Notification option is turned on for an app, it displays banners or alerts within Notification Center, and when the Show on Lock Screen option is turned on, those same banners and alerts are displayed on the device's Lock screen. The device is woken up from Sleep mode to display the app-related alert, alarm, or notification on the Lock screen, even when the device continues to be locked.

When applicable, tap on the Sounds option to customize the audible alert associated with the app.

As you review each app listed under the Notification Style heading, tap on it to reveal a secondary submenu pertaining specifically to that app.

Notifications can be viewed as a banner or alert on the Lock screen and within Notification Center, and/or as a badge on the app icon (displayed on the Home screen).

Some apps have additional options. For example, the Calendar submenu under Notifications (shown in Figure 1.6), displays another submenu that allows you to separately customize alerts, alarms, and notifications related to Upcoming Events, Invitations, Invitee Responses, Shared Calendar Changes, and Events Found in Mail. The submenu that appears (shown in Figure 1.7) for each of these enables you to determine where related notifications are displayed, plus which Alert Style should be used.

By selecting an Alert Style, you choose whether a banner or alert is displayed on the screen, even when you are using another app.

If you choose Banners, a pop-up window appears at the top of the screen with the alert-related information. It appears for a few seconds, and then automatically disappears.

Figure 1.6

Depending on the app, there can be several levels of submenus that enable you to customize how each app exchanges information with Notification Center.

Figure 1.7

New iOS 9 options give you greater control over what information is displayed by Notification Center, plus you can choose how, when, and where that information is displayed.

If you choose the Alerts option, a pop-up window displays on the iPhone or iPad's screen until you tap on it to dismiss or address the alarm. The Calendar app generates alerts by default if you set an alarm for an upcoming event.

If you select the None option, no app-specific banner or alert is displayed while you're using the iPhone or iPad. You can, however, have a custom sound played to get your attention by tapping on the Sounds option.

By turning on the virtual switch associated with the Badge App Icon option (when applicable), the app you're customizing can display a badge on the Home screen along with its app icon. Some, but not all, apps can utilize Home screen badges.

> **NOTE** A badge (as shown in Figure 1.8) is a small red-and-white circular graphic that can appear in the upper-right corner of an app icon on your device's Home screen. The badge contains a number used to graphically show you that something relating to a specific app has changed. For example, a badge appears on your Mail app icon when you've received new incoming email messages, indicating how many unread messages you have waiting in your inbox.

Figure 1.8

On this iPhone 6s Home screen, the Chase Bank, Mail, and Messages apps display badges.

Also from the submenu associated with customizing app-specific Notification Center options, you can adjust the sounds generated if that app is capable of playing sounds with alerts, alarms, or notifications.

From the Calendar submenu in the Notification Center settings, tap on the Upcoming Events option, for example, and then tap on the Sounds option to access another submenu that enables you to choose a sound to be associated with event alarms. The default sound for this specific option is called Chord.

Turn on the virtual switch associated with Show In Notification Center if you want alerts related to that app to be displayed in the Notification Center window.

Finally, you can determine whether notifications generated by a particular app should be displayed on the Lock screen when your device is otherwise in Sleep mode. When enabled, the phone or tablet is woken up automatically to display new notifications on the Lock screen for anyone to see, without the device first needing to be unlocked.

NOTIFICATION CENTER QUICK TIPS

- Avoid getting bombarded by excessive notifications from apps that aren't too important to you by manually setting Notification Center to work only with apps that you deem important.

- At the very bottom of the Notification Center settings on the iPhone are two features: AMBER alerts and Emergency Alerts. When turned on, if the government issues an AMBER alert in your area or a message is broadcast over the Emergency Broadcast System, an alert appears on your device.

- To protect your privacy, consider setting up Notification Center to refrain from having alerts displayed on your Lock screen. To do this, tap on each app under the Notifications Style heading, and turn off the Show on Lock Screen option.

▓ As you customize how Notification Center displays notifications, the options available to you vary by app. For example, for the Messages app, you can assign Notification Center to repeat alerts between zero and ten times, at two-minute intervals, to get your attention. You also can opt to preview an incoming message in alerts and banners, and in the Notification Center window.

CONTROL CENTER (iPHONE/iPAD)

Control Center (shown in Figure 1.9) grants you quick access to a handful of smart-phone- or tablet-related functions and apps. In the Settings app, tap the Control Center option to choose whether to make Control Center accessible from the Lock screen or while using other apps.

Figure 1.9

Control Center (shown here on the iPhone) gives you quick access to a bunch of commonly used features and functions.

When the Access on Lock Screen option is turned on, you can swipe your finger from the bottom of the screen up to display Control Center from the Lock screen. When the option is turned off, Control Center is accessible only after the device is unlocked. If Access Within Apps is turned off, you can access Control Center from the Home screen, but not while you're using an app.

> **TIP** If you play a lot of games that require a lot of onscreen tapping or swiping near the bottom of the screen, you might want to disable Control Center to keep it from opening accidently and disrupting your game. To do this, launch Settings, tap on the Control Center option, and then turn off the virtual switch that's associated with the Access within Apps option.

DO NOT DISTURB (iPHONE/iPAD)

This feature enables you to temporarily turn off your iPhone or iPad's capability to notify you about incoming calls or text messages, as well as app-specific alerts, alarms, or notifications. From the Do Not Disturb menu option within Settings, it's possible to fully customize this feature.

At any time, you can manually turn on the Do Not Disturb feature by turning on the virtual switch that's labeled Manual (shown in Figure 1.10). This feature can also be manually turned on from the Control Center. Turn on the Scheduled switch to preset times when you want this mode to automatically activate.

Figure 1.10

It's possible to manually turn on the Do Not Disturb feature anytime from the Do Not Disturb submenu within Settings by turning on the Manual virtual switch.

GENERAL (iPHONE/iPAD)

When you tap the General option in the Settings app, various other options become available. Unless otherwise noted, each option is available using an iPhone or iPad. Because many of these options remain consistent from iOS 8, only the most important or new options are discussed here. Thus, some of the General options include the following:

- **About**—At the top of this screen is the Name field. Here, you can create a unique name for your mobile device, such as "Jason's iPad mini 4" or "Jason's iPhone 6s." Naming your device is useful if you have multiple devices linked to the same iCloud/Apple ID account. The rest of this About screen includes details about your device, including what version of the iOS is installed, information pertaining to the cellular network it's connected to (if applicable), and how its internal storage is utilized.

- **Software Update**—Use this option to update the iOS operating system wirelessly, without having to connect your iPhone or iPad to your primary computer and use the iTunes sync procedure.

- **Siri**—Enable or disable Siri functionality on compatible devices, and adjust specific settings related to this feature. See Chapter 2, "Using Siri, Dictation, and CarPlay to Interact with Your Mobile Device," for more information about using Siri.

> **TIP** Many of the newer iPhone and iPad models offer an always turned on "Hey Siri" feature that can be activated from within Settings. When activated, instead of pressing and holding the Home button for two seconds to activate Siri (which can be done from any iOS mobile device), you simply need to say the words, "Hey Siri," followed by your verbal command or question.

> **TIP** From the Siri menu in Settings, you can give Siri a male or female voice, as well as an American, British, or Australian accent. To do this, tap on the Siri option, followed by the Siri Voice option.

- **Spotlight Search**—Tap this option to determine which portions of your iPhone or iPad are searched when you use the Spotlight Search feature. When using one of the newer iOS mobile devices, turn on the Siri Suggestions option so that your iPhone or iPad can recommend apps, people, locations, and other content (based on recent usage) before you type anything into the Spotlight Search field.

☑ **TIP** To access Spotlight Search from the Home screen, perform a swipe downward that originates from the center of the screen to make the Spotlight Search screen appear.

If you swipe from the top of the screen, you open the Notification Center, so be sure your swipe originates from the center. Separate Search fields also appear in some other apps.

You can access a more robust Spotlight Search screen from the first page of the Home screen by swiping horizontally from left to right.

📝 **NOTE** Turn on Location Services for Spotlight Search to show nearby businesses or points of interest as part of your search results. For example, if you enter "Chinese Food" in the Spotlight Search field, listings for local Chinese food restaurants are displayed. Tap on one of these listings to launch the Maps app and learn more about it.

To turn on Location Services related to Spotlight Search, launch Settings, tap on the Privacy option, and tap on the Location Services option. At the bottom of the Location Services screen, tap on System Services and then make sure the switch for Safari & Spotlight Suggestions is on.

- **Handoff & Suggested Apps**—Handoff enables you to start performing a task on one iOS mobile device (or Mac) and continue it on another Mac or iOS mobile device linked to the same iCloud account. From this submenu, you can also set the Suggested Apps feature, which enables the App Store to recommend specific apps based on your location or what you're working on. These recommendations appear in the app switcher and the Lock screen.

- **Multitasking (iPad)**—The options available from the Multitasking submenu within Settings allow you to customize finger gestures used to navigate between apps when using the tablet.

- **Storage & iCloud Usage**—Tap on this option to see how the storage capacity of your device and your iCloud account are being utilized. Tap on the Manage Storage option under the Storage heading to view storage space utilized by individual apps installed on your iPhone or iPad and manage that content. Tap on the Manage Storage option under the iCloud heading to see how your online ("cloud-based") storage space is being utilized and manage content. At the bottom of the iCloud Manage Storage screen, tap on the Change Storage Plan option to purchase additional online storage space for your iCloud account.

- **Background App Refresh**—This enhanced feature enables you to control the capability of apps to automatically access the Internet to refresh app-specific content and/or Location Services data when the device has Internet access. Turning off this feature helps extend battery life and cuts down on your cellular data usage. You will, however, need to manually update apps each time you launch them. This feature can also be turned on/off on an app-by-app basis from within Settings.

- **Auto-Lock**—Anytime your iPhone or iPad is turned on, if you don't do anything for a predetermined amount of time, it can be set to automatically switch into Sleep mode to conserve battery life and secure the device.

- **Restrictions**—This feature provides a way to "childproof" your iPhone or iPad by enabling an authorized guest user (such as your child) to gain access exclusively to apps or content that you choose. To activate it, tap the Restrictions option, and then tap Enable Restrictions from the submenu. Set a passcode for the restrictions. You can then customize which apps are allowed, block the installation or deletion of apps, prevent in-app purchases, or set ratings limits for content.

> **! CAUTION**   If you choose to utilize the Restrictions feature, make sure you remember the passcode you associate with it. If you forget the passcode, it might be necessary to erase your entire iOS device and reload everything from scratch. Do not give this passcode to your child or the person you're allowing to use your mobile device.

- **Keyboard**—You can make certain customizations from the Settings screen that impact how your virtual keyboard responds as you're typing. It's possible to make supplemental keyboard layouts accessible, customize the Text Replacement feature, plus adjust settings, such as whether Auto-Capitalization, Auto-Correction, Check Spelling, and Dictation are turned on. You can add the popular emoji keyboard from the Keyboards option in the Keyboards submenu of Settings.

- **Reset (iPhone/iPad)**—Every so often, you might run in to a problem with your iPhone or iPad resulting in a system crash or the need to reset specific settings. For example, to restore your iPhone or iPad to its factory default settings and erase everything stored on it, tap on the Reset option, and then tap on the Erase All Content and Settings option. In general, you should refrain from using any of these settings unless you're instructed to do so by an Apple Genius or a technical support person. If you upgrade to a new iOS mobile device and want to return your old device to factory settings and erase all of your data and content, so you can safely give away or sell the device, use the Erase All Content and Settings option found in the Reset submenu of Settings.

! CAUTION Before using any of the options found under the Settings Reset option, which could potentially erase important data from your iPhone or iPad, be sure to perform a manual iCloud Backup or iTunes sync and create a reliable backup of your device's contents. See Chapter 5 for step-by-step directions for how to do this.

You'll probably never need to tinker with or adjust several options found under the General heading. Leave them at their default settings. Others you'll need to utilize often as you use your iPhone or iPad for different tasks.

DISPLAY & BRIGHTNESS (iPHONE/iPAD)

The Display & Brightness options enable you to control the brightness of your iPhone or iPad's screen, plus customize the default text size and typestyle. In general, you should leave the virtual switch for the Auto-Brightness feature turned on, and then only use the Brightness slider when you manually need to adjust the screen to accommodate a specific lighting situation.

Drag the white dot on the Auto-Brightness slider to the right to make the screen brighter, or to the left to make the screen darker.

When the Auto-Brightness virtual switch is turned on, your device takes into account the surrounding lighting where you're using your Phone or iPad, and then adjusts the screen's brightness accordingly. This can also be set from the Control Center. In addition, some apps, such as iBooks, have their own Brightness sliders built in to the app.

WALLPAPER (iPHONE/iPAD)

The capability to choose a custom graphic to be used as the wallpaper behind your device's Lock and Home screen has its own option within Settings. From the main Settings menu, tap on the Wallpaper option to adjust this.

NOTE Your iPhone or iPad has more than two dozen preinstalled wallpaper designs built in, plus you can use any digital images stored in the Photos app as your Lock screen or Home screen wallpaper. In Figure 1.11, you see a thumbnail graphic of an iPhone or iPad's Lock screen (left) and its Home screen (right).

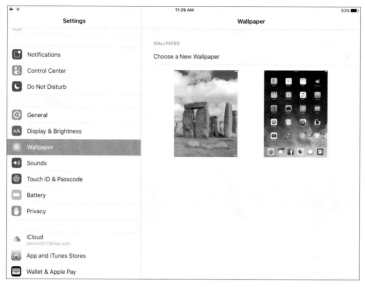

Figure 1.11

Tap on the Choose a New Wallpaper option to select a new graphic or photo to be used behind your Lock and/or Home screen as a Wallpaper.

To change the Wallpaper, tap on the Choose a New Wallpaper option. Tap on the Dynamic, Stills, or Live thumbnail to reveal iOS 9's built-in Wallpaper options, or select a photo from an Album that's listed under the Photos heading.

iOS 9 What's New The new Live wallpapers (available for the iPhone 6s and iPhone 6s Plus) animate when you place your finger on them as they're being displayed within the Lock or Home screen. They work better on the Lock screen where they're not covered with app icons.

Next, the graphic or image you select is displayed in full-screen mode. Three command options, labeled Set Lock Screen, Set Home Screen, and Set Both, are displayed (shown in Figure 1.12).

After making your selection, when you return to the iPhone or iPad's Lock screen or Home screen, you see your newly selected wallpaper graphic displayed.

Instead of choosing one of the preinstalled wallpaper graphics, you also have the option of using photos you've transferred to your iOS device and have stored in the Photos app, or photos you've shot using the Camera app.

To select one of your own photos to use as your Lock screen or Home screen wallpaper, tap on the Wallpaper option in Settings, followed by the Choose a New Wallpaper option. Next, tap on an Album thumbnail that's listed under the Photos heading.

When the thumbnails related to the contents of the image Album you selected are displayed, tap on the thumbnail that represents the image you want to use as your Wallpaper. As soon as a preview screen is displayed, if necessary, use your finger to move the image around on the screen. You can also zoom in or out, in some cases. When this is possible, the Perspective Zoom On/Off option will be displayed in the lower-right corner of the preview screen.

Now, tap on the Set Lock Screen, Set Home Screen, or Set Both option to save your selection. Figure 1.13 shows a custom Lock screen on an iPhone, while Figure 1.14 shows a custom Home screen on an iPad.

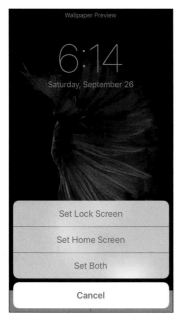

Figure 1.12

Decide whether the selected wallpaper will be used on the Lock screen, Home screen, or both.

Figure 1.13

A newly selected Lock screen graphic, chosen from a photo stored on the iPhone 6s in the Photos app.

Figure 1.14
A still wallpaper selected from within Settings is now displayed as the Home screen wallpaper, behind the app icons (shown here on the iPad Air 2).

> **!CAUTION** If the image you opt to use is not sized appropriately for both the portrait and landscape aspect ratio on the iOS mobile device's screen, the image can appear distorted or not fill the entire screen when you rotate your device.

SOUNDS (iPHONE/iPAD)

Tap on this option to adjust the overall volume of the iPhone or iPad's built-in speaker (or the volume of the audio you hear through headsets), as well as to turn on or off various audible tones and alarms your phone or tablet generates.

From this menu, it's possible to assign specific audio tones, sounds, or ringtones to specific types of app-specific alerts and alarms, plus turn on or off the click noise associated with pressing keys on the iPhone or iPad's virtual keyboard.

It's also possible to turn on the Vibrate mode so that the iPhone handset shakes, instead of or in addition to playing a ringtone. You can control the ringer volume using an onscreen slider and adjust the custom ringtones and audio alerts associated with various features and functions of your iPhone. Your device has a built-in library of different audio alarms and alerts, as well as ringtones built in, plus you can download additional ringtones from the iTunes Store.

☑ TIP In addition to customizing ringtones and the wallpaper, it's possible to customize the vibration patterns used by your device, such as when an incoming call is received. To do this, launch Settings, tap on the Sounds option, and from under the Sounds and Vibration Patterns heading, tap on any of the listed options, such as Ringtone or New Mail.

Next, tap on the Vibration option that's displayed at the top of the submenu for the option you selected. Choose one of the patterns from the Vibration submenu, or tap on Create New Vibration to create your own pattern for the selected option.

☑ TIP Manually adjust the ringer and speaker volume using the Volume Up and Volume Down buttons located on the left side of your handset.

You also can choose different vibration patterns to alert you to different things from the Sounds option within Settings. Volume controls are also accessible from the Control Center.

TOUCH ID & PASSCODE (iPHONES AND iPAD)

Determine whether your device's Touch ID (Home button sensor) can be used to identify your fingerprint and unlock the device and/or approve online purchases. Turn on the Apple Pay option to activate Apple Pay on your iPhone 6, iPhone 6 Plus, iPhone 6s, or iPhone 6s Plus. Tap on the Add a Fingerprint option displayed as part of this menu to securely scan and store your fingerprint(s). These fingerprint scans cannot be accessed by Apple or third parties.

✎ NOTE If your iPhone or iPad is equipped with a Touch ID sensor, options pertaining to setting up and using this fingerprint scanner feature are found under the Touch ID & Passcode option within Settings. Devices not equipped with Touch ID, however, simply have a Passcode option available to them within Settings.

☑ TIP Consider storing the fingerprint for the thumb and index finger on both of your hands, so you can use Touch ID with any of those fingers based on how you're holding the device.

BATTERY (iPHONE/iPAD)

This submenu enables you to display the Battery Life Percentage remaining on your device in the top-right corner of the screen in addition to the Battery Status Bar. From this menu, you can also see how the use of individual apps that are running on your iPhone or iPad are impacting the device's overall battery life. Tap on the Last 24 Hours or Last 7 Days tab, and then view the apps listed below the Battery Usage heading if you're wondering why your iPhone or iPad's battery is draining too quickly. Shut down specific apps and keep them from running in the background when not in use to extend battery life.

From the Battery submenu screen, if you tap on the new clock icon, information about how much time each app has been used is displayed along with each app's listing.

PRIVACY (iPHONE/iPAD)

This menu option in Settings gives you much greater privacy control in terms of how information is shared between apps and shared with other people.

From this Settings submenu screen, it's possible to control specifically which apps have access to the iOS device's Location Services feature, for example, plus which other apps can share data with certain pre-installed apps (including Contacts, Calendar, Reminders, and Photos).

Certain apps and services, such as Maps, HomeKit, or Find My iPhone (or Find My iPad), utilize the capability to pinpoint your exact location. It's important to customize the Location Services options if you're concerned that certain apps can potentially share this information.

When the master virtual switch for Location Services option is turned on, your iPhone or iPad can fully utilize its GPS capabilities, in addition to crowd-sourced Wi-Fi hotspots and cell towers, to determine your exact location. When it's turned off, your device cannot determine (or broadcast) your location. However, some of your apps will not function properly.

> **TIP** When the Location Services option is turned on and you snap a photo or shoot video using the Camera app, the exact location where that photo or video was shot is recorded and saved. This feature is deactivated if you turn off the Location Services option. You can also leave the master Location Services feature for your device turned on, but turn off this feature with specific apps, such as the Camera app.

> **NOTE** From the Privacy menu within Settings, determine which apps can share information with each other and with the public when you use Facebook, Twitter, Instagram, or other online social networking apps.

iCLOUD (iPHONE/iPAD)

Learn all about using iCloud with your iPhone or iPad in Chapter 5.

APP AND iTUNES STORES (iPHONE/iPAD)

Choose which Apple ID account you want to associate with the iPhone or iPad you're using and manage that account by tapping on the Apple ID option displayed near the top of this menu.

From below the Automatic Downloads heading determine whether the device you're using will automatically download content acquired from other computers or mobile devices that are linked to the same iCloud (Apple ID) account. This relates to Music, Apps, Books, and App Updates acquired from the iTunes Store, iBook Store, and App Store.

It's also possible to turn on/off the Installed Apps option, which enables your device to recommend apps based on your location or what you're currently doing. These recommendations appear on the Lock screen and app switcher screen.

WALLET & APPLE PAY (iPHONE)

If you're using an iPhone 6, iPhone 6 Plus, iPhone 6s, iPhone 6s Plus (or a newer iPhone model), you have the ability to set up and use Apple Pay.

From the Wallet & Apple Pay option within Settings, add or delete debit and credit cards associated with the Wallet app and the Apple Pay feature.

> **TIP** To speed up making payments using Apple Pay in stores, turn on the Double-Click Home Button option. Then from the Lock screen, quickly press the Home button twice to launch the Wallet app and select the stored debit or credit card with which you want to pay. When this option is turned off, you must manually launch the Wallet app from the Home screen.

From under the Transaction Defaults heading, you can choose a default debit or credit card to use with Apple Pay transactions plus store your default shipping address, email, and phone number. This speeds up the checkout process.

> **NOTE** The verification process for linking a credit, debit, or store credit card varies based on the card issuer. Follow the onscreen prompts.

If you're using an older model iPhone that does not have a Touch ID sensor, the Wallet app can still be used to manage store/company reward cards or member-ship cards that are set up to utilize Wallet functionality.

MAIL, CONTACTS, CALENDARS (iPHONE/iPAD)

If you use your iPhone or iPad to help manage your life, you probably rely heav-ily on Mail, Contacts, and Calendars. From the Settings app, you can customize a handful of options pertaining to each of these apps. From here, you also must set up your existing email account(s) to work with your smartphone or tablet.

For information about how to use the Settings app to customize the Mail app-related settings, see Chapter 11, "Send and Receive Emails, Texts, and Instant Messages with the Mail and Messages Apps." You can find details about custom-izing the settings of the Contacts and Calendar apps in Chapter 13, "Tips for Using Calendar, Contacts, Reminders, and Notes."

> **TIP** Under the Calendars heading of the Mail, Contacts, Calendars option, one useful setting is Default Alert Times. Tapping on this option reveals the Default Alert Times menu screen, from which it's possible to automatically set advance alarms for birthdays, events, and all-day events stored in the Calendar app. Each of these options can be individually set to alert you at 9:00 a.m. on the day of the event, one or two days prior, or one week before the event, based on your preference.
>
> If you fill in the Birthday field as you create contact entries in the Contacts app, these dates can automatically be displayed in the Calendar app to remind you of birthdays. The advance warning of a birthday gives you ample time to send a card or a gift.

> **TIP** From the Default Alert Times submenu screen, turn on the Time To Leave option if you want your device to determine how long it will take you to travel from your current location to the next event in the Calendar app based on distance and current traffic conditions. In addition to turning on this feature from within Settings, the location of your event must be entered into the Location field for the event.

MORE APP-SPECIFIC OPTIONS WITHIN SETTINGS

As you scroll down on the main Settings menu on your iPhone or iPad, you'll see specific apps listed, including some of the core preinstalled apps (such as Notes, Reminders, Messages, FaceTime, Maps, Safari, News, Music, Videos, Photos & Camera, iBooks, Podcasts, and Game Center).

As you continue scrolling down, listings for Twitter, Facebook, Flickr, and Vimeo lead to submenus that offer the capability to fully customize integration with these online social networking services with many of the apps you'll soon be using.

USER-INSTALLED APPS

By scrolling toward the bottom of the Settings menu, you'll discover a listing of other individual apps that you have installed on your iPhone or iPad, and that have user-adjustable options or settings available. Tap on one app listing at a time to modify these settings. Remember, as you install new apps in the future, additional app listings will be added to this section of the Settings menu and can be modified accordingly.

CONTROL CENTER GIVES YOU QUICK ACCESS TO POPULAR FEATURES AND FUNCTIONS

At any time, regardless of what you're doing on your iPhone or iPad, it's possible to access the Control Center. To do this, simply place your finger near the bottom of the screen and swipe upward. This causes the Control Center window to appear.

On the iPhone, several circular icons appear near the top of the Control Center window, each of which enables you to control a frequently used iPhone feature (refer to Figure 1.9). From left to right, the icons include the following:

- **Airplane Mode**—Quickly place your iPhone or iPad into Airplane mode.

- **Wi-Fi**—Turn Wi-Fi on or off with a single tap, without having to access Settings.

- **Bluetooth**—Turn Bluetooth on or off so that your iPhone or iPad can link to Bluetooth devices it has already been paired with.

- **Do Not Disturb**—Manually turn on the Do Not Disturb feature after you've customized this option from within Settings.

- **Rotation Lock**—Normally, when you rotate your iPhone sideways, the screen automatically switches from portrait to landscape mode. To prevent this from happening when the phone is rotated, turn on the Rotation Lock feature by tapping on its icon.

> **!CAUTION** If you turn on the Rotation Lock, this could prevent you from accessing certain app-specific features or views, depending on which app you're using. For example, turning on Rotation Lock prevents you from using the Week view in the Calendar app.

Displayed below these icons is the screen brightness slider, and below that are the Music app controls, which enable you to play currently selected music (or Playlists) without launching the Music app.

Moving down within Control Center, there are two additional command buttons, labeled AirDrop (left) and AirPlay (right). Tap on AirDrop to quickly activate this feature and determine which content or data you want to wirelessly share with nearby iPhone, iPad, or Mac users. Tap the AirPlay button to select where AirPlay-compatible apps will direct content.

If you have a Bluetooth device linked with your smartphone or tablet, the AirPlay button is replaced with a button that represents the Bluetooth device, such as a wireless headset.

> **TIP** When AirDrop is turned on, your iPhone or iPad is discoverable by any iPhone, iPad, or Mac user that's in your immediate vicinity that also has the AirDrop feature turned on (or just by people included in your Contacts database). You can then wirelessly transfer data from certain apps, such as Contacts and Photos. To protect your privacy when out in public, consider keeping this feature turned off unless you specifically want to use it.

Displayed along the bottom of the Control Center window on the iPhone are four app-related icons. Tap on the flashlight icon to turn on the iPhone's flash so that it serves as a bright flashlight. Tap on the Timer icon to set and manage timers (that is, access the World Clock, Alarm Clock, Stopwatch, and Timer feature). Tap on the Calculator icon to launch the Calculator app quickly. Finally, tapping on the Camera icon offers yet another way to quickly launch the Camera app and begin snapping photos.

The Control Center on the iPad is similar to that of the iPhone; however, as you can see from Figure 1.15, the layout of the options is different. The Control Center on the tablet is displayed as a bar across the bottom of the screen.

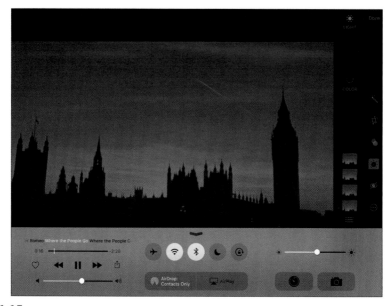

Figure 1.15

While the Photos app is running, the Control Center feature on the iPad is displayed along the bottom of the screen.

The Music controls and volume slider are displayed on the left, the five command icons (Airplane Mode, Wi-Fi, Bluetooth, Do Not Disturb, and Rotation Lock) are displayed near the center, and the Clock/Alarm and Camera app icons and screen brightness slider can be found on the right. The AirDrop and AirPlay/Bluetooth icons are displayed near the bottom center of the Control Center window.

To close the Control Center window, tap anywhere near the top of the iPhone or iPad's screen, or tap on the down-pointing arrow icon displayed near the top of the window.

ORGANIZE APPS ON YOUR HOME SCREEN WITH FOLDERS

If you're like most iPhone and iPad users, you'll probably be loading a handful of third-party apps onto your device. After all, there are well over 1.5 million third-party apps to choose from. To make finding and organizing your apps easier from the iPhone or iPad's Home screen, and to reduce onscreen clutter, you can place app icons in folders.

Utilizing the Folders feature is easy. From the Home screen, tap and hold down any app icon until all the app icons begin shaking on the Home screen. Using your finger, drag one app icon on top of another, to automatically place both of those apps into a new folder.

You can organize your apps in folders based on categories, like Games (shown in Figure 1.16), Travel, or Productivity, or you can enter your own folder names, and then drag and drop the additional app icons into the folders you create. After your app icons are organized, simply press the Home button again on the iPhone or iPad to save your folders and display them on your Home screen.

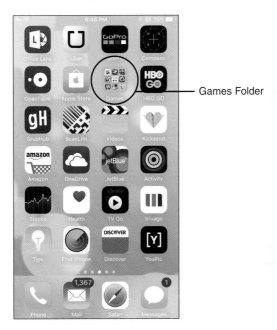

Games Folder

Figure 1.16

On this iPhone, a Games folder has been created.

To open a folder, tap on its icon displayed on the Home screen. Tap on any of the contained app icons to launch one of the apps. Figure 1.17 shows a Games folder that contains several popular game apps.

Figure 1.17

This Games folder was created to organize the game apps currently installed on this iPhone 6s. Using folders helps to eliminate clutter on your Home screen.

> **📝 NOTE** As you're creating app folders, you are no longer limited in terms of how many apps you can place into each folder.

If you later want to remove an app icon from a folder so that it appears as a stand-alone app icon on your Home screen, simply press and hold any of the folder icons until all the onscreen icons start to shake. The folder's contents are displayed.

When the app icons are shaking, simply drag the app icons, one at a time, back onto the Home screen. Each is then removed from the folder. Press the Home button to finalize this action.

MOVING APP ICONS AROUND ON THE HOME SCREEN

To move app icons around and reorganize them on the Home screen, press and hold down any app icon with your finger. When the app icons start to shake, you can use your finger to drag one app icon at a time around on the Home screen.

Your iPhone or iPad can extend the Home screen across multiple pages. (Switch pages by swiping your finger from left to right, or right to left when viewing the Home screen.)

To move an app icon to another Home screen page, while it's shaking, hold it down with your finger and slowly drag it to the extreme right or left, off of the screen, so that it bounces onto another of the Home screen's pages.

When you switch pages, the row of up to four app icons displayed at the very bottom of the iPhone's screen (or up to six app icons on the iPad's screen) remains constant. Place your most frequently used apps in these positions so that they're always visible from the Home screen.

As the app icons are shaking on the Home screen, you can delete the icons that display a black-and-white "X" in the upper-left corner from your iPhone or iPad by pressing that "X" icon. The preinstalled (core) apps related to iOS 9, such as Contacts, Calendar, Reminders, Notes, News, iCloud Drive, Maps, App Store, and Settings, cannot be deleted. They can only be moved.

> **TIP** Although it is not possible to delete any of the apps that come pre-installed on your iPhone or iPad, you can place the core apps that you seldom or never use in a separate folder to remove unwanted clutter from your Home screen.

DISCOVER WHAT'S POSSIBLE FROM THE LOCK SCREEN

The Lock screen enables you to do more than just unlock your device or prevent unauthorized people from using it.

From within Settings, you can opt to turn off most of this functionality to protect your privacy. Thus, if you turn on Passcode Lock, strangers cannot pick up and use your phone or tablet or access any content from it.

The Lock screen automatically displays the current time and date, the Slide To Unlock feature, as well as the Camera icon. You can also set it up so app-specific alerts or banners are displayed on the Lock screen when applicable, plus you can decide whether you want the ability to access the Control Center directly from the Lock screen. These features can be customized from within Settings.

> **TIP** To unlock the Lock screen and access your Home screen, swipe any-where on the screen from left to right. You don't have to place your finger directly on the Slide To Unlock slider.

When you have the Continuity feature turned on, if there was an app you were using on your Mac or another mobile device that's linked to the same iCloud account, a tiny icon for that app appears in the lower-left corner of the Lock screen. By tapping on this icon, you can launch the app and pick up exactly where you left off. This works really well with Safari when surfing the Web, for example.

> **TIP** To launch the Camera app from the Lock screen, instead of tapping on the app, place your finger on the app icon and swipe upward.

MANAGE YOUR CUSTOMIZED NOTIFICATION CENTER SCREEN

Accessing the Notification Center window/screen from the iPhone or iPad at any time continues to be possible simply by placing your finger near the top of the screen and swiping downward. The Notification Center displays all alerts, alarms, and notifications generated by your device in one place.

As you now know, the Notification Center screen displays additional content beyond just app-specific notifications. For example, along the top of the Notification Center are two command tabs: Today and Notifications. (In landscape mode, the iPad displays similar information, plus widget-related information, but in a slightly different format.) Tap on Today to see the current day and date, along with the weather forecast, plus a preview of upcoming appointments from the Calendar app. Scroll down on this screen to see a preview of tomorrow's schedule. This content is automatically displayed on the left side of the iPad's Notification Center screen.

Tap on the Notifications tab to see items recently generated by all compatible apps running on your phone or tablet. The name and app icon for each compatible app is displayed, followed by the preselected number of alerts, alarms, or notifications related to that app. (Keep in mind that which apps are displayed and the number of alerts, alarms, or notifications from each app can be customized from within Settings.)

To clear all notifications related to an app that's displayed in Notification Center, tap on the small "X" icon that's displayed to the right of the app's name and icon.

Tap on the Widgets tab (iPad) to access installed and active, app-specific widgets that are accessible to you. This content is displayed on the Today screen on an iPhone.

TIP To control the order in which content is displayed within the Notification Center window/screen, tap on the Edit button displayed near the bottom of the screen.

To further customize what information is displayed, launch Settings, select the Notifications option, and then under the Notifications View, tap on the Sort Order option and/or turn on or off the Group By App option.

To sort and view Notifications based on the date and time each alert, alarm, or notification was generated, tap on the Sort By Time option and then select the Recent option.

TIP When viewing an item from within Notification Center, swipe sideways to access a mini-menu of available options, or tap on the item to launch the related app to review the item.

When looking at incoming email message items from within Notification Center, for example, swipe from right to left across the listing to reveal an "X," Mark As Read, and Trash button pertaining to that message. Menu options vary based on what app the item is related to.

If you're using an iPhone 6s or iPhone 6s Plus, you can use the Peek and Pop options to preview an email by holding your finger on a message listing and then launching the Mail app to work with that message by pressing your finger a bit harder on the listing or preview.

IN THIS CHAPTER

- Introduce yourself to Siri
- Learn to use Siri with your iPhone or iPad
- Use the Dictation feature as an alternative to the virtual keyboard
- Use your iPhone with CarPlay in your vehicle

2

USING SIRI, DICTATION, AND CARPLAY TO INTERACT WITH YOUR MOBILE DEVICE

Siri is designed to be a virtual assistant that responds to commands, questions, and requests that you say, as opposed to type, into your mobile device. Siri has access to the content stored in your iPhone or iPad, as well as an ever-growing arsenal of Internet-based resources that can be used to quickly gather information or answers that you need within seconds after you state your request.

☑ TIP   Simply say, "Hey Siri," to activate Siri from most newer iPhones or iPads (that utilize the M9 processor). Older devices must be plugged in to an external power source to activate Siri using the "Hey Siri" feature. When you do this, the familiar, "What can I help you with?" screen appears and you hear Siri's "ready" tone.

You can also press and hold down the Home button for 2 seconds to activate Siri at any time.

It's possible to deactivate the "Hey Siri" feature from the Siri menu within Settings. Simply turn off the virtual switch associated with the Allow "Hey Siri" option.

It's important to realize that Siri does not understand everything, and this feature does have its limitations in terms of what it can do and which apps it works with. When you get accustomed to working with Siri, however, this feature can make you more efficient when using your iPhone or iPad.

In addition to using cutting-edge voice recognition, Siri uses advanced artificial intelligence, so it doesn't just understand what you say, it interprets and comprehends what you mean, and then translates your speech to text. And if you don't initially provide the information Siri needs to complete your request or command, you're prompted for more information.

☑ TIP   To get the most out of the Siri feature, turn on your iOS device's master Location Services functionality, and then make sure Location Services is set up to work with Siri.

To do this, launch Settings, tap on the Privacy option, and then tap on the Location Services option. Turn on the virtual switch that's associated with Location Services.

WHAT YOU SHOULD KNOW BEFORE USING SIRI

For Siri to operate, your phone or tablet must have access to the Internet via a cellular or Wi-Fi connection. Every time you make a request or issue a command to Siri, your iOS mobile device connects to Apple's data center. Thus, if you're using a cellular data connection, some of your monthly wireless data allocation gets used up (if cellular data allocation, such as 5GB per month, is imposed by your wireless service provider).

> **TIP** Because a Wi-Fi connection is typically significantly faster than a cellular data connection, Siri often responds faster to your requests and commands when you use a Wi-Fi connection.

You should also understand that heavy use of the Internet, especially when connected via a cellular data connection, depletes the battery life of the iPhone or iPad faster. So, if you constantly rely on Siri throughout the day, the battery life of your device will be shorter.

> **CAUTION** If your iPhone or iPad is placed in Airplane mode (and Wi-Fi connectivity is turned off), Siri does not function. You'll receive a verbal message stating that Siri is unavailable.

CUSTOMIZING SIRI

To customize the Siri feature, launch Settings, tap on the General option, and then tap on the Siri option. From the Siri submenu (shown in Figure 2.1), there's a master switch for this feature. You can also turn on/off the "Hey Siri" function with the virtual switch labeled Allow "Hey Siri."

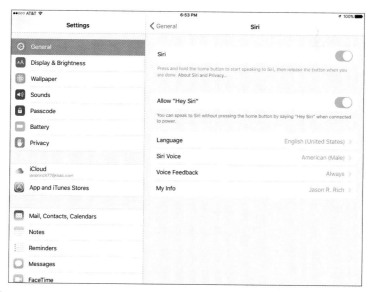

Figure 2.1

Be sure to customize Siri from within Settings. This needs to be done only once; however, you can alter these settings whenever you wish.

(iOS 9) WHAT'S NEW The first time you turn on the "Hey Siri" feature, your iPhone or iPad asks you to speak several Siri-related commands so that the device can learn what your voice sounds like. Follow the onscreen prompt and say what's requested. This process takes under one minute and only needs to be done once.

Tap the Language option to select your native language, and then tap on the Siri Voice option to choose between giving Siri a male or female voice, as well as an American, Australian, or British accent. Siri functions the same as a male or female, so which voice and accent you choose is a matter of personal preference.

The Voice Feedback option enables you to control whether Siri speaks its responses to each request, or just displays related content on the iPhone or iPad's screen. When using the hands-free capabilities of Siri in your car via CarPlay, no content is displayed on the screen. Siri says everything, so you can keep your eyes on the road.

It's important that Siri be able to greet you properly. Tap on the My Info option and then select your own entry from your Contacts database. Within this entry, be sure to include as much information as possible because Siri uses this information to assist you.

For example, if you have a Home and Work address in your own Contacts entry, from anywhere you are, you can activate Siri and say, "How do I get home from here?" or "How do I get to work from here?," and Siri knows exactly where you're talking about.

TIP By default, Siri addresses you by your first name, based on the information in your own Contacts entry. However, at anytime, you can activate Siri and say, "Siri, call me [insert nickname]." Siri remembers your request and addresses you by that name in the future.

Siri also utilizes information stored in the Related Name fields as you create or edit a contact in the Contacts app. By tapping on this field, you can add a relationship title, such as mother, father, brother, or sister when creating or editing Contact app entries.

> **✓ TIP** At any time, teach Siri who your relatives are who already have entries within your Contacts database. Simply activate Siri and say, "[Insert name] is my father," for example. Siri will remember these relationships in the future.

Then, when using Siri, if you say, "Call Mom at home," Siri knows exactly to whom you're referring. Otherwise, if you activate Siri and say, "Call my mom at home," the first time you use Siri for this task, you're asked who your mother is.

As long as you have a Contact entry for your mother stored in the Contacts app, when you say your mother's real name, Siri links the appropriate contact and remembers this information. This applies to any nickname or title you have for other people, such as "wife," "son," "mother," "dad," or even "Uncle Jack."

WAYS TO ACTIVATE SIRI

If you want to use Siri, you first must activate it. There are multiple ways to do this:

- Use the "Hey Siri" function. This works when the device is in Sleep mode but not when the iPhone or iPad is powered off altogether.
- Press and hold the Home button on your iPhone or iPad for 2 seconds.
- Press and hold the Call button on your wireless Bluetooth headset that is paired with your iPhone or iPad. This enables you to speak to Siri on your device from up to 30 feet away.
- If you're using Apple EarPods or an original Apple headset (headphones), press the middle button on the controls found on the cable.
- Press the CarPlay button built in to the steering wheel or dashboard of your car when your iPhone is linked with your vehicle.

> **✓ TIP** If you're using your iOS device with a Bluetooth headset, when you activate Siri, to the right of the microphone icon will be a Bluetooth icon. Tap on it to choose between using the iPhone's built-in microphone or your headset's microphone when talking to Siri.

When Siri is activated, the message "What can I help you with?" displays on the screen, along with a rainbow-colored, animated wave graphic (shown in Figure 2.2). On some iPhone and iPad models, you'll simultaneously hear Siri's activation tone. When not listening for spoken commands, a microphone icon replaces the animated wave graphic. Tap on this microphone to activate or reactivate Siri.

Once activated, you have about 5 seconds to begin speaking before the feature deactivates. To reactivate it, simply tap on the microphone icon or repeat one of the previously mentioned steps.

As soon as Siri is activated, speak your question, command, or request. For the most accurate results when using Siri, speak directly into the iPhone, iPad, or headset. Try to avoid being in areas with excessive background noise. Also, speak as clearly as possible so Siri can understand each word in your sentences.

Figure 2.2

When Siri is activated (shown here on the iPhone), the "What can I help you with?" message appears, and you hear Siri's activation tone.

DISCOVER HOW SIRI CAN HELP YOU

The great thing about Siri is that you don't have to think too much about how you phrase a command, question, or request. Siri automatically interprets what you say.

> **✓ TIP** When you're in a quiet area, activate Siri and then speak. Stop speaking when you're finished, and Siri responds accordingly.
>
> However, if you're in a noisy area, Siri might have trouble determining when you've stopped speaking. To avoid this problem, press and hold down the Home button as you speak to Siri. When you're finished speaking, release the Home button so Siri can process your request.

To get the most out of using Siri—with the least amount of frustration as a result of Siri not being able to comply with your requests—you must develop a basic understanding of which apps this feature works with and how Siri can be used with those apps.

In general, Siri can be used with most of the apps that come preinstalled with iOS 9, plus Siri can find information on the Internet by performing web searches. You can use Dictation mode, however, in any app where the microphone key appears on the iPhone or iPad's virtual keyboard.

> **✎ NOTE** Dictation mode offers an easy way to speak into your iPhone or iPad and have what you say translated into text and inserted into the app you're using instead of typing.

The following sections provide a sampling of what Siri can be used for, as well as tips for how to use Siri effectively. Apple and third-party app developers are continuously working to upgrade Siri's capabilities, so you might discover additional functionality as you begin using Siri with various apps.

> **✓ TIP** For an up-to-date summary of Siri's capabilities and a sampling of how to phrase commands or requests to work with Siri's newest features, visit this page of Apple's website: www.apple.com/ios/siri.

SIRI QUICK TIPS

■ Siri is one of the few features that work from the Lock screen. Thus, even if you have the Passcode Lock feature turned on, someone can potentially pick up your device and access your data using Siri without your permission. To keep this from happening, set up the Passcode feature on your device. Then turn off the Siri option found in the Touch ID & Passcode submenu of the Settings app.

■ Siri can be used to verbally launch any app. To do this, activate Siri and say, "Launch [app name]." If it's a game you want to play, simply say, "Play [game name]." Another option is to say, "Open [app name]."

■ For more information about how Siri can be used, activate Siri and say, "What can you do?" or after activating Siri, wait a few seconds and then tap on the Help ("?") icon displayed in the lower-left corner of the screen.

> **NOTE** Siri is compatible with FaceTime, Messages, Calendar, Maps, Twitter, Facebook, Music, Mail, Weather, Stocks, Clock, Contacts, Notes, Settings, Safari, iTunes, iBooks, and Podcasts. New to iOS 9, Siri now understands commands related to the Photos, App Store, Twitter, and Facebook apps, as well as third-party apps that allow you to control compatible equipment from your iPhone or iPad using Apple's HomeKit protocols. It also works with the Voicemail option of the Phone app (on the iPhone).
>
> Siri also responds to requests or questions related to almost anything having to do with sports, movies, restaurants, music, weather, locations, or stocks.
>
> Plus, Siri can look up information when you pose almost any type of question, or it can be used to verbally control almost any iPhone/iPad-related feature that's adjustable from within Settings or Control Center. For example, you can activate Siri and say, "Turn on Airplane mode." or "Turn off Do Not Disturb."

FIND, DISPLAY, OR USE INFORMATION RELATED TO YOUR CONTACTS

Every field within a Contact's entry is searchable and can be accessed by Siri. Or you can ask Siri to look up a specific contact for you and display that contact's Info screen.

Again, the more information you include in each entry stored in your Contacts database, the more helpful Siri can be. To have Siri look up and display information stored in Contacts, say something like the following:

■ "Look up John Doe in Contacts."

■ "What is John Doe's phone number?"

■ "What is John Doe's home phone number?"

■ "What is John Doe's work address?"

■ "Where does John Doe live?"

■ "Where does John Doe work?"

TIP   When Siri displays the Info screen for a Contact, it is interactive; therefore, you can tap on a displayed phone number to initiate a call, or tap on an email address to launch the Mail app to send email to that address. If you tap on a regular address, the Maps app launches, and if you tap on a website URL, Safari launches and opens that web page.

Siri can also use information stored in your Contacts database to comply with various other requests, such as

- **"Send John Doe a text message"**—This works if you have an iPhone-labeled phone number, iMessage username, or email address saved in John Doe's Contacts entry. On the iPhone, it also works with the phone's SMS text messaging feature if you have a phone number in someone's Contacts entry that's associated with the "mobile" label.

- **"Send John Doe an email"**—This works if you have an email address saved in John Doe's Contacts entry.

- **"How do I get to John Doe's home?"**—This works if you have a home address saved in John Doe's Contacts entry. The Maps app launches, and directions from your current location are displayed.

- **"When is John Doe's birthday?"**—This works if you have a date saved in the Birthday field in John Doe's Contacts entry.

- **"What is John Doe's wife's name?"**—This works if you have a spouse's name saved in John Doe's Contacts entry.

INITIATE A CALL

Initiate a call by activating Siri and then saying, "Call [name] at home," or "Call [name] at work." This works if that person has a Contacts entry associated with their name, as well as a phone number labeled Home or Work, respectively.

You could also say, "Call [name]'s mobile phone," or "Call [name]'s iPhone." If you just use the command call, and that person has several phone numbers in their Contacts entry, Siri gives you the option to select which number you want to call.

NOTE   When issuing a command to Siri, you have flexibility in terms of what you say. For example, say, "Call John Doe at work," "Call John Doe work," or "Call the work number for John Doe," and in all these cases, Siri initiates a call to John Doe's work number.

Alternatively, if someone's contact information or phone number is not stored in your iPhone, you can say, "Call" or "Dial" followed by each digit of a phone number. Thus, you'd say, "Call 212 555 1212."

> **✓ TIP** You can also ask Siri to look up a business phone number or address by saying, "Look up [business name] in [city, state]." Or, you could say, "Look up [business type, such as a dry cleaner] in [city, state]."

On the iPhone, when Siri finds the phone number you're looking for, Siri says, "Calling [name] at [location]," and then automatically initiates a call to that number by launching the Phone app. Siri also has the capability to initiate FaceTime video calls. Use a command, such as, "FaceTime with [name]."

> **✓ TIP** On the iPhone or iPad, Siri works with FaceTime, so you can say, "FaceTime Natalie," or "Make a FaceTime call to Natalie" to initiate a video call. You can also use FaceTime to initiate an audio-only call by saying, "Make a FaceTime audio call to Natalie."

SET UP REMINDERS AND TO-DO ITEMS

If you constantly jot down reminders to yourself on scrap pieces of paper or sticky notes, or manually enter to-do items into the Reminders app, this is one Siri-related feature you'll truly appreciate.

To create a reminder (to be utilized by the Reminders app), complete with an alarm, simply activate Siri and say something like, "Remind me to pick up my dry cleaning tomorrow at 3 p.m." Siri then creates the to-do item, displays it on the screen for your approval, and then saves it in the Reminders app. At the appropriate time and day, an alarm sounds and the reminder message is displayed.

> **✓ TIP** When creating a Reminder using Siri, you can provide a specific date and time, such as "tomorrow at 3 p.m." or "Friday at 1 p.m." or "July 7th at noon." You can also include a location that Siri knows, such as "Home" or "Work." For example, you could say, "Remind me to feed the dog when I get home," or "Remind me to call Emily when I get to work."

READ OR SEND TEXT MESSAGES

When you receive a new text message but can't look at the screen (such as when you're driving), activate Siri and say, "Read new text message." After Siri reads the incoming message, you're given the opportunity to reply to that message and dictate your response.

Using Siri with the Messages app, you can also compose and send a text/instant message to anyone in your Contacts database by saying something like, "Compose a text message to John Doe."

You are asked to select an email address or mobile phone number to use. To bypass this step, say, "Send a text message to John Doe's mobile phone," or "Send a text message to John Doe's iPhone." Then, Siri says, "What do you want to say to John Doe?" Dictate your text message.

When you're finished speaking, Siri says, "I updated your message. Ready to send it?" The transcribed message is displayed on the screen, along with Cancel and Send icons. You can tap an icon or speak your reply.

CHECK THE WEATHER OR YOUR INVESTMENTS

The Weather app can display an extended weather forecast for your immediate area or any city in the world, and the Stocks app can be used to track your investments. However, Siri has the capability to automatically access the Web and obtain weather information for any city, as well as stock-related information about any stock or mutual fund.

After activating Siri, ask a weather-related question, such as

- **"What is today's weather forecast?"**—Siri pinpoints your location and provides a current forecast.

- **"What is the weather forecast for New York City?"**—Of course, you can insert any city and state in your request.

- **"Is it going to rain tomorrow?"**—Siri accesses and interprets the weather forecast, and then vocalizes, as well as displays a response. Siri determines your current location before providing a forecast.

- **"Should I bring an umbrella to work?"**—Siri knows the location of your work and can access and then interpret the weather forecast to offer a vocalized and displayed response.

If you have stock-related questions (using the iPhone or iPad), you can ask about specific stocks by saying something like

- "What is [company name]'s stock at?"

- "What is [company]'s stock price?"
- "How is [company name]'s stock performing?"
- "Show me [company name]'s stock."

When you request stock information, you get a verbal response from Siri along with information about that stock displayed on the iPhone or iPad's screen, as you can see in Figure 2.3.

Figure 2.3

Siri can tell you how a specific stock is performing. Here, the command "Siri, show me Apple stock," was spoken.

FIND INFORMATION ON THE WEB OR GET ANSWERS TO QUESTIONS

If you want to perform a web search, you can manually launch the Safari browser, and then use a keyboard to find what you're looking for in the Search field. Or, you can ask Siri to perform the search for you by saying something like

- "Look up the [company] website."
- "Access the website cnn.com."
- "Find [topic] on the web."

- "Search the web for [topic]."
- "Google information about [topic]."
- "Search Wikipedia for [topic]."
- "What is the definition of [insert word]?"

You also can ask a question, and Siri seeks out the appropriate information on the Web.

> **NOTE** When you ask Siri a question that requires your iPhone or iPad to seek out the answer on the Internet, this is done through Apple using Wolfram Alpha. To learn more about the vast topics you can ask Siri about, from unit conversions to historical data, visit www.wolframalpha.com/examples.

SCHEDULE AND MANAGE MEETINGS AND EVENTS

Like many of the apps that come preinstalled with iOS 9, the Calendar app is fully compatible with Siri, which means it's possible to use Siri to create or modify appointments, meetings, or events by using your voice. To do this, some of the things you can say include

- "Set up a meeting at 10:30 a.m."
- "Set up a meeting with Drew at noon tomorrow."
- "Meet with Emily for lunch at 1:00 p.m."
- "Set up a meeting with Rusty about third-quarter sales projections at 4:00 p.m. on December 12th."

> **TIP** Siri can also be used to reschedule or cancel events stored in the Calendar app. For example, you could say, "Move my 2 p.m. meeting to 4:00 p.m.," or "Cancel my 6:00 p.m. dinner with Rusty."
>
> To obtain an overview of your schedule, ask a question like, "What does the rest of my day look like?," or "When is my next appointment?" You can ask about a specific event as well, by asking, "When is my next meeting with Kevin?" or "Where is my next meeting?"
>
> Siri can also tap the Calendar and Maps app simultaneously if you ask a question like, "How do I get to my next meeting?" This works if you've filled in the Location field when creating an event in the Calendar app.

SEND EMAIL AND ACCESS NEW (INCOMING) EMAIL

If you want to compose an email to someone, activate Siri and say, "Send an email to [name]." If that person's email address is listed in your Contacts database, Siri addresses a new message to that person. Siri then says, "What is the subject of your email?" Speak the subject line for your email. When you stop speaking, Siri says, "Okay, what would you like the email to say?" You can now dictate the body of your email message.

When you're finished speaking, Siri composes the message, displays it on the screen, and then says, "Here is your email to [name]. Ready to send it?" You can now respond "yes" to send the email message, or say "cancel" to abort the message. If the message isn't what you want to say, you can edit it using the virtual keyboard, or ask Siri to "Change the text to…."

Meanwhile, if you're expecting an incoming email from someone, you can activate Siri and say, "Any new email from [insert name]?" and not have to first manually launch the Mail app.

Siri also now has the capability to search through the subjects of your emails. So, you can activate Siri and say, "Do I have any emails about [insert subject]?"

SET AN ALARM OR TIMER

Siri can control the Clock app that comes preinstalled on your iOS device so that it serves as an alarm clock or timer. You can say something like, "Set an alarm for 7:30 a.m. tomorrow" or "Set a recurring wakeup call for 7:30 a.m." to create a new alarm. Or, to set a 30-minute timer, say, "Set a timer for 30 minutes." A countdown timer is displayed on the iPhone or iPad's screen, and an alarm sounds when the timer reaches zero.

You can also simply use "Hey Siri" and ask "What's today's date?"; "What time is it?"; or "How many days until Christmas?" if you're too busy to look at the iPhone or iPad's screen, such as when you're driving.

GET DIRECTIONS USING THE MAPS APP

Pretty much any feature you can use the Maps app for—whether it's to find the location or phone number for a business, obtain turn-by-turn directions between two addresses, access public transit information, or map out a specific address location—you can access using Siri.

To use Maps-related functions, say things like the following:

- "How do I get to [location]?"
- "Show [address]."

- "Directions to [contact name or location]."

- "Find a [business type, such as gas station] near [location]."

- "Find a [business or service name, such as Starbucks Coffee] near where I am."

- "Where is the closest [business type, such as post office]?"

- "Find a [cuisine type, such as Chinese] restaurant near me."

- "What time does [insert store name] close tonight?"

- "Where is a good barber?" (When you ask a question like this, Siri relies on Yelp! Reviews and other information to provide highly recommended businesses or restaurants.)

If multiple businesses or locations are found that are directly related to your request, Siri asks you to select one, or all related matches are displayed on a detailed map.

CONTROL THE MUSIC APP

In the mood to hear a specific song that's stored on your iPhone or iPad? Maybe you want to begin playing a specific playlist, you want to hear all the music stored on your iOS device by a particular artist, or you want to play a specific album? Well, just ask Siri. You can control the Music app or the Apple Music service using your voice by saying things like the following:

- "Play [song title]."

- "Play [album title]."

- "Play [playlist title]."

- "Play [artist's name]."

- "Play [music genre, such as pop, rock, or blues]."

You can also issue specific commands, such as "Shuffle my [title] playlist," or speak commands, such as "Pause" or "Skip" as music is playing.

> **TIP** If you subscribe to Apple Music and use the Music app, activate Siri and request to hear any of the songs in the online-based iTunes Store music library.
>
> You can request to play (stream) music by song title, album title, or artist. Start by activating Siri and saying, "Play [song title]," Play [song title] by [artist name]," or "Play [album title]." Without an Apple Music subscription, you're limited to hearing the digital music you own.

As you're listening to music on your mobile device, if you want to hear similar music, activate Siri and say, "Play more music like this," or if you want to hear music that's popular, say something like, "Siri, play the number one Country song right now."

When streaming music from Apple Music, to purchase a song or album, activate Siri and say, "Buy this song" or "Buy this album."

If you happen to be somewhere and hear a song being played and want to know the name of the song or who sings it, activate Siri and say, "What song is this?" or "Who sings this?" Siri will listen for a few seconds and then provide information about the music that's playing on the radio, in an elevator, or on TV, for example.

FORGET STICKY NOTES—DICTATE NOTES TO YOURSELF

Siri is compatible with the Notes app and enables you to create and dictate notes. To create a new note, activate Siri and begin a sentence by saying, "Note that I... " You can also say, "Note: [sentence]." What you dictate is saved as a new note in the Notes app.

> **NOTE** When using the Siri or dictation feature, your iPhone or iPad can capture and process up to 30 seconds of your speech at a time.

SIRI KNOWS ALL ABOUT SPORTS, MOVIES, ENTERTAINMENT, AND RESTAURANTS, TOO

If you're looking for the latest scores related to your favorite professional team or sporting event, just ask Siri. It's also possible to ask sports-related questions and then have Siri quickly research the answers via the Internet. When it comes to sports, here are some sample questions or requests you can use with Siri:

- "Did the Yankees win their last game?"
- "What was the score of last night's Patriots game?"
- "What was the score the last time the Yankees and Red Sox played?"
- "Show me the baseball scores from last night."
- "When do the Dallas Cowboys play next?"

- "Who has the most home runs on the New York Mets?"
- "Show me the roster for the Patriots."
- "Are any of the Bruins players currently injured?"

When it comes to movies, Siri can also help you decide what to go see, determine where movies are playing, look up movie times, and provide details about almost any movie ever made. Here are some sample questions or requests you can use with Siri that relate to movies:

- "Where is [movie title] playing?"
- "What's playing at [movie theater]."
- "Who directed the movie [movie title]."
- "Show me the cast from [movie title]."
- "What's playing at the movies tonight?"
- "Find the closest movie theater."
- "Show me the reviews for [movie title]."
- "What movie won Best Picture in [year]?"
- "Buy two tickets to see [movie title] tonight at the [movie theater name]."

If you're looking to try out a new restaurant or want to learn more about a local dining establishment, Siri knows all about restaurants too. Plus, thanks to Yelp! and Open Table integration, you can view detailed information about restaurants, make dining reservations, or read reviews.

Here are some examples of how Siri can be used when you want to know more about restaurants:

- "Where's the closest Japanese restaurant?
- "Find a good Italian restaurant in Boston."
- "Table for two at Palm Restaurant in Boston for 7 p.m."
- "Show me reviews for [restaurant name] in [city]."

In Figure 2.4, the question, "Siri, what's a good steak restaurant in Boston?" was asked. A series of listings based on Yelp! ratings was displayed. Tap on a listing for more details about a particular restaurant (shown in Figure 2.5). When Siri locates restaurant information, thanks to Yelp!, details about that establishment, including its location, phone number, hours of operation, entree price range, and a star-based rating, are displayed.

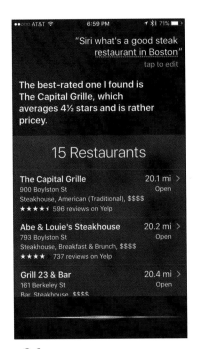

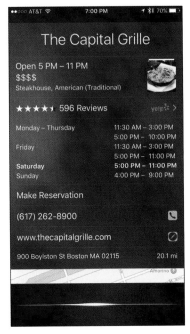

Figure 2.4

Activate Siri, and say, "Siri, what's a good restaurant in Boston?" Siri displays a list based on Yelp! ratings.

Figure 2.5

The restaurant information Siri displays is interactive. For example, tap on the phone number to initiate a call to that restaurant or tap on the listed address to launch the Maps app and get detailed directions.

MORE SIRI QUICK TIPS

- Siri is a mathematical genius. Simply say the mathematical calculation you need solved, and Siri presents the answer in seconds. For example, say, "What is 10 plus 10?," "What's the square root of 24?," or "What is 20 percent of 500?" This feature is particularly useful for helping you calculate the server's tip when you receive the check at a restaurant.

- When asking Siri to look up businesses, landmarks, popular destinations, or restaurants, in addition to just displaying a location on a map, Siri integrates with the Yelp! online service to provide much more detailed information about many businesses and restaurants.

- Send a Tweet or update your Facebook status using your voice. Activate Siri and say something like, "Send a Tweet that says, 'I am at Starbucks, come join me.'" To update your Facebook status, say something like, "Write on my wall, 'I just landed in New York City and I am leaving the airport now.'"

- When dictating a Tweet, you can add the phrase, "Tweet with my location," to have Siri publish your current location with the outgoing Tweet you're dictating.

- If you need to turn on or off certain iPhone or iPad features, activate Siri and say, "Turn on Wi-Fi" or "Turn off Bluetooth."

- When traveling overseas, use Siri to do currency conversion calculations. For example, activate Siri and ask, "How many U.S. dollars is 500 yen?"

- With the Photos app, you can activate Siri and say, "Show me my selfies," or "Show my photos from New York City." You can also be more specific and say something like, "Show my selfies from yesterday," or "Show selfies from my Florida vacation."

- Along with knowing about sports, TV shows, movies, restaurants, and music, Siri can quickly give you information about books. For example, activate Siri and say, "Show me books by Jason Rich" or "What are the best-selling books right now?"

PRACTICE (WITH SIRI) MAKES PERFECT

Right from the start, Siri will probably understand most of what you say. However, as you begin using this feature often, you will become acquainted with the best and most efficient ways to communicate questions, commands, and requests to generate the desired response.

Keep in mind that Siri translates what you say phonetically, so periodically, you might encounter names or commands that Siri can't understand or match up with correctly spelled information stored on your iPhone or iPad. This occurs most frequently with unusual names that sound vastly different from how they're spelled or used.

> **! CAUTION** Before allowing Siri to send any message or text, be sure to proofread it carefully on your device's screen. Keep in mind that some words sound the same when spoken, and Siri might choose the wrong word when translating your speech to text. This could lead to embarrassing situations or dramatically change the meaning of what you intended to say.

Siri can streamline how you interact with your device and make certain tasks much easier to accomplish. Based on the questions you ask, you might also discover that Siri has a sense of humor. For example, try asking, "Siri, what do you look like?," "Siri, are you attractive?," or "What is the best smartphone on the market?"

USE DICTATION MODE INSTEAD OF THE VIRTUAL KEYBOARD

In many situations when the iPhone or iPad's virtual keyboard appears, a microphone key is located to the left of the spacebar. When you tap on this microphone key, Dictation mode is activated (shown in Figure 2.6). An animated sound wave graphic displays on the screen as you speak.

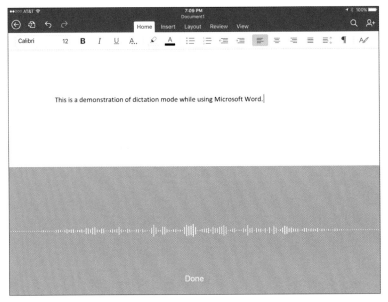

Figure 2.6

Use Dictation mode to enter text using your voice instead of typing on the virtual keyboard. It's shown here on an iPad running Microsoft Word.

You can now say whatever text you were going to manually type using the virtual keyboard. You can speak for up to 30 seconds at a time. When you're finished speaking, it's necessary to tap the Done key so that your device can translate your speech into text and insert it into the appropriate onscreen field.

For the fastest and most accurate results, speak one to three sentences at a time, and have your device connected to a Wi-Fi Internet connection.

> **TIP** While using Dictation mode, you can easily add punctuation just by saying it. For example, you can say, "This is a sample dictation period," and Siri adds the period (".") at the end of the sentence. You can also use words like "open parenthesis" or "close parenthesis," "open quotes" or "close quotes," or "comma," "semicolon," or "colon" as you dictate.

CONNECT OR LINK YOUR IPHONE TO YOUR CAR TO USE THE CARPLAY FEATURE

Over the past few years, Apple has worked with most of the world's major car manufacturers to integrate the iPhone with the stereo system or infotainment system built in to many vehicles. This functionality varies depending on the make, model, and year of your car.

In some cases, if your vehicle is CarPlay compatible, there is a Lightning port for your iPhone built in to the car. When you plug in your iPhone, your smartphone charges, plus it integrates directly with the car's in-dash infotainment system. This enables you to activate the iPhone's navigation capabilities via the Maps app, Siri functionality, and music capabilities by pressing the CarPlay button built in to your steering wheel or dashboard, for example.

In other cases, your vehicle establishes a wireless Bluetooth connection with your car and enables you to play music that's stored on your iPhone via your car's stereo or that your iPhone streams from the Internet via Apple Music, Spotify, Pandora, or another compatible music streaming app. It's also possible to use the Phone feature to make and receive calls hands-free while you're driving.

Every vehicle manufacturer is implementing iPhone integration differently, and this functionality is only built in to 2013 through 2016 (or later) model year vehicles. If you have an older car, you must use third-party accessories to link your iPhone to the vehicle.

Typically, when you use Siri, information that's requested is displayed on the iOS device's screen. CarPlay functionality, however, offers much of the same functionality as Siri but turns off the iPhone's screen altogether. Thus, Siri offers only verbal responses to a user's requests, commands, and questions.

This is a much safer solution for drivers who must pay attention to the road, yet want to access content from their Internet-connected iOS mobile device to initiate calls, look up information, access email or text messages, or obtain turn-by-turn driving directions to a specific location.

> **TIP** If you've invested in an Apple Watch, you also have full access to Siri from the watch when it is wirelessly paired to your iPhone. To activate Siri from the watch, press the Digital Crown for about two seconds until the Siri screen is displayed, and then start speaking into the watch.

3

STRATEGIES FOR FINDING, BUYING, AND USING THIRD-PARTY APPS

The collection of preinstalled apps that comes with iOS 9 enables you to begin utilizing your iPhone or iPad for a wide range of popular tasks without first having to find and install additional apps. However, one of the things that has set the iPhone and iPad apart from its competition and made these devices among the most sought-after and popular throughout much of the world is the vast library of optional apps available for them.

All the apps currently available for your iOS device can be obtained from Apple's online-based App Store. Then, as needed, iOS 9 can automatically update your apps to ensure you're always working with the most recently released version.

NOTE Although some apps are tweaked to work exceptionally well on the latest iPhone or iPad models, such as the iPhone 6s or iPhone 6s Plus, all iPhone-specific apps can scale themselves automatically to accommodate the iPhone model you're using, whether it has a 4", 4.7", or 5.5" display. Likewise, apps for the iPad (as well as universal iPhone/iPad apps) automatically adapt to the screen size of the tablet you're using.

APP STORE BASICS

There are two ways to access the App Store: directly from your iPhone or iPad (using the App Store app that comes preinstalled on your device) or using the iTunes software on your primary computer.

The App Store app is used exclusively for finding, purchasing (if applicable), downloading, and installing apps directly onto your device from the App Store. Other apps are used to access additional types of content. The iTunes software on your primary computer is used to access the App Store, as well as many other types of content.

HOW NEW APPS INSTALL THEMSELVES

If you're shopping for apps directly from your iPhone or iPad, tap on the Price icon, followed by the Buy icon, to make a purchase. Free apps display a Get icon in place of the Price icon. You might be asked to supply your Apple ID password (or place your finger on your device's Touch ID sensor, a.k.a. the Home button) to confirm the transaction. The app automatically downloads and installs itself on your device. After it is installed, its app icon appears on your iPhone or iPad's Home screen and is ready to use.

You can also shop for apps from your primary computer and transfer them to your iPhone or iPad, or sync apps between your various mobile devices using the iTunes Sync process or iCloud.

TIP Instead of manually entering your Apple ID password to confirm an app purchase (or acquire a free app), if your iOS mobile device is equipped with a Touch ID sensor as part of its Home button, you can simply scan your fingerprint to approve the transaction. For this to work, the feature must be turned on once from within Settings. To do this, launch Settings, tap on the Touch ID & Passcode option, enter your device's passcode, and then turn on the virtual switch that's associated with the App and iTunes Stores option.

> ⌇ **NOTE** The tiny "+" icon in the top left corner of a Buy or Get button indi-
> cates that the app is universal and will run on both the iPhone and iPad.

RESTORING OR REINSTALLING APPS YOU'VE ALREADY DOWNLOADED

If you have Family Sharing set up via iCloud (see Chapter 5, "Use iCloud and the iCloud Drive App from Your iPhone or iPad"), you can share apps you acquire with up to five other family members without having to repurchase that app. With or without Family Sharing, you can also install the app on all of your own iOS mobile devices that are linked to the same iCloud account, as long as the app is compat-ible with each device.

To download an app onto your iPad that has already been purchased or down-loaded onto another computer or device, tap on the Purchased icon that's dis-played at the bottom of the screen in the App Store app. On the iPhone, tap on the Updates icon, and then tap on the Purchased option that's displayed near the top of the Updates screen. All your app purchases to date are displayed.

> ⌇ **NOTE** At the top of the Purchased screen on the iPhone or iPad, tap on
> the All tab to view all of the apps you've purchased to date for that device. You
> also have the option to tap on the Not On This iPhone/Not On This iPad tab to
> view apps you've acquired in the past that are not currently installed on the device
> you're using.

Instead of a Get or Price icon being associated with each app description, an iCloud icon indicates the app is available through your iCloud account. Tap on the iCloud icon to download the app (without having to pay for it again) to the iOS device you're currently using. You can only install already purchased apps that are compatible with that iOS device. For example, you can't install an iPad-specific app onto an iPhone or iPod touch. You can, however, install iPhone-specific or univer-sal apps onto an iPad, iPad Pro, or iPad mini.

☑ TIP   From the Settings app, you have the option of having your iOS device automatically download and install any new (and compatible) apps, music, or eBooks purchased using your Apple ID on any other computer or device. To set this up, launch Settings, select the App and iTunes Stores option from the main Settings menu, and then adjust the Automatic Downloads options, which include Music, Apps, Books, and Updates. You also can decide whether this feature works with a cellular data Internet connection or just when a Wi-Fi connection is available. To exclusively use a Wi-Fi connection, turn off the virtual switch associated with the Use Cellular Data option.

WHERE TO FIND APPS, MUSIC, AND MORE

If you're shopping for apps, music, movies, TV shows, podcasts, audiobooks, eBooks, ringtones, or other content from your primary computer, with the goal of transferring what you acquire to your iPhone or iPad later via the iTunes sync process or via iCloud, use the latest version of the iTunes software on your Mac or PC computer.

However, from your iPhone or iPad, you can acquire and enjoy different types of content using a handful of different apps. Table 3.1 explains which app you should use to acquire and then enjoy various types of content on your iOS device.

Table 3.1   How to Acquire and Enjoy Various Types of Content on Your iPhone or iPad

Content Type	Buy with App	Run with App
Apps	App Store	The app itself that you download and install
Digital editions of publications (including newspapers and magazines)	App Store	The digital publication's proprietary app
Music	iTunes Store	Music
Movies	iTunes Store	Videos
TV Shows	iTunes Store	Videos
Podcasts	Podcasts	Podcasts
Audiobooks	iTunes (or the optional Audible app)	iBooks (or the optional Audible app)
eBooks*	iBooks (to access iBook Store)	iBooks

Content Type	Buy with App	Run with App
PDF files	Mail, iCloud, iTunes Sync	iBooks or another PDF reader app
iTunes U Personal Enrichment and Educational Content	iTunes U**	iTunes U
Ringtones (and Alert Tones)	iTunes Store	Phone, FaceTime, Messages (or other apps that generate audible alarms or ringtones)

eBooks can also be purchased from Amazon.com and read using the free Kindle app, or purchased from BN.com and read using the free Nook app.

**The iTunes U app serves as a gateway to a vast selection of personal enrichment and educational courses, lectures, workshops, and information sessions that have been produced by leading educators, universities, and other philanthropic organizations. All iTunes U content is provided for free.*

EVERYTHING YOU NEED TO KNOW ABOUT APPS

Apps are individual programs that you install on your iPhone or iPad to give it additional functionality, just as you utilize different programs on your primary computer. For the iPhone or iPad, all apps are available from one central (online-based) location, called the App Store.

When you begin exploring the App Store, you'll discover right away that there are in excess of 1.5 million apps to choose from. They are divided into different categories to help make it easier and faster to find what you're looking for.

The App Store's main app categories include Games, Kids, Books, Business, Catalogs, Education, Entertainment, Finance, Food & Drink, Health & Fitness, Lifestyle, Magazines & Newspapers, Medical, Music, Navigation, News, Photo & Video, Productivity, Reference, Social Networking, Sport, Travel, Utilities, and Weather.

COMPATIBILITY: DOES THE APP RUN ON MULTIPLE DEVICES?

In terms of compatibility, all iOS apps fall into one of these three categories:

1. **iPhone-specific**—These are apps designed exclusively for the various iPhone models that might not function properly on the iPad. Most iPhone-specific apps will run on an iPad but do not take advantage of the tablet's larger screen.

2. **iPad-specific**—These are apps designed exclusively for the iPad. They fully utilize the tablet's larger display and do not function on the iPhone or on other iOS devices. All iPad-specific apps do, however, function flawlessly on all iPad and iPad mini models, as well as the iPad Pro.

3. **Universal**—These are apps designed to work on all iOS devices, including any model iPhone or iPad. These apps detect which device they're running on and adapt.

> **TIP** When reading the App Store description of any app, tap on the Details tab and scroll down to the Information heading. Here, you can see a listing of which iOS devices the app is compatible with. Look for the Compatibility listing that's found under the Information heading (see Figure 3.1).

Figure 3.1

From an app's Description screen, you can see which iOS mobile devices the app is compatible with. Look for the Compatibility heading.

> **TIP** If you own two or more iOS devices, such as an iPhone and an iPad (or an iPod touch), and all the devices are linked to the same Apple ID (iCloud) account, you can purchase a universal (or iPhone-specific) app once but install it on all your iOS devices. This can be done through iTunes Sync or via iCloud after an app is initially purchased or downloaded.

When you're browsing the App Store from your iPhone, by default it displays all iPhone-specific apps followed by universal apps, but it does not display iPad apps. When you're browsing the App Store from your iPad, iPad-specific, universal, and iPhone-specific apps are all listed. Tap on the iPhone or iPad tab that's displayed near the top of the screen when viewing many areas of the App Store.

If you're shopping for apps using the iTunes software on your primary computer, click the iPhone or iPad tab that's displayed near the top center of the iTunes screen (shown in Figure 3.2) to select which format apps you're looking for.

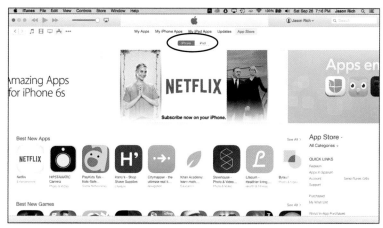

Figure 3.2

When shopping for apps using the iTunes software on your primary computer (in this case, a Mac), click the appropriate tab to indicate which format apps you're looking for, keeping in mind that iPhone-specific apps will run on an iPad (but not take advantage of the tablet's larger screen), but iPad-specific apps do not run on an iPhone.

> **✓ TIP** Because some app developers release the same app in both an iPhone-specific and an iPad-specific format, many iPad-specific apps have "HD" for High-Definition in their title, to help differentiate them from iPhone or universal apps. Some iPad-specific apps include the words "for iPad" in their title.

QUICK GUIDE TO APP PRICING

Regardless of whether you use the App Store app from your mobile device or visit the App Store using the iTunes software on your primary computer, you must set up an Apple ID account and have a major credit card or debit card linked to the account to make purchases.

> **TIP** If you don't have a major credit card or debit card that you want to link with your Apple ID account, you can purchase prepaid iTunes Gift Cards from Apple or most places that sell prepaid gift cards.
>
> iTunes Gift Cards are available in a variety of denominations and can be used to make app and other content purchases. They are distinct from Apple Gift Cards, which are only redeemable at Apple Stores or Apple.com.

The first time you access the App Store and attempt to make a purchase, you are prompted to enter your Apple ID account username and password or set up a new Apple ID account, which requires you to supply your name, address, email, and credit card information. For all subsequent online app purchases, you simply need to enter your Apple ID password (or place your finger on your device's Touch ID sensor), and the purchase is automatically billed to your credit or debit card or deducted from your iTunes Gift Card balance.

> **TIP** An Apple ID account can also be referred to as an iTunes Store account. To learn more about how an Apple ID account works or to manage your account, visit www.apple.com/support/appleid. The same Apple ID you use to make purchases can also be used as your username when you're using FaceTime for video calling, Messages to access the iMessage service, or to access your iCloud account.

Originally, when the App Store opened, there were two types of apps: free apps and paid apps. The free apps were often demo versions of paid apps (with limited functionality) or fully functional apps that displayed ads in the app. Paid apps were typically priced between $.99 and $9.99.

As the App Store has evolved, additional payment options and fee structures for apps have been introduced, giving app developers new ways to generate revenue, and iPhone and iPad uses different methods of paying for apps and content.

The following sections summarize the different types of apps from a pricing standpoint.

FREE APPS

Free apps cost nothing to download and install on your phone or tablet. Some programmers and developers release apps for free out of pure kindness to share their creations with the iPhone- and/or iPad-using public. These are fully functional apps.

There are also free apps that serve as demo versions of paid apps. In some cases, certain features or functions of the app are locked in the free version, but are later made available if you upgrade to the paid or premium version of the app.

A third category of free apps comprises fully functional apps that display ads as part of their content. In exchange for using the app, you must view ads. These ads typically offer the option to click on special offers from within the app or learn more about a product or service being advertised.

> ☐✐ **NOTE** Many free apps that contain ads also have a paid app counterpart that's ad-free.

A fourth category of free apps serves as a shell for premium (paid) content that must be loaded into the app to make it fully functional. For example, many newspaper and magazine publishers offer free apps related to their specific publications but require users to pay for the actual content of the newspaper or magazine, which later gets downloaded into the app.

The final type of free app enables the user to make in-app purchases to add features or functionality to the app or unlock premium content. The core app, without the extra content, is free, however.

> ☐✓ **TIP** Some fully functional apps are free because they're designed to promote a specific company or work with a specific service. For example, to use the free HBOGo app, you must be a paid subscriber of the HBO premium cable channel.
>
> Likewise, to use the free Netflix app, you must be a paid subscriber to this streaming movie service. The AmEx app is useful only to people with an American Express Card, but the free Target app is useful to anyone who shops at Target stores.

PAID APPS

After you purchase an app, you own it and can use it as often as you'd like, usually without incurring additional fees (although in-app purchases might be possible). You simply pay a fee for the app upfront, which is often between $.99 and $9.99. Typically, future upgrades of the app are free of charge.

SUBSCRIPTION-BASED APPS

Each full-length digital edition of a magazine or newspaper requires its own proprietary app (also available from the App Store) to access and read that publication's content.

These apps are typically free, and then you pay a recurring subscription fee for content, which automatically gets downloaded into the app. Many digital editions of newspapers, such as the *New York Times* and the *Wall Street Journal*, utilize a subscription app model, as do hundreds of different magazines.

Typically, the main content of the digital and printed version of a publication are identical. However, you can view the digital edition on your iPhone or iPad and take advantage of added interactive elements built in to the app.

If you're already a subscriber to the print version of a newspaper or magazine, some publishers offer the digital edition free, while others charge an extra fee to subscribe to the digital edition as well. Or you can subscribe to just the digital edition of a publication.

With some publications, you can download the free app for a specific newspaper or magazine and then purchase one issue at a time from within the app, including past issues. There is no long-term subscription commitment, but individual issues of the publication still must be purchased and downloaded. Or you can purchase an ongoing (recurring) subscription and new issues of that publication will automatically be downloaded to your iPhone or iPad as they become available.

 **WHAT'S NEW** New to iOS 9 is the News app. As you'll discover in Chapter 15, "Customize Your Reading Experience with iBooks and the News App," many leading publications now offer content for free. You can fully customize what topics or publications you're interested in reading, and the News app presents all related content (potentially acquired from many sources) to you in an easy-to-read way. There are no subscription fees to access or read content. When using the News app, you only have access to select articles and content, not the digital edition of an entire publication, however.

IN-APP PURCHASES

Some apps allow you to purchase additional content or add new features and functionality by making in-app purchases. The capability to make in-app purchases has become very popular and is being used by app developers in a variety of ways. If an app offers in-app purchases, they are listed under the In-App Purchases heading within the app description screen in the App Store.

!CAUTION The price you pay for an app does not translate directly to the quality or usefulness of that app. Some free or very inexpensive apps are extremely useful and packed with features and can really enhance your experience using your iPhone or iPad. There are also costly apps that are poorly designed, filled with bugs, or don't live up to expectations or to the description of the app offered by the app's developer or publisher.

The price of each app is set by the developer or programmer that created or is selling the app. Instead of using the price as the only determining factor if you're evaluating several apps that appear to offer similar functionality, be sure to read the app's customer reviews carefully, and pay attention to the star-based rating the app has received. These user reviews and ratings are a much better indicator of the app's quality and usefulness than the price.

HOW TO SHOP WITH THE APP STORE APP

From your iPhone or iPad's Home screen, to access the App Store, tap on the blue-and-white App Store app icon. Your device must have access to the Internet via a cellular or Wi-Fi connection.

When you access the App Store app (shown in Figure 3.3 on the iPad), a handful of command icons at the top and bottom of the screen are used to navigate your way around the online-based store.

Figure 3.3

The main App Store app screen on the iPad. Find, purchase, download, and install apps directly from your tablet.

If you already know the name of the app you want to find, purchase, download, and install, tap on the Search field, which is located near the upper-right corner of the screen in the iPad version. On the iPhone, tap on the Search option displayed at the bottom of the App Store app's screen (as shown in Figure 3.4).

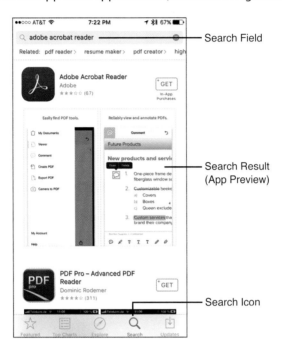

Figure 3.4

From your iPhone, tap on the Search icon to search for any app in the App Store by name or keyword.

Using the virtual keyboard, enter the name of the app. Tap the Search key on the virtual keyboard to begin the search. You can also perform a search based on a keyword or phrase, such as "word processing," "to-do lists," "time management," or "photo editing."

In a few seconds, matching results are displayed on the App Store screen in the form of app previews.

If you're shopping for apps from your iPad, as you browse the App Store, iPad-specific and universal apps are displayed if you tap on the iPad Only option near the top of the screen in most areas in the App Store.

> **TIP** At the bottom center of the main App Store screen on the iPad are several command icons, labeled Featured, Top Charts, Explore, Purchased, and Updates. On the iPhone, the icons along the bottom of the screen are labeled Featured, Top Charts, Explore, Search, and Updates. If you don't know the exact name of an app you're looking for, these command icons will help you browse the App Store and discover apps that might be of interest to you.

THE FEATURED ICON

Tap on the Featured icon near the bottom of the App Store screen to see a listing of what Apple considers "Featured" apps. These are divided into a handful of categories, such as Best New Apps or Popular Apps.

Either flick your finger from right to left to scroll horizontally through the apps listed, or tap on the See All option that's displayed to the right of the category heading.

Near the top of the screen are large graphic banners that constantly change. When you refer to Figure 3.4, for example, one of the banners says "Great Apps & Games for iOS 9"; however, it constantly scrolls and often showcases specific apps.

THE TOP CHARTS ICON

When you tap on the Top Charts command icon, located near the bottom center of the App Store app's screen, a listing of Paid, Free, and Top Grossing apps are displayed (shown in Figure 3.5). These charts are based on all app categories.

To view charts related to a specific app category, such as Business or Games, first tap on the Top Charts button, and then tap on the Categories button and choose a specific category.

MANAGE YOUR ACCOUNT AND REDEEM ITUNES GIFT CARDS

When you scroll down to the very bottom of the Featured screen in the App Store, you'll see several command buttons.

Tap on the Redeem button to redeem a prepaid iTunes Gift Card. Tap on the Apple ID [Your Apple ID Username] button to manage your Apple ID account and update your credit card information, for example. When the Apple ID window appears, tap on the View Apple ID option. When prompted, enter your password.

Tap on the Apple ID account button to manage your recurring paid subscriptions, as well. When the Account Settings screen is displayed, scroll down to the
Subscriptions heading and tap on the Manage button. You can then modify or
cancel your paid recurring subscriptions to digital newspapers or magazines,
for example. If you don't yet have any active subscriptions, this option does not
appear.

Figure 3.5

*From the App Store app on the iPad, tap on the Top Charts icon at the bottom of the screen to
view a list of popular free, paid, and top-grossing apps.*

Tap on the Send Gift option to send an iTunes Gift Card to someone else. Their gift
will arrive via email and they can redeem it almost instantly from the App Store,
iTunes Store, or iBook Store.

FEATURES OF AN APP LISTING

As you browse the App Store, each screen is composed of many app listings (or more
information-packed app previews). Each listing promotes a specific app and displays
the app's title, graphic icon or logo, what category the app falls into, and its price.

Within an app preview (refer to Figure 3.4), the app's title, its logo/graphic, the
app's developer, its average star-based rating, how many ratings the app has
received (the number in parentheses), the price icon, and a sample screenshot
from the app itself are displayed.

LEARN BEFORE YOU BUY: ACCESSING THE APP'S DESCRIPTION PAGE

Before committing to a purchase, as you're looking at an app's listing or preview in the App Store, tap on its title or graphic icon to view a detailed description. When you do this on the iPhone, the App Store screen is replaced with a detailed description of the app. On the iPad, a new app description window is displayed over the App Store screen.

An app description screen (shown in Figure 3.6) displays the app's title and logo near the top of the screen, along with its price icon (or Get icon if it's a free app), average star-based rating, and the number of ratings it has received.

Figure 3.6

From an app's description screen, you can learn all about a specific app. This information can help you decide whether it's of interest to you or relevant to your needs.

You then see three command tabs, labeled Details, Reviews, and Related. Tap on the Details tab to view a detailed description of the app. Tap on the Reviews tab to view a star-based ratings chart for that app, as well as detailed text-based reviews written by your fellow iPhone and iPad users. Tap on the Related tab to view similar apps that are available from the App Store.

Displayed immediately below the Details, Reviews, and Related tab are sample screen shots from the app itself. Swipe your finger horizontally to scroll through the sample screen shots, or scroll down to view the Details, Reviews, or Related information, based on which command tab you've tapped.

WHAT'S OFFERED WHEN YOU TAP THE DETAILS TAB

Immediately below the sample screen shots from the app is a text-based description of the app from the app's developer. This is a sales tool designed to sell apps.

Below the description is information about what new features have been added to the app in the most recent version. Look for the What's New heading.

Displayed beneath the What's New heading, if applicable, is the Supports heading. Here, you can quickly determine whether the app is compatible with Apple's Game Center online service, for example. As you scroll down on this screen, the Information section offers more useful facts about the app.

Below the Information section, tap on the In-App Purchases option, if this option is available, to discover what in-app purchases are available and their cost.

Tap on the Version History option to see information about all revisions to the app that have been released since it was first introduced.

Tap on the Developer Apps link to discover other apps available from the same developer or publisher. Tap on the Developer Website option to access the website operated by the app developer or the app-specific website. When you do this, Safari automatically launches and then loads the applicable website.

WHAT'S OFFERED WHEN YOU TAP THE REVIEWS TAB

When you tap on the Reviews tab, the App Store Ratings chart is displayed (shown in Figure 3.7). This graphically shows how many ratings the app has received, its overall average rating, and the total number of ratings. A top rating is five stars.

Below the App Store Ratings chart are text-based reviews that have been written by other App Store customers.

> **TIP** As you're looking at an app's Description screen, sharing details about an app with others are offered when you tap on the Share icon displayed near the top-right corner of the Description screen. For example, the Gift option enables you to purchase and send a paid app to someone else.

WHAT'S OFFERED WHEN YOU TAP THE RELATED TAB

These are listings for other apps, usually similar in functionality to the app you're looking at.

On the iPhone, to exit an app's description page and continue browsing the App Store, tap on the left-pointing arrow icon that's displayed near the top-left corner of the screen. On the iPad, tap anywhere outside the app's description window.

Star-Based Rating Chart

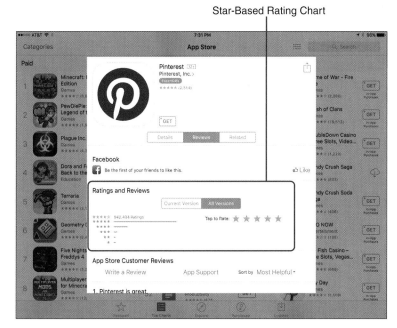

Figure 3.7
Every app description contains an average rating and a rating summary chart. Use it to quickly see what other users think about the app you're currently looking at.

KEEP YOUR APPS CURRENT WITH THE UPDATES COMMAND ICON

One of the command icons that's constantly displayed at the bottom of the App Store app's screen is the Updates icon. This is used to keep your currently installed apps up to date. More information about this feature is included in the section, "Keep Your Apps Up to Date with the Latest Versions."

NOTE If you opt to shop for apps using the iTunes software on your Mac or PC, you can transfer those apps to your iOS mobile device using the iTunes Sync process or download your purchases from iCloud by tapping on the Purchased option in the App Store app on your mobile device.

To learn more about using the iTunes software on your computer and the iTunes Sync process, visit www.apple.com/support/itunes.

QUICK TIPS FOR FINDING APPS RELEVANT TO YOU

As you explore the App Store, it's easy to get overwhelmed by the sheer number of apps that are available for your iOS device. If you're a new iPhone or iPad user, spending time browsing the App Store introduces you to the many types of apps that are available, and provides you with ideas about how your phone or tablet can be utilized in your personal or professional life.

However, you can save a lot of time searching for apps if you already know the app's exact title, or if you know what type of app you're looking for. In this case, you can enter either the app's exact title or a keyword description of the app in the App Store's Search field to see a list of relevant matches. If you're looking for a word-processing app, you can either enter the search phrase "Microsoft Word" into the App Store's Search field, or enter the search phrase "word processor" to see a selection of word processing apps.

If you're looking for vertical market apps with specialized functionality that caters to your industry or profession, enter that industry or profession (or keywords associated with it) in the Search field. For example, enter keywords like "medical imaging," "radiology," "plumbing," "telemarketing," or "sales."

As you're evaluating an app before downloading it, use these tips to help you determine whether it's worth installing on your phone or tablet:

- Figure out what type of features or functionality you want to add to your iPhone or iPad.

- Using the Search field, find apps designed to handle the tasks you have in mind. Chances are, you can easily find a handful of apps created by different developers that are designed to perform the same basic functionality. You can then pick which is the best based on the description, screenshots, and list of features each app offers.

- Check the customer reviews and ratings for the app. This useful tool quickly determines whether the app actually works as described in its description. Keep in mind that an app's description in the App Store is written by the app's developer and is designed to sell apps. The customer reviews and star-based ratings are created by fellow iPhone or iPad users who have tried out the app firsthand. If an app has only a few ratings or reviews and they're mixed, you might need to try out the app for yourself to determine whether it will be useful to you.

- If an app offers a free version, download and test that first before purchasing the premium version. You can always delete any app that you try out but don't wind up liking or needing.

> **✓ TIP** If you discover an app that looks interesting but you don't want to purchase or install it right away, access the Description screen for that app, and then tap on its Share button. You can then either email yourself information about the app or tap on the Add to Wish List button to add it to a list of apps you're interested in.
>
> You can later view your Wish List by tapping on the Wish List icon that on the iPhone is displayed in the top-right corner of the App Store's Featured screen. On the iPad, the Wish List icon is located to the immediate left of the Search field (in the top-right corner of the App Store screen.)

KEEP YOUR APPS UP TO DATE WITH THE LATEST VERSIONS

Periodically, app developers release new versions of their apps. iOS 9 can automatically update your installed apps as long as your iPhone or iPad has access to the Internet.

To customize this auto-update option, launch Settings and then tap on the App and iTunes Stores option. From the App and iTunes Stores menu, set up automatic downloads for Music, Apps, Books, and Updates. Make sure the virtual switch associated with the Updates option is turned on.

Next, scroll down to the Use Cellular Data option. Choose whether you want apps to update using a cellular data connection to the Internet. Keep in mind that some apps which have a large file size associated with them will require a Wi-Fi Internet connection to update.

At any time, you can see which apps have been updated and read a summary of what functionality or features have been added to the app update (as well as which bugs have been fixed) by launching the App Store app and tapping on the Updates option.

If an app listed on the Updates screen has an Open button associated with it, the app has been recently updated. The date of the update is listed. Tap on the app icon or its title to read about the update. Tap on the Open button to launch the app and use it on your iPhone or iPad.

From the Updates screen, if an Open button is not displayed, you might see a progress meter indicating the app is currently being updated and downloaded to your device. If an update is available but has not yet been downloaded and installed, an Update button, instead of an Open button, is displayed with that app.

As you're viewing the Updates screen, apps are listed in chronological order, based on when they were updated. Pending updates, if any, are displayed near the top of the screen (shown in Figure 3.8).

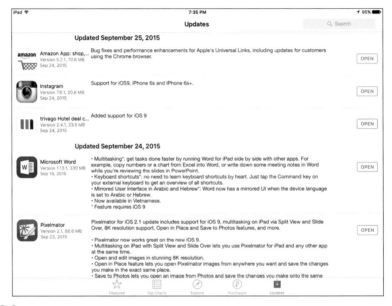

Figure 3.8
iOS 9 can automatically download and install updates to apps. The Updates screen shows which apps have been recently updated and what's new in those updates.

MANAGE YOUR KIDS' APP ACQUISITIONS

As a parent, you can control what apps your child is allowed to purchase, install, and ultimately use on their iOS mobile device or yours. You can also control their online spending when it comes to apps and in-app purchases in several different ways.

To determine which apps and content your child is allowed to use on an iOS mobile device, activate the Restrictions options. To do this, launch Settings on the device, tap on the General option, and then tap on the Restrictions option.

From the Restrictions submenu, tap on Enable Restrictions and then turn on the virtual switches associated with iTunes Store, Apple Music Connect, Podcasts, News, iBooks Store, Installing Apps, Deleting Apps, and In-App Purchases to limit what your child can do.

Under the Allowed Content heading, tap on the Apps option and determine what apps your child will be able to access, based on the App Ratings.

When you set up iCloud's Family Sharing, it's possible to set up your child's iOS mobile device so he or she needs to ask you for permission (via a text message to your iPhone or iPad) before acquiring any new apps or content. This feature also gives parents greater control over apps installed on a child's device.

It's also possible to set up an iTunes Allowance for your child and give them a prede-termined amount of money to spend in the App Store, iTunes Store, and iBook Store each month. To learn more about this option, visit www.apple.com/itunes/gifts.

> **NOTE** In addition to the apps that come preinstalled with iOS 9, Apple offers a handful of optional Made By Apple apps, such as Pages (similar to Microsoft Word), Numbers (similar to Microsoft Excel), Keynote (similar to Microsoft PowerPoint), iMovie (video editing), Apple Store (online shopping via the Apple.com Online Store or an Apple retail store), GarageBand (music composi-tion and editing), and iTunes U (educational programming). These are available for free from the App Store.

IN THIS CHAPTER

■ Use AirDrop to share content with other nearby Mac, iPhone, and iPad users

■ Utilize your iPhone or iPad with AirPlay-compatible equipment

■ Print files wirelessly to a compatible AirPrint printer

■ Discover iOS 9's Continuity and Handoff functionality

4

SYNC, SHARE, AND PRINT FILES USING AIRDROP, AIRPLAY, AIRPRINT, AND HANDOFF

When it comes to syncing and sharing files and data (including app-specific data), your iOS mobile device is equipped with several tools, including AirDrop, AirPlay, AirPrint, Continuity, and Handoff.

The AirDrop tool enables your iPhone or iPad to wirelessly transfer certain types of files (including photos) and app-specific data to other iPhones, iPads, and Macs that are in close proximity, and that also support the AirDrop function.

To turn on the AirDrop feature on your iPhone or iPad, launch Control Center by swiping your finger upward from the very bottom of the screen. When the Control Center appears, tap on the AirDrop option.

From the AirDrop menu (shown in Figure 4.1), choose whether you want to utilize AirDrop to communicate with any other nearby users (Everyone) or only with people within your Contacts database (Contacts Only). It's also possible to turn off the feature altogether.

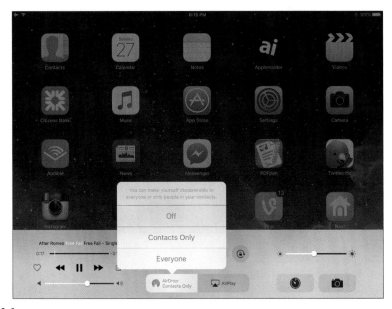

Figure 4.1

Access the AirDrop menu from the Control Center. (Shown here on an iPad.)

When it's turned on, use this feature to send content from the Share menu that's built in to compatible apps. For example, if you want to send a photo to another AirDrop user (or one of your other compatible Macs or mobile devices), launch Photos, view and select the photo(s) you want to send, and then tap on the Share icon.

When the Share menu is displayed (shown in Figure 4.2), thumbnails representing people in close proximity who have AirDrop turned on are displayed. Tap on the intended recipient, and the selected photos are wirelessly sent.

> **NOTE** AirDrop is available only when using iPhones and iPads released within the last few years that are running iOS 8 or iOS 9.
>
> If you want to use AirDrop between an iOS mobile device and a Mac, the Mac must have been released in 2012 or later and be running OS X Yosemite or OS X El Capitan.

Possible AirDrop Recipient

Figure 4.2

Select AirDrop from the Share menu of compatible apps to send app-specific content to other iOS mobile devices and Mac users.

> **TIP** In addition to the Photos app, the AirDrop feature is supported by the Share menu found in other apps, including Contacts, Maps, Notes, Safari, iBooks, and iTunes Store.

After you receive content via AirDrop, to access that content, launch the relevant app. For example, to view, organize, or edit photos you receive, open the All Photos/ Camera Roll album in the Photos app. If you receive a Contacts entry, it is automatically added to your Contacts database and is accessible from the Contacts app.

> **Caution** To avoid receiving unwanted content from strangers when you're in public places such as an airport or theater, consider turning off the AirDrop feature from within Control Center and turning it on only when it's needed. Alternatively, you can turn on AirDrop but set it up so only content from people with entries in your Contacts app's database will be received.

STREAM CONTENT FROM YOUR iPHONE OR iPAD TO OTHER COMPATIBLE DEVICES USING AIRPLAY

AirPlay is a wireless feature that enables your mobile device to stream content such as photos, videos, or audio, to an AirPlay-compatible device, such as Apple TV, a Mac, or AirPlay-compatible speakers.

To use AirPlay, your iOS mobile device and the other AirPlay-compatible device must be connected to the same wireless home network (via Wi-Fi). Then, when you turn on the AirPlay feature, the two compatible devices automatically establish a wireless connection.

After the connection is made, an AirPlay icon appears within compatible apps, such as Music, Videos, and Photos, enabling you to transfer (stream) what you would otherwise see on your iPhone or iPad's screen, or what would be heard through the device's speaker, to another compatible device.

In addition to being able to stream photos and video (including iTunes Store TV show and movie purchases and rentals), you can use AirPlay to connect external speakers (without cables) to your iOS mobile device and then stream music (from Apple Music, Pandora, Spotify, or iTunes Radio, for example) or other audio (such as audiobooks or podcasts) from your device to those compatible speakers.

When it's available, one of the easiest ways to turn AirPlay on or off is to access it from Control Center. Tap on the AirPlay icon, and then choose where you want to stream the content to. In Figure 4.3, you see that an iPad is wirelessly connecting to Apple TV to stream a TV show saved in the iPad and display it on an HD television set via Apple TV.

> **TIP** It's possible to use AirPlay to present PowerPoint or Keynote digital slide presentations on a TV or monitor that has an Apple TV connected to it. What appears on the TV is exactly what's displayed on your smartphone or tablet.

> **MORE INFO** AirPlay-compatible speakers are available from a handful of different companies, starting around $49.95. To learn more about AirPlay and compatible equipment, visit https://support.apple.com/en-us/HT204289.

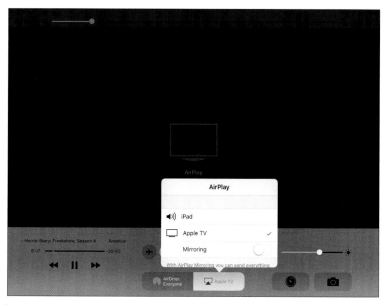

Figure 4.3
The AirPlay icon and menu found in Control Center.

PRINT FILES WIRELESSLY USING AN AIRPRINT-COMPATIBLE PRINTER

Another wireless feature offered by iOS 9 is AirPrint. It enables compatible apps to wirelessly send documents, data, or photos to be printed on an AirPrint-compatible laser, ink jet, or photo printer. For this feature to work, the iOS mobile device and the printer must be connected to the same wireless network.

> 🔍 **MORE INFO** Dozens of different AirPrint-compatible printers are now available, from companies such as Brother, HP, Canon, Lexmark, and Epson. To learn more about AirPrint-compatible printers, visit https://support.apple.com/en-us/HT201311.

After you've set up an AirPrint-compatible printer, use the Print feature that's built in to many apps, such as Pages, Notes, Safari, Maps, and Photos. The Print option is often found in the Share menu of these apps, although this can vary.

> ☑ **TIP** If you're not using an AirPrint-compatible printer, it's possible to install specialized software on your Mac, such as handyPrint (www.netputing.com/handyprint) or Printopia (www.decisivetactics.com/products/printopia), to enable your printer to work with the AirPrint feature of your iPhone or iPad, as long as your Mac is turned on.

CONTINUE A TASK ON ONE DEVICE EXACTLY WHERE YOU LEFT OFF ON ANOTHER USING HANDOFF

Handoff is an iOS feature that works with many apps that come preinstalled with iOS 9, as well as the iWork for iOS apps. It's also compatible with a growing number of third-party apps.

Basically, this feature enables you to begin a task on one of your Mac(s) or iOS mobile devices and then pick up exactly where you left off on another Mac or iOS mobile device that's linked to the same iCloud account and is within Bluetooth range (about 33 feet).

> ✎ **NOTE** To use the Handoff feature between your iPhone and a Mac, the Mac must be running the latest version of OS X Yosemite or OS X El Capitan.

To enable the Handoff feature on your mobile device, launch Settings, tap on General, and then tap on the Handoff & Suggested Apps option. Turn on the virtual switch associated with the Handoff option. This must be done on each of your iOS mobile devices.

Also, make sure the device you're using is connected to the same wireless network as the device(s) with which you want to use these features and that Bluetooth is turned on.

When Handoff is turned on, start performing a compatible task on one of your Macs or iOS mobile devices. Then, to pick up what you were doing on a different iPhone or iPad, wake up the device, and from the Lock screen, place your finger on the app icon displayed in the lower-left corner of the screen, and swipe upward (shown in Figure 4.4). You can also access the app switcher. Apps available via Handoff will be displayed at the bottom of the screen.

Handoff icon for
Safari web browser

Figure 4.4
*When it's possible to take advantage of the Handoff feature, upon waking up your iPhone or
iPad, place your finger on the Handoff app icon displayed in the lower-left corner of the Lock
screen and swipe upward.*

> **NOTE** When you attempt to use the Handoff feature from the Lock
> screen, it is still necessary to unlock the iPhone or iPad you're currently using
> before accessing the app that you were using on your other computer or iOS
> mobile device.

> **NOTE** To pick up what you were previously doing while currently using
> a Mac, simply open the app you were previously using on your other Mac or iOS
> mobile device.

Handoff is one of iOS 9's Continuity features. Another Continuity feature, and one
of the coolest if you're an iPhone user, is that when you receive an incoming call
on your phone, when the Continuity/Handoff feature is also active on your iPad

and/or Mac, you can answer that incoming call and engage in the phone conversation from one of these other devices.

Your iPhone continues to host the call, but the wireless connection between your iPhone and iPad (or iPhone and Mac) enables you to use the Mac or iPad's built-in microphone and speaker(s) as a speakerphone.

> **NOTE** For this aspect of the Handoff feature to work, your iPad or Mac must be linked to the same Wi-Fi network as your iPhone, plus both devices must be signed in to the same iCloud account and have Bluetooth turned on. T-Mobile users have access to this feature, but the devices do not need to be linked to the same Wi-Fi account.

When an incoming call is displayed on your iPad or Mac's screen, tap or click on the Answer icon to answer the call. If you want to initiate a call from your iPad or Mac (via your iPhone), tap or click on a phone number that's displayed in the Contacts, Calendar, or Safari apps, or tap on one of the recent contact thumbnails displayed on the Spotlight Search screen.

Another nice feature of Handoff is that you can now send and receive SMS and MMS text messages via your cellular service provider's texting network (as opposed to Apple's Internet-based iMessage service) from your iPad or Mac(s). These incoming or outgoing messages use the Messages app running on your iPhone (with its cellular connection) as a conduit.

> **MORE INFO** To determine whether your iOS mobile device or Mac is compatible with iOS 9's Continuity, Handoff, Instant Hotspot, Phone Calling, and SMS features, visit this page of Apple's website: https://support.apple.com/en-us/HT204689.
>
> To use the Personal Hotspot feature, which enables you to create a Wi-Fi hotspot from your iPhone (for your other Wi-Fi-compatible mobile devices linked to the same iCloud account), this feature must be supported by your iPhone's cellular service provider and your service plan.

IN THIS CHAPTER

- How to sync files, documents, photos, and data via iCloud
- Get acquainted with the iCloud Drive feature and the iCloud Drive mobile app
- Take advantage of iCloud's Family Sharing feature to share purchased content with up to five other family members

USE iCLOUD AND THE iCLOUD DRIVE APP FROM YOUR iPHONE OR iPAD

iCloud is Apple's cloud-based service, which has been designed from the ground up to work seamlessly with all iOS mobile devices and Macs. Functionality for using iCloud's various features and functions is built in to the iOS 9 operating system, as well as the Mac's operating system.

Now, more than ever, if you're an iPhone, iPad, and/or Mac user, setting up an iCloud account is essential in order to take full advantage of the latest features and functions built in to your smartphone, tablet, and/or computer.

WHAT'S NEW The new iCloud Drive app comes preinstalled with iOS 9. This app enables you to directly access the online-based iCloud Drive aspect of your iCloud account to directly view, manage, or share data, documents, photos, and/or files that you have stored online. Your iPhone or iPad requires Internet access to use the iCloud Drive app.

While setting up an iCloud account continues to be free, if you need to utilize more than the 5GB of online storage space that comes with each account, you must purchase additional online storage. The monthly fee structure for additional iCloud online storage space is shown in Table 5.1.

Table 5.1   iCloud Online Storage Space Fees*

iCloud Online Storage Space	Monthly Fee
5GB	Free
50GB	$0.99
200GB	$2.99
1TB	$9.99

* This new fee structure went into effect September 16, 2015. Charges for the monthly fees are automatically billed to the debit or credit card linked to your Apple ID account as a recurring charge, once you acquire additional online storage space. For more information on pricing outside the U.S., visit https://support.apple.com/en-us/HT201238.

> **! CAUTION** The included 5GB of online storage space, plus any additional space you pay for, can be utilized to store your app-specific data, backup files, photos, and your personal files.
>
> In the past, online storage needed to store your photos as part of iCloud's My Photo Stream and Shared Photo Streams was provided for free. This is no longer the case, however. Using iCloud Photo Library, which is managed from the Photos app on your iPhone, iPad, and/or Macs, photo storage now utilizes some of your 5GB online storage allocation and any additional storage space you purchase (based on the size of your personal photo library).
>
> However, the additional online storage space that's needed for your iTunes Store, App Store, iBook Store, and other content purchases continues to be free.

To see and manage how your iCloud online storage space is actually being utilized, launch Settings and tap on the iCloud option. Then tap on the Storage option.

From the Storage screen (shown in Figure 5.1), you see how much online storage space is currently available, as well as how much is being utilized by photos, backups, documents, data, mail, and your other stored content.

Figure 5.1
The Storage screen enables you to see how your iCloud account's online storage is currently being utilized. (The iCloud account shown here has been upgraded to have 1TB of online storage space.)

> **TIP**   To conserve online storage space within your iCloud account, delete iCloud Backup files for old devices, or backups that are redundant and no longer needed.
>
> To do this, launch Settings, tap on the iCloud option, tap on the Storage option, and then tap on the Manage Storage option.
>
> Under the Backups heading (shown in Figure 5.2), tap on any of your device-specific listings. Then, to delete that old or unwanted backup, tap on the Delete Backup option.

Figure 5.2
To free up online storage space, consider deleting old or unwanted backup files.

Each iCloud account also includes a free @icloud.com email account, which you can use to send and receive email from any devices linked to your iCloud account. Once it's set up, iCloud automatically keeps your email account synchronized via the Mail App.

> **NOTE** If you have an older Apple ID account that has an associated @mac.com or @me.com email address, its @icloud.com equivalent can automatically be used as the email address that's associated with your iCloud account.

CONTENT SAVED TO iCLOUD IS AVAILABLE ANYWHERE

By default, as soon as you establish your free iCloud account, anytime you acquire and download content from the iTunes Store, App Store, or iBook Store, a copy of that content automatically gets saved in your iCloud account, and immediately becomes available on all of your compatible computers and iOS mobile devices (including Apple TV) that are linked to that iCloud account. This includes all past purchases and downloads.

So, if you hear an awesome new song on the radio (or on iTunes Radio), you can immediately purchase and download it from the iTunes Store using your iPhone. As always, that song becomes available on your iPhone within a minute. Then, thanks to iCloud, you can access that same song from your primary computer, iPad, iPod touch, and/or Apple TV device, without having to repurchase it. This feature also works with TV shows and movies purchased from the iTunes Store.

> **NOTE** Thanks to iCloud's Family Sharing feature, it's now possible for up to six family members to have their own independent Apple ID/iCloud accounts, but share some or all of their purchased content from the iTunes Store, App Store, and iBook Store. Family Sharing is covered later in this chapter.

Another benefit to using iCloud is that syncing can be done from anywhere via the Internet, without using iTunes Sync or requiring a physical cable connection between your iOS mobile device and your primary computer.

> **NOTE** The iTunes Sync process is still possible by installing the iTunes software onto your primary computer, and then connecting your iOS mobile device using the supplied USB cable, but this process for backing up and syncing data is less convenient than using iCloud. (The Wi-Fi iTunes Sync process can be done without a cable, as long as both devices are linked to the same wireless network.)
>
> Because using the iTunes Sync process is now considered an antiquated way to sync and back up data, this book focuses on using iCloud. If you're still interested in using iTunes Sync, however, visit Apple's website (https://support.apple.com/en-us/HT203977) for more information on how to use this feature.

If you ever opt to delete a purchase from your iOS mobile device, for whatever reason, you always have the option of downloading and installing it again, free, from iCloud.

☑ **TIP**   Depending on how you set up the iTunes Store, App Store, and iBook Store to work with iCloud, you can automatically have all of your computers and iOS mobile devices download all new music, app, and eBook content you purchase, or this can be done manually.

To adjust these Automatic Downloads settings, launch Settings, select the App and iTunes Stores option, and then set the virtual switches associated with Music, Apps, and Books that are listed under the Automatic Downloads heading.

It's possible to also set up your iPhone or iPad to automatically update all of your apps as new versions of previously installed apps get released. To do this, turn on the virtual switch associated with the Updates option that's listed below the Music, Apps, and Books options.

Due to their large file sizes, automatic downloads are not possible for TV show episodes or movies acquired from the iTunes Store. However, you can download these purchases manually onto all your computers and/or iOS mobile devices linked to the same iCloud account.

✎ **NOTE**   Although your iTunes Store music purchases might represent a portion of your overall personal digital music library, chances are that library also includes CDs (which you have ripped into digital format), as well as online music purchases and downloads from other sources (such as Amazon.com).

For an additional fee of $24.99 per year, you can upgrade your iCloud account by adding the iTunes Match services. This grants you full access to your entire personal digital music library (including non-iTunes Store purchases) from all of your computers and devices that are linked to the same iCloud account. To learn more about iTunes Match, visit www.apple.com/itunes/itunes-match.

Alternatively, for $9.99 per month, you can sign up for the Apple Music service and have access to almost every song in the iTunes Store's digital music library (more than 43 million songs) via the Music app.

ACCESS YOUR PURCHASED iTUNES STORE CONTENT FROM ANY DEVICE

If you do not have the Automatic Downloads option enabled, you can still manually load iTunes Store purchases onto your device by following these steps:

1. Make sure that your iOS device is connected to the Web via a cellular data or Wi-Fi connection.

2. Launch the iTunes Store app on your device. If prompted, when the Apple ID Password window pops up on your screen, use the virtual keyboard to enter

your Apple ID password. (You can also use your device's Touch ID to scan your fingerprint.)

3. Tap on the Purchased icon near the lower-right corner of the iTunes Store app's screen. Then, near the top center of the screen, tap on the Music, Movies, or TV Shows tab.

4. On an iPhone, to access already purchased content, launch the iTunes Store app, tap on the More ("…") icon near the bottom-right corner of the screen, and then tap on the Purchased option. Select Music, Movies, or TV Shows; then choose the content you want to download onto the phone.

5. On the iPad, in a column on the left side of the screen is an alphabetical listing of artists, music groups, or TV shows, depending on which category of content you selected. Tap one to see what is available under that listing (shown in Figure 5.3). If you chose Movies in step 3, you can directly select a movie.

6. On the iPhone, after selecting a content type, past purchases are listed in alphabetical order. Tap on a song listing, and then tap on its iCloud icon to download that song onto the device you're currently using. On the iPad, this is possible from a single screen that displays both purchase listings and respective iCloud icons.

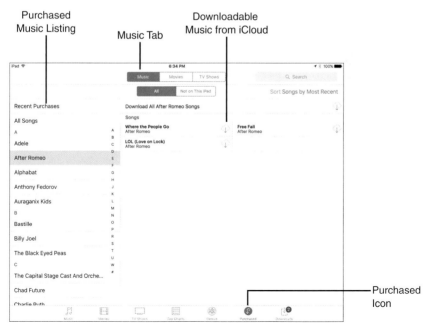

Figure 5.3

From the iTunes Store app, access and download your previous purchases by tapping on the Purchased icon. Here, the Music option has been selected.

> **TIP** To see a listing of your most recently purchased content, tap on a category (Music, Movies, or TV shows, for example), and then tap on the Recent Purchases option.

7. Tap on the iCloud icons, one at a time, to select content you want to download onto the iPhone or iPad you're currently using. Or to download all the listed content, tap on the Download All option at the top of the list.

> **TIP** If you've acquired audiobooks, an additional tab is displayed alongside the Music, Movies, and TV Shows options for this content.

8. Within minutes, the content you selected to download is available to enjoy on the iOS mobile device you're currently using.

9. Exit the iTunes Store app by pressing the Home button.

10. Launch the Music or Videos app on your iOS mobile device to experience the newly downloaded (or re-downloaded) content.

USE iCLOUD TO SYNC YOUR APP-SPECIFIC DATA, DOCUMENTS, AND FILES

Most cloud-based file-sharing services serve mainly as a place in cyberspace to remotely store files. However, you must manually transfer those files to and from the "cloud." This functionality is possible using the iCloud Drive feature.

However, thanks to iCloud's integration with iOS 9, many of the core apps that come with the latest version of this mobile operating system, as well as a growing number of third-party apps, automatically keep data and files created or managed using those apps synchronized with other devices and computers linked to the same iCloud account.

From within Settings on your iPhone or iPad, turn on or off iCloud support for all compatible apps on your device. In terms of iOS 9's preinstalled apps, those compatible with iCloud data syncing include Contacts, Calendars, Reminders, Safari, Notes, Photos, News, Wallet, and Mail (relating only to your free iCloud-related email account).

TIP iCloud Keychain can automatically store the usernames, passwords, and credit card information (for online purchases) related to all the websites you visit. Thus, you no longer need to manually sign in to websites when you revisit them, nor do you need to remember each username and password you associated with a website-related account.

When this feature is turned on once on each of your iOS mobile devices and Macs, your iCloud Keychain database syncs automatically with iCloud and all computers and iOS mobile devices linked to your iCloud account.

NOTE Bank- and personal finance-related websites purposely do not support the iCloud Keychain feature. When visiting sites that require added security, iCloud Keychain might be able to remember your username, but it cannot automatically remember your password.

MORE INFO iCloud is fully compatible with Apple's optional iWork apps, which include Pages (word processing), Numbers (spreadsheet management), and Keynote (for digital slide presentations).

The Microsoft Office apps (Word, Excel, PowerPoint, OneNote, and Outlook) now support iCloud, as well as Dropbox, and Microsoft's own OneDrive service (https://onedrive.live.com/about).

When you turn on the iCloud functionality related to the Contacts app, for example, your iOS mobile device automatically syncs your Contacts app database with iCloud. Thus, if you add or update an entry on your iPhone, it automatically synchronizes with the Contacts app running on your other iOS devices, as well as the compatible contact management software that's running on your computers (such as the Contacts app or Microsoft Outlook on your Mac). This is also true if you delete a Contacts entry from one device. It is almost instantly deleted from all of your other computers and iOS mobile devices linked to the same iCloud account. (Keep in mind, there is no "undo" option related to this feature.)

As you surf the Web using Safari, when you turn on iCloud syncing functionality related to this app, all your Bookmarks and Bookmark Bar data, along with your Reading List information and open browser window/tabs data, are synced via iCloud.

To share your photos between iOS devices, your primary computer, and/or an Apple TV device, from the iCloud submenu within Settings, tap on the Photos option to turn on the iCloud Photo Library feature.

CUSTOMIZING iCLOUD TO WORK WITH YOUR APPS

It's important to understand that the app-related synchronization feature offered by iCloud is different from iCloud Backup, which creates a complete backup of your iOS mobile device that gets stored online as part of your iCloud account.

When you set up iCloud to work with a specific compatible app, that app automatically accesses the Web, connects to iCloud, and then uploads or downloads app-related files, documents, or data as needed. iCloud then shares (syncs) that app-specific data with your other computers and devices that are linked to the same iCloud account.

To customize which of your compatible apps utilize iCloud functionality, follow these steps:

1. Launch Settings from your iPhone's or iPad's Home screen.

2. Tap on the iCloud option.

3. When the iCloud screen appears (shown in Figure 5.4), at the top of the screen, make sure the Apple ID–linked email address that's associated with your iCloud account is displayed next to the Account option. If it's not, use your existing Apple ID to create or access an iCloud account by tapping on the Account option.

4. Below the Account option is a list of all preinstalled iCloud-compatible apps on your iOS device. To the right of each listing is a virtual on/off switch. To turn on the iCloud functionality associated with a specific app, set its related virtual switch to the on position.

5. When you have turned on the iCloud functionality for all the apps that you want to synchronize via iCloud, press the Home button to exit Settings and save your changes.

6. Repeat this process on each of your iOS mobile devices. If you have an iPhone and an iPad, you must turn on the iCloud functionality for Contacts, for example, on both devices to keep Contacts data synchronized via iCloud on both devices.

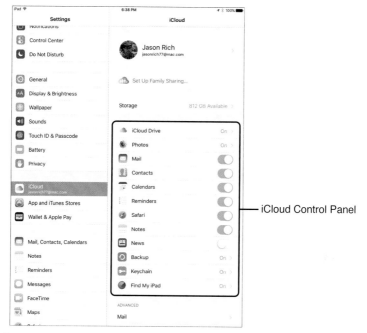

Figure 5.4

Turn iCloud functionality on or off for specific preinstalled Apple apps from the iCloud menu within Settings.

NOTE From the iCloud Drive Settings menu, there is a list of apps you have installed on your iPhone or iPad that allow you to store content, data, or files within iCloud Drive. Turn on or off the virtual switch for each app to activate this feature.

To access the iCloud Drive menu, launch Settings, tap on the iCloud option, and then tap on the iCloud Drive option.

NOTE After you've turned on the iCloud functionality for specific apps, to stay synchronized, each computer or device must have access to the Internet. For this use of iCloud on your iPhone or iPad, a cellular or a Wi-Fi Internet connection works fine. For certain other iCloud features, such as managing iCloud Photo Library functions or iCloud Backup, your iPhone or iPad requires a Wi-Fi Internet connection.

ACCESS YOUR APP-SPECIFIC DATA ONLINE FROM iCLOUD.COM

Another benefit of using iCloud to sync your app-specific data is that using any computer or Internet-enabled device, you can visit www.iCloud.com to run online versions of iOS 9 preinstalled apps populated with all your app-specific data.

To do this, log in to iCloud.com using your iCloud username and password (which is typically your Apple ID username and password). Online versions of the Mail, Contacts, Calendar, Photos, iCloud Drive, Notes, Reminders, Pages, Numbers, Keynote, News Publisher, Find My…, and Settings apps are available. This is shown on a Mac using the Safari web browser in Figure 5.5.

Figure 5.5

Log in to www.iCloud.com to access your app-specific content using online versions of popular iPhone and iPad apps.

If you forget your iPhone at home, for example, you can still securely access your complete Contacts database, your schedule, your to-do lists, and your notes from any Internet-enabled computer, whether or not that computer is typically linked to your iCloud account.

After you log in to iCloud.com, click on the onscreen app icon for the app you want to use.

☑ **TIP** From iCloud.com, it's possible to access and manage files you manually store in the iCloud Drive portion of your iCloud account. This includes nonapp-
specific files. To do this, log in to iCloud.com and click on the iCloud Drive icon.
You can then access or manage your files from the iCloud Drive screen (shown in
Figure 5.6).

Displayed near the top center of the iCloud Drive screen, from left to right, are
command icons for creating a new file folder, as well as uploading, downloading,
deleting, and/or sharing (via email) selected files.

As you'll see later in this chapter, the new iCloud Drive app that comes preinstalled with iOS 9 works almost exactly like this online iCloud Drive app, but from
your mobile device.

Figure 5.6
*From the iCloud Drive screen accessible from iCloud.com, it's possible to access and manage files
you've manually stored in this area of your iCloud account.*

❗ **CAUTION** If you're using someone else's computer to access iCloud.
com, be sure to log off from the iCloud service when you're finished. To do this,
click on your username in the top-right corner of the screen, and click on the
Sign Out option.

AUTOMATICALLY TRANSFER DOCUMENTS USING iCLOUD

In addition to the iCloud compatibility built in to many of the core (preinstalled) apps that are included with iOS 9, a growing number of other apps also offer iCloud compatibility and enable you to easily and automatically transfer or synchronize app-related documents and files.

If you turn on iCloud functionality within compatible third-party apps, when you create or revise a document or file, that revision is stored on your iOS device and on iCloud. It then syncs with that same app running on other iOS mobile devices, Macs, or PCs linked with your iCloud account.

The synchronization process happens automatically and behind the scenes, assuming that your iOS devices and primary computer are connected to the Internet.

> **TIP** Many iCloud features are now accessible from Windows-based PCs. However, you must download and install the free iCloud for Windows software onto your PC, which is available from this page of Apple's website: www.apple.com/icloud/setup/pc.html.

As with all apps running on your iPhone or iPad, iCloud functionality must be turned on in compatible third-party apps. How to do this varies by app, but it's typically done from the app's Settings, Setup, or Preferences menu. You can also adjust this setting from the iCloud Drive submenu within Settings. To access it, launch Settings, tap on the iCloud option, and then tap on the iCloud Drive option.

CREATE A PHOTO LIBRARY USING iCLOUD

Apple has recently redesigned and streamlined iCloud's photo sharing, backup, syncing, and sharing capabilities. Everything is now done through the iCloud Photo Library portion of your iCloud account and can be managed from the Photos app that comes bundled with iOS 9, as well as the OS X Yosemite or El Capitan version of the operating system and Photos app for the Mac.

iCloud Photo Library automatically syncs your complete personal photo library with all the computers and mobile devices linked to the same iCloud account (including Windows PCs). Plus, it's possible to share specific albums (or a group of selected photos from within an album) with specific people, yet keep the rest of your photo library private.

To customize options related to iCloud Photo Library, launch Settings, tap on the iCloud option, and then tap on the Photos option. From the Photos submenu (shown in Figure 5.7), turn on the virtual switch associated with iCloud Photo Library, and if you want to be able to share certain albums with others, turn on the iCloud Photo Sharing option. This must be done on all of your iOS mobile devices and from the iCloud Preference Pane on your Mac or Control Panel on PC computers.

Figure 5.7

From the Photos menu within Settings on your iPhone or iPad (shown here), it's possible to customize the iCloud Photo Library feature.

> **NOTE** One goal of iCloud Photo Library is to give you full online access to your entire digital images library, anytime, from any of your computers or iOS mobile devices. As a result of this content being readily available via the Internet, the need to store digital images on your mobile device will be reduced, so you will ultimately be able to free up internal storage space within your iPhone or iPad.
>
> Depending on the size of your entire digital photo library, it might become necessary, however, to purchase additional iCloud online storage space in order to store all of your digital images.

USING A UNIQUE APPLE ID FOR iCLOUD

When you first create an iCloud account, you're encouraged to use your existing Apple ID and username. This is to entice Apple computer and mobile device users to use the same Apple ID to make all of their iTunes Store, App Store, and iBook Store, purchases, plus use that same Apple ID to access Apple's online-based iMessage instant messaging service, use the FaceTime video calling service, and use all of iCloud's other functionality.

To create and manage your Apple ID account(s), visit https://appleid.apple.com from any computer or Internet-enabled device. When you set up iCloud, or try to use iMessage or FaceTime, or try to access the iTunes Store or iBook Store for the first time, you also have the option to create an Apple ID account.

> ✓ **TIP**   From your iPhone or iPad, to view and manage your Apple ID account, launch Settings, tap on the App and iTunes Stores option, and then tap on the Apple ID option displayed at the top of the submenu screen. Tap on the View Apple ID option to access and manage your account, or tap on the iForgot option to recover a forgotten Apple ID username or password.

BACKING UP WITH iCLOUD

Another useful feature of iOS 9 is the capability to create a backup of your iOS device wirelessly and have the related backup files stored online ("in the cloud"). To use this iCloud Backup feature, your iOS mobile device must be connected to the Internet via Wi-Fi. Your primary computer is not needed. Thus, the backup can be created from anywhere, and you can later restore your device from wherever a Wi-Fi Internet connection is present.

When activated, your iOS mobile device automatically creates a backup to iCloud once per day. For this to happen, your iPhone or iPad also must be connected to an external power source. However, at any time, you can manually create a backup of your device to iCloud from within Settings. This can be done when your device is running on battery.

Follow these steps to activate and use the iCloud Backup feature on an iPhone or iPad:

1. Connect your device to the Internet via a Wi-Fi connection.
2. From the Home screen, launch Settings.
3. Tap on the iCloud option.

4. Scroll down and tap on the Backup option.

5. Turn on the virtual switch that's associated with the iCloud Backup option.

6. The Back Up Now option appears near the bottom of the Backup screen (as shown in Figure 5.8). Tap on it to manually begin creating a backup of your iOS mobile device at any time.

Figure 5.8

Manage and launch the iCloud Backup feature from the Backup screen, accessible from within the Settings app.

TIP The first time you use the iCloud Backup feature to create a wireless backup of your iOS device, the process could take up to an hour (or longer), depending on how much data you have stored on your device. After the backup process begins, a progress meter is displayed at the bottom of the Backup screen within Settings.

In the future, the iCloud Backup process takes place once per day, automatically, when your iOS device is not otherwise in use. These backups save all newly created or revised files and data only, so subsequent iCloud Backup procedures are much quicker.

At the bottom of the Backup screen within Settings, the time (and date, if it's not the current day) of the last backup is displayed.

The purpose of creating and maintaining a backup of your device is so that you have a copy of all your apps, data, files, content, and personalized settings stored if something goes wrong with your device. If and when you need to access the backup to restore your device using iCloud, when prompted, choose the Restore from iCloud option.

Likewise, if your iPhone or iPad gets lost or stolen and is ultimately replaced, you can restore the content from your old device onto the new one.

> **TIP** To be able to restore your iOS mobile device completely from an iCloud Backup, you also need to turn on and be syncing app compatible apps. Turn on these app-specific features from the iCloud Control Panel screen, which is accessible by launching Settings and tapping on the iCloud option.

FAMILY SHARING ALLOWS FOR THE SHARING OF PURCHASED CONTENT

Thanks to iCloud's Family Sharing feature, up to six people can share some or all of their content purchases, while each person retains his or her own private iCloud account. At the same time, a separate Family folder is set up within the Photos app that enables participating family members to share selected photos by placing them in this Family album. All the other photos, however, remain private.

> **NOTE** When you set up Family Sharing, a separate Family calendar is automatically created in each participant's Calendar app. This calendar is shared with other family members, while all other Calendar-related data remains private.

To set up a Family Sharing account, one adult in the family needs to turn on this feature and then invite up to five other family members. To do this, launch Settings, tap on the iCloud option, and then tap on the Set Up Family Sharing option (refer to Figure 5.4).

One drawback to this feature is that the person setting up Family Sharing must choose one iCloud account associated with a credit card from which all purchases by all family members will be paid from this point forward. (This doesn't apply to gift cards, which are deducted from only the specific user's account.)

One useful feature of Family Sharing is the ability for family members to share their whereabouts with each other via the free Find My Friends app (which comes preinstalled with iOS 9). As you're setting up Family Sharing, you can activate this feature by tapping on the Share Your Location option.

Then, from the Family submenu screen, tap on the Add Family Member option and enter the name or email address for each family member who will participate.

Remember, you need to select a single Shared Payment Method that can be used to purchase content via this account in the future. By using Family Sharing, parents can now preapprove their kids' spending for online content and in-app purchases, plus set spending limits.

As soon as this feature is set up and the family members respond to the email invitation to participate, each person's music, TV shows, movies, eBooks, and compatible apps become available to everyone else. However, it's possible for each family member to keep selected content purchases and/or photos private.

> **NOTE** It's a good idea for parents to set up the Family Sharing feature for their younger kids and create a separate Apple ID account for each child who the parent maintains control over. To do this, launch Settings, tap on the iCloud option, tap on the Family option, and then tap on the Create an Apple ID for a Child option.

> **TIP** Before a family member accepts a Family Sharing invitation, his iOS mobile device (or Mac) must already be signed into his personal iCloud account.

When everyone is active with Family Sharing, to access each other's previously purchased content, launch the iTunes Store app, iBooks app (to access iBook Store), or the App Store app (to access apps), and tap on the Purchased option. Select a family member from the displayed menu. The purchased content already acquired by that family member (using the person's own Apple ID account) is displayed and becomes downloadable by others. All new purchases are considered acquired by the primary account used to manage the Family Sharing option.

> **TIP** If you're a parent, turn on the Ask To Buy option when setting up the Family Sharing feature. Then, anytime a child (under age 18) who is linked to the account wants to make a content purchase, the parent receives a text message asking them to approve the purchase. This approval is also required when a child wants to acquire free content.

In addition to the other Family Sharing features, events can be created and shared within an automatically created Family calendar using the Calendar app. Any participating family member can create an event with the Calendar app, like they normally would, and choose the Family calendar in the Calendar option in the New Event screen.

To view the Family calendar from the Calendar app, tap on the Calendars option, and then tap on the Family option to select the Family calendar for viewing.

Any participating member can add or delete events from the Family calendar; however, any other calendars being managed by each person's Calendar app remain separate and private.

> **NOTE** Just like the Family calendar accessible by all participating family members, a Family list is also created automatically in the Reminders app. This allows for centralized lists to be accessed and viewed by all participating family members, while at the same time, by default, all other lists stored in each person's Reminders app are kept private (unless you opt to share your other lists as well.)

> **NOTE** Using the Find My Friends app, it's possible to deactivate the Share My Location feature and block family members from viewing your current location. This cannot be done from a child's Apple ID/iCloud account if the account was set up as a "Child Account."

Like all of iCloud's features and functions, what's possible with Family Sharing will evolve over time.

USING THE NEW iCLOUD DRIVE APP ON YOUR MOBILE DEVICE

The new iCloud Drive app enables you to access the individual folders that contain data, documents, files, photos, and other content that you manually stored online on your iCloud Drive.

When you access a file, you can either preview it from within the iCloud Drive app or open and work with it using a compatible app. For example, if it's a Word document, you can open that document using the Word or Pages app. If it's a PDF file, you can open and view it using any PDF reader app.

Like any app that comes preinstalled with iOS 9, iCloud Drive has an app icon that appears on your device's Home screen. Tap on the app to launch it. Your mobile device must have Internet access for this app to work.

If the app icon for iCloud Drive does not appear on your Home screen, launch Settings, tap on the iCloud option, tap on the iCloud Drive option, and then turn on the virtual switch that's associated with Show on Home Screen.

As soon as you launch the iCloud Drive app, default folders for specific apps are displayed, as are folders you created from your primary computer (shown in Figure 5.9).

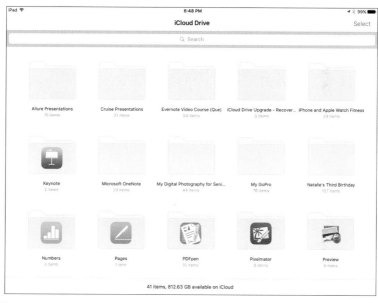

Figure 5.9

The main screen of the iCloud Drive app on an iPad when it's connected to the Internet.

Tap on any folder to open it and view its contents, or tap on any file icon or listing to preview it using the iCloud Drive app (shown in Figure 5.10).

When you're previewing content, tap on the Share icon to access a menu that enables you to share that content via text message or email, or open that content within a specific (compatible) app already installed on your mobile device. In some cases, you will first need to tap on the Download to View option that's displayed to view that content on your mobile device's screen.

To transfer the PowerPoint file (previewed in Figure 5.10) that's stored on your iCloud Drive to the PowerPoint app on the iPad being used, tap on the Copy to PowerPoint icon displayed after tapping on the Share icon (shown in Figure 5.11).

Figure 5.10

You can preview most types of files and content stored in iCloud Drive from directly within the
iCloud Drive app by tapping on its icon or listing. Shown here is a PowerPoint presentation.

Figure 5.11

When previewing a file, it's possible to open it in another compatible app and work with it or
share it via email with someone else. To do this, tap on the Share icon.

As needed, the file or content is automatically downloaded from iCloud Drive, stored in your mobile device, and loaded into a compatible app.

> **Tip** As you're previewing content or files, tap on the Trash icon to delete the file, or tap on the Folder icon to move that file to a different folder within iCloud Drive. When you tap on the Folder icon, a listing of folders in your iCloud Drive is displayed. Tap on the listing for the folder where you want to move the file or content.

Located at the top of the screen when you launch the iCloud Drive app is a Search field (refer to Figure 5.9). Type a keyword or search phrase to quickly find a file stored online in the iCloud Drive portion of your iCloud account.

To custom sort how the iCloud Drive folders and files are displayed on the screen, tap on the Date, Name, or Tags tab displayed below the Search field. Tap on the View icon, located to the right of these tabs, to switch between an icon view and a listing view of your stored folders and files. If you don't see these tabs, place your finger near the center of the screen and swipe downward, so you're looking at the very top of the screen (just below the Search field).

> **Tip** Tap on the Select option displayed in the top-right corner of the iCloud Drive app's screen to select one or more files or folders by tapping on them. As soon as you tap on the Select option, the New Folder, Move, and Delete options are displayed at the bottom of the screen.
>
> After selecting one or more files, tap on the New Folder, Move, or Delete option to handle that task. When you tap on New Folder, you can create a new folder within your iCloud Drive account. Tap on the Move option to move the selected file into a different online-based folder. Tap on the Delete option to delete the selected content.

When using the iCloud Drive app, displayed at the bottom of the main screen is a summary of how many individual files are stored online, as well as how much of your allocated online storage space is still available. Thanks to iCloud Drive, it's possible to store content online and not keep it stored on your mobile device (or computer). This frees up internal storage space. Yet, as long as your mobile device or computer has Internet access, the files stored in iCloud Drive are always accessible when they're needed.

The same content that you can access from the iCloud Drive app on your mobile device can also be accessed from iCloud.com by clicking on the iCloud Drive app icon when using the web browser of any Internet-connected computer.

> **! CAUTION** Anything you do in the iCloud Drive app in terms of creating new folders, moving files, or deleting content happens instantly. There is no "undo" option, and this impacts what can be accessed via iCloud Drive from all your other computers and mobile devices linked to the same iCloud account.

iCLOUD: MANY USES, ONE STORAGE SPACE

Keep in mind that you are not required to use all of iCloud's various features. You can turn on only those features you believe are beneficial to you, based on how you typically use your iPhone and/or iPad and what content, data, and information you want to synchronize or back up to your iCloud account.

IN THIS CHAPTER

- Use the Maps app to obtain turn-by-turn directions between two locations
- Find and display any address, landmark, point-of-interest, or business on a map
- Get real-time public transportation information via the Maps app

NAVIGATING WITH THE MAPS APP

In addition to overall improvements in accuracy and integration with other apps, the preinstalled Maps app now includes real-time mass transit information for buses, trains, subways, and ferries related to many major cities around the world.

MORE INFO To discover what cities around the world are supported by various Maps app features, like public transportation (Transit) or turn-by-turn navigation, visit this page of Apple's website: www.apple.com/ios/feature-availability. Keep in mind that this list is updated often.

(iOS 9) WHAT'S NEW The Maps app now offers the Nearby feature that allows you to quickly find businesses or services that are nearby simply by tapping on a category icon, such as Food, Drinks, Shopping, Travel, Services, Fun, Health, or Transport (shown in Figure 6.1).

To view these Nearby icons, tap on the Search field in the Maps app. They're also displayed on the Spotlight Search screen when you access the Home screen and then swipe from left to right.

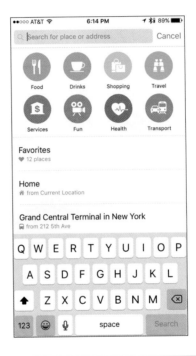

Figure 6.1

Tap on the Search field in the Maps app to access the new Nearby feature. Use it to quickly find a nearby business or service that you're looking for by first tapping on a category icon.

The Maps app requires continuous Internet access to function. Although the app works with a Wi-Fi connection, if you plan to use the app's turn-by-turn directions feature, you must use a cellular data connection (which uses up some of your monthly wireless data allocation with each use) because you'll be in motion and will quickly leave the wireless signal radius of any Wi-Fi hotspot.

That being said, a Wi-Fi connection can be used to preload driving or public transportation directions prior to your departure. If your route changes, however, your iOS mobile device will not be able to help if it cannot connect to the Internet.

Using the Maps app with Siri (which is very convenient) requires even more cellular data usage.

> **☑ TIP** To use the Maps app, the main Location Services feature in your iPhone or iPad (as well as Location Services for the Maps app) must be turned on. To do this, launch Settings, tap on the Privacy option, and then tap on Location Services. From the Location Services menu screen, turn on the virtual switch displayed near the top of the screen (associated with Location Services). Then, scroll down and tap on the Maps option. Be sure that the While Using The App option is selected.

> **❗CAUTION** Just as when using any GPS device, do not rely 100 percent on the turn-by-turn directions you're given. Pay attention as you're driving and use common sense. If the Maps app tells you to drive down a one-way street or drive along a closed road, for example, ignore those directions and seek out an alternative route.

GET THE MOST FROM USING THE MAPS APP'S FEATURES

In addition to providing detailed maps, the Maps app is capable of displaying useful information with each map, including real-time, color-coded traffic conditions showing traffic jams and construction, which can be graphically overlaid onto maps. Plus, when you look up a business, restaurant, point of interest, or landmark, the Maps app seamlessly integrates with Yelp! to display detailed information about specific locations.

The Yelp! information screens are interactive, so if you're using an iPhone and tap on a phone number, you can initiate a call to that business or restaurant. Likewise, if you tap on a website URL (on either an iPhone or iPad), Safari launches and the applicable website automatically loads and displays.

> **☑ TIP** To enhance the capabilities of the Yelp! integration, download and install the optional (and free) Yelp! app from the App Store. Without the Yelp! app, when appropriate, the Maps app transfers you to the Yelp! website.

> **NOTE** Yelp! is a crowd-sourced online database that contains more than 83 million reviews related to local businesses, stores, restaurants, hotels, tourist attractions, and points of interest. Reviews are created by everyday people who share their experiences, thoughts, and photos. Beyond user-provided reviews, Yelp! offers details about many businesses and restaurants, often including menus.

Although Maps offers a lot of functionality packed into a standalone app, it's also designed to work with many other apps. For example, as you're viewing an entry in the Contacts app, when you tap on an address, the Maps app launches and displays that address on a map. You can then quickly obtain detailed directions to that location from your current location, or from any address you select. This also works with any address displayed in any other app, such as Calendar, Mail, Messages, Notes, or Safari.

> **TIP** Anytime you receive a text message or view a Calendar event that has an address included with it, iOS 9 automatically determines you're looking at an address and turns it into an active link. Tap on this link to launch the Maps app and view the address or obtain directions to or from that address.

Plus, you can utilize many features built in to the Maps app using voice commands and requests, thanks to Siri. For example, regardless of what you're doing on the iPhone or iPad, it's possible to activate Siri and say, "How do I get home from here?" or "Where is the closest gas station?" and then have the Maps app provide you with the directions and map you need.

> **TIP** If you're using one of the newer model iPhones that support the "Hey Siri" feature, this is extremely useful for controlling your iPhone while driving, for example, because you don't need to look at or touch the display to obtain information.
>
> For example, you can simply say, "Hey Siri, how do I get home from here?" or "Hey Siri, where is the closest Starbucks?"

> **TIP** When you're viewing a map using the Maps app, tap on the My Location icon (which looks like a northeast-pointing arrow) displayed near the bottom-left corner of the screen to pinpoint and display your current location on the map. Your location is displayed using a pulsating blue dot.

OVERVIEW OF THE MAPS APP'S SCREEN

The main screen of the iOS 9 edition of the Maps app sometimes displays a tiny compass in the upper-right corner of a map, as well as a map scale in the top-left corner of a map. The compass displays automatically when North isn't toward the top of the screen. The map scale appears if you're scrolling around a map using your finger or zooming in or out.

Displayed near the top-left corner of the screen is the Directions option. On the iPhone, this looks like a curved arrow that's pointing to the right. On the iPad, the option actually says "Directions."

Use the Search field located at the top center of the Maps screen to find and map out any address. You can enter a complete address (house/building number, street, city, state) or provide less specific information, such as just a city, state, or country. Enter United States to see a map of the entire country. Enter California to view a map of the state.

You also have the option of entering Los Angeles, California, to view a more detailed map of the city, or you can enter a specific street address located within Los Angeles to view it on a detailed map that shows specific streets (and street names).

> **TIP** When viewing a map on the screen after typing a location or address in the Search field, for example, if the Maps app's 3D Flyover featured is offered for that area, a message that says "3D Flyover Tour of [insert city]" is displayed below the Search field. To switch to the viewing mode, tap on the Start option displayed to the right of this message. More information about 3D Flyover is offered later in this chapter.

This Search field is also used to find businesses, restaurants, points of interest, landmarks, and tourist destinations. When the Maps app finds the location you're looking for, you can zoom in or zoom out manually on that map to see more or less detail. Plus, you can change the Map view and switch between the Standard, Satellite, 3D, Transit, or 3D Flyover views. To do this, tap on the Info icon located in the bottom-right corner of the screen and tap on applicable menu options (shown in Figure 6.2).

Figure 6.2
With a few onscreen taps, it's possible to dramatically alter the appearance of a map and how information is presented to you. You can also overlay traffic details on the map, for example, by tapping on the Show Traffic option.

TIP In the Search field, enter the name of any contact that has an entry stored in the Contacts app to find and display an address for that contact. The Maps app searches the contents of your iOS device (including the Contacts app), followed by a web-based search, if applicable.

Anytime a specific location is identified on the map, such as results of a search, those results are displayed using a virtual red push-pin. Tap on a push-pin to view more details about that location and to access a separate Location Information screen (iPhone) or window (iPad).

Continuously displayed near the bottom-left corner of the main Maps screen is the My Location icon (it looks like a northeast-pointing arrow). At anytime a map is displayed, tap on this icon to locate and display (or update) your current location on the map.

This feature is useful if you look up another destination and then want to quickly see where you're located in comparison to that other location. However, when you're using the Maps app for turn-by-turn directions, your iPhone/iPad keeps track of your location in real time, and displays this on the map as you're in motion.

As you're viewing a map, the main Maps app screen includes a Share icon (iPhone) or option (iPad) that's displayed in the top-right corner of the screen. Tap on this Share icon/option to reveal a Share menu (shown in Figure 6.3), from which you can share location details with others, add the location to the Maps app's Favorites list, or print the current map (using an AirPrint-compatible printer).

> **TIP** To add a location to the Maps Favorites listing, when viewing a location on a map, tap on the Share icon and then from the Share menu (see Figure 6.3) tap on the Add to Favorites icon.

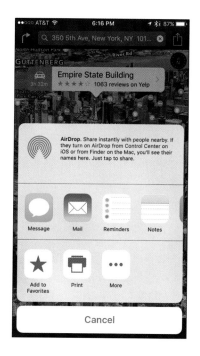

Figure 6.3

The Share menu built in to the Maps app enables you to share your location with others or save the location in the Maps Favorites listing.

> **✓ TIP**   To access your Favorites menu in the Maps app, tap on the Search field that's located in the top center of the screen. Displayed below the Nearby icons is the Favorites option. Tap on this to reveal your list of manually saved Favorites locations. When this list is visible, tap any item to reopen the map of that location.

Anytime you tap on the Search field within Maps, below the Nearby icons and Favorites heading is a Home button. Tap on this to quickly get directions from your current location to your Home address. Below that is a listing of recent searches you've performed in the Maps app, which includes the places you've used the app to travel to.

Tap on any listing displayed on the Search Results screen to obtain detailed directions to or from that location.

VIEW A MAP FROM MULTIPLE PERSPECTIVES

As you're viewing a map on the screen, place one finger on the screen and drag it around to move the map around. To rotate the map, place two fingers (slightly separated) on the screen, and rotate your fingers clockwise or counterclockwise. To then return to the north-up orientation, tap on the compass icon that's displayed on the screen.

Use a reverse-pinch finger gesture to zoom in or a pinch finger gesture to zoom out. If you're using the Satellite, 3D, or 3D Flyover map view, it's possible to zoom in very close and then drag your finger around the map to take a bird's-eye tour of the area.

THE MAPS APP'S INFO SCREEN

The Info icon is displayed near the bottom-right corner of the main Maps screen. When you tap on this circular "i" icon, a menu is displayed that enables you to quickly switch between the various map views available, based on the mapped location. Simply tap on the labeled tabs that are displayed to customize your map view (refer to Figure 6.2).

From the Info window, it's possible to drop a virtual pin on any location displayed on the currently viewed map, plus show or hide color-coded traffic details on the map, for example.

THE DROP A PIN OPTION

When you tap on the Drop A Pin option, the full Maps screen returns with a new push-pin displayed. Using your finger, drag the push-pin to the desired location on the map. The new push-pin is displayed in purple instead of red. After you place a push-pin, it's possible to view detailed information about that particular location, including its exact address. You can then tap on the displayed Info icon to view a location menu that offers a handful of menu options, including Directions, Create New Contact, Add To Existing Contact, Remove Pin, Add Bookmark, or Report An Issue.

THE SHOW/HIDE TRAFFIC OPTION

Regardless of which map view you're looking at, you can have color-coded real-time traffic information superimposed on the map. This feature can help you avoid traffic jams and construction, and enables you to seek an alternative route before you get stuck in the traffic.

> **NOTE** Mild traffic is showcased using orange, while heavy traffic is depicted in red. When construction is being done on a roadway, separate construction icons (in yellow or red) are displayed on the map.

> **TIP** The Show Traffic feature works much better when you're viewing a zoomed-in version of a map that shows a lot of street-level detail.

THE MAP VIEW TABS

Displayed in the Maps app's Info window are the three map view command tabs: Standard, Transit, and Satellite. The Standard map view (shown in Figure 6.4) displays a traditional-looking, multicolored map on the screen. Street names and other important information are labeled and displayed on the map.

The Satellite view uses high-resolution and extremely detailed satellite imagery to show maps from an overhead view (shown in Figure 6.5).

The Transit map shows information such as bus, subway, and train stations (and their routes) on the displayed map (shown in Figure 6.6).

Figure 6.4

The Standard map view shows a traditional, multicolored map with street names and other points of interest listed on it.

Figure 6.5

The Satellite map view uses high-definition satellite imagery to display map locations.

> **TIP** Anytime you're viewing a map, it's possible to switch between a 2D and 3D map view by tapping on the Show 2D/3D Map option displayed as part of the Info menu. Which you use is a matter of personal preference. When using 3D view, place two fingers on the screen simultaneously, and move them up or down to alter the tilt angle of the view.

> **TIP** When you look up any business using the Maps app, if you then view the location of the business with the Satellite view, you can often determine the best place to park nearby. Consider dropping a pin on that location, and then using turn-by-turn directions to get you to that spot. There are also third-party apps, like Parker, that can help you find a parking spot or paid parking lot within a major city.

Figure 6.6

Get an overview of an area's public transportation system when you tap on the Transit map view tab.

OBTAIN TURN-BY-TURN DIRECTIONS BETWEEN TWO LOCATIONS

The turn-by-turn directions feature of the Maps app is not only easy to use, it's also extremely useful. Begin using this feature from the main Maps app screen. Tap on the Directions icon located near the top-left corner of the screen.

The Start and End fields, as well as the reverse directions icon and recently displayed location results (if applicable), are displayed (shown in Figure 6.7).

In the Start field, the default option is your current location; however, to change this, tap on the field and enter any starting address. Then tap on the End field and enter any ending address.

iOS 9 WHAT'S NEW Below the Start and End fields are the Home, Work, and Favorites icons. Tap on the Home icon to quickly obtain directions from your current location to your home address. Tap on the Work icon to obtain directions from your current location to your work address, or tap on the Favorites icon to view your list of saved (bookmarked) locations. Then choose one of those listings to obtain directions from your current location to that location.

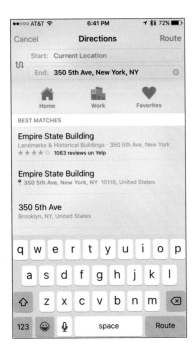

Figure 6.7

Fill in the Start and End fields to obtain detailed, turn-by-turn directions between any two locations that you choose.

> **TIP** Also displayed below the Start and End field are recent locations you've utilized within the Maps app. Scroll up or down this list using your finger, or tap on any entry to use it as your Start or End location.

> **TIP** In the Start and End field, you can enter a contact entry's name, a full address, a city and state, just a state, or just a country. You can use two-letter state abbreviations, and you don't have to worry about using upper- and lowercase letters. For example, you can type "New York, NY," "new york, ny," or "New York, New York," and get the same result. This goes for contacts or business names as well.

When the Start and End fields have been filled in, tap on the Route option that's displayed near the top-right corner of the window. There's also a Route button on the virtual keyboard.

A route overview map (shown in Figure 6.8) is displayed. The green push-pin represents your starting location and the red-push pin represents your ending location.

Figure 6.8

A route overview map shows your start and end location on one map, plus up to three possible driving routes to get there.

ios 9 **WHAT'S NEW** Displayed at the top of the Route map are three tabs labeled Drive, Walk, and Transit. Tap the Drive tab to receive turn-by-turn driving directions. Tap on the Walk tab if you prefer to walk to your destination. Tap on the Transit tab if you plan to use public transportation to reach your destination (and you're in a city supported by this new Transit feature).

Tap on the Drive tab displayed at the top of the Route screen if you plan to drive to your selected destination and want turn-by-turn directions. Between one and three possible routes between the start and end locations are displayed.

The primary route is outlined on the route overview map with a dark blue line. One or two alternative routes may be outlined with light blue lines. Associated with each route is an approximate travel time.

> **TIP** Turn on the Show Traffic option to display current traffic conditions along the three routes, and then choose the one with the least congestion or construction. Tap on any of the route lines to select your route. The route highlighted with the dark blue line is the default (recommended) route.

When you're ready to begin your journey, tap on the Start option that's displayed near the bottom center of the screen. You're then given real-time, turn-by-turn directions. Just like when using a standalone GPS device, the Siri voice guides you through each turn, while also displaying related information on the main map screen (shown in Figure 6.9).

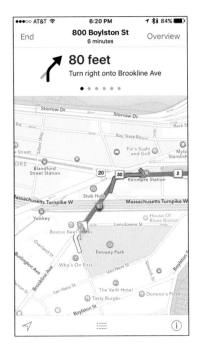

Figure 6.9

The Maps app shows detailed turn-by-turn directions on the map screen and speaks to you as you're driving.

> **iOS 9 WHAT'S NEW** If you're wearing an Apple Watch that's paired with your iPhone, navigation information is automatically and simultaneously displayed on your watch.

While the turn-by-turn directions are being displayed, a variation of the Standard map view is used. Your ETA, as well as how much time is left in your trip, and the distance from your destination are displayed on the screen. At any time, tap the Overview option to return to the route overview map, or tap the End option to exit out of the turn-by-turn directions feature and return to the main Maps screen. When available, you can switch to the 3D view option. Look for the 3D icon to be displayed in the bottom-right corner of the screen when applicable.

Follow the voice and onscreen prompts until you reach your destination. If you press the Home button, you can return to the Home screen (or access the app switcher by pressing the Home button twice quickly) and launch another app while the Maps feature is still running, and then return to the turn-by-turn directions by tapping on the blue bar that says Touch To Return To Navigation. It's displayed near the top of the screen when using a different app (and the Map app, with the navigation feature active, is simultaneously running in the background).

> (iOS 9) **WHAT'S NEW**   When using the Maps app's turn-by-turn directions feature, you're now warned about upcoming construction or traffic while you're driving. This allows you to quickly find an alternative route, before you get delayed.

> **TIP**   To view text-based directions to your destination, enter Start and End locations using the Directions feature of the Maps app, but before tapping Start to obtain the directions, tap on the Details option, which can be found just above the Info icon when viewing the route overview screen. Also, the Overview option appears if you tap on the screen during the navigation process.

LOOK UP CONTACT ENTRIES, BUSINESSES, RESTAURANTS, LANDMARKS, AND POINTS OF INTEREST

One of the other primary uses of the Maps app is to find and display addresses, contacts, businesses, points of interest, or landmarks on a map screen. To do this, from the main Maps screen, simply type what you're looking for into the Search field. In Figure 6.10, "Space Needle" was entered into the search field.

Figure 6.10

The Seattle Space Needle in Seattle, Washington, is shown here using the 3D map view.

> ✅ **TIP**   If you're looking for businesses or services in your immediate area, tap on the My Location icon first, so the iPhone or iPad pinpoints your location, and then enter what you're searching for, or tap on one of the Nearby icons. No city or state needs to be entered. However, if you don't tap on the My Location icon first, you must enter into the Search field what you're looking for, followed by the city, a comma, and the state, to find local search results. Otherwise, the Maps app defaults to the last search location.
>
> If the business or service is considered a major point of interest, such as the Seattle Space Needle, The White House, The Empire State Building, Disney World, or O'Hare Airport, you do not need to include the city or state in the Search field.

USE THE INTERACTIVE LOCATION SCREENS TO FIND MORE INFORMATION

Once search results are displayed on the map in the form of virtual push-pins, tap on any push-pin to view an information banner for a location on a map. In Figure 6.11, a search for Apple Store locations in New York City was performed and displayed on the map.

Figure 6.11

The results of a search for Apple Stores in the New York City area appear as red virtual push-pins on the map.

Tap on one push-pin, and then tap the left side of the information banner to obtain "quick" turn-by-turn directions from your current location. Or, tap on the ">" arrow displayed to the right of the banner listing to view an interactive Location Information screen.

A separate and informative Location Information screen (shown in Figure 6.12) displays details about that search result using details from the Maps app, the Internet, and from Yelp!. This information includes the phone number, address, website URL, hours of operation, and other information for that search result. The information displayed depends on whether it's a business, restaurant, point of interest, or tourist attraction.

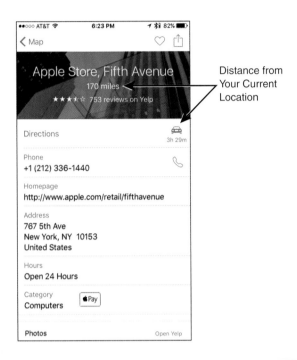

Distance from Your Current Location

Figure 6.12

A detailed Location Information screen combines location information with details about that location obtained from Yelp!. Information about the Apple Store on Fifth Avenue in Manhattan is shown here.

On any Location Information screen, you'll see a Directions option. Tap on it to obtain directions to or from your current location to the address listed on the screen.

Tap on the More Info On Yelp! option to launch the Yelp! app or visit the Yelp! website to view more detailed information about that location.

Create New Contact, Add To Existing Contact, and Report A Problem options are also available by scrolling down in the Location Information screen (iPhone) or window (iPad).

Displayed next to the Reviews option is an Open Yelp option. Tap on it to view all the individual reviews that others have published on Yelp! that are related to the selected location.

Another potentially useful feature offered within each Location Information window is the Popular Apps Nearby listing. This showcases a handful of optional third-party apps relevant to that specific area or location. From this listing, you might find apps from local stores, malls, tourist attractions, or media outlets, for example.

> **☑ TIP** If you look up information about a restaurant, the Location
> Information screen features Yelp!-related information, including the type of food
> served, the menu price range (using dollar sign symbols), the hours of operation,
> and potentially a website link that enables you to view the restaurant's menu. You
> can also determine whether the restaurant delivers or accepts reservations.
>
> If reservations are accepted, use the optional Open Table app to make reservations
> online. Activate Siri and say, "Make a reservation for [insert number of people] for
> [insert day and time]," or initiate a call from an iPhone to the restaurant by tapping
> on the phone number field. When applicable, the Info or Yelp! screen for a busi-
> ness also tells you whether Apple Pay is accepted at that location.

THE MAPS APP'S FLYOVER VIEW

The Flyover map view is offered for many major cities, although it doesn't really
serve a navigation purpose. This feature, however, can be used to help you get
acquainted with the layout of a city, and enables you to take a virtual tour of its
skyline from your iPhone or iPad.

When available, the 3D option normally displayed as a map view option is replaced
with the 3D Flyover icon. Tap on it to switch to a stunning Flyover map view. New
to iOS 9, an animated virtual tour showcasing a city's landmarks is offered. Shown
in Figure 6.13 is a virtual tour of London, England.

NAVIGATE A CITY'S PUBLIC TRANSPORTATION SYSTEM

Built in to the Maps app for a growing number of cities around the world is extensive public transportation information relating to buses, trains, subways, and ferries. This feature is customized for every city that it works with. Displayed on the
map are applicable bus/train/subway stations and routes, and based on where you
are and where you're headed, current (real-time) schedules are offered.

What's great about the Transit feature is that you can manually enter your Start and
End locations and then choose the Transit option or ask Siri to guide you. Once you
enter your Start and End locations and then tap on the Transit option, the Maps app
offers walking directions to the closest bus, subway, or train station, and then tells you
exactly what bus, subway, or train to take and provides the appropriate schedule, as
well as how long each leg of the trip will take and when you need to make a transfer.

Tap on the Overview option at any time to see a list that details each leg of your trip and what mode of public transportation the Maps app recommends you use (shown in Figure 6.14).

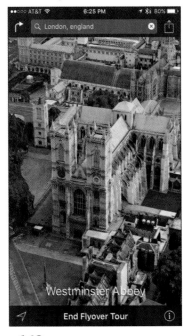

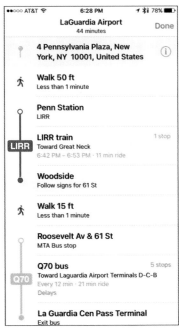

Figure 6.13

The Maps app offers a stunning 3D Flyover view of many popular cities around the world, including London (shown here).

Figure 6.14

The Transit feature of the Maps app works just like the Turn-By-Turn Navigation feature (used when driving), but it explains how to utilize the local public transportation system. Tap on the Overview option to view this comprehensive step-by-step listing, as opposed to receiving real-time, step-by-step driving directions.

MAPS QUICK TIPS

- After tapping the Directions option to obtain directions between two addresses, a Reverse icon is displayed to the immediate left of the Start and End. Tap it to switch the addresses you have in the Start and End fields to obtain reverse directions.

- When using the Maps app, your iPhone or iPad accesses the Internet extensively. This drains the device's battery faster. If you use this feature from your car often, consider investing in a car charger that plugs into your car's 12-volt or USB jack. This way, your iPhone/iPad's battery remains charged (and can recharge) while it's being used.

■ Using the Maps app for turn-by-turn directions via a cellular data Internet connection requires a significant amount of wireless data usage. Using this feature will help to deplete your monthly cellular data allocation unless you're subscribed to an unlimited wireless service plan (or a plan with a generous amount of cellular data). Also, if you're using international roaming to access the Internet from abroad, using Maps with a cellular data connection can get very expensive.

■ The Maps app works with iCloud and automatically syncs your Favorites list with all your other computers and mobile devices linked to the same iCloud account. You can also use the Handoff feature to switch from using your iPhone to your iPad or Mac (or vice versa) when using the Maps app, without having to reenter information.

IN THIS CHAPTER

▪ Learn to use the Facebook and Twitter functionality that's integrated into iOS 9

▪ Discover how to use the official Facebook and Twitter app

▪ Discover other online social networking apps for services like YouTube and Instagram

7

MAKE THE MOST OF ONLINE SOCIAL NETWORKING APPS

One of the reasons why online social networking services have become so incredibly popular around the world is because access to these services is incredibly easy from any smartphone, tablet, or computer. In some cases, social media accounts for services like Twitter and Instagram can also be managed from an Apple Watch that's paired with your iPhone.

Available for free from the App Store are official apps from all of the major social networks that enable you to fully manage your online account, stay in touch with your online friends, and share photos, videos, or other content while you're on the go.

Meanwhile, iOS 9 has Facebook, Twitter, Flickr, and/or Vimeo integration built in to the Share menu of many apps. This means you can quickly create and publish app-specific content without actually launching a social networking app. Other third-party apps used for managing social media accounts also now show up in the Share menu.

> **✓ TIP**   Almost any iPhone or iPad app that has a Share button now enables you to share app-specific information by publishing it on Facebook and/or Twitter from within the app you're using.

To begin using any of the popular online social networking services from your iPhone or iPad, you first must set up a free account with that service. This can be done either by visiting the service's main website (such as www.facebook.com or www.twitter.com) on your primary computer, using Safari on your mobile device, or by clicking on the new account setup-related option offered in the official iOS mobile app for that service.

After you've set up an account, enter your username and password into the social networking app on your iPhone or iPad.

> **! CAUTION**   Many of the online social networking apps automatically tap in to the Location Services function of your iPhone or iPad and display your exact location anytime you publish a new posting to that service (or upload a new photo or video). To prevent this and protect your privacy, do not grant permission for a specific online social networking app to access your mobile device's Location Services as you're first setting it up.
>
> Anytime thereafter, it's possible to customize privacy-related settings for many apps by launching Settings and tapping on the Privacy option. Next, tap on the Location Services option (at the top of the screen). Tap on the option for each app (including the social media apps) to adjust how that selected app will utilize the Location Services feature built in to your device. For example, if you tap on the Facebook option, under the Allow Location Access heading, you can choose between the Never, While Using the app, or Always options.
>
> Most services, like Twitter or Instagram, also enable you to add your location to a posting, but only if you want to.
>
> Many people opt to leave Location Services turned on, but as they're using a social networking service from their mobile device, they pay attention to when this feature is going to be utilized and opt to include or leave out their location when creating a new post or uploading content.

> **✓ TIP**   Facebook (www.Facebook.com), as well as the Facebook app, offers its own Privacy Settings menu that you should access and customize based on your level of comfort sharing information as you begin using this service. Tap on the More menu icon and select the Privacy Shortcuts option or the Settings option to do this.

FACEBOOK, TWITTER, FLICKR, AND VIMEO INTEGRATION IS BUILT IN TO iOS 9

If you already have a Facebook, Twitter, Flickr, or Vimeo account, you must set up the iOS 9 integration functionality for each of these services separately, plus download and install the official app for each of the services on which you're active.

Setting up account integration with iOS 9 (and many of the apps that come preinstalled on your iOS mobile device) must be done once per account on each of your iOS mobile devices.

> **NOTE** This integration allows options for the compatible online social networking services to be displayed as part of the Share menu of many apps, including Photos.
>
> If you don't turn on integration with a service, these options will not be accessible from the Share menu of the apps you use.

To set up iOS 9 integration for each service, follow these steps:

1. Launch Settings from the Home screen.

2. Scroll down to the Twitter, Facebook, Flickr, or Vimeo option that's displayed as part of the main Settings menu. Tap on the app you want to configure.

3. Tap on the Username and Password option and enter the appropriate information (shown in Figure 7.1).

4. Tap on the Sign In option.

5. If you haven't already done so, tap on the Install button displayed next to the app logo to download and install the official app. Once the app is downloaded, you must sign in to the service from the app, and once again supply your account username and password (this time, while using the app).

6. When the app is installed, if applicable, tap on the Settings option below the app icon on the service-specific menu within Settings to customize specific features of the online social networking app.

7. Near the bottom of the service-specific menu within Settings, under the heading Allow These Apps To Use Your Account, turn on or off the virtual switches associated with specific apps. Your Calendar and Contacts apps can sync with your Facebook account if you allow it.

8. When applicable, tap on the Update Contacts button that's also displayed on the service-specific menu within Settings. This enables your iPhone or iPad to access your online account and compare your online friends with the entries

you already have in the Contacts app. When appropriate, the Contacts app pulls additional information from services such as Facebook and adds details to each applicable Contacts entry. For example, when you do this for the Facebook app, Contacts adds Profile pictures, birthdays, and other information listed on the Facebook profile to your Contacts entry.

Figure 7.1

Add your existing Twitter account information to the Twitter submenu within Settings, and then tap Sign In to log in to your account. This enables iOS 9 and many apps to include a Share via Twitter option as part of the app's Share menu.

TIP If you manage multiple Twitter accounts, repeat steps 1–4 for each account after selecting the Twitter option from the main Settings menu. Later, you can select from which account you publish new content as you use the Tweet command from within the Share menu of various apps.

From the Share menu of many apps (shown in Figure 7.2), you can now publish new content directly to your compatible online social networking account. However, if you want to fully manage your account and interact directly with your online friends, you must download and install the official app for each service on which you're active. Find these apps by performing a search in the App Store or looking in the Social Networking category.

Figure 7.2

After you turn on Facebook, Twitter, Flickr, and/or Vimeo integration, options for publishing content to these services appear in the Share menu of many compatible apps, including Photos.

MANAGE YOUR FACEBOOK ACCOUNT USING THE OFFICIAL FACEBOOK APP

The official Facebook app offers much of the same functionality for managing your Facebook account as using the web browser on your primary computer to access www.facebook.com. However, the Facebook app is custom designed to fully utilize the iPhone or iPad's touchscreen and format content for the screen size of the iOS mobile device you're using.

TIP On the iPad, more content is displayed when you use the official Facebook app in landscape mode.

TIP   Every two weeks or so, Facebook updates its official app, as well as the Facebook Messenger app. Facebook Messenger is the instant messaging component of Facebook that enables you to communicate with your Facebook friends in real time via instant messages (text), Internet-based voice calls, or video calling through Facebook.

If you use Facebook to manage your own Page or Group, separate official Facebook apps (Facebook Page Manager and Facebook Groups) are available for free from the App Store to allow you to manage Pages or Groups directly from your mobile device.

Found along the bottom of the official Facebook app are News Feed, Requests, Messenger, and Notifications icons, as well as the More menu icon. Tapping on these icons gives you access to the majority of Facebook's features and functions from your mobile device (shown in Figure 7.3).

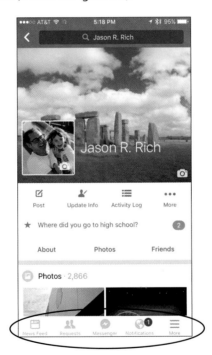

Figure 7.3
Access most of Facebook's features and functions from the icons displayed along the bottom of the Facebook app's screen.

Tap on the More icon to access the Facebook app's main menu. At the top of this menu is your Facebook name. Tap on this to access your own online profile and Facebook page.

Available from this More menu (shown in Figure 7.4) are a handful of other options for managing all aspects of your Facebook account. For example, under the Settings option, tap on the Privacy Shortcuts option to customize your Facebook Privacy settings, which is highly recommended.

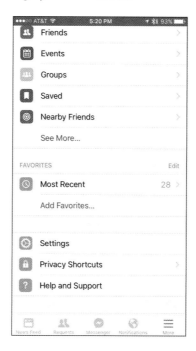

Figure 7.4

Spend a few minutes customizing the various settings offered from this More menu, especially the Privacy Shortcuts-related settings.

From along the bottom of the screen, tap on the News Feed icon to view your live newsfeed and see the posts and status updates of your Facebook friends.

Tap on the Requests icon to respond to incoming friend requests, plus view a listing of People You May Know. When you tap on the Messenger icon, your iPhone/iPad exits out of the Facebook app and launches the separate Facebook Messenger app, which is also available for free from the App Store. It is used to communicate with other Facebook users.

Displayed on the right side of the iPad screen when using the Facebook app (or when you tap on the icon in the top-right corner of the iPhone screen), you can see a listing of your Facebook friends and whether they're currently online and using Facebook or logged in to Facebook using their mobile device.

> **✓ TIP** Tap on the Nearby Friends option to view a listing of your friends who have recently used the Check In feature and posted their current location online. You can then determine their proximity to you, based on your current location. For this feature to work, you must have the Location Services feature that's associated with Facebook set to "Always."

Tap on the Notifications option to view listings for new content that's been created or updated by your online friends. The information shown here depends on how you set up the Facebook Activity Log, News Feed Preferences, and Privacy Shortcuts from the More Menu.

Use the Search field displayed at the top of the screen to enter a name, keyword, or search phrase, based on what you're looking for. For example, if you're looking for the Facebook page for your favorite TV show, movie, hobby, area of interest, company, public figure, or celebrity, type it into the Search field.

When viewing the News Feed, at the top of this screen are the Status, Photo, and Check In options. Use one of these options to update your own Facebook wall or status.

When you tap on the Status icon, you can publish content on your Facebook wall. This can include text, photos, your current location, tags for the people you're currently with, and an icon-based activity or emotion update.

When you tap on the smiley face emoticon when updating your Status, you can tap on the Feeling option to choose an option (and icon) for how you're currently feeling, or you can choose an activity icon, such as Watching…, Eating…, Playing…, or Traveling To…. Doing this, however, is an optional part of a status update.

As you're composing your status update, tap on the To field to determine who will be able to see it. Tap on the Post option to publish your status update online.

By tapping on the Photo option, you can choose one or more photos that are stored in your iPhone or iPad and publish them on Facebook—as a new Album, within an Existing Album, or on your Facebook wall. Tap on the Camera icon to snap a photo from within the Facebook app to publish online.

The Check In option enables you to publish a status update that automatically includes your current location. Your online friends and people following you will be able to see where you are when they tap on the Nearby Friends option.

PARTICIPATE IN CHATS USING THE FACEBOOK MESSENGER APP

To participate in a real-time text, audio-, or video-based chat with one of your Facebook friends, you now must use the Facebook Messenger app, which you can launch from the Home screen or from within the Facebook app by tapping on the Messenger icon.

> **TIP** You can also launch the Facebook Messenger app by tapping on someone's name when you view the listing of friends who are currently online (displayed on the right side of the Facebook app on the iPad, or when you tap on the icon displayed in the top-right corner of the iPhone.)

When viewing your friends list in the official Facebook app, a green dot displayed with a friend's name indicates that person is currently on Facebook. A cell phone icon to the right of his name indicates he's accessing Facebook from his mobile phone or tablet.

If a message such as Active 4m Ago, Active 5H Ago, or Active 2D ago is displayed, this tells you the last time that person was active on Facebook. The "M" stands for minutes, the "H" stands for hours, and the "D" stands for days.

After tapping on a Facebook friend's name to initiate or return to a chat, the Facebook Messenger app automatically launches and a chat window is displayed (shown in Figure 7.5). The app also enables you to set up and participate in group chats/conversations. To do this, select more than one person when initiating a new chat.

When using the instant messaging feature of Facebook Messenger, text bubbles down the left side indicate what your friend types, while the text bubbles down the right side show what you've typed.

> **TIP** In the top-right corner of the Facebook Messenger chat window is a phone and video camera icon. Tap on the phone icon to initiate a voice call with that person via the Internet (which is free), or tap on the video camera icon to initiate a video call with that person (also free). Either of these features is a great alternative to traditional long-distance or international phone calls, which typically cost a lot.

When using the instant messaging aspect of Facebook Messenger to send text, type what you want to send in the Type A Message field displayed at the bottom of the screen.

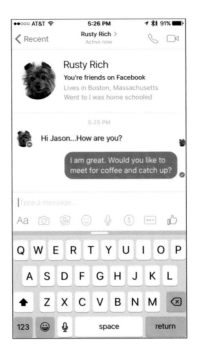

Figure 7.5

Participate in real-time text chats with your Facebook friends via the Facebook Messenger app.

Tap on any of the icons displayed with this field to add a photo, audio clip, animated GIF graphic, or another type of compatible content.

If you want to include an emoji in your text-based message, tap on the smiley face icon that appears between the 123 and microphone (Dictation) keys near the bottom of your mobile device's virtual keyboard, and select one or more emoticons by tapping on them.

> **TIP**   Instead of turning on the Do Not Disturb feature, if you want to keep someone from disturbing you via Facebook Messenger, it's possible to "mute" and then "unmute" a specific conversation. To do this, tap on the person's username (at the top of the screen). When viewing the Contact screen, tap on the Notifications option. You can then "mute" that person for 15 minutes, 1 hour, 8 hours, 24 hours, or until you manually unmute them by returning to this menu screen.
>
> It's also possible to block someone altogether. To do this, from the Contact screen, tap on the Block option.

READ YOUR NEWS FEED USING THE FACEBOOK APP

After launching the Facebook app, the News Feed is shown by default. However, if you were using the Facebook app previously and chose a different feature, when you reopen the app, the last feature used will be shown. To then view the News Feed, tap on the News Feed icon at the bottom of the screen to discover what your friends are up to. When the News Feed screen is displayed, along the top of the screen, tap the Status option to update your own status.

Scroll down to read your current News Feed. The postings are displayed in reverse chronological order, with the most recent or most recently commented-upon posts listed first. You can, however, change how information is presented by adjusting the app's Sort Order and See First options.

Just below the poster's name is the time the post was published or updated (as well as the person's location, if this information was shared by the poster). Along the bottom of each posting are three icons.

Tap Like (the thumbs-up icon) to "Like" the post. If you want to add a comment related to the post, tap the Comment icon, and then type a public message. If you want to share the post with your friends on your own Facebook wall, tap the Share icon.

> **NOTE** At the time of this writing, Facebook announced plans to add a variety of emote buttons, in addition to Like.

> **! CAUTION** If you're active on several online social networking services, be mindful of the permissions you grant to these apps.
>
> Many of them, like Facebook, Instagram, and Twitter, are now designed to work together and share information. (In some cases, a third-party app that's compatible with multiple services must be used.) For example, if you post a new photo on Instagram (using the official Instagram app), that same photo/posting can automatically appear on Facebook as a status update, and be published as a tweet via your Twitter account.
>
> You can customize how these various services interact and determine what information they share by visiting their main websites (such as www.facebook.com or www.twitter.com) and logging in to your account.

MANAGE YOUR TWITTER ACCOUNT(S) USING THE OFFICIAL TWITTER APP

The official Twitter app enables you to manage one or more Twitter accounts from your iPhone or iPad. Using the app, it's possible to compose and publish new tweets (outgoing messages), access your Twitter feed and see what the people you're following are up to, manage your account's followers, send private messages to other Twitter users, and discover interesting content using the Search feature with keyword (hashtag) searches and/or by tracking what's currently trending on Twitter.

> **(iOS 9) WHAT'S NEW** From the Home screen, if you're using an iPhone 6s or iPhone 6s Plus, place and hold your finger gently on the Twitter app icon to reveal a menu that allows you to quickly perform a search, compose and publish a new tweet, or compose a new (private) message (shown in Figure 7.6).

Figure 7.6

Use your iPhone 6s or iPhone 6s Plus's 3D Touch screen to access this Twitter-related menu by gently resting your finger on the Twitter app icon.

When composing a tweet with the official Twitter app (shown in Figure 7.7), or by selecting the Twitter option from the Share menu of any compatible app, the Compose Tweet screen (iPhone) or window (iPad) is displayed.

Figure 7.7

Manage all aspects of your Twitter account, which include composing and sending tweets using the official Twitter app.

Use the virtual keyboard or the Dictation feature to compose an outgoing tweet to publish to your Twitter feed. It's also possible to use Siri to compose and publish content to either Facebook or Twitter using voice commands.

A tweet can be up to 140 characters in length. Aside from text, you can also attach a photo that's taken using the iPhone or iPad's built-in camera (or a photo that's already stored on your mobile device), include a website URL, or add your exact location to the tweet.

> **TIP** As you're composing a tweet, a character counter is displayed in the Compose Tweet screen/window. Keep in mind that when you attach a photo, website URL, or your location to the tweet, this utilizes some of the 140 characters you have available.

To find and follow your real-life friends who are already active on Twitter, launch the Twitter app, tap on the Add Friends icon, and then use the Find People tools that are built in to the app.

One nice feature of the official Twitter app is that you can manage multiple accounts and quickly switch between them. As you're composing a tweet, if you have multiple accounts, simply tap on your Twitter username in the Compose Tweet screen/window, and you can choose from which of your accounts you want to send the tweet.

You can create or update your personal profile at any time from within the Twitter app. To do this, launch the app, tap on the Me option, and then tap the Edit Profile option. Tap the Save button to save your changes.

> **NOTE** Visit the App Store to discover dozens of additional third-party apps that enable you to easily manage one or more Twitter accounts. Many of these third-party apps, such as Twitterific, TweetCaster, or Tweetbot, are paid apps that offer extra functionality that's not found in the official Twitter app, while others are free (but offer in-app purchase options).

DISCOVER THE OFFICIAL APPS FOR OTHER POPULAR ONLINE SOCIAL NETWORKING SERVICES

Official (free) apps from virtually all the popular online social networking services are available from the App Store. You can also find some third-party (paid) apps that offer a different mix of features and functions for managing one or more online social networking accounts.

THE YOUTUBE APP

As an online-based video sharing service, YouTube offers millions of hours worth of free videos you can watch on demand. The official YouTube app enables you to stream the service's content from anywhere your iOS mobile device has an Internet connection.

If you want to access your YouTube account, watch YouTube videos, or upload your own YouTube videos from an iPhone or iPad, the easiest way to do this is using the official YouTube app. Alternatively, you can visit www.youtube.com from the Safari web browser.

> ☑ **TIP** When you sign in to the YouTube service from within the app, the YouTube app's main menu adds a My Subscriptions heading. Below it are details about all of the YouTube Channels to which you subscribe. Tap on any of these listings to quickly find the latest videos from your favorite YouTubers.

Displayed under the Best of YouTube heading in the YouTube app's main menu, tap on the category for videos you're interested in viewing. Or from the main YouTube screen, tap on the Search icon and then in the Search field enter any keyword or phrase to quickly find videos you might be interested in related to any topic whatsoever.

When you tap on a video listing, what's displayed on the screen (shown in Figure 7.8) is similar to what you see when accessing YouTube from your primary computer.

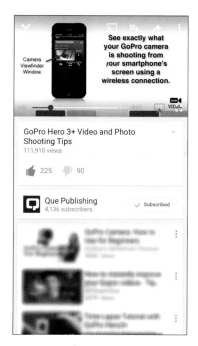

Figure 7.8

The official YouTube app enables you to watch unlimited videos for free or manage a YouTube channel and publish your own videos to share with others. Use the onscreen controls to manage a video as it's playing.

This includes a video window in which the YouTube video plays. Tap on the video window to access onscreen controls to play or pause the video, view the time slider, and tap the Full Screen mode icon or the AirPlay icon. Turn the iPhone sideways to view the video in full-screen mode (as shown in Figure 7.9).

Figure 7.9

Turn your iPhone sideways to view a streaming YouTube video in full-screen mode. On an iPad, tap on the Full-Screen icon displayed in the bottom-right corner of the video window.

NOTE Videos you watch using the YouTube app are streamed to your mobile device. These videos are not, however, saved on your device. To avoid quickly using up your monthly cellular wireless data allocation, if applicable, opt to use this app with a Wi-Fi Internet connection.

THE INSTAGRAM APP

Instagram is a social networking service that enables users to create and share an ongoing stream of individual photos. Each photo can include a caption, keywords, and your location.

What's great about Instagram is that instead of using the Camera app to snap pictures, you can use the Instagram app to take photos and/or use the app's powerful photo editing tools to quickly edit or enhance a photo before sharing it online. Unlike other photo sharing services, Instagram crops images into a square shape (shown in Figure 7.10).

Instagram offers a fun and easy way to share moments of your life in the form of snapshots taken using the camera built in to your iOS mobile device (shown in Figure 7.11).

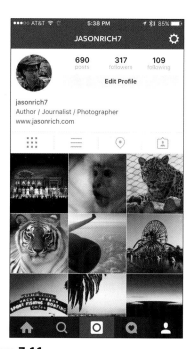

Figure 7.10

Snap or select a photo, crop it, and then edit it using powerful, but easy-to-use tools, before publishing it on Instagram.

Figure 7.11

Instagram users can share individual photos and manage their online account using the official Instagram app.

TIP To view photos posted by strangers, tap on the Search icon displayed near the bottom of the screen. Then, simply scroll down. You can also use the Search Users and Hashtags feature to quickly find and view images with specific keywords associated with them.

IN THIS CHAPTER

- Tips and tricks for shooting, editing, and sharing photos and videos from your iPhone or iPad
- Discover the image editing tools built in to the Photos app
- Take advantage of the Camera app's new Selfie and Live Picture features when using an iPhone 6s or iPhone 6s Plus

8

SHOOT, EDIT, AND SHARE PHOTOS AND VIDEOS

Every day, more than 1.3 billion photos are taken on smartphones and tablets around the world. People love taking photos, and thanks to the two digital cameras built in to all the iPhone and iPad models released within the past few years, plus improvements made to the iOS 9 edition of the Camera and Photos apps, it has never been easier or more fun to shoot, edit, view, print, and share your digital images or video clips.

iOS 9 WHAT'S NEW The iPhone 6s and iPhone 6s Plus not only offer a 12-megapixel rear-facing camera (with a flash) and a 5-megapixel front-facing camera (with a new feature that allows the smartphone's screen to serve as a flash), but when used with the iOS 9 edition of the Camera app, it's possible to use the new Selfie picture taking feature, plus snap what Apple calls "Live Photos," that can be viewed on any Apple computer or mobile device.

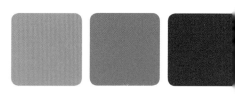

> **NOTE** The new Live Photo option enables you to snap a photo but capture it as a two- to three-second mini-movie that can later be viewed as an animated image on any iPhone, iPad, iPod touch, Mac, Apple TV, or Apple Watch that's using the Photos app or is capable of displaying digital photos in other ways. For example, you can use a Live Photo as your custom watch face on the Apple Watch or as the Lock screen wallpaper on your iPhone or iPad.
>
> A Live Photo can still be treated as a regular digital image file. It can be shared online, emailed, or printed, for example.

Whether you're using one of these latest iPhone models or an older iPhone (or any iPad model for that matter), it's possible to take crystal-clear photos and create large and vibrant full-color prints from your digital image files or share those images using options offered by the Photos app's Share menu.

> **WHAT'S NEW** When using the iPhone 6s or iPhone 6s Plus and viewing the Home screen, instead of launching the Camera app by tapping on its app icon, place and hold your finger gently on the app icon to reveal a new menu that enables you to access the new Selfie picture taking feature, record a video, record a Slo-mo video, or take a regular photo by tapping on one of the listed options (shown in Figure 8.1).

SOME CAMERA APP FEATURES ARE AVAILABLE ONLY ON CERTAIN iPHONE AND iPAD MODELS

The Camera app continues to be one of the core apps that come preinstalled with the iOS 9 operating system. The same version of the Camera app is installed on all iOS mobile devices. However, based on which iPhone or iPad model you're using, some of the features and functions of the Camera app might not be available to you.

Features such as the new Selfie picture taking mode and the ability to shoot "Live Photos," for example, work only with the latest iOS mobile devices that offer 3D Touch functionality built in to the device's touchscreen.

THE CAMERA AND PHOTOS APPS ARE CHOCK FULL OF FEATURES

When it comes to taking, viewing, editing, and sharing pictures using your iPhone or iPad, the Camera and Photos apps each offer a collection of powerful features, like zoom capabilities, a panoramic shooting mode, a timer, a time-lapse shooting mode, plus easy-to-use autofocus sensors that help ensure your photos are blur-free and utilize the available lighting in the best way possible.

Figure 8.1

Quickly launch a specific feature of the Camera app directly from the Home screen by placing and holding your finger on the Camera app icon for about 2 seconds and utilizing the iPhone 6s or iPhone 6s Plus's new 3D Touch functionality.

METHODS FOR LOADING DIGITAL IMAGES INTO YOUR iPHONE OR iPAD

Before you can view, edit, print, and share your favorite digital images, you first must either shoot them using the Camera app or transfer the images into your iOS device.

> **NOTE** Facebook, Twitter, Instagram, and other third-party apps enable you to access and use your iPhone or iPad's built-in cameras without using the Camera app. It's also possible for these apps to access the Photos app's image folders, such as the All Photos or Favorites folder.

> **NOTE** If you activate the iCloud Photo Library feature offered by the Photos app (which enables you to sync all of your digital images between all iOS mobile devices and computers linked to the same iCloud account), your main photos album where all of your photos are stored, including all newly shot photos, is called "All Photos." However, when iCloud Photo Library is turned off, the main album where you'll initially find all photos you take using your iPhone or iPad is called "Camera Roll."

Aside from shooting images using one of your iOS device's built-in cameras, there are several ways to import photos and then store them in the Photos app:

■ Use the iTunes sync process with the Photos app running on a Mac or PC. By linking your iPhone or iPad with your computer (via the supplied USB cable), you can transfer photos or entire albums.

■ Load photos from your online-based iCloud Photo Library from within the Photos app.

> **TIP** If multiple images are attached or embedded within an incoming email, from the Mail app, when you use your finger and hold it on one of the images, a Save [number] Images option is displayed in addition to the Save Image option. Use the Save [number] Images option to save all the photos within the email at once to the All Photos/Camera Roll album in the Photos app.

■ Receive and save photos sent via text/instant message. Tap on the image you receive using the Messages app, and then tap on the Save command.

■ Save images directly from a website as you're surfing the Web. Hold your finger on the image you're viewing in a website. If it's not copy-protected, after a second or two a menu appears, enabling you to save the image or copy it to your device's virtual clipboard (after which you can paste it into another app). Tap on the Save Image or Copy options, respectively (shown in Figure 8.2).

■ Images can be sent to your iPhone or iPad wirelessly via AirDrop. For this feature to work, AirDrop must be turned on, which can be done from the Control Center. Launch Control Center, tap on the AirDrop option, and then select Contacts Only or Everyone. You can then send images to other AirDrop-compatible computers or mobile devices, or receive images sent to you using this method. Received photos are automatically placed in your All Photos/Camera Roll album.

■ Use the optional Camera Connection Kit ($29, available from Apple Stores or Apple.com) to load images from your digital camera or its memory card directly into your iPhone or iPad.

Figure 8.2

Tap on the Save Image option to save an image in your iPhone or iPad that you discover on a web page.

USE THE CAMERA APP TO TAKE PHOTOS OR SHOOT VIDEO

There are a variety of ways you can launch the Camera app to begin shooting photos or video quickly.

WAYS TO LAUNCH THE CAMERA APP

There are several easy ways to launch the Camera app, including the following:

■ From the Home screen, tap on the Camera app icon.

■ From the Lock screen, place your finger on the camera icon that's displayed in the bottom-right corner of the screen, and then swipe your finger upward.

■ Tap on the Camera app icon that's displayed in the Control Center.

- On an iPhone 6s or iPhone 6s Plus, press on the Camera app icon displayed on the Home screen to reveal a pop menu for using specific Camera app features (refer to Figure 8.1).

- Activate Siri and say, "Launch the camera app." If you're using one of the newer iPhones or iPads, simply say, "Hey Siri, launch the Camera app," without having to press and hold down the Home button.

- If the Camera app is already running in the background, access the App Switcher and select the Camera app.

HOW TO SHOOT PHOTOS OR VIDEO WITH THE CAMERA APP

The main camera viewfinder screen appears as soon as you launch the Camera app on an iPhone, iPod touch, or iPad. Figure 8.3 shows the main Camera app viewfinder screen on an iPhone 6, while Figure 8.4 shows the Camera app on the iPhone 6s (which offers the Live Photo feature). Figure 8.5 shows the Camera app's viewfinder screen on an iPad.

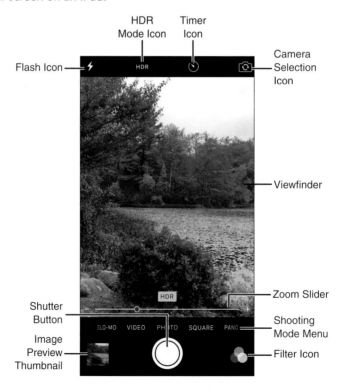

Figure 8.3

From the Camera app's main screen (shown here on the iPhone 6), you can snap digital photos or shoot video.

Figure 8.4

The Camera app on the iPhone 6s (or iPhone 6s Plus) offers the new Live Photo icon displayed at the top-center of the screen.

Figure 8.5

The Camera app looks slightly different on an iPad but offers much of the same functionality.

TIP To snap a Live Photo (iPhone 6s or iPhone 6s Plus), first tap on the Live Photo icon displayed at the top center of the viewfinder screen to turn on this feature. Then take a photo as you normally would by utilizing any of the Camera app's other features and functions. Keep in mind that the Live Photo feature works only when the Camera app is set to Photo mode (not Square, Time Lapse, or Pano mode, for example). It does still work, however, with the Timer feature turned on.

When using the Camera app on any iOS mobile device, the main area of the screen serves as your camera's viewfinder.

On the iPhone, along the bottom of the screen are several command icons and options. When using the Camera app with the iPad, all command icons and options are displayed along the right margin of the screen.

NOTE If you're using an older iPhone or iPad model, such as an iPhone 4s, iPhone 5, or iPad 3, some of the features and functions discussed in this chapter (such as HDR mode, Live Photo, and Burst shooting mode) are not available to you.

To view the last photo you shot (or the last video clip recorded), tap on the Image Preview thumbnail displayed in the bottom-left corner of the viewfinder screen. You can then use the Photo app's viewing and editing functions on that image.

At the bottom center of the screen on the iPhone is the camera's round Shutter button. Tap on this to snap a photo or to start and stop the video recording pro-cess. In Video mode, the Shutter button icon transforms from a bright red circle into a red square (pause button) when you tap on it to begin shooting a video clip.

> **TIP** In Photo mode, if you press and hold down the Shutter button, Burst shooting mode automatically activates on newer iPhone and iPad models. This feature enables you to shoot multiple photos in quick succession (several frames per second) without having to keep pressing the Shutter button.
>
> This feature is ideal for capturing a fast moving subject, for example, and allows you to capture an action or event that happens very quickly. You can always delete the unwanted (extra) photos after choosing your favorite image(s) from the sequence.
>
> Images shot using Burst shooting mode are placed in a separate album in the Photos app called Bursts.

OVERVIEW OF THE CAMERA APP'S SHOOTING MODES

From the Shooting Mode menu, your options include Time-Lapse, Slow-Mo, Video, Photo, Square, and Pano. This menu is displayed directly above the Shutter button. Use your finger to manually scroll left or right to select your shooting mode. The active shooting mode is highlighted in yellow and displayed directly above the Shutter button.

> **NOTE** If you're using an iPhone 6s or iPhone 6s Plus, the new Selfie shooting mode allows you to snap a photo while using the smartphone's screen as your flash. This can be accessed from the Home screen using the Camera app's Pop menu, or from the main Camera app's viewfinder screen. Make sure the flash option is set to on or auto.

■ The **Time-Lapse** feature enables you to set up the Camera app to automati-cally keep snapping one photo at a time (the time interval is dynamically set by the iOS device) until you manually turn off this function. This feature works best if you mount the iOS mobile device on a tripod, or use it with a stand. It's great for capturing changes that happen in a single scene over time, such as a sunrise or sunset. The content created when using the Time Lapse feature is stored in the Photos app as a video, not as a series of photos.

> **NOTE** When shooting with Time Lapse mode, the longer you leave the feature turned on (so the Camera app keeps taking photos automatically over an extended period of time), the longer the interval is between shots. Typically, if you leave this feature turned on long enough, the images are condensed into a 30- to 40-second mini-movie that shows the animated time-lapsed images.

■ The **Slo-Mo** option enables you to shoot high-action video but play it back in slow motion. When using the iPhone 6/6s/6 Plus/6s Plus, you can capture slow-motion video at up to 240 frames per second, as opposed to 120 frames per second using the iPhone 5s and some iPad models. This shooting mode is ideal if you're shooting a fast-moving subject or a high-action activity.

■ The **Video** shooting mode is used to shoot 1080p HD-quality video using your iPhone or iPad. Depending on which device you're using, it's possible to shoot at 30 or 60 frames per second. Keep in mind that your iPhone or iPad is ideal for shooting relatively short video clips. These HD video files take up a tremendous amount of storage space, so if you want to shoot long home videos, consider using a dedicated video camera.

> **NOTE** From within Settings, you can select the video shooting resolution. The options vary based on the device you're using. If you're using an iPhone 6s or iPhone 6s Plus, for example, it's possible to shoot 4K resolution video at 30 frames per second (or you can choose a lower resolution).
>
> To adjust the default video resolution on any iPhone or iPad, launch Settings, tap on the Photos & Camera option, and then tap on the Record Video option and/or Record Slo-Mo option.
>
> Keep in mind that the higher the resolution you select, the larger your video files will be. Larger files require more internal storage space.

■ The **Photo** shooting mode is what you'll use most of the time when taking pictures. It allows you to snap regular, rectangular-shaped digital images.

■ The **Square** shooting mode automatically precrops images as you're shooting to be compatible with services such as Instagram. You wind up with square images.

▤ The **Pano** shooting mode launches the Camera app's panoramic mode, which is ideal for shooting vast landscapes, skylines, or large groups of people (shown in Figure 8.6). You wind up with a long, rectangular image.

Figure 8.6

The Pano (panoramic) shooting mode is ideal for shooting images of vast landscapes, large groups of people, or very wide areas.

> ☑ TIP   In addition to the Time-Lapse option, the Camera app offers a Timer option. To turn this on, tap on the Timer icon and then set the timer for 3 or 10 seconds. Doing this determines how long the Camera app waits between the time you press the Shutter button and when an image is actually taken and saved. This feature is available on most iPhone and iPad models.

The iPhone and iPad each have two built-in cameras—one in the front and one on the back of the device. The front-facing camera makes it easier to snap photos of yourself (that is, take a "selfie" or participate in video calls via FaceTime or Skype).

The rear-facing camera (which enables you to take much higher-resolution photos or video) enables you to photograph or record whatever is in front of you. Tap on the camera-shaped icon located in the top-right corner of the viewfinder screen to switch between cameras.

> ☑ TIP   Unless you're taking a "selfie," which is a photo of yourself, use the rear-facing camera whenever possible. This is a much higher-resolution camera. Using it will enable you to shoot more detailed, vibrant, and higher-quality images or video.

TAKE ADVANTAGE OF THE HDR SHOOTING FEATURE

The HDR feature offered by the Camera app stands for High Dynamic Range. It can be used with the rear-facing camera only. When turned on, this feature captures the available light differently, and can help you compensate for a photo that would otherwise be over- or underexposed.

When you take a photo using HDR mode, the iPhone or iPad actually captures several separate images simultaneously and then automatically blends them into a single image in a fraction of a second. By doing this, it's possible to capture more depth and contrast, plus make better use of available lighting. The result is often a more detailed and vibrant photo.

You can decide whether the original photo and the HDR version of a photo are both saved in the All Photos/Camera Roll album or just the HDR version of the image is saved. To make this adjustment, launch Settings, tap on the Photos & Camera option, and then turn on or off the virtual switch associated with the Keep Normal Photo option.

Depending on which iPhone or iPad model you're using, you might have access to HDR Auto mode. This allows the camera to decide whether a photo benefits from this feature. Turning on HDR Auto mode takes some of the guesswork out of picture taking, and often results in better-quality images.

The HDR button is displayed near the top center of the Camera app's viewfinder screen on the iPhone, or just above the Shutter button on the iPad. Tap it to toggle the HDR mode when taking photos.

On the latest iPhones and iPads are three HDR-related options: On, Off, or Auto. If HDR Auto is available (shown in Figure 8.7), it enables you to consistently capture the most vibrant photos in a wide range of lighting situations.

> **NOTE** When you turn on the HDR mode, this automatically turns off the flash that's built in to the iPhone, which could otherwise be used with the smartphone's rear-facing camera.

HOW TO UTILIZE THE iPHONE'S BUILT-IN FLASH

On the iPhone, the flash icon is located in the upper-left corner of the Camera's viewfinder screen. It controls whether the iPhone automatically uses the built-in flash when needed as you're shooting photos or video with the rear-facing camera. Tap the icon, then tap the On, Off, or Auto option to toggle this feature.

The Auto option is offered only on the newer iPhone models released within the past few years. The Auto option enables the smartphone to analyze the available light for you and automatically determine whether the flash is needed.

Keep in mind that even in low-light situations, you can often achieve better results if you shoot photos using the HDR shooting mode, as opposed to using the flash.

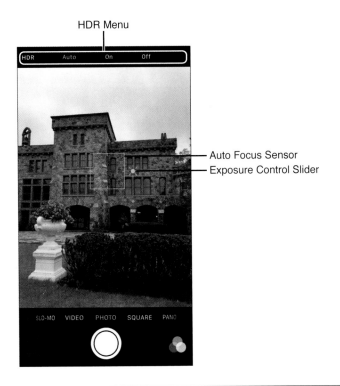

HDR Menu

Auto Focus Sensor
Exposure Control Slider

Figure 8.7
On the latest iPhone and iPad models, you can set HDR mode to On, Off, or Auto mode by tapping on the option at the top of the screen. On older iPhone and most iPad models, only the On or Off options are available.

> **NOTE** Starting with the iPhone 5 series, the smartphone includes what Apple calls a True Tone flash. This is really two flashes that work together and emit light in different colors. As a result, the Camera app analyzes the available light in each shooting situation and enhances it, while monitoring the natural colors within a photo.
>
> The True Tone flash automatically reduces the red-eye effect when taking pictures of people and can often reduce or eliminate unwanted shadows in photos.

> **iOS 9 WHAT'S NEW** When using the iPhone 6s or iPhone 6s Plus, if you activate the flash when using the front-facing camera, the screen of your iPhone automatically serves as a simulated flash to brighten up your face when the ambient light isn't adequate. Make sure the Camera app's flash option is turned on for this to work.

TAKE ADVANTAGE OF THE AUTOFOCUS AND EXPOSURE CONTROL OPTIONS

As you're looking at the Camera app's viewfinder and framing your shot, be sure to force the app to focus in on your intended subject by tapping on the screen directly over where your subject appears.

When you do this, the Autofocus Sensor box appears in the viewfinder, and the Camera app then focuses in on your intended subject.

If you're shooting people, however, the Camera app automatically identifies each person's face in a photo and focuses in on those faces. An Autofocus Sensor box appears around each person's face.

> **TIP** In addition to the Autofocus Sensor, depending on which iOS mobile device you're using, a manual Exposure Control slider might also be displayed. It looks like a sun-shaped icon that appears to the immediate right of the Autofocus Sensor.
>
> When this Exposure Control slider is displayed (refer to Figure 8.7), place your finger on the sun-shaped icon and slide it upward or downward to manually adjust the exposure before snapping the photo.

HOW TO SNAP A PHOTO

Snapping a single digital photo using the Camera app is simple. Follow these steps:

1. Launch the Camera app.
2. Make sure the shooting mode is set to Photo or Square.
3. Choose which of your device's two cameras you want to use by tapping on the camera selection icon.
4. Compose your image by holding up your device and pointing it at your intended subject(s).
5. If desired, set the Timer feature.
6. To add a special effect to the image as you're shooting, tap on the Filter icon and then select one of the eight displayed filters by tapping on its preview image (shown in Figure 8.8). The filter thumbnail serves as the shutter button for snapping a photo when you tap on it.

Figure 8.8

As you're shooting a photo, you can choose one of the eight image filters to add an effect. Choose None (in the center) to shoot without using a filter. You can always add a filter later when editing a photo using the Photos app.

7. Choose the intended subject of your photo, such as a person or an object. Tap your finger on the screen where your subject appears in the viewfinder. An Autofocus Sensor box appears on the screen at the location you tap (refer to Figure 8.7). Where this box is positioned is what the camera focuses on (as opposed to something in the foreground, background, or next to your intended subject).

8. If necessary, use the Exposure Control slider (refer to Figure 8.7) to manually adjust the exposure just before snapping a photo. Keep in mind that using the Photos app, you can later adjust or correct a variety of problematic issues within a photo, including its exposure, contrast, saturation, color, and shadows. These are some of the editing tools built in to the iOS 9 edition of the Photos app.

☑ **TIP**   As you're holding your iPhone or iPad to snap a photo or shoot video, be sure your fingers don't accidentally block the camera lens that's being utilized. On the more recent iPhone models, next to the rear-facing camera lens is a tiny flash. Keep your fingers clear of this, as well.

9. If you want to use the Camera app's zoom feature, use a pinch motion on the screen. A zoom slider (shown in Figure 8.9) appears directly above the Shooting Mode menu and the Shutter button. Use your finger to move the dot on the slider to the right to zoom in, or to the left to zoom out. Alternatively, use a pinch or reverse-pinch finger gesture to manage the zoom level while shooting.

Figure 8.9

As you're framing an image, zoom in (or out) on your subject using the onscreen zoom slider. Use a pinch finger gesture on the screen to make this slider appear, and then move it to the right or left to increase or decrease the zoom level.

10. Decide whether you want to use HDR mode or the built-in flash (iPhone only) when taking the photo. (You can also choose neither of these options.) Another option, on some more recently released iPhones, is to set both the flash and HDR mode to Auto, and then let the Camera app decide which feature to use. On the iPad, set HDR mode to Auto to allow the Camera app to decide whether this feature is needed. (iPads do not have a rear-facing built-in flash.)

11. When you have your image framed in the viewfinder, tap on the Shutter button to snap the photo. You can also press the Volume Up (+) or Volume Down (-) buttons on the side of your iPhone/iPad, which serve as a Shutter button when using the Camera app.

12. The photo is saved in the All Photos/Camera Roll album of the Photos app. You can now shoot another photo or view the photo using the Photos app.

> **NOTE** All regular photos are automatically stored in the All Photos/ Camera Roll album as they're taken. The iOS 9 edition of the Photos app automatically places selfies into a separate Selfies album and sorts your panoramic shots into a Panoramas album.
>
> Videos are placed in a separate Videos folder, and Slo-mo video clips are stored in an album called Slo-mo.
>
> When you use the Burst shooting mode, these groups of images are clustered together and placed in the Bursts album.
>
> All these albums are automatically created for you. In the Photos app, you can move images into the Favorites album or custom-named albums you create manually.

HOW TO SHOOT A PANORAMIC PHOTO

To take advantage of the panoramic shooting mode to snap a photo of a landscape, city skyline, or a large group of people, follow these steps:

1. Launch the Camera app.

2. Swipe on the Shooting Modes menu and select the Pano shooting mode.

3. Position your iPhone or iPad's viewfinder to the extreme left of your wide-angle shot. (When using the Pano shooting mode, hold the smartphone or tablet upright in portrait mode, unless you're shooting a very, very tall object).

> **TIP** If you tap on the large arrow icon in the viewfinder, you can switch the panning direction from right to left, instead of left to right as you're capturing a panoramic shot.

4. Tap the Shutter button, and then slowly and steadily move your iPhone or iPad from left to right (shown in Figure 8.10). If you go too fast, a message appears on the screen telling you to slow down.

Figure 8.10

When taking panoramic shots, the viewfinder screen looks very different on your iPhone or iPad.

5. The panorama slider moves from left to right as you capture your image. Tap the Shutter button again when you're finished, or continue moving the iOS device to the right until the entire length of the image has been captured.

6. The panoramic photo is saved in the Panoramas folder of the Photos app. You can then view, edit, or share it from within Photos.

> **TIP** When viewing a panoramic photo, hold your iPhone or iPad in landscape mode; however, when shooting a panoramic shot, hold it in portrait mode.

HOW TO SHOOT HD VIDEO

From the Camera app, you can easily shoot stunning HD video. Follow these basic steps for shooting video using your iPhone or iPad:

1. Launch the Camera app.

2. Select the Video shooting mode option from the Shooting Mode menu. (If you want to shoot slow-motion video, select the Slo-Mo option, if it's offered by your iOS mobile device.)

3. Tap the camera selection icon to choose which camera you want to use. You can switch between the front- and the rear-facing camera at any time. On older iPhone/iPad models, the rear-facing camera shoots lower-resolution video, as opposed to 1080p HD resolution video.

> **(iOS 9) WHAT'S NEW** The iPhone 6s and iPhone 6s Plus is capable of shooting 4K resolution video using the rear-facing camera.
>
> On any iPhone, set the video recording resolution by launching Settings, tapping on the Photo and Camera option, and then tapping on the Record Video and/or Record Slo-Mo options. The available options are listed on the Record Video submenu screen, as well the amount of internal storage space needed to record each minute of video.
>
> For example, when the iPhone 6s or iPhone 6s Plus records video in 4K resolution, this requires 375MB of internal storage space per minute.

4. If applicable, tap on the Flash icon that's displayed near the top-left corner of the screen (iPhone) to turn on the flash and use it as a continuous light source while filming video.

5. Hold your iPhone or iPad up to the subject you want to capture on video. Set up your shot by looking at what's displayed on the screen.

6. In the viewfinder, tap on your intended subject to make the autofocus sensor appear. If necessary, and if your device supports this feature, you can also manually adjust the Exposure Control using the displayed slider.

7. When you're ready to start shooting video, tap on the Shutter button. The red dot turns into a red square. This indicates you're now filming. Your iPhone or iPad captures whatever action you see on the screen, as well as any sound in the area.

8. As you're filming video, notice a timer displayed on the screen (shown in Figure 8.11). Your only limit to how much video you can shoot is based on the amount of available memory in your iOS device and how long the battery lasts. However, this app is designed more for shooting short video clips, not full-length home movies.

9. As you're filming, tap anywhere on the screen to focus in on your subject using the app's built-in autofocus sensor.

10. To stop filming, tap again on the Shutter button. Your video footage is saved. You can now view, edit, and share it from within the Photos app (or a video app, such as iMovie).

TIP Although the Photos app enables you to trim your video clips as well as view and share the videos, if you want to edit your videos, plus add titles and special effects, use Apple's feature-packed iMovie app, which is available from the App Store. For more information about iMovie, visit www.apple.com/apps/imovie.

Video Timer

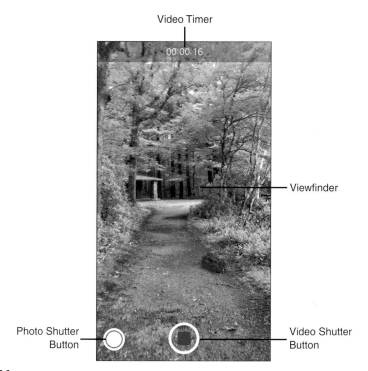

Viewfinder

Photo Shutter Button

Video Shutter Button

Figure 8.11

When shooting video on your iPhone or iPad, make sure the timer (displayed at the top center of the screen) is counting up. This indicates you're actually recording.

TIP Depending on which iPhone or iPad model you're using, at the same time you're shooting video, you might discover a second, circular (white) Shutter button displayed to the left of the primary Shutter button (refer to Figure 8.11). When available, this second Shutter button can be used to snap high-resolution digital images at the same time you're shooting HD video.

USING THE PHOTOS APP TO VIEW, EDIT, ENHANCE, PRINT, AND SHARE PHOTOS AND VIDEOS

Use the Photos app to view images stored on your iOS device or in your iCloud account. The iOS 9 version of the Photos app includes a robust selection of photo editing and image enhancement tools.

> ✅ TIP   Images in the Photos app are auto-sorted based on when or where they were shot. Years displays thumbnails of all images shot within a particular year and includes details about where those images were shot.
>
> Collections (shown in Figure 8.12) breaks down a Years grouping to display images based on when and where they were taken. Moments enables you to display thumbnails of images within a Collection that represent one location or date.
>
> As you're viewing thumbnails in the Moments view, tap on one of them to view a single image. Or, at the bottom of the screen, tap on Photos, Shared, or Albums to view a different set of images stored on your mobile device.

On the iPhone, the functionality of the Photos app is almost identical to the iPad version; however, the appearance of some of the screens and the position of certain command icons and menus differs due to the size of each device's screen.

To exit out of the Moments or Collections thumbnail view, use the options displayed at the top-left corner of the screen. From the Years view, tap on a collection (within the main area of the screen) or tap on the Photos, Shared, or Albums icon that's displayed along the bottom of the screen.

When viewing Moments, each group of photos that are shot at the same place and in the same time frame are automatically grouped together into an event.

As you're viewing these events, tap on the associated Share button to quickly share all images in that event, or select and share specific images from it via AirDrop, Messages, or iCloud. Tap on the Select option at the top-right corner of the screen to choose one or more events or thumbnails. Once selected, tap either the Share or Trash icon in the top-left corner of the screen to manage those images.

VIEW AN IMAGE IN FULL-SCREEN MODE

When viewing thumbnails of your images, tap on any single image thumbnail to view a larger version of it. The Edit icon is displayed in the upper-right corner of the screen.

On the iPhone (shown in Figure 8.13), the Share, Favorites, and Trash icons are displayed along the bottom of the screen, while on the iPad, these icons are grouped together near the top-right corner of the screen (with the Edit option).

Shooting Location

Date Range

Photos Icon

Figure 8.12

The Photos app offers several ways to sort and view image thumbnails. This is an example of the Collections view.

Along the bottom-center of the screen are thumbnails for all the images stored in the album you're currently accessing.

> **TIP** By tapping on the Favorites (heart-shaped) icon associated with each image, you can place that image into a separate Favorites album and then opt to view or share only those images.

As you're viewing a photo, tap on it to hide or show the Edit option, Share icon, Favorites icon, and Trash icon, which automatically appear and then disappear after a few seconds when you first open a photo. Tap on the Edit icon to reveal the Photo app's image editing options (shown in Figure 8.14).

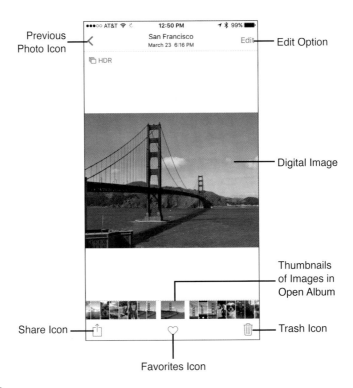

Previous Photo Icon

Edit Option

Digital Image

Thumbnails of Images in Open Album

Share Icon

Trash Icon

Favorites Icon

Figure 8.13
The Edit option and the Share, Favorites, and Trash icons are all displayed when viewing a single image on your iPhone or iPad's screen.

To exit the single-image view and return to the multi-image thumbnail view, tap anywhere on the screen to make the command icons appear, then tap on the left-pointing arrow-shaped icon displayed in the upper-left corner of the screen.

EDITING VIDEOS

When you tap on the thumbnail for a video clip, you have the option of playing that clip from within the Photos app. The Share, Favorite, and Trash icons are displayed on the screen.

Tap on the Edit option to access the video trimming (editing) feature. Then to trim a video clip, look at the filmstrip display of the clip and move the left and/or right editing tabs accordingly to define the portion of the clip you want to edit and keep.

The box around the filmstrip display (representing the portion of the video you want to keep) turns yellow, and the Done option appears (shown in Figure 8.15). Before tapping on the Done option, tap on the Play icon to preview your newly edited (trimmed) video clip.

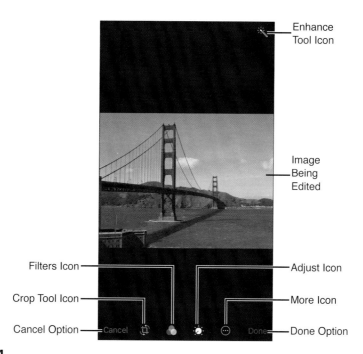

Enhance
Tool Icon

Image
Being
Edited

Filters Icon

Crop Tool Icon

Cancel Option

Adjust Icon

More Icon

Done Option

Figure 8.14

After tapping the Edit option, the command icons you use to edit and enhance images are displayed.

Figure 8.15

Use the Photos app to trim video clips, but use the optional iMovie app to fully edit videos.

If it's okay, tap on the Done option to save your changes. The Save As New Clip option appears. Tap on it. To gain access to a comprehensive and powerful set of video editing tools, download and install Apple's iMovie app onto your mobile device.

TOOLS FOR EDITING PHOTOS

When you tap on the Edit option while viewing a single image, several command icons are displayed on the screen (refer to Figure 8.14). These icons provide the tools for quickly editing and enhancing your image. Your options are explained in the next sections.

ENHANCE

The Enhance icon looks like a magic wand. When you tap on it, you can utilize a one-touch editing tool that automatically adjusts multiple aspects of a photo at once, including its contrast, exposure, and color, to make the image look better and make colors appear more vibrant. This feature can be turned on or off and is not manually adjustable.

CROP

Use the Crop tool shown in Figure 8.16 to manually adjust the cropping of the image by dragging one of the corners of the white frame horizontally, vertically, or diagonally. The Crop tool also enables you to straighten a photo and readjust its angle by placing your finger on the straightening dial and moving it. Tap on the Image Rotation icon to rotate the image 90 degrees.

> **TIP** After using any of the Crop-related tools, be sure to tap the Done option to save your changes. Alternatively, tap Cancel to exit out of this option without saving your changes.

> **TIP** As you're cropping an image, tap on the Aspect Ratio icon to select an aspect ratio, such as Original, Square, 2:3, 3:5, 3:4, 4:5, 5:7, or 9:16. Unless you need the image in a specific size, choose the Original option and then use the Crop tool to adjust your image. Selecting an aspect ratio forces the basic dimensions to stay intact as you crop the image. This enables you to make accurately formatted prints later, without throwing off the image dimensions.

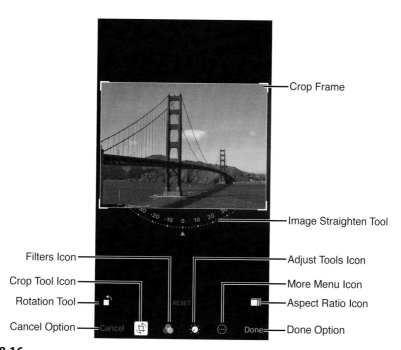

Figure 8.16

Tap on the Crop icon to access tools for cropping, straightening, and/or rotating an image.

FILTERS

The Photos app offers a handful of preinstalled special effect filters. After tapping on the Filters icon, select the filter you want to apply to your image with a single on-screen tap. A preview of the altered image is displayed. To save the changes, tap Done. To discard the changes, tap Cancel, or tap on another filter.

> **NOTE** In addition to the filters that come preinstalled with the Photos app, third-party developers can now create optional filters you can use with the Photos app.

ADJUST

The Photos app enables you to edit or enhance many different aspects of a photo. Begin by tapping on the Adjust icon. Then, from the Adjust submenu, tap on the Light, Color, or B&W option. Each one of these options reveals another submenu that offers a variety of editing tools.

THE LIGHT TOOLS

When you tap on the Light tool, a slider appears that enables you to manually increase or decrease the overall lighting effect within the image being viewed (shown in Figure 8.17).

LIGHT   ——More Menu Icon

Figure 8.17

It's possible to use a slider to manually adjust the master Light tool.

When you tap on the More menu icon (after tapping on the Light option), another submenu with options for Exposure, Highlights, Shadows, Brightness, Contrast, and Black Point is displayed (shown in Figure 8.18).

Tap on any of these options to reveal a separate slider you can use to manually adjust that option. Keep in mind that you can mix and match the use of these options to create truly customized visual effects.

THE COLOR TOOLS

When you tap on the Color icon, a master Color slider is displayed. Use your finger to manually adjust this feature. Tap on the More menu icon to reveal additional Color-related options, including Saturation, Contrast, and Cast.

Each of these tools (shown in Figure 8.19) has its own slider that you can manually adjust. Again, after making a change, be sure to tap on the Done option to save your edits. Alternatively, tap Cancel/Close to exit out of the selected editing tool without making any changes.

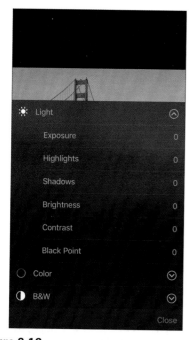

Figure 8.18

Tap on the More menu icon to reveal additional light-related editing and image enhancement tools.

Figure 8.19

After tapping on the Color icon, tap the More menu icon to access tools for adjusting the Saturation, Contrast, and Cast within a photo.

THE B&W TOOLS

Tap on the B&W icon to instantly convert a full-color image into black and white. It's then possible to manually adjust the black, white, and grayscale colors using the B&W slider that's displayed.

By tapping on the More menu icon after selecting the B&W editing tool, additional submenu options enable you to manually adjust the image's Intensity, Neutrals, Tone, and Grain, which all relate directly to the black-and-white effect (shown in Figure 8.20).

After making a change, tap Done to save your edits or Cancel/Close to exit out of the selected editing tool without making any changes.

Figure 8.20
Not only can you convert a full-color photo into black and white, but you can then fully customize the black-and-white effect using a series of sliders related to the Intensity, Neutrals, Tone, and Grain settings.

PRINTING PHOTOS

iOS 9 is fully compatible with Apple's AirPrint feature, so if you have a photo printer set up to work wirelessly with your smartphone or tablet, it's possible to create prints from your digital images using the Print command in the Photos app. Follow these steps to print an image:

1. Launch the Photos app from the Home screen.

2. From the main View Images screen, tap on any thumbnail to view an image in full-screen mode. You might need to open an album first by tapping on the Album's thumbnail if you have the Albums viewing option selected.

3. Tap on the full-screen version of the image to make the various command icons appear.

4. Tap on the Share icon.

5. From the Share menu, select the Print option.

6. When the Printer Options submenu appears, select your printer, determine how many copies of the print you'd like to create, choose the size of the desired print(s), and then tap on the Print icon.

> 🔎 **MORE INFO**   To print wirelessly from your iOS device using the AirPrint feature, you must have a compatible printer. To learn more about AirPrint, and to configure your printer for wireless printing from your iPhone or iPad, visit https://support.apple.com/en-us/HT201311.

THIRD-PARTY APPS FOR ORDERING PRINTS FROM YOUR IMAGES

If you want to order professional quality prints directly from your iPhone or iPad and have them shipped to your door within a few days, you can use one of several apps (such as FreePrints) available from the App Store.

The free KickSend app, for example, determines your current location and tells you which one-hour photo labs are in close proximity. You can then upload your photos to the desired lab directly from your iPhone or iPad, and within 30 to 60 minutes pick up your prints at the selected location. KickSend is easy to use, and works with participating Walgreen's, CVS Pharmacy, Target, and Wal-Mart locations.

The free Shutterfly app also enables you to order prints directly from your iOS mobile device, plus it gives you the option to create custom photo gifts, such as coffee mugs, mouse pads, iPhone cases, T-shirts, and other products that showcase your images. Enlargements can also be ordered, as can canvas prints and other types of wall art that showcase your favorite photos.

SHARING PHOTOS AND VIDEOS

After you have selected one or more images, tap the Share icon to access the Share menu (shown in Figure 8.21).

SEND IMAGES WIRELESSLY VIA AIRDROP

If you're within close proximity to another Mac, iPhone, or iPad and the other computer or iOS mobile device also has the AirDrop feature turned on, you can wirelessly send images from within the Photos app using the AirDrop feature. This feature becomes active only when others nearby can receive an AirDrop transmission.

Figure 8.21
From the Share menu, you can share your photos with others in a variety of ways.

SEND IMAGES VIA TEXT/INSTANT MESSAGE

Tap this option to send images via the Messages app. When the New Message window appears, fill in the To field with the recipient's cell phone number or iMessage account username. Tap the plus-sign icon to send the same message to multiple recipients.

You can optionally add text to the photos that are attached to the message. To add more images to the outgoing message, tap on the Camera icon. When you're ready, tap the Send option to send the photos and message.

EMAIL UP TO FIVE IMAGES AT A TIME

When looking at thumbnails for images in an album, tap on the Edit button to select between one and five images, and then tap on the Share icon.

Select the Mail option from the Share menu and fill in the To field when prompted. If you want, edit the Subject field, and/or add text to the body of the email, and then tap the Send button.

> **NOTE** After you tap the Send button, you are asked to choose an image size. On the iPhone, a pop-up window appears. On the iPad, tap on the Image Size option, displayed to the right of the From field.
>
> The smaller the file size you choose, the faster it sends, but the image's resolution and file size are reduced. In general, unless you know the recipient can use a smaller and lower resolution image size, choose the Actual Size option.

When viewing a single image, tap on the Share icon, select Mail, fill in the To field, and edit the Subject. If you want, add text to the body of the message, and then tap the Send button.

TWEET A PHOTO TO YOUR TWITTER FOLLOWERS

To tweet a photo, after tapping the Share icon while viewing a single photo in full-screen mode, select the Tweet option. Compose your tweet message (which will already have the selected image attached), and then tap the Send icon.

It's also possible to tweet photos from the official Twitter app or from a third-party Twitter-related app such as Twitterific (available from the App Store).

PUBLISH PHOTOS ON FACEBOOK

To publish one or more photos to Facebook with an optional text-based status update, tap the Facebook icon displayed in the Share menu. From the Facebook window, tap the Album option to choose an existing Facebook Photos Album to which the image should be added.

Next, tap the Location option to publish the location where the image was shot on Facebook along with the photo. Tap on the Audience option to decide who can view the image(s) on Facebook. Your options include Public, Friends, Friends Except Acquaintances, Only Me, Close Friends, or people within a specific Facebook group you've created.

To the left of the photo thumbnail, use the virtual keyboard to enter a caption for the image(s) you're about to upload, and then tap the Post option (displayed at the top-right corner of the Facebook window) to publish the photos.

> **TIP** An alternative to using the Photos app to publish photos to Facebook is to use the official Facebook app. This gives you additional options, such as the ability to tag photos with the names of the people who appear in them. Plus, the Facebook app enables you to add special-effect filters to images before uploading them.

UPLOAD IMAGES TO FLICKR

Flickr is an online-based photo sharing service and photo lab operated by Yahoo!. To upload selected images to your existing Flickr account, select the images from within the Photos app, tap the Share icon, and then tap the Flickr option. You then can choose an album to which your selected images are uploaded.

It's also possible to use the official Flickr app to upload and manage your account from your iPhone or iPad.

SHARE PHOTOS VIA OTHER COMPATIBLE APPS

Displayed in the Share menu, when applicable, are app icons for third-party apps you have installed that work with the Photos app to share photos. For example, if you have the Facebook Messenger app installed on your device, you can send photos via instant message using this service.

You'll also discover options for iCloud Photo Sharing and Notes displayed as part of the Share menu. To place photos online in a particular iCloud album that you want to share with other people, tap on the iCloud Photo Sharing option, and then fill in the prompts offered in the iCloud window that appears.

To export one or more photos from the Photos app and place them into the newly redesigned Notes app, tap on the Notes icon and then choose which existing note you want to place the photos into, or select the New Note option to create a new note in the Notes app from scratch that displays the exported photos.

> **NOTE** To control which third-party apps (which are compatible with the Photos app) appear in the Share menu associated with the Photos app, tap on the More option. Then, turn on or off the virtual switch that's associated with each app. When a switch for a listed app is turned on, that app appears in the Share menu.

> **NOTE** Displayed along the bottom of the Share menu are the Copy, Slideshow, AirPlay, Hide, Assign to Contact, Use as Wallpaper, Print, and More icons. Tap on any of these icons to manage the selected photo(s) in the Photos app.

COPY AN IMAGE TO ANOTHER APP

From within the Photos app, you can store a photo in your iOS device's virtual clipboard and then paste that photo into another compatible app. To copy a photo into your device's virtual clipboard, follow these steps:

1. From within the Photos app, select a single photo and view it in full-screen mode.
2. Tap on the image to make the command icons appear.
3. Tap on the Share icon.
4. Tap on the Copy icon. The photo is now stored in the virtual clipboard.
5. Launch a compatible app and then hold your finger down on the screen to use the Paste option and paste your photo from the clipboard into the active app.

CREATE A SLIDESHOW

To create and display an animated slideshow featuring selected images, launch Photos and select a group of images. Next, tap the Share icon and choose the Slideshow option.

From the Slideshow Options screen, choose to display the image on the iPhone (or iPad) or via Apple TV. Select your Transition effect from the menu, and decide whether you want music to accompany the presentation. By turning on the virtual switch associated with Play Music, you can choose music that's stored in the Music app of your iOS mobile device. To begin the Slideshow, tap on the Start Slideshow option.

SHOW IMAGE ON A TELEVISION VIA AIRPLAY

Instead of viewing an image in full-screen mode on your iPhone or iPad, tap the AirPlay icon and select Apple TV to wirelessly transmit the image to your HD television set. To use this feature with an HD TV, you need the optional Apple TV device. To use the feature with a Mac, be sure AirPlay on your Mac is turned on.

ASSIGN IMAGE TO CONTACT

To link an image stored in the Photos app to a specific contact in the Contacts app, follow these steps:

1. From within the Photos app, select a single photo and view it in full-screen mode.
2. Tap on the image to make the various command icons appear.
3. Tap on the Share icon.
4. Tap on the Assign to Contact option.

5. An All Contacts window is displayed. Scroll through the listing, or use the Search field to find the specific entry with which you want to associate the photo.

6. Tap on that person's or company's name from the All Contacts listing.

7. When the Choose Photo window opens, use your finger to move or scale the image. What you see in the box is what will be saved.

8. Tap on the Use icon to save the photo and link it to the selected contact.

9. When you launch Contacts and access that person's entry, the photo you selected appears in the entry.

USE AS WALLPAPER

As you're viewing a photo, you can assign it to be the wallpaper image used on your Home screen or Lock screen by tapping on the Share icon and then choosing the Use As Wallpaper option. When the image is previewed on the screen, tap on the Set button. From the Set Lock Screen, Set Home Screen, or Set Both menu, choose where you want the selected image displayed.

> **NOTE** Before tapping on the Set button when previewing a potential wallpaper image that's one of your photos, it's possible to use a reverse pinch finger gesture to zoom in on the image, and then hold one finger on the image and drag it around to reposition it.

DELETING PHOTOS STORED ON YOUR iOS DEVICE

To delete one image at a time as you're viewing them in full-screen mode, simply tap on the Trash icon displayed on the screen.

To select and delete multiple images at once as you're looking at thumbnails, tap on the Select button. Tap on each thumbnail that represents an image you want to delete. A checkmark icon appears within each image thumbnail indicating that the image has been selected. Tap on the Trash icon to delete the selected images.

TAKE ADVANTAGE OF iCLOUD PHOTO LIBRARY

Turn on the iCloud Photo Library feature from within Settings on all your iOS mobile devices as well as from the iCloud Control Panel on your Mac and/or PC computers, and you'll be able to sync your entire digital photo library across all your computers, maintain an online backup of your images, and share groups of selected images (or entire albums) with other people.

To turn on iCloud Photo Library on each of your iOS mobile devices, launch Settings, tap on the iCloud option, tap on the Photos option, and then turn on the virtual switch associated with the iCloud Photo Library option. Use the other options in this submenu to customize the iCloud Photo Library feature on the device you're using.

Keep in mind that, based on how many digital photos are in your entire digital photo library, it might be necessary to upgrade your iCloud account and acquire additional online storage space (for a monthly fee). Refer to Chapter 5, "Use iCloud and the iCloud App from Your iPhone or iPad," for more information about using iCloud.

THE PHOTOS APP SUPPORTS iCLOUD'S FAMILY SHARING

One aspect of iCloud's Family Sharing feature is what Apple refers to as the Family Album. One single Family album becomes accessible by up to six family members, who can then freely add, edit, delete, and share images stored within that Family album. Everyone's other image albums remain private and separate from the Family album.

When you turn on the Family Sharing feature within iCloud, the Family Album is automatically created. From within the Photos app, you can move images from the All Photos album (or another album) into the Family album, so they become viewable by participating family members.

MOVE IMAGES BETWEEN ALBUMS

To copy selected images from one album to another as you're viewing thumbnails for images within a specific album, tap on the Select option. Then, one at a time, tap on the images you want to copy into another album. A check mark appears on each image thumbnail you select.

Tap on the Add To option, and then tap on which album from the displayed listing you want to move the selected images to. For example, you can choose the Family album if you have iCloud Family Sharing activated.

To create a new album from scratch, scroll down in the Add To Album screen and tap on the New Album option. When prompted, type a title for the new Album and then tap the Save button.

Create as many separate albums as you need within the Photos app to properly group together and organize your images. As you create a new album, it syncs with iCloud Photo Library if you have this feature turned on.

IN THIS CHAPTER

- How to use the calling features you'll find useful
- How to manage Favorites, Recents, Contacts, and Voicemail
- Take advantage of iOS 9's Continuity feature to answer incoming calls to your iPhone from your iPad or Mac

MAKE AND RECEIVE CALLS WITH AN iPHONE

Although your iPhone is capable of handling a wide range of tasks, one of its core purposes is to serve as a feature-packed cell phone. Your iPhone makes and receives voice calls using a cellular network that's operated by the service provider you selected when the phone was activated. The Phone app that comes preinstalled on your iPhone offers a vast selection of calling features that make it easy to stay in touch with people.

> **TIP** If you're an iPad user, you can also make and receive Voice-over-IP (Internet-based) phone calls using Skype or a similar app. These calls can be made to or received from any landline or cell phone.
>
> You can participate in Skype-to-Skype calls for free. For other calls, Skype charges a very low per-minute rate (typically $0.02 or less per minute).

In addition to voice-over-IP calls, Skype can be used for free video calls with Mac, PC, iOS mobile device, Android, or Windows mobile device users. Using FaceTime for video or audio-only calls, however, works only with other Mac or iOS mobile device users.

Skype is also ideal for saving money when you're making international calls from the United States, or to avoid hefty international roaming charges when you're calling home to the United States when traveling overseas.

Yet another Internet calling option is to use the audio calling feature offered by Facebook Messenger to initiate calls with your Facebook friends.

After you set up and activate your new iPhone with a cellular service provider and choose a calling plan, the iPhone is capable of receiving incoming calls and enables you to make outgoing calls using the Phone app.

In the United States, a growing number of popular cellular service providers offer iPhone compatibility. When you purchase an iPhone, you must decide in advance which wireless service provider to sign up with (a two-year service agreement with a hefty early termination fee is typically involved). You can, however, purchase an "unlocked" iPhone with no service contract, and then pay a month-to-month fee for service. This requires you to pay an unsubsidized price for the iPhone and then pay between $30 and $120 per month for voice, data, and text services.

NOTE Many cellular service providers offer other plans that allow you to pay for the iPhone over time and upgrade to the newest model iPhone each year, when it's released. For example, AT&T calls this the Next plan.

Choose a wireless service provider that offers the best coverage in your area, the most competitively priced calling plan based on your needs, and the extra features you want or need. When looking at coverage area maps for various service providers, focus on 4G LTE coverage, as opposed to 3G or plain 4G service.

Not all wireless service providers enable iPhone users to talk and surf the Web at the same time. Likewise, some offer better international roaming coverage than others, while some are more generous when it comes to monthly wireless data allocation.

Keep in mind that the iPhone hardware is slightly different based on which wireless service provider you choose, so you typically can't switch providers after you've acquired the iPhone.

iOS 9 WHAT'S NEW If you utilized Apple's new iPhone Upgrade Program to acquire an iPhone 6s or iPhone 6s Plus, what you received is an unlocked phone that comes with AppleCare+ and can be used with many cellular service providers throughout the world.

Depending on which iPhone model you select, the monthly payment is between $32.41 and $44.91 for up to 24 months (after which time you own the phone), or you can trade in the phone after 12 months and receive the newest iPhone model. If you do this, the monthly payments required to own the phone begins again. This monthly fee is in addition to the monthly fee for the cellular service.

There are no finance charges associated with this plan. You simply divide up the cost of the phone and pay for it over a predetermined number of months, such as 18 months or 24 months.

TIP For your iPhone to make or receive calls, it must be turned on and *not* in Airplane mode. Unless you're using the Call Over Wi-Fi function (which not all cellular service providers support), a decent cellular service signal, which is displayed in the upper-left corner of the screen in the form of dots, is also a necessity. The more dots you see (up to five), the stronger the cellular signal (which is based on your proximity to the closest cell towers).

ANSWERING AN INCOMING CALL

Regardless of what you're doing on your iPhone, when an incoming call is received, everything else is put on hold and the Phone app launches, unless the iPhone is turned off, in Airplane mode, or the Do Not Disturb feature is turned on, in which case incoming calls automatically go to voicemail.

To control the volume of the ringer, press the Volume Up or Volume Down buttons on the side of your iPhone; or to turn off the ringer (which causes the phone to vibrate when an incoming call is received), turn on the Mute button on the side of the iPhone.

TIP While your iPhone is still ringing, to silence the ringer and send the incoming call to voicemail after a 5- to 10-second delay, press the Power button or the Volume Up or Volume Down button once. To send the incoming call immediately to voicemail, double tap on the Power button, or tap the Decline option displayed on the screen when the phone is not locked at the time the incoming call is received.

You also can silence the iPhone's ringer by switching on the Mute button (located on the side of the iPhone, above the Volume Up button). Your phone vibrates instead of ringing when an incoming call is received.

To control the Vibrate feature, launch Settings, tap on the Sounds option, turn on the virtual switch that's associated with Vibrate On Ring and/or Vibrate On Silent, and then tap on the Ringtone option that's found under the Sounds and Vibration Patterns heading to select a custom vibration pattern when incoming calls are received.

Yet another way to be left alone is to put your phone in Do Not Disturb mode. This can be done automatically at certain predetermined times, or manually whenever you want to be left alone. To do this, access Control Center and tap on the Do Not Disturb icon.

There are several ways to answer an incoming call. If you're doing something else on your iPhone and it starts to ring, the caller ID for the incoming caller appears, along with a green-and-white Accept button and a red-and-white Decline icon (as shown in Figure 9.1). Tap the Accept button to answer the call. If you tap Decline or wait too long to answer, the call automatically goes to voicemail.

Figure 9.1

Your iPhone notifies you when an incoming call is received. You can then answer or decline the call. This screen appears as long as the phone is not locked when the incoming call is received.

If you're using your iPhone with EarPods, ear buds, or a headset with a built-in microphone, you can answer an incoming call by pressing the Accept button on the headset.

> **TIP** When you receive an incoming call, displayed above the Decline and Accept buttons (or the Slide To Answer slider on the Lock screen) are two other options (refer to Figure 9.1) labeled Remind Me and Message.
>
> When you tap on Message, a menu containing four prewritten text messages, along with a Custom button, is displayed. Tap on one of the message buttons to send that message to the caller via text/instant message. Or tap on the Custom button to type a custom message to send to that caller. The incoming call is automatically transferred to voicemail.
>
> To customize the prewritten messages available from the Message option, launch Settings, tap on the Phone option, and then tap on the Respond with Text option. Displayed on the Respond with Text menu screen are three customizable fields, under the heading, "Can't Talk Right Now." Tap on one of these fields to replace one of the default messages with your own.
>
> The other option for managing incoming calls is the Remind Me option. When you tap on this button, the incoming call is sent to voicemail, but you can quickly set a reminder (and alarm) for yourself to call that person back in one hour, when you leave your current location, or when you get home. For these last two options to function, Locations Services related to the Phone app must be turned on from within Settings.

If the iPhone is in Sleep mode (or on the Lock screen and locked) when an incoming call is received, unlock the phone by swiping your finger from left to right on the Slide to Answer slider, which automatically takes the phone out of Sleep mode, unlocks it, and answers the incoming call (shown in Figure 9.2). Notice that the iPhone's Lock screen displays the Remind Me and Message icons but does not display an Accept or Decline button.

> **NOTE** Answering the phone using an optional Bluetooth headset automatically unlocks the phone if it's in Sleep mode.

Figure 9.2

When an incoming call is received while the phone is in Sleep mode (locked), you need to unlock the phone to automatically answer it.

> **TIP**   If you're too busy to answer an incoming call on your iPhone, you can let the call go to voicemail or set up call forwarding so that the incoming call automatically gets rerouted to another phone number, such as your home or office number. To set up call forwarding and turn this function on or off as needed, launch Settings, and then tap on the Phone option.
>
> From the Phone submenu in Settings, you can view your iPhone's phone number, set up and turn on call forwarding, turn on or off call waiting, and decide whether you want your iPhone's number to be displayed on someone's caller ID when you initiate a call.
>
> Also from Settings, you have the option of enabling the International Assist feature, which makes initiating international calls much less confusing.

After you answer an incoming call, you have a few additional options. You can hold the iPhone up to your ear and start talking, or you can tap the Speaker icon to use your iPhone as a speakerphone. You can also use the phone with a wired or Bluetooth (wireless) headset, which offers hands-free operation. The headset option is ideal when you're driving, plus it offers privacy (versus using the iPhone's speakerphone option).

> **! CAUTION** If you're driving, choose a headset that covers only one ear, or use the Speaker option for hands-free operation. Refrain from holding the phone up to your ear or covering both ears with a headset. (See the section, "A Few Thoughts About Wireless Headsets," for headset considerations.) Make sure you're familiar with state and local laws in your area related to the use of cell phones while driving.

When using a Bluetooth headset, you don't need to hold the phone up to your ear to carry on a conversation. If you're using a headset, tap on the headset's answer button when you receive an incoming call to answer it. There's no need to do anything on your iPhone.

When you're in a compatible car (or in a vehicle equipped with an iPhone Hands-Free Kit), take advantage of the vehicle's CarPlay or Hands-Free compatibility. This enables your phone to link to your vehicle and use the in-dash infotainment system or stereo system to make and receive calls, utilizing your vehicle's built-in microphone and stereo system speakers to interact with the other party. The call is still handled by your iPhone, but the iPhone is operated hands-free (and eyes-free).

USE THE HANDOFF FEATURE TO ANSWER INCOMING iPHONE CALLS ON YOUR iPAD OR MAC

When Continuity is activated, as long as your iPhone is within wireless proximity to your iPad or Mac (they can typically be up to 33 feet apart), it's possible to answer an incoming call that's made to your iPhone from your iPad (shown in Figure 9.3) or Mac.

> **NOTE** All Macs and iOS mobile devices that are set up to work with iOS 9's Continuity features must be linked to the same iCloud account and have Bluetooth and Wi-Fi turned on. Keep in mind that some older iPhones and iPads do not support the Continuity/Handoff features. Only models purchased in 2012 or later (and that are running OS X Yosemite or El Capitan) support this feature.

Figure 9.3

When an iPhone and iPad are linked to the same iCloud account and have the Handoff option turned on, it's possible to answer an incoming call on the iPad.

To set up this feature, launch Settings, tap on the General option, and then tap on the Handoff & Suggested Apps option. From the Handoff & Suggested Apps sub-menu, turn on the virtual switch that's associated with the Handoff option. Next, repeat this process on your iPad.

When the feature is turned on, your iPhone automatically maintains a wireless link to your iPad and/or Mac. When an incoming call is received, all connected devices ring, Caller ID information is displayed, and you can Accept or Decline the call from any connected device.

On the iPad or Mac, the tablet or computer acts like a speakerphone by taking advantage of the built-in microphone and speaker(s). You can also pair a Bluetooth wireless headset to your iPad and/or Mac.

To initiate a call from your iPad or Mac via your iPhone and the Handoff feature, tap on any displayed phone number from within the Contacts, Calendar, or Safari apps (on your iPad or Mac), for example, to initiate a call to that number using the computer or tablet you're currently working with.

MANAGING THE DO NOT DISTURB FEATURE

To activate and customize the Do Not Disturb feature, launch Settings and tap on the Do Not Disturb option. To later enable or disable this feature, access the Control Center and tap on the crescent moon–shaped icon (shown in Figure 9.4).

Figure 9.4

Accessing the Do Not Disturb feature can easily be done from Control Center.

When turned on, a moon icon is displayed on the iPhone's or iPad's status bar, and all calls and alerts are silenced.

This feature can be turned on or off at any time, or you can schedule specific times you want Do Not Disturb to be activated, such as between 11:00 p.m. and 7:00 a.m. on weekdays. From the Do Not Disturb menu in Settings (shown in Figure 9.5), you can also determine whether certain callers are allowed to reach you when the phone is in Do Not Disturb mode.

Keep in mind that when your iPhone is turned off, all incoming calls are forwarded directly to voicemail, and it is not possible to initiate an outgoing call. Likewise, incoming text messages, FaceTime calls, and other communications from the out-side world are not accepted when an iPhone is turned off, in Do Not Disturb mode, or in Airplane mode. Instead, notifications for these missed messages are displayed in Notification Center (depending on how you set up Notification Center), within their respective apps, and potentially on the Lock screen when you turn on the device or turn off Airplane mode.

(for example, when you're told to press 1 for English, press 2 to speak with an operator, press 3 to track an order, and so on).

- **Speaker (or Audio Source)**—Tap the Speaker icon to switch from Handset mode (in which you hold the iPhone up to your ear to have a phone conversation) to Speaker mode, which turns your iPhone into a speakerphone. If you're using your iPhone with a Bluetooth headset, a third Headset option (which may be listed as Headset, or the name of your headset) is displayed, and this menu feature is labeled Audio as opposed to Speaker.

- **Add Call (+)**—During a conversation with someone, you can initiate a conference call and bring a third party into the conversation by tapping on Add Call, as described later in this chapter.

- **FaceTime**—If the person to whom you're talking is also using an iPhone, iPad, or Mac, and both devices have access to an Internet connection, tap on the FaceTime icon to switch from a traditional phone call to a real-time video call using the FaceTime app. This is a free service.

> **TIP** In addition to being able to launch FaceTime from the Phone app and switch from a normal call to a video call, you can also use the separate FaceTime app to initiate a video or audio only call from your iPhone that utilizes the Internet, as opposed to a cellular network.

- **Contacts**—While you're conversing on the phone, you can access your Contacts database and look up someone's information by tapping on this option.

- **End**—Tap on the large red-and-white End button or tap the end call button on your headset, if applicable, to terminate the call.

> **TIP** Your phone conversation can continue while you're using other apps. Depending on your wireless service provider, you might even be able to participate in a phone conversation and surf the Web at the same time.
>
> To launch another app, press the Home button and tap on its app icon from the Home screen. Or to access the app switcher, double-tap on the Home button, and then tap on any app icon that appears.
>
> When you view the Home screen while still on the phone, a green-and-white banner shows, "Touch to return to call," along with a call timer. Tap on this green bar to return to the Phone app.

RESPOND TO A CALL WAITING SIGNAL WHILE ON THE PHONE

As you're chatting it up on the phone, if someone else tries to call you, you hear a call waiting tone, and a related message appears on your iPhone's screen. You can control the Call Waiting feature from the Settings app.

When a second call comes in, the caller ID information of the new caller is displayed on the screen, along with several command icons and buttons (shown in Figure 9.7). These commands are End & Accept, Send To Voicemail, or Hold & Accept.

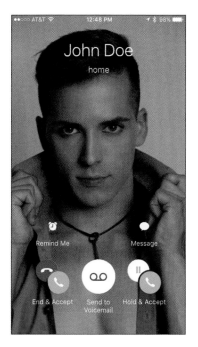

Figure 9.7

When you're on a call and you simultaneously receive another incoming call, in addition to hearing the Call Waiting signal, you're given several onscreen options.

If you place the first call on hold and answer the new incoming call, you have the opportunity to merge the two calls and create a conference call or switch between the two calls and speak with each person individually (while the other is on hold).

> **☑ TIP** When the call waiting signal goes off on your iPhone, only you hear it. Thus, the person you're speaking with on the other end of the line does not know you've received another call. So before tapping the End & Accept or Hold & Accept button, be sure to tell the person you were originally speaking with what's going on.

While engaged in a conference call on your iPhone, the names of the people with whom you're engaged in a call are displayed along the top of the screen, along with an Info icon. Tap on the circular "i" icon to the right of this information to reveal a new screen that enables you to manage any of the parties involved with the conference call.

While you're engaged in a three-way call (with two other parties), you can tap on the Add Call option again to add more parties to the conference call.

On the secondary Conference Call Info screen, associated with each name/Caller ID number is an End button and a Private button. Tap on End to disconnect that party, or tap Private to speak with just that party privately and place the other party (or parties) on hold. You can then reestablish the conference call by tapping on the Back button to return to the previous Conference Call screen, and then tap on the Merge Calls icon again.

MAKING CALLS FROM YOUR iPHONE

There are several ways to initiate a phone call from your iPhone; however, you typically must first launch the Phone app. Then, you can do the following:

- Dial a number manually using the keypad.
- Access a listing from your Contacts database (from within the Phone app), choose a number, and dial it.
- Use Siri (which is explained in Chapter 2, "Using Siri, Dictation, and CarPlay to Interact with Your Mobile Device"). This can be done anytime, regardless of what app is running on your iPhone or whether you're looking at the Home screen.

> **☑ TIP** If you're using one of the newer iPhone models and the "Hey Siri" feature is active, simply say "Hey Siri, call [insert name]" or "Hey Siri, call [insert name] at [insert location, such as home or work]" to initiate a call.

- Redial a number from the Phone app's Recents call log.
- Select and dial a phone number from the Phone app's Favorites list.
- Dial a number displayed in another compatible app or iOS 9 feature, such as Maps, Messages, Mail, Safari, Contacts, or the Notification Center window. When you tap on a displayed phone number, it dials that number and initiates a call using the Phone app.

MANUAL DIALING

To initiate a call by manually dialing a phone number, follow these steps:

1. Launch the Phone app from the Home screen.
2. Tap on the Keypad icon displayed at the bottom of the screen.
3. Using the numeric phone keypad, dial the number you want to reach, including the area code. If you're making an international call, include the country code as well.
4. If you make a mistake when entering a digit, tap the small "X" icon that's displayed near the top-right corner of the screen.

> **TIP** As you're manually entering a phone number, if you want to create a Contacts entry for it, tap on the "+" icon that's displayed in the top-left corner of the screen, and then tap on the Create New Contact or Add To Existing Contact option.

5. When the phone number is entered and displayed at the top of the screen, tap the green-and-white Call button to initiate the call.
6. The display on the iPhone changes to display a "Calling" message until the call connects, at which time the Call Menu screen is displayed.

> **NOTE** You can also use the Cut, Copy, and Paste features of iOS 9 to copy a phone number displayed in another app, and then paste it into the phone number field on the Keypad screen. Or, if you tap on a phone number displayed in the Contacts app, listed in an incoming email, or displayed while surfing the Web using Safari, for example, the Phone app automatically launches and a call to that number is initiated.

DIALING FROM A CONTACTS ENTRY IN THE PHONE APP

From within the Phone app, it's possible to look up any phone number stored in your personal contacts database that's associated with the Contacts app. The Phone and Contacts apps work nicely together on your iPhone. To use this feature, follow these steps:

1. Launch the Phone app from the Home screen.

2. Tap on the Contacts icon displayed at the bottom of the screen.

3. An alphabetized listing of the contacts stored in the Contacts app is displayed. At the top of the screen is a blank Search field. Using your finger, either scroll through the alphabetized list of contacts or use the iPhone's virtual keyboard to find a stored listing.

4. Tap on any listing to view its complete Contacts entry. This might include multiple phone numbers, such as Home, Work, and Mobile. Then tap on the phone number you want to dial.

5. The display on the iPhone changes. A "Calling" message is displayed until the call connects, at which time the Call Menu screen is displayed.

REESTABLISH CONTACT FROM THE SPOTLIGHT SEARCH SCREEN'S RECENTS LISTING

Regardless of what you're doing on your iPhone (or iPad), when you access the expanded Spotlight Search screen, you see icons representing the last few people you've had contact with and can quickly reinitiate contact with any of them.

To do this from the Home screen, swipe from left to right to access the Spotlight Search screen. Tap on a person's profile photo/icon, and then tap the appropriate command icon to quickly call or message that person.

USE THE CALL OVER WI-FI CALLING FEATURE

Typically, when you initiate a call from your iPhone, it connects to the cellular network you've subscribed to, such as AT&T Wireless, Verizon Wireless, Sprint, or T-Mobile (if you're in the United States). Thanks to the Call Over Wi-Fi feature, if you're not in a good cellular network coverage area but your compatible iPhone is within a Wi-Fi hotspot, you can make a call to any landline or other cellphone via the Internet.

For iPhone 6/6 Plus/6s/6s Plus users, once a Wi-Fi call is initiated, if you leave the Wi-Fi hotspot, your call is automatically transferred to the cellular network's Voice

Over LTE feature, if your cellular service supports this option. Likewise, if you're using the Voice Over LTE feature and a Wi-Fi signal becomes available, the call is seamlessly transferred to the Wi-Fi network; otherwise, the call is dropped if the Wi-Fi signal is lost.

If available, to manually initiate calls using the Call Over Wi-Fi feature, as opposed to a cellular network, launch Settings, tap on the Phone option, and then turn on the virtual switch that's associated with the Wi-Fi Calling option.

> **NOTE** When Apple introduced Call Over Wi-Fi in September 2014, T-Mobile was the only cellular service provider in the United States supporting it. Since then, AT&T Wireless, Verizon Wireless, and other service providers have announced support for this feature but only with certain cellular service plans.

MANAGING YOUR VOICEMAIL

Your unique iPhone phone number comes with voicemail, which enables people to leave you messages if you're not able to speak with them when they call.

Just as with any voicemail service, you can record your outgoing message, play back missed messages from your iPhone, or call your iPhone's voicemail service and listen to your calls from another phone.

RECORD YOUR OUTGOING MESSAGE

To record your outgoing voicemail message, which is what people hear when they call your iPhone and you don't answer, follow these steps. Or you can have a computer-generated voice instruct callers to leave a message.

1. Launch the Phone app from the Home screen.
2. Tap on the Voicemail icon, displayed in the lower-right corner of the screen.
3. In the upper-left corner of the Voicemail screen, tap on the Greeting option.
4. From the Greeting screen (shown in Figure 9.8), tap on the Default option to skip recording a message and have a computer voice use a generic message. Or tap on the Custom option to record your own outgoing voicemail message.
5. After you tap the Custom option, tap on the Record option that's also displayed on the Greeting screen. Hold the phone up to your mouth and begin recording your message.
6. When you're finished recording, tap on the Stop option. You can now play back your message by tapping on the Play option, or tap on the Save option to save your message and activate it.

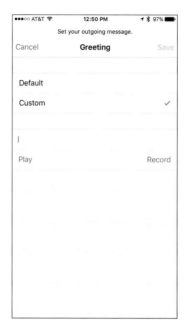

Figure 9.8

The Greeting screen in the Phone app. From here, you can record an outgoing greeting.

HOW TO PLAY AND DELETE VOICEMAIL MESSAGES

It's possible to listen to voicemail messages either from your iPhone or by calling your iPhone's voicemail from another phone.

LISTEN TO VOICEMAIL FROM YOUR IPHONE

From your iPhone, to listen to and then save or delete an incoming voicemail message, follow these steps:

1. Launch the Phone app from the Home screen, or by swiping on a voicemail notification appearing on the Notification Center screen, for example.
2. Tap on the Voicemail icon that's displayed in the bottom-right corner of the screen.
3. Under the Voicemail heading seen at the top of the screen is a listing of missed voicemail messages. Tap on a message to highlight it.

> **NOTE** When you see a blue dot to the left of a voicemail message listing, this indicates it's a new, unheard message. After you listen to the message, the blue dot disappears. When you tap on the message to listen to it, the blue dot changes into a Pause/Play icon.

4. After a message is highlighted, tap on the small play/pause icon (shown in Figure 9.9). The message begins playing. It might, however, take a few seconds for the message to load. A brief pause should be expected.

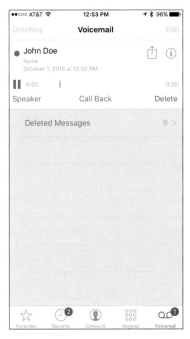

Figure 9.9
Listen to and manage incoming voicemails from the Phone app.

5. Near the bottom of the voicemail listing is a slider that depicts the length of the message, along with Speaker, Call Back, and Delete options. As your message plays, the timer slider moves to the right. You can listen to parts of the message again by moving this slider around with your finger.

6. When you're finished listening to the message, you can leave the listing alone (which keeps the message saved on your phone) or tap the Delete option to erase it. You also have the option of calling back the person who left the message by tapping on the Call Back option.

7. To exit the voicemail options, tap on any of the other command icons displayed at the bottom of the Phone app's screen, or press the Home button on your iPhone.

> **TIP** You might find it easier to listen to your voicemail messages via speaker phone, by first tapping on the Speaker or Audio option that's displayed below the timer slider.

> **TIP** If you accidentally delete an important voicemail, don't panic. From the voicemail screen, scroll to the very bottom of your voicemail message list and tap on the Deleted Messages icon. Tap on a message to highlight it, and then tap on the Undelete icon.

CREATE AND USE A FAVORITES LIST

From within the Phone app, you can create a Favorites list, which is a customized list of your most frequently dialed contacts. To access this list, launch the Phone app, and then tap on the Favorites icon that's displayed in the bottom-left corner of the screen.

To add a contact to the Favorites list, tap on the plus-sign (+) icon that you see in the upper-right corner of the screen. Select any listing from your Contacts database and tap on it. When the complete listing for that entry appears, tap on the specific phone number you want listed in your Favorites list. The newly created Favorites listing appears at the end of your Favorites list.

> **TIP** Each favorites entry can have one name and one phone number associated with it, so if a Contact entry has multiple phone numbers listed, choose one. If you want quick access to someone's home, work, and mobile numbers from your Favorites list, create three separate entries for that person.
>
> When you create the entry in Favorites, the type of phone number (Home, Work, Mobile, iPhone, and so on) is displayed to the right of the person's name. A Favorites listing can also relate to someone's FaceTime identifier (their iPhone number, Apple ID, or the email address they used to set up their FaceTime account).

To edit the contacts already listed in your Favorites list, tap on the Edit option in the upper-left corner of the screen. After tapping Edit, change the order of your Favorites list by holding your finger on the rightmost icon next to a listing, and then dragging it upward or downward to the desired location. Or delete a listing by tapping on the red-and-white negative-sign icon displayed to the left of a listing. When you're finished making changes, tap on the Done icon that's displayed in the upper-left corner of the screen.

> **TIP** As you're viewing your Favorites list, tap on the Info ('i') icon, shown to the right of each listing. This enables you to view that person's entire entry from within your Contacts database.

To dial a phone number listed in your Favorites list, simply tap on its listing. The Phone app automatically dials the number and initiates a call.

TIP If you want to block incoming calls from a specific phone number, create a contact in the Contacts app that includes the phone number you want to block. Next, launch Settings and tap on the Phone option. Tap in the Blocked option, and then tap on the Add New option. Select the contact entry that contains the number you want to block. This number is added to your Blocked incoming call list.

You will not receive phone calls, messages, or FaceTime calls from people on the blocked list. To remove a number of the Blocked list, while viewing the Blocked submenu, tap the Edit option, and then tap on the Remove (negative sign) icon that's associated with a specific listing.

Use this feature to block calls from known telemarketers, obnoxious debt collectors, or people you're trying to avoid.

ACCESSING YOUR RECENTS CALL LOG

The Phone app automatically keeps track of all incoming and outgoing calls. To access this detailed call log, launch the Phone app from the Home screen, and then tap on the Recents icon displayed at the bottom of the screen.

At the top of the Recents screen are two command tabs, labeled All and Missed, along with an Edit option. Tap on the All tab to view a detailed listing of all incoming and outgoing calls, displayed in reverse-chronological order. Missed incoming calls are displayed in red. Tap on the Missed tab to see a listing of calls you didn't answer. Tap on the Edit option to delete specific calls from this listing, or tap on the Info ("i") icon to view more details about that caller, including their recent call history with you.

TIP Missed calls are also displayed in the Notification Center window on your iPhone or as an icon badge or alert on your Home screen, depending on how you set up Notifications for the Phone app in the Settings app. To customize the Notifications options for the Phone app, launch Settings from the Home screen and tap on the Notifications option. From the Notifications screen in Settings, tap on the Phone option. You can adjust how your iPhone alerts you to missed calls by personalizing the options on this Phone screen.

Each listing in the Recents call log displays the name of the person you spoke with (based on data from your Contacts database or the Caller ID feature) or their phone number. If it's someone from your Contacts database, information about which phone number (home, work, mobile, or such) the caller used appears below the name.

If the same person called you, or you called that person, multiple times in a row, a number in parentheses indicates how many calls were made to or from that person. This is displayed to the right of the name or phone number.

On the right side of the screen, with each Recents listing, is the time the call was made or received. To view the Contacts entry related to that person, tap on the right-pointing blue-and-white arrow icon associated with the listing. At the top of a contact's entry screen are details about the call itself, including its time and date, whether it was an incoming or outgoing call, and its duration.

To call someone back who is listed in the Recents list, tap anywhere on that listing except for on the blue-and-white arrow icon.

DO YOU TALK TOO MUCH? KEEPING TRACK OF USAGE

Some iPhone voice plans come with a predetermined number of talk minutes per month. Some plans offer unlimited night and weekend calling, but calls made or received during the day count against your monthly minute allocation.

> **! CAUTION** Contact your wireless service provider (or read your service agreement carefully) to determine the time period that's considered prime day-time, versus night or weekend, because it varies greatly. Unlimited night and weekend calling does not start until 9:00 p.m. with some wireless service providers. If you have a truly unlimited calling plan, however, this is not a concern.

If your plan does have a monthly allocation for talk minutes, if you go over your monthly minute allocation, you may be charged a hefty surcharge for each additional minute used.

> **TIP** Each wireless service provider that supports the iPhone offers a free app for managing your wireless service account. It's available from the App Store. Use it to manage all aspects of your account, pay your monthly bill, and view your voice, data, and text-messaging use at any time. You can also set the alert option in the app to remind you each month when the bill is due for payment.

CUSTOMIZING RINGTONES

Thanks to the iTunes Store, you can purchase and download custom ringtones for your iPhone. You can use one ringtone as your generic ringtone for all incoming calls, or you can assign specific ringtones to individual people.

> **TIP** iOS 9 comes with more than two dozen preinstalled ringtones. To shop for ringtones, launch Settings, select Sounds, and from the Sounds menu screen, tap on the Ringtone option. Tap on the Store option that's displayed near the top-right corner of the Ringtone menu screen (within Settings).
>
> When you purchase and download a new ringtone, it becomes available on your iPhone's internal ringtones list. Most ringtones from the iTunes Store cost $1.29 each.
>
> Using the iTunes software on a PC or Mac, or using a specialized app, such as Ringtone Maker, Ringtone Wizard, or Ringtone Pro, it's also possible to create your own ringtones using music or audio from your iTunes library.

To choose a default ringtone for all your incoming calls, launch Settings and select the Sounds option. From the Sounds menu screen, scroll down to the Ringtone option and tap on it. A complete listing of ringtones stored on your iPhone is displayed.

CUSTOM RINGTONES FOR SPECIFIC CONTACTS

To assign a custom ringtone to a specific person so that you hear it when that person calls your iPhone, follow these steps:

1. Launch the Contacts app from the iPhone's Home screen.

2. From the All Contacts screen, find the specific contact with whom you want to link a custom ringtone. You can scroll through the listing or use the Search field to find a contact.

3. When the contact is selected and you're looking at that Contacts entry, tap the Edit option that's displayed in the upper-right corner of the screen.

4. From the Info screen that displays that contact entry's data, scroll down to the Ringtone field and tap on it (shown in Figure 9.10).

5. When the Ringtone screen appears, select a specific ringtone from the list that you want to assign to the contact and tap on it. You can choose a specific song (purchased from iTunes) or ringer sound that reminds you of that person.

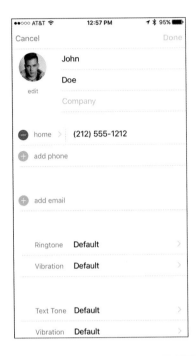

Figure 9.10

It's possible to choose a custom ringtone for each entry in the Contacts app.

6. Tap on the Done icon to save your selection and return to the contact's Info screen.

7. When that contact calls you, you will hear the ringtone you just linked to that contact (as opposed to the default ringtone).

> **TIP** Also from a Contact's entry screen in the Contacts app, it's possible to choose a special vibration pattern for the phone when that person calls. To do this, tap on the Vibration option and choose a vibration pattern from the Vibration menu, or scroll to the bottom of this screen and tap on the Create New Vibration option to create a custom vibration pattern for that contact.

MORE INFORMATION ABOUT BLUETOOTH WIRELESS HEADSETS

Many states have outlawed using a cellphone while driving unless you have a wireless headset or hands-free feature on your phone. Although the speakerphone feature of your iPhone counts as a hands-free feature, to ensure the best possible call quality while you're driving, invest in a wireless Bluetooth headset.

Not only can you use a wireless Bluetooth headset while driving, but you can keep it on your person throughout the day and use it whenever you make or receive calls using your iPhone.

Using a headset enables you to keep your hands free while you're talking so you can easily access other apps or iPhone features during a phone conversation. If you invest in only one accessory for your iPhone, and you plan to use the iPhone to make and receive phone calls, a wireless Bluetooth headset is a worthwhile investment (although a good-quality iPhone case is also highly recommended).

Bluetooth wireless headsets are priced as low as $20 but can cost as much as $200. If you want to ensure the highest-quality phone conversations possible, so that people can hear you and you can hear them, even if there's background noise present, invest in a good-quality Bluetooth wireless headset that includes a noise-canceling microphone and a good-quality speaker. Plus, choose a headset that's comfortable to wear and has a long battery life.

IN THIS CHAPTER

- Get acquainted with the Health app on the iPhone
- Discover how the Health app works with other apps and equipment, including Apple Watch
- Use the new Wallet app to manage Apple Pay and reward/membership cards from your iPhone

10

IMPROVE YOUR HEALTH AND MANAGE YOUR WEALTH USING YOUR iPHONE

Built in to iOS 9 are a vast assortment of tools available to app developers that make it possible to create cutting-edge apps related to health and fitness.

Thanks to how third-party app developers continue to utilize these tools, and because fitness equipment and medical device manufacturers continue building iPhone compatibility and integration into their products, what is now possible using your smartphone (and optional Apple Watch) makes leading a healthier and more active lifestyle, eating a well-balanced diet, and getting a good night's sleep much more efficient.

> ### ⌕ MORE INFO
> If you're interested in learning much more about the health and fitness capabilities of your iPhone and the Apple Watch, pick up a copy of *Apple Watch and iPhone Fitness Tips and Tricks* (Que) by Jason R. Rich. This informative, full-color book is now available from wherever books are sold or from www.quepublishing.com. This book covers all aspects of improving and monitoring your fitness, activity, health, diet, sleep, and mental health using the iPhone and (optional) Apple Watch.

DISCOVER THE iPHONE-SPECIFIC HEALTH APP

Among all the other app icons displayed on your iPhone's Home screen is an app called Health. On its own, the Health app can't do much. However, for people who are fitness, health, and/or nutrition conscious, the Health app works as a "dashboard" along with a growing number of other workout, fitness, diet, and lifestyle apps, and it can help you monitor and analyze your daily activity, food intake, and sleep patterns.

Beyond just working with other apps, the Health app is designed to integrate and communicate with optional equipment, including the Apple Watch, as well as a vast selection of other fitness and medical devices, including heart rate monitors, fitness/workout machines, digital scales, and various types of sleep and blood sugar monitors, for example.

The Health app is designed to gather information from these sources wirelessly and help you track your progress and/or share specific data with appropriate professionals, when applicable.

What's nice about the Health app is that it's fully customizable. You determine what data it collects automatically, or what information you manually enter into it, and then you decide exactly how that data is used and whether it can be shared. If you ultimately choose to share certain information stored in the app, such as your fitness or workout progress with a personal trainer, you can still keep other medical data private.

> ### ✓ TIP
> To discover what apps are designed to work with Health, visit the App Store, tap on the Explore icon that's displayed near the bottom of the screen, and then tap on the Health & Fitness or Medical options.

START USING THE HEALTH APP RIGHT AWAY

Without allowing your iPhone to communicate with the Apple Watch or other optional fitness or medical equipment, the Health app's capabilities are limited to being a secure personal database for medical, diet, sleep, and health-related information that you manually enter into the app, or that you import from other apps installed on your iPhone.

To get started using the Health app, launch it from the Home screen. By default, the Dashboard screen is displayed. This is where collected data from optional apps and equipment is displayed in one centralized place. Using this data, you can easily track your health, fitness, diet, and/or sleep patterns. Tap on the Day, Week, Month, or Year tabs that are displayed along the top of the screen to sort and display this information, if applicable.

Displayed along the bottom of the screen are four command icons, labeled Dashboard, Health Data, Sources, and Medical ID. Tap on the Health Data icon to access a menu of categories related to the types of data the Health app is capable of collecting, tracking, analyzing, and sharing.

This list was expanded in the iOS 9 edition of the Health app. As you can see from Figure 10.1, options include Body Measurements, Fitness, Me, Nutrition, Reproductive Health, Results, Sleep, and Vitals.

Tap on any of these options to manually enter relevant data. For example, tap on the Me option to enter your Birthdate, Biological Sex, and Blood Type. Tap on Nutrition to manually track your intake of specific food types or the nutritional aspects of the food you eat. For example, from the Nutrition menu, tap on Caffeine, and then each time you consume a caffeinated beverage, tap on the Add Data Point option (shown in Figure 10.2).

From the Add Data screen, the time and date are automatically recorded (however, you can tap on these fields to override them), and then you're prompted to enter your consumption amount. As you do this over time, you can tap on the Day, Week, Month, or Year tabs displayed at the top of the Caffeine screen, for example, to display how much caffeine you consume, and analyze what times of day you're most apt to consume it. As you tap on each tab, this information is also displayed in chart form on the screen.

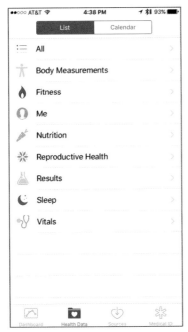

Figure 10.1

This is the main Health Data menu that's displayed when you tap on the Health Data icon.

Figure 10.2

You can manually track your intake of various types of foods or other nutrition-related information using the Health Data option built in to the Health app.

> **✅ TIP**   As you're tracking specific types of nutritional intake data, whether it's caffeine, fiber, iron, potassium, sodium, sugar, or total fat, for example, turn on the virtual switch associated with the Show On Dashboard option (refer to Figure 10.2) to display this particular information on the app's main Dashboard.
>
> Tap on the Share Data option to specify exactly which apps and outside sources you're willing to share this particular data with.

When it comes to selecting which apps and optional equipment you want to utilize with the Health app, this is controlled by tapping on the Sources icon. From here, you control which apps and equipment can transmit data to, or retrieve data from, the Health app. If no optional apps or equipment are being used, the word None is displayed under the Apps heading.

This app works best when used with the Apple Watch, a Bluetooth scale, a compatible fitness/activity tracker, and/or sleep monitoring device.

> **NOTE** When you pair your iPhone with the Apple Watch, the Activity app is automatically installed on your iPhone. This app collects your real-time activity data from the Apple Watch and then formats and shares it with the Health app, and it displays your activity-related data in a variety of easy-to-understand and colorful formats.

EVERY iPHONE USER SHOULD UTILIZE THE HEALTH APP'S MEDICAL ID FEATURE

Whether you use any additional apps or equipment with the Health app, consider using the Medical ID tool built in to the app. This is basically a digital summary of vital medical information that can be made available to doctors, paramedics, or medical personnel in case of an emergency.

To use the Medical ID component of the Health app, tap on the Medical ID icon (in the lower-right corner of the screen). From the Medical ID welcome screen, tap on the Create Medical ID option and then tap on each field to manually enter medical information about yourself (shown in Figure 10.3).

Here, you can list your medical conditions, emergency contacts, primary care physician, your birthday (age), height, weight, blood type, and whether you want to be an organ donor. For easy identification, also include a photo of yourself in the app.

> **TIP** After filling in these fields with your personal data, it's possible to later edit it by tapping on the Edit option displayed in the top-right corner of the screen.
>
> At the top of this Medical ID Edit Screen is a virtual switch associated with the Show When Locked option. Turn on this option if you want a doctor or emergency medical professional to be able to access your Medical ID information from your locked iPhone, without knowing its passcode.

> **TIP** Tap on the Medical ID Edit option to reveal additional fields that you can manually fill in. The more information you include, the more helpful it could be to doctors in an emergency situation. For example, be sure to fill in the Medical Notes and Allergies & Reactions fields, as well as the Medications field with an up-to-date listing of medications you take.

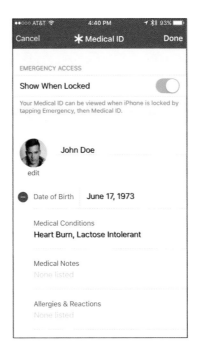

Figure 10.3
By filling in the Medical ID component of the Health app with your personal data, it can later be accessed by medical professionals in an emergency situation.

HOW TO VIEW MEDICAL ID INFORMATION ON ANY iPHONE

In an emergency situation, to access the Medical ID information from a locked iPhone, turn on the phone and from the Lock screen swipe from left to right. The Touch ID or Enter Passcode screen is displayed.

Located in the bottom-left corner of this screen is an option labeled Emergency. Tap on this to access the emergency phone dialing screen. Next, tap on the Medical ID option displayed in the lower-left corner to view the Medical ID information stored in the phone. Doing this does not grant someone full access to the phone.

MANAGE APPLE PAY AND MORE USING THE WALLET APP

One new app that comes preinstalled with iOS 9 (on the iPhone only) is called Wallet. This is a redesigned version of the now defunct Passbook app, which came preinstalled with iOS 8.

The Wallet app serves two main purposes—to securely store your debit card, major credit card, and store credit card information so you can use Apple Pay from your iPhone; and to store and help you manage various reward and membership cards from companies you do business with or organizations you belong to (such as AAA).

> **TIP** To discover third-party apps, stores, and organizations with apps that support the Wallet app, launch the Wallet app, and from the introductory screen (shown in Figure 10.4), tap on the Find Apps for Wallet option.

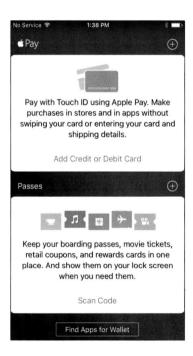

Figure 10.4

The first time you launch the Wallet app, this introductory screen is displayed. Tap on the Find Apps for Wallet option to discover third-party apps from companies and organizations that support it.

SET UP AND USE APPLE PAY FROM YOUR iPHONE

If you want to set up and begin using Apple Pay from your iPhone, you must be using an iPhone model that has a Touch ID sensor built in and that supports this feature (the iPhone 6, iPhone 6 Plus, iPhone 6s, or iPhone 6s Plus). From the Wallet introductory screen (refer to Figure 10.4), tap on the Add Credit or Debit Card option, or tap on the "+" icon displayed to the right of the Apple Pay heading.

> **Note** The iPad Air 2, iPad mini 3, iPad mini 4, and iPad Pro support Apple Pay, but only when it's used to make purchases from within apps. (You cannot make Apple Pay purchases at retail stores using an iPad.)

Later, once you have cards stored in the Wallet app, to add an additional credit or debit card, tap on the "+" icon displayed to the right of the Apple Pay heading (shown in Figure 10.5).

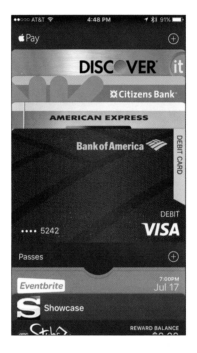

Figure 10.5

Use the Wallet App to create a virtual wallet that securely stores digital versions of your compatible credit and debit cards.

After you store information about at least one compatible credit or debit card in the Wallet app, you can use the app to make purchases/payments using Apple Pay at participating retail stores, or when making online purchases while using compatible apps on your smartphone.

Instead of handing a retail store's cashier your plastic debit or credit card, you simply need to hold your iPhone close to the cash register or credit card swiper, launch the Wallet app, select the debit or credit card you want to pay with (or use the app's default card that you preselect), and then place your finger on the iPhone's Touch ID sensor to authorize the purchase and make your payment.

> ## 🔍 MORE INFO
> Not all debit or credit card issuers (banks and financial institutions) currently support Apple Pay, although the list of supporting card issuers in the United States and Europe is growing rapidly.
>
> To determine whether your card issuer supports Apple Pay, enter your debit or credit card information into the Wallet app or visit https://support.apple.com/en-us/HT204916.
>
> To view an up-to-date list of retail stores, supermarkets, restaurants, pharmacies, and hotels, for example, that currently accept Apple Pay, visit www.apple.com/apple-pay/where-to-use-apple-pay. From this web page, scroll down to also view a list of third-party iPhone apps that accept Apple Pay.

There are several reasons why using Apple Pay is more secure than making a purchase using a traditional (plastic) debit or credit card. For example, the merchants do not see your name, nor do they receive your actual credit/debit card number, expiration date, security code, and/or card PIN.

The credit card issuer processes the payment using an encrypted code. Also, a purchase can only be authorized by you via Apple Pay using the Touch ID sensor to scan your fingerprint. So, even if someone steals your iPhone, they can't access your card details or use the card without your fingerprint scan.

> ## 🗒 NOTE
> If using Apple Pay to make a debit card purchase at a retail store, you might be required to enter the PIN associated with the card or provide a signature to complete a transaction. This varies, and is determined by your financial institution and the amount of the purchase.

Meanwhile, if your traditional (plastic) credit or debit card gets stolen, the thief could use that card to make purchases until you call the card issuer and report the card lost or stolen. Unauthorized use of a credit/debit card by someone else, and potential identity theft, is no longer as much of a threat when using the Wallet app and Apple Pay.

ADDING DEBIT/CREDIT CARD DETAILS TO THE WALLET APP

To add one or more credit or debit cards to the Wallet app, which is a process that needs to be done only once per card, tap on the "+" icon displayed to the right of the Apple Pay heading when you launch the Wallet app.

To proceed, your iPhone must be signed in to your iCloud account. After viewing the Add Card Screen (shown in Figure 10.6), tap on the Next option displayed in the top-right corner.

You'll notice that the rear-facing camera of your iPhone becomes active. While in a well-lit area, position your credit or debit card within the onscreen frame, and your iPhone automatically scans the card and imports your name and card number into the Wallet app (shown in Figure 10.7).

Figure 10.6
Read this information screen about Apple Pay and the Wallet app; then tap on the Next option.

Figure 10.7
Using the rear-facing camera built in to your iPhone, it's possible to scan each of your credit or debit cards into the Wallet app.

> **TIP** To manually enter credit or debit card details, instead of scanning the card, tap on the Enter Card Details Manually option displayed at the bottom of the screen (refer to Figure 10.7).

From the Card Details screen that appears next, enter the Expiration Date and Security Code from your card into the Wallet app (shown in Figure 10.8).

At this point, the verification process varies, based on the card issuer. Follow the onscreen prompts to complete the verification processes, which typically takes 30 seconds or less.

Figure 10.8
Enter the Expiration Date and Security Code when prompted for the debit or credit card you're storing in the Wallet app.

> **NOTE** Some card issuers require you to call the customer service number that is displayed on the card verification screen to activate your card in the Wallet app for use with Apple Pay.

Once the credit or debit card has been verified and activated by your card issuer, a digital version of that card (that displays only the last four digits of the card number) is displayed in the Wallet app (refer to Figure 10.5).

You're now ready to use that credit or debit card to make Apple Pay purchases. If you want to add additional cards to the Wallet app, repeat this process for each card.

> **TIP** There are two ways to set the default card, which is the one preselected each time you launch the Wallet app.

First, place your finger on one of the virtual cards displayed under the Apple Pay heading (refer to Figure 10.5), hold your finger down on the screen, and drag that card's graphic to the top of the pile. A message is displayed stating that the card you selected and placed at the top of the pile is now your default card (shown in Figure 10.9).

Alternatively, to select a default card, launch Settings, tap on the Wallet & Apple Pay option, and then tap on the Default Card option found below the Transaction Defaults heading. Be sure to customize the Shipping Address, Email, and Phone Number fields as well.

Figure 10.9
You can change your default credit or debit card in the Wallet app at any time.

Once you have one or more credit or debit cards stored in the Wallet app, when you're ready to make a payment at a retail location, launch the Wallet app and select the card you want to use by tapping on the graphic for a card displayed below the Apple Pay heading.

When prompted by the cashier, hold the iPhone up to the cash register or credit card swiper, and then place your finger on the iPhone's Touch ID sensor for a few seconds to authorize the payment (shown in Figure 10.10).

Figure 10.10

The only way to authorize Apple Pay to initiate a payment using the selected credit or debit card (or store credit card) is to use the Touch ID sensor to scan your fingerprint.

> **TIP** There are two ways to launch the Wallet app. First, tap on the Wallet app icon from the Home screen. Second, from the Lock screen, quickly double-press the Home button, without first having to unlock the phone and manually launch the Wallet app.
>
> To use this second option, be sure to turn on the virtual switch associated with the Double-Click Home Button option that can be found by launching Settings and then selecting the Wallet & Apple Pay option.

To delete or edit a credit or debit card stored in the Wallet app, launch Settings, tap on the Wallet & Apple Pay option, and then tap on the listing for a card that appears below the Cards heading.

To change the Billing Address associated with the card, tap on the Billing Address option. To delete the card altogether from the Wallet app, tap on the Remove Card option displayed at the bottom of the card's submenu screen within Settings.

USE THE WALLET APP TO MANAGE REWARD CARDS, MEMBERSHIP CARDS, AND MORE

A growing number of retail stores and organizations that have iPhone apps are beginning to support the Wallet app as well and allow users to manage their reward and/or membership cards from the Wallet app. For example, Dunkin' Donuts, Walgreen's, Panera, and AAA were among the first companies and organizations to support the Wallet app for this purpose. To use this functionality, it is often necessary to also install the app from that company.

In addition, most of the major airlines allow you to store not just Frequent Flier membership cards in the Wallet app, but also digital versions of upcoming flight boarding documents.

Meanwhile, movie theaters and ticket services (like Ticketmaster and Live Nation) allow you to store digital tickets you purchase online in the Wallet app and present those tickets at the movie theater, event, or show.

Many movie theater chains that have reward programs also support the Wallet app to store membership card details, so you can view, manage, and redeem reward points earned from within the app.

TIP How businesses opt to support and utilize the Wallet app varies greatly. To find third-party apps from businesses that support the Wallet app, at any time launch the App Store app and type **Wallet** in the Search field.

When the Apps for Wallet window is displayed (see Figure 10.11), tap on the Browse Now option. Then browse the App Store's offerings to download and install the (free) apps from companies and organizations that you want to use (see Figure 10.12).

TIP To add membership or reward card details from participating companies and organizations into the Wallet app, launch the app and tap on the "+" icon displayed next to the Passes heading (again, refer to Figure 10.5). Next, scan the plastic card into the Wallet app by tapping on the Scan Code to Add a Pass option.

Alternatively, import the appropriate information directly from the store or organization's own iPhone app. Directions for how to do this are supplied in the compatible app.

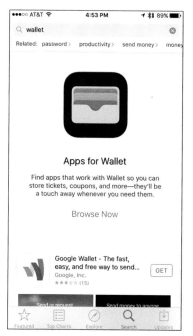

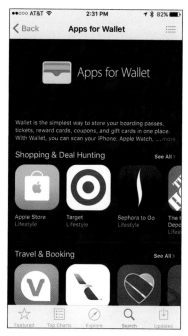

Figure 10.11

From the App Store app, access an up-to-date selection of third-party apps that support the Wallet app.

Figure 10.12

Browse the App Store to find (free) apps from companies or organizations you frequently do business with, such as the Apple Store, Target, Home Depot, Walgreen's, Ticketmaster, or AAA.

Once you set up Apple Pay to work with the Wallet app and begin storing compatible company/organization reward and membership cards in the app, you'll quickly discover that not only is Apple Pay more secure than making a purchase using a traditional, plastic credit/debit card, the checkout process is typically faster, plus you can dramatically slim down your actual wallet.

🔍 **MORE INFO** To learn more about how Apple Pay and the Wallet app work, visit www.apple.com/apple-pay.

☑ **TIP** To delete a card that's stored in the Wallet app, view that card with the app, and then tap on the Info ("i") icon that's displayed in the bottom-right corner of the screen. Tap on the Delete option that appears there.

IN THIS CHAPTER

■ How to send and receive emails using the Mail app

■ Quickly manage emails from your inbox(es)

■ How to send and receive text, audio, and video messages using your cellular service provider's text-messaging service or the iMessage service

11

SEND AND RECEIVE EMAILS, TEXTS, AND INSTANT MESSAGES WITH THE MAIL AND MESSAGES APPS

If you're someone who's constantly on the go, being able to send and receive emails from virtually anywhere there's a cellular or Wi-Fi Internet connection enables you to stay in touch, stay informed, and be productive from wherever you happen to be.

The Mail app offers a comprehensive set of tools, features, and functions to help you compose, send, receive, and organize emails from one or more existing accounts. From your iPhone or iPad, you can simultaneously manage your personal and work-related email accounts, as well as the free email account that's provided when you set up an iCloud account.

Before you can begin using the Mail app, it's necessary to set up your existing email accounts from within Settings.

> [Note icon] **NOTE**   If you don't yet have an email account, there are several ways to get one. You can sign up for a free Apple iCloud account, which includes an email account. In addition, Google offers free Gmail accounts (http://mail.google.com), and Yahoo! offers free Yahoo! Mail accounts (http://features.mail.yahoo.com), both of which are fully compatible with your iOS device's Mail app.

HOW TO ADD EMAIL ACCOUNTS TO THE MAIL APP

Use the Add Account tool available within Settings to initially set up your iOS device to work with your existing email account(s). This process works with virtually all email accounts, including industry-standard POP3 and IMAP email services.

If you have an email account through your employer that doesn't initially work using the setup procedure outlined in this chapter, contact your company's IT department or Apple's technical support for assistance.

> [Note icon] **NOTE**   The process for setting up an existing email account to use with your iPhone or iPad and the Mail app needs to be done only once per account.

Follow these steps to set up your iOS device to work with each of your existing email accounts:

1. From the Home screen, launch Settings.

2. Tap on the Mail, Contacts, Calendars option.

3. Tap on the Add Account option displayed near the top of the screen, below the Accounts heading.

4. Select the type of email account you have. Your options include iCloud, Microsoft Exchange, Google Gmail, Yahoo! Mail, AOL Mail, Microsoft Outlook.com, and Other (shown in Figure 11.1). Tap on the appropriate option. If you have a POP3 or IMAP-compatible email account that doesn't otherwise fall into one of the provided email types, tap on the Other option, and follow the onscreen prompts.

   If you have an existing Yahoo! email account, for example, tap on the Yahoo! option. When the Yahoo! account setup screen appears (shown in Figure 11.2), enter your account name, email address, password, and a description for the account.

TIP   As you're adding an email account from within Settings, the account name should be your full name (or whatever you want to appear in the From field of outgoing emails). You can opt to use just your first name, a family name (such as "The Anderson Family"), or a nickname, based on what you want to share with the recipients of your emails. The Description can be anything that helps you personally differentiate that account from your other accounts, such as Home Email, Work Email, or Yahoo! Email. This is something that you see only on your device.

Figure 11.1

Choose the type of email account you'd like to add by tapping on the appropriate menu option.

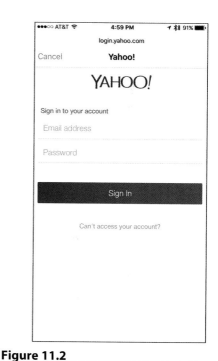

Figure 11.2

If you're setting up a Yahoo! Mail account, tap on the Yahoo! option, and then fill in your existing account information.

5. Tap on the Next option. Your iOS device connects to the email account's server and confirms the account details you've entered. The word Verifying appears on the screen.

6. After the account has been verified, a new window with options is displayed. They're probably labeled Mail, Contacts, Calendars, Reminders, and Notes,

although depending on the type of email account you're setting up, some of these options might not be available. They're used to determine what additional app-specific data can be linked with the Mail account, such as your Contacts database, the schedule from your Calendar app, your to-do list from the Reminders app, or your notes from the Notes app.

! CAUTION   If you're already syncing app-specific data for Contacts, Calendar, Reminders, and/or Notes with iCloud, do not also sync them with Yahoo!, Google, or a Microsoft Exchange–compatible account, or you could wind up with duplicate records or entries in each app. Likewise, if you're already syncing your app-specific data with Google, don't also sync this information using iCloud.

7. Tap on the Save option. An Adding Account message is briefly displayed, and details about the email account you just set up are added to your iOS device. The account is now ready to use via the Mail app.

8. If you have another existing email account to set up, from the Mail, Contacts, Calendars screen in the Settings app, tap on the Add Account option again, and repeat the preceding procedure. Otherwise, exit the Settings app and launch the Mail app from the Home screen.

Depending on the type of email account you're setting up, the information for which you're prompted varies slightly.

TIP   If you plan to set up a POP3 or IMAP email account, in addition to your existing email address and password, you might be prompted to enter your host name [mail.example.com] and outgoing mail server information [smtp.example.com]. Obtain this information from your email account provider, Internet service provider, or the IT department at your company before attempting to set up this type of account on your iPhone or iPad.

After the account is set up, it is listed in Settings under the Accounts heading when you tap on the Mail, Contacts, Calendars option.

> **TIP** When you purchase a new iOS device, it comes with free technical support from AppleCare for 90 days. If you purchased AppleCare+ with your iOS device, you have access to free technical support from Apple for two years. This includes the ability to make an in-person appointment with an Apple Genius at any Apple Store, and have someone set up your email accounts on your iPhone or iPad for you.
>
> To schedule a free appointment, visit www.apple.com/retail/geniusbar. Or call Apple's toll-free technical support phone number and have someone talk you through the email setup process. Call 800-APL-CARE (275-2273).

HOW TO CUSTOMIZE MAIL OPTIONS FROM SETTINGS

To customize options available in the Mail app, launch Settings and select the Mail, Contacts, Calendars option. In the Mail, Contacts, Calendars submenu screen (shown in Figure 11.3) are a handful of customizable features for managing your email accounts.

Figure 11.3

From Settings, you can customize a handful of settings relating to the Mail app.

TIP You should customize each email account separately. This includes how your iOS device displays new incoming email details in Notification Center, as well as how alerts or banners are utilized for each account. To set this up for each account, launch Settings, tap on Notifications, select the Mail option, and then one at a time, tap on the listing for each of your email accounts. There's also a separate listing for VIP, which enables you to set separate alerts for important incoming emails from people included in the Mail app's VIP list that you create.

At the top of the Mail, Contacts, Calendars screen within Settings is a listing of the individual email accounts you have already linked with the Mail app. Below this is the Fetch New Data option. Use this to determine how often your iOS device automatically accesses the Internet to check for and download new incoming email messages from each email account's server.

TIP From the Fetch New Data screen, either enable or disable the Push feature. When turned on, your iPhone or iPad automatically accesses and displays new incoming emails as they arrive on your email account's server. When the Push feature is turned off, select how often you want to check for new emails. Your options include Every 15 Minutes, Every 30 Minutes, Hourly, or Manually. Customize this setting separately for each of your email accounts.

The benefit of using the Fetch feature set to Manually is that you can greatly reduce your cellular data usage. This is important if you have a monthly data allocation through your cellular service provider. If you have an account that offers unlimited wireless data, or you utilize a Wi-Fi connection, this is not a concern. Using the Fetch feature can also help you extend your device's battery life.

By scrolling down on the Mail, Contacts, Calendars menu screen, you see the Mail heading. Below this heading are the following customizable options relating to how the Mail app manages your email accounts and email messages:

- **Preview**—As you look at your Inbox (or any mailbox) using the Mail app, determine how much of each email message's body text is visible from the mailbox summary screen, in addition to the From, Date/Time, and Subject. Choose None, or between one and five lines of the email message to preview.

TIP The Preview option also impacts the email-related notifications that appear in the Notification Center if you assign it to continuously monitor the Mail app. You can adjust this in Settings by tapping on the Notifications option found in the main Settings menu.

■ **Show To/Cc Label**—Decide whether to view the To and Cc fields when viewing the preview screen for emails.

■ **Swipe Options**—This feature enables you to manage the Inbox of your email accounts. As you're looking at the previews of each message in your inbox, swipe from left to right, or right to left, across each message listing to access menu options (shown in Figure 11.4). Tap on this menu option to configure which Mail-related command(s) become available to you by swiping across a message listing.

Figure 11.4

Access commonly used commands for managing incoming messages by swiping your finger across a message listing.

☑ TIP   Tap on Swipe Options in the Mail, Contacts, Calendars submenu to determine which email management–related commands become available to you when you swipe left to right (or right to left) across a message listing when viewing an Inbox.

When you swipe from left to right, it's possible to choose whether the Mark As Read, Flag, Move Message, or Archive command is made available. If you select the None option, the left to right swipe feature is disabled.

When you swipe right to left, choose whether the Mark As Read, Flag, or Move Message command becomes available in addition to the Trash and More options (which are default options).

Choose the email message commands you most often use to organize your incoming messages so you can access them faster (refer to Figure 11.4).

■ **Flag Style**—When you flag an email as important, the Flag style determines whether the Mail app displays a flag-shaped icon or a colored dot next to each flagged email message.

■ **Ask Before Deleting**—This option serves as a safety net to ensure that you don't accidentally delete an important email message from your iOS device. When this feature is turned on, you're asked to confirm your message deletion request before an email message is actually deleted. By default, with some email service providers, you cannot delete email messages stored on your email account's server. When you delete a message from the Mail app, it is deleted from your iPhone or iPad, but is still accessible from other devices. Check with your mail service provider to see how this feature is set up and whether it is changeable.

■ **Load Remote Images**—When an email message has a photo or graphic embedded in it, this option determines whether the image is automatically downloaded and displayed with the email message. You can opt to refrain from automatically loading graphics with email messages to reduce the amount of data transferred to your iPhone or iPad (which is a consideration if you're connected to the Internet via a cellular data network). You still have the option to tap on the placeholder icon in the email message to manually download the images in a specific message.

> **NOTE** In addition to reducing your cellular data usage, disabling the Load Remote Images option can help you cut down on the amount of spam (unsolicited emails) you receive, because remote image loading can be tracked by the senders of spam and used to verify valid email addresses.
>
> When turned off, displaying images embedded within an email requires an additional step on your part, because you now must tap the image icon to load the image if you want to view it.

■ **Organize by Thread**—This feature enables you to review messages in reverse chronological order if a single message turns into a back-and-forth email conversation in which multiple parties keep hitting Reply to respond to messages with the same subject. When turned on, this makes keeping track of email conversations much easier, especially if you're managing several email accounts on your iPhone or iPad. If it's turned off, messages in your Inbox are displayed in reverse chronological order as they're received, not grouped by subject.

- **Always Bcc Myself**—When this feature is turned on, a copy of every outgoing email is sent to your Inbox. Typically, all outgoing messages automatically get saved in a Sent folder that's related to that account. If your email account type does not enable you to access sent emails from another computer or device, using the Bcc Myself option compensates for this. When you send an email message from your iPhone/iPad, using this feature ensures that the message becomes accessible from your primary computer.

- **Mark Addresses**—By tapping on this option, you can enter a portion of an email address, and then be alerted each time an email is received that meets that search criteria. For example, if you do business with many people who work at Widget.com, anyone with an email address ending with widget.com, such as johndoe@widget.com, sales@widget.com, or janedoe@wideget.com, can be automatically flagged in your Inbox to get your attention. All you have to do is store "widget.com" in the Mark Address field. This feature is particularly useful if you work in a corporate environment.

- **Increase Quote Level**—When turned on, anytime you reply to a message or forward a message, the content of that original email appears indented, making it easier to differentiate between the message you add and the original message being replied to or forwarded. This option impacts message formatting, not actual content.

- **Signature**—For every outgoing email that you compose, you can automatically add an email signature. The default signature is "Sent from my iPhone" or "Sent from my iPad." However, by tapping on this option within Settings, it's possible to create customized signatures for each email account. A signature might include your name, mailing address, email address, phone numbers, and so forth.

- **Default Account**—If you're using the Mail app to manage multiple email accounts, when you reply to a message or forward a message, it is always sent from the email account to which the message was originally sent. However, if you tap on the Compose New Email icon to create a new email from scratch, the email account from which the message is sent is whichever you have set up as the Mail app's default account. If you want to change this account for a specific email, simply tap on the From field as you're composing a new email and select one of your other accounts.

TIPS FOR VIEWING YOUR INCOMING EMAIL

When you launch the Mail app, the Inbox for your various email accounts is displayed. You can opt to display incoming messages for a single email account, or display the incoming messages from all of your email accounts by selecting the All Inboxes option.

Even though Mail enables you to simultaneously view incoming emails from multiple accounts within a single listing (on the same screen), behind the scenes, the app automatically keeps your incoming and outgoing emails, and your various email accounts separate. So if you opt to read and respond to an email from your work-related Inbox, for example, that response is automatically sent out from your work-related email account and saved in the Sent Folder for that account.

Viewing all the Inboxes for all of your accounts simultaneously makes it faster to review your incoming emails, without having to manually switch between email accounts.

If you have multiple email accounts being managed from your iOS device, to view all of your Inboxes simultaneously, or to switch between Inboxes, follow these steps:

1. Launch the Mail app.

2. The Inbox you last looked at is probably displayed. If only one email account is set up to work with your iPhone or iPad, the last email you viewed is displayed.

3. Tap on the left-pointing, arrow-shaped Mailboxes option displayed in the upper-left corner of the screen to select which Inbox you want to view. If you're looking at a particular account's Inbox, the arrow-shaped option is labeled Back.

4. From the menu that appears, the first option displayed is All Inboxes. Tap on this to view a single listing of all incoming emails. Or tap on any single email account that's listed on the Mailboxes screen.

> **☑ TIP**   Tap on the VIP mailbox listing to view only emails from your various inboxes that have been received from people you've added to your VIP List. When you tap on the VIP option, these emails are displayed in a single list, although it is comprised of VIP messages from all the accounts you're managing on your iPhone or iPad.
>
> Below the VIP listing under the Inboxes heading is a Flagged listing. This enables you to view a separate mailbox comprised of only emails you've previously flagged as being important. Again, this is a comprehensive list from all the accounts you're managing on your iPhone or iPad. The Mail app keeps the messages sorted behind the scenes, based on which account each is associated with.

COMPOSING AN EMAIL MESSAGE

From the Mail app, it's easy to compose an email from scratch and send it to one or more recipients. To compose a new email, tap on the Compose icon. On an iPhone, the Compose icon can be found in the lower-right corner of the screen in the Mail app. On an iPad, the Compose icon is displayed in the upper-right corner of the screen.

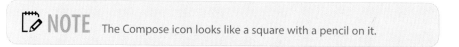

NOTE The Compose icon looks like a square with a pencil on it.

When you tap on the Compose icon, a blank New Message email message template appears on the iPhone or iPad's screen. Using the virtual keyboard, fill in the To, Cc, Bcc, and/or Subject fields (as shown in Figure 11.5). You must fill in the To field with a valid email address for at least one recipient. The other fields are optional.

Figure 11.5

Tap on the Compose icon to create an email from scratch and send it from your iOS device.

You can send the same email to multiple recipients by either adding multiple email addresses to the To field, or by adding additional email addresses to the Cc and/or Bcc fields.

If you're managing one email account from your iOS device, the From field is auto-matically filled in with your email address. However, if you're managing multiple email addresses from the iPhone or iPad, tap on the From field to select which email address you want to send the message from, if you don't want to use the default account.

> **✓ TIP** As you fill in the To field when composing an email, the Mail app automatically accesses your Contacts database to match up entries. This can save you time because you don't have to manually enter that email address. If you know that the person you're sending an email to already has an entry that includes the person's email address in your Contacts database, you can type that person's name in the To field.
>
> The Mail app also remembers email addresses from people not in your Contacts database, but with whom you've corresponded through email via the app. Also, when you begin manually entering an email address, the Mail app offers sugges-tions. Either select a suggestion or continue typing.

Next, tap on the Subject field and use the virtual keyboard to enter the subject for your message. As you do this, the subject appears at the very top center of the Compose window (replacing the New Message heading).

> **✓ TIP** When using almost any app with a Share menu, to compose and send an email that contains app-specific content without first launching the Mail app, tap on the Share icon, and then select Mail.
>
> A New Message screen appears with the related app-specific content already attached to that outgoing email message. Use the virtual keyboard to compose your email, and then tap on the Send icon. The email message is sent and you are returned to the app you were using.

To begin creating the main body of the outgoing email message, tap in the main body area of the Compose Message screen and begin using the virtual keyboard (or an optional external keyboard) to compose your message. You also have the option of tapping on the Dictation key and then dictating your message using the Dictation feature.

! **CAUTION** If you have the Auto-Capitalization, Auto-Correction, or Check Spelling features turned on, as you type, the iPhone or iPad automatically corrects anything that it perceives as a typo or misspelled word. Be very careful when using these features because they are notorious for plugging the wrong word into a sentence. Especially if you're creating important business documents and emails, make sure you carefully proofread whatever you type before sending it. Typically, these features are helpful, but they do have quirks that can lead to embarrassing and unprofessional mistakes.

To control the Auto-Capitalization, Auto-Correction, and Check Spelling features, launch Settings, tap on the General option, select the Keyboard option, and then turn on or off the virtual switch associated for each option displayed in the Keyboard menu screen.

TIP When turned on, the QuickType feature monitors what you're typing in real time and anticipates what you're about to type (based on the context of what you're typing). It then suggests appropriate words or phrases.

Use this feature to speed up and improve the accuracy of your typing. The QuickType suggestions are displayed as tabs just above the virtual keyboard (shown in Figure 11.6). Tap on a suggestion tab to select that word and insert it into your message. Then continue typing.

The signature you set up from within Settings for the selected From account is automatically displayed at the bottom of each newly composed message. You can return to Settings to turn off the Signature feature, or change the signature that appears. A signature can also be edited or added manually directly from the Compose screen as you create or edit each message.

When your email is fully written and ready to be sent, tap on the Send option. In a few seconds, the message is sent from your iOS device, assuming that it is connected to the Internet. A copy of the message appears in your Sent or Outbox folder.

As a message is being sent, a "Sending" notification appears near the bottom of the Mail app's screen.

NOTE The Mail app enables you to format your outgoing email messages and include **bold**, *italic*, and underlined text (as well as combinations, like bold-italic text).

Figure 11.6
The QuickType features works nicely when composing emails using the Mail app. Notice the suggested text displayed in tabs just above the virtual keyboard.

To format text in an email message you're composing, type the text as you normally would using the virtual keyboard. After the text appears in your email, hold your finger on a word to make the Select, Select All, Paste, Quote Level, Insert Photo or Video, and Add Attachment command tabs appear above that word.

Tap on Select, and then use your finger to move the blue dots that appear to highlight the text you want to modify. When the appropriate text is highlighted in blue, tap the right-pointing arrow that appears above the text (next to the Cut, Copy, and Paste commands), and then tap on the **B**/U option. A new menu appears above the highlighted text with three options labeled Bold, Italics, and Underline. Tap on one or more of these tabs to alter the highlighted text. On the iPad, all options are listed and no scrolling is required.

WHAT'S NEW If you're using one of the newer iPad models, displayed in the top-right corner of the virtual keyboard is a text formatting icon, as well as an Attach Photo and a File Attachment icon (shown in Figure 11.7).

On most newer iPad models, it's possible to tap on a word, and then tap on the **B**/U icon to select and format text after it's been typed, or select your type style option before you begin typing. This icon also makes it easier to quickly change the type style while you're typing.

Tap on the Attach Photo icon to select and import a photo into your email, or tap on the File Attachment icon to attach a file, document, or photo that's stored in iCloud Drive to your outgoing email.

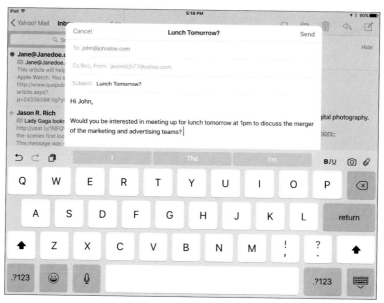

Figure 11.7

Newer iPad models now display Undo, Redo, Paste, Type Style, Attach Photo, and Attach File icons on a toolbar that appears just above the virtual keyboard when composing an email.

WHAT'S NEW When using any iPad model running iOS 9, you can more accurately move the cursor around on the screen (to select content to cut and paste, for example) by placing two fingers on the screen simultaneously over the cursor and then dragging your fingers around on the screen.

Also, if you're using an external keyboard with your iPad, press the Control, Command, or Options key to see available shortcuts new to iOS 9.

INSERT A PHOTO OR VIDEO INTO YOUR OUTGOING EMAIL

As you're composing an outgoing email, to insert a photo or video clip that's stored on your iPhone or iPad into that email, place and hold your finger anywhere in the body of the email where you want to embed the photo or video.

> **NOTE** On the iPhone, tap on the right-pointing arrow displayed to the right of the Select, Select All, and Paste commands to access the Insert Photo or Video option.

When the Insert Photo or Video tab is displayed, tap on it. Select the photo you want to insert into the email by selecting an album and then tapping on an image or video thumbnail. The photo/video you selected is previewed in the Choose Photo window. Tap on the Use button to insert the photo or video into your email.

You can repeat this process to include multiple images within an email (up to five), keeping in mind that the overall file size associated with the outgoing email is often limited by your email service.

> **TIP** When you insert a photo into an outgoing email you are prompted to choose the image size. Your options include Small, Medium, Large, and Actual Size. Each is accompanied by the file size of the image(s) you're sending. Tap on one of these options when prompted.
>
> On the iPad, tap on the Images option displayed to the right of the Cc:/Bcc, From field, and then tap on the Small, Medium, Large, or Actual Size tab on the newly displayed Image Size field to customize the image file size.

INSERT AN ATTACHMENT WITHIN AN EMAIL

One new iOS 9 feature in the Mail app is the capability to add a file attachment to an outgoing email you're composing. To do this, place and hold down your finger in the body of the email where you want to insert the file. From the menu that appears tap on the Add Attachment option.

If you're using an iPad, simply tap on the File Attachment icon displayed to the extreme right on the new toolbar found above the virtual keyboard.

Your iOS mobile device accesses your online-based iCloud Drive folders and allows you to select a file stored on your iCloud account (not within your iPhone or iPad).

> **NOTE** Refer to Chapter 5, "Use iCloud and the iCloud Drive App from Your iPhone or iPad," for more information about managing files, data, photos, and documents using iCloud Drive.

Select the file you want to attach to the outgoing email by tapping on its icon or listing, and then tap on the Done option. The selected files are attached to the outgoing email message (shown in Figure 11.8).

Attached Word Document

Figure 11.8

The iOS 9 edition of the Mail app enables you to attach many different types of files (including a Word document as shown here) to an outgoing email using the Attach File command.

USING SELECT, SELECT ALL, CUT, COPY, AND PASTE

The iOS operating system offers Select, Select All, Cut, Copy, and Paste commands, which are accessible from many iPhone or iPad apps, including Mail. Using these commands, you can quickly copy and paste content from one portion of an app to another, or from one app into another app, whether it's a paragraph of text, a phone number, or a photo, for example.

> **iOS 9 WHAT'S NEW** When using the iPad's new Split Screen feature, you can display two apps at once on your tablet's screen and then easily select, copy, and paste app content between the two apps.

To use these commands, use your finger to hold down on any word or graphic element on the screen for one or two seconds, until the Select and Select All tabs appear above that content. To select a single word or select the content you want to copy or cut, tap on the Select tab. Or to select all the content on the screen, tap the Select All tab.

After text (or a graphic element, such as a photo) is selected, tap on the Cut tab to delete the selected content from the screen (if this option is available in the app you're using), or tap the Copy tab to save the highlighted content in your iPhone or iPad's virtual clipboard.

Now, move to where you want to paste the saved content. This can be in the same email or document, for example, or in another app altogether. Choose the location on the screen where you want to paste the content, and hold your finger on that location for two or three seconds. When the Paste tab appears, tap on it. The content you just copied is pasted into that location.

(iOS 9) WHAT'S NEW   On the iPad, displayed above the virtual keyboard are Undo, Redo, and Clipboard icons. Tap on the Undo icon to go one step back and undo the last thing you did when composing the email. Tap on the Redo icon to counteract what the Undo command just did.

When you select content in an outgoing email, for example, the Cut, Copy, and Paste command icons are displayed on the top-left side of the virtual keyboard. Tap the scissor-shaped icon to use the Cut command. The icon that looks like two sheets of paper represents the Copy command, and the clipboard-shaped icon works as the Paste command.

TIP   In the Mail app, as you use the Select, Select All, Cut, Copy, and Paste commands, notice a Quote Level option that appears on the menu above the highlighted text or content you select. Tap on this to increase or decrease the indent of that content, which impacts how it's formatted on the screen.

HOW TO SAVE AN UNSENT DRAFT OF AN EMAIL MESSAGE

If you want to save a draft of an email without sending it, as you're composing the email message, tap on the Cancel button that appears in the upper-left corner of the Compose message window. Two command buttons appear: Delete Draft and Save Draft. To save the unsent draft, tap on Save Draft.

You can return to it later to modify and send it. To do this, from the main Inbox screen in Mail, tap on the left-pointing Mailboxes icon that looks like an arrow displayed at the upper-left corner of the screen. From the Mailboxes screen, scroll down to the Accounts heading and tap on the listing for the email account from which the email draft was composed.

When you see a list of folders related to that email account, tap on the Drafts folder. Tap on the appropriate listing to open the email message. You can now edit the message or send it.

TIPS FOR READING EMAIL

After you launch the Mail app, you can access the Inbox for one or more of your existing email accounts, compose new emails, or manage your email accounts. Just like the Inbox on your main computer's email software, the Inbox of the Mail app (shown in Figure 11.9 on an iPhone, and Figure 11.10 on an iPad) displays your incoming emails.

> **TIP** As you're looking at the inbox for any of your email accounts (or the All Inboxes mailbox), to the left of each email message preview you might see a tiny graphic icon (refer to Figure 11.10). A blue dot represents a new and unread email (or an email that has been marked as unread). A solid blue star represents a new and *unread* email from someone on your VIP list, while a gray star icon represents a *read* email from someone on your VIP list.
>
> An orange flag-shaped icon displayed to the left of an email preview means that you have manually flagged that message (or message thread) as urgent. Instead of a flag icon, a blue dot with an orange circle can be displayed indicating a message is urgent and unread. Just an orange dot will appear after it's read. You can choose between a flag or a dot icon from Settings.
>
> A curved, left-pointing arrow icon means that you have read and replied to that message, while a right-pointing arrow icon means you've read and have forwarded that message to one or more people.
>
> A bell icon means that the Notify Me option has been turned on in relation to that message.
>
> If no tiny icon appears to the left of an email preview listing, this means the message has been read and is simply stored in that inbox (or mailbox).

Figure 11.9

The Inbox screen of the Mail app displays a listing of your incoming emails on the iPhone.

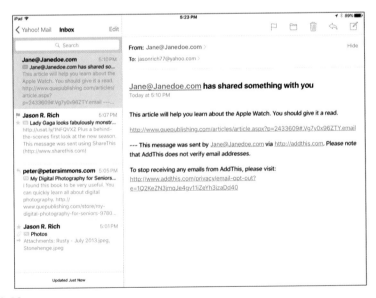

Figure 11.10

On the iPad, the Inbox provides a listing of your incoming emails on the left side of the screen (in the Inbox sidebar).

THE MAIL APP'S INBOX

When you're viewing your Inbox(es), a list of the individual emails is displayed. Based on the customizations you make from the Settings app that pertain to the Mail app, the Sender, Subject, Date/Time, and up to five lines of the message's body text can be displayed for each incoming message listing.

> **NOTE** If you're using the Mail app on an iPad while holding the tablet in portrait mode, place your finger near the left side of the screen and swipe to the right to open the Inbox sidebar.

On the iPhone, when viewing your Inbox and the listing of incoming (new) email messages, tap on any message listing to read that message in its entirety. When you do this, a new message screen appears. At the bottom of this screen is a series of command icons for managing that email.

> **iOS 9 WHAT'S NEW** If you're using an iPhone 6s or iPhone 6s Plus, take advantage of the Peek and Pop features to quickly review emails. As you're looking at the Inbox listing, place and hold your finger down gently on a specific email listing. A preview of that entire email message is displayed. If you want to open and read the message, press down on the screen a bit harder when the preview is visible.

On the iPad, the email message that's highlighted in gray on the left side of the screen is the one that's currently being displayed, in its entirety, on the right side of the screen. Tap on any email listing on the left side of the screen to view the entire message on the right side of the screen. Icons at the top of the screen are used for managing that email.

At the top of the Inbox message listing are two command icons, labeled Mailboxes (or the name of the mailbox you're viewing) and Edit.

Located at the top of the Inbox message listing is a Search field. You might need to swipe your finger downward along the Inbox to reveal it. Tap on this Search field to make the virtual keyboard appear, enabling you to enter a search phrase and quickly find a particular email message. You can search the content of the Mail app using any keyword, a sender's name, a date, or an email subject, for example. You can also use your device's Spotlight Search feature to quickly locate content within email messages.

THE EDIT BUTTON

Located on top of a mailbox's message listing (to the right of its heading) is the Edit button. Tap on this option to quickly select multiple messages from a mailbox, such as your inbox, to delete or move to another mailbox (or folder), as shown in Figure 11.11.

> **TIP** After tapping the Edit button, manually select one or more message listings to move or delete, or tap on the Mark All option to select all the messages in that Inbox. It's then possible to Flag or Mark As Read/Unread all the selected messages.

> **TIP** If you tap on the Mark button displayed to the left of the Trash and Move buttons, you can then flag them or mark one or more emails as read or unread. You can also move selected messages to your Junk folder.

After you tap the Edit button, an empty circle icon appears to the left of each email message preview listing. To move or delete one or more messages from the current mailbox's listing (which could be your Inbox, VIP, Archive, or Junk mailbox), tap on the empty circle icon for that message. A blue-and-white check mark fills the empty circle icon when you do this, and the Mark, Move, and Trash options are displayed at the bottom of the screen.

After you've selected one or more messages, tap the Trash button to quickly delete one or more messages simultaneously from the mailbox (which sends them to the Trash folder), or tap the Move button and then select to which folder you want to move those email messages. Tap on the Mark option to Flag the message, mark it as unread, or move it to the Junk folder.

To exit this option without doing anything, tap on the Cancel button displayed at the top of the Inbox listing, to the right of the Inbox heading.

HOW TO DELETE INDIVIDUAL INCOMING MESSAGES

As you're looking at the listing of messages in your Inbox (or any mailbox), to delete individual messages, one at a time, swipe your finger from right to left over a message listing. Tap on the red-and-white Trash option to delete the message.

Tap on the More option to access a menu (shown in Figure 11.12) that offers the Reply, Forward, Mark, Notify Me, and Move Message options. You can also tap on the orange Flag option to flag or unflag that message.

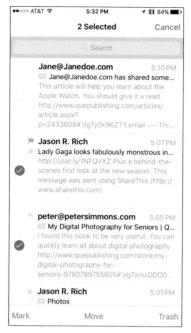

Figure 11.11

Tap the Edit button, and then manage your incoming messages, mark them, delete them in quantity, or move them to the Trash folder.

Figure 11.12

After swiping from right to left across a message listing in your Inbox, tap on the More option to reveal this menu.

> **TIP** Another way to delete a message from your Inbox, or any mailbox, is to tap on a message listing to view that message and then tap on the Trash icon.

HOW TO VIEW YOUR EMAILS

When a single email message is selected from the Inbox listing, that message is displayed in its entirety. At the top of the message, see the From, To, Cc/Bcc (if applicable), Subject, and the Date/Time it was sent.

In the upper-right corner of the email message is a blue Hide command. If you tap on this, some of the message header information will no longer be displayed. To make this information reappear, tap on the More option.

As you're reading an email, tap on the flag icon to flag that message and mark it as urgent, or mark the email as unread. These options appear within a pop-up menu. When you flag a message, an orange flag (or an orange dot) becomes associated with that message, which is displayed in the message itself (to the right of the date and time), and in the inbox (mailbox) in which the message is stored. Plus, from your Inboxes menu, if you tap on the Flagged option, you can view a separate mailbox that contains only flagged (urgent) messages.

TAKE ADVANTAGE OF THE MAIL APP'S VIP LIST FEATURE

In addition to flagging individual messages as important, the Mail app can automatically highlight all emails sent from particular (important) senders, such as your boss, specific clients, close friends, or family members. Once you add a sender to your VIP List, all their incoming emails are marked with a star-shaped icon instead of a blue dot icon that represents a regular, new incoming email.

To add someone to your VIP List, as you're reading an email from that person, tap on the From field (their name/email address). A Sender screen (iPhone) or window (iPad) appears. Located toward the middle of this window, tap on the Add To VIP button. This adds and keeps that sender on your custom VIP list until you manually remove them.

To later remove someone from your VIP list, read any of their email messages and again tap on the From field. When the Sender window appears, tap on the Remove From VIP button (which has replaced the Add To VIP button).

TIP From the Mailboxes menu, tap on the VIP listing to view a special mailbox that displays only incoming emails from people on your VIP list. Using the VIP List feature helps you quickly differentiate important emails from spam and less important incoming emails that don't necessarily require your immediate attention.

HOW TO DEAL WITH INCOMING EMAIL MESSAGE ATTACHMENTS

The Mail app enables you to access certain types of attachment files that accompany an incoming email message. Dozens of different file formats are compatible with the Mail app. As you add third-party apps that support other file formats, they become recognized by the Mail app. This includes files related to text, photos, audio clips, video clips, PDFs, and eBooks, as well as iWork and Microsoft Office documents and files.

To open an attached file using another app, in the incoming email message, tap and hold down the attachment icon for one to three seconds. If the attachment is compatible with an app that's installed on your iPhone or iPad, you're given the option to transfer the file to that app or directly open or access the file using that app.

If an incoming email message contains an attachment that is not compatible or accessible from your iOS device, you can't open or access it. In this case, you must access this content from your primary computer.

ORGANIZE EMAIL MESSAGES IN FOLDERS

Email messages can easily be moved into another folder, enabling you to better organize your emails. Here's how to do this:

1. From the Inbox listing, tap the Edit button that's located above the Inbox listing. Or, if you're viewing an email message, swipe your finger from right to left across the message listing.

2. Tap the Move option. A menu that offers various folders and options available for that email account are displayed.

3. Tap on the Move Message option, and then tap on the mailbox folder to which you want to move the message. The email message is moved to the folder you select.

> **NOTE** The Move option is also available by swiping from right to left across a message listing from your inbox and then tapping on the More option.

> **TIP** As you're managing incoming and outgoing emails, the Mail app uses the default mailboxes that are already associated with that email account, such as Inbox, Drafts, Sent, Trash, and Junk. For some accounts, you are limited to only these default mailboxes. However, for many types of email accounts, you can create additional mailboxes and then move messages into those mailboxes to organize them.
>
> To create a custom mailbox (assuming that your account allows for this feature), from the Inbox, tap on the Mailboxes icon. When the Mailboxes screen appears, under the Accounts heading, tap on the account for which you want to create a mailbox. A listing of the existing mailboxes for that account is displayed.
>
> Tap on the Edit button at the top of the screen. Then, tap on the New Mailbox icon that appears at the bottom of the screen. Enter the name of the mailbox you want to create, and then tap on the Save button. Your new mailbox is now displayed with that email account. The process works the same on the iPhone and iPad, but the position of the icons varies slightly.

FORWARDING, PRINTING, AND REPLYING TO MESSAGES

As you're reading incoming emails, it's possible to forward a message to some-one else, reply to the message, or print the email by tapping on the left-pointing, curved-arrow icon displayed when you're viewing an email.

When you tap on this icon, as you're reading any email message, a menu offers the following options: Reply, Forward, Save Image, and Print. If the message you're viewing has more than one recipient, an additional option, Reply All, appears.

To reply to the message you're reading, tap on the Reply (or Reply All) option. An email message template appears on the screen that already contains the content of the message you're replying to. Refer to the "Composing an Email Message" section for details on how to write and send an email message from the Mail app.

To forward the email you're reading to another recipient, tap on the Forward icon. If an attachment is associated with the email, you're asked, "Include attachments from original email?" with two options displayed on the screen, Include and Don't Include. Tap on the appropriate response.

When you opt to forward an email, a new message template appears on the screen. However, the content of the message you're forwarding appears in the body of the email message. Start the message-forwarding process by filling in the To field. You can also modify the Subject field (or leave the message's original subject), and then add to the body of the email message with your own text. This text appears above the forwarded message's content.

> **TIP** To forward an email to multiple recipients, enter each person's email address in the To field of the outgoing message, separating each address with a comma (,), or tap on the plus icon (+) that appears to the right of the To field to add more recipients.

When you're ready to forward the message, tap on the Send option, or tap the Cancel button to abort the message-forwarding process.

If you have an AirPrint-compatible printer set up to work with your iOS device, tap the Print option that appears when you tap the left-pointing curved-arrow icon as you're reading an email.

MAIL APP QUICK TIPS

- To refresh your Inbox, swipe your finger downward on the inbox screen (iPhone) or column (iPad).
- As you're reading email, if the text is difficult to see, you can automatically increase the size of all text displayed in the Mail, Contacts, Calendar,

Messages, and Notes apps by adjusting the Accessibility option within Settings. To make this font size adjustment, launch Settings. Select the General option, and then tap on the Accessibility option. From the Accessibility menu screen, tap on the Large Text option.

■ As you're reading emails, all of the touchscreen finger motions you've learned work on the section of the iOS device's screen that's displaying the actual email messages. You can scroll up or down and zoom in or out.

■ While looking at the Home screen on an iPhone 6s or iPhone 6s Plus, press and hold down on the Mail app icon to make the app's Pop menu appear. Four options appear, including All Inboxes (view the Inbox for all of your accounts on a single screen), VIP (view the VIP inbox), Search (enter a keyword or search phrase to find in any of your incoming or outgoing emails), and New Message (used to compose a new message from scratch).

TIP The Mail app also has a Notify Me feature. As you're reading an email, tap on the flag icon and then select the Notify Me option to activate this feature for the message you're reading. Then, when you receive a response from anyone related to this email thread, you are automatically notified. The bell-shaped Notify Me option also appears to the right of the Subject field when composing an email.

COMMUNICATE EFFECTIVELY WITH THE MESSAGES APP

Text messaging and instant messaging were designed to make communications between two or more people fast and easy. Today, "texting" has become a preferred and highly efficient form of communication.

In addition to sending and receiving text-based messages, the Messages app supports the sending and receiving of photos, video messages, and video clips, emoticons, and audio messages.

NOTE If the person you're communicating with via the Messages app has an entry in your Contacts app database, and that entry contains the person's photo, it is displayed in the Messages app; otherwise, the person's initials are displayed by default if the entry contains no photo. Or, if there's no Contacts entry at all for the person, a generic head graphic is used.

Most iPhone service plans have three components: voice, data, and text messaging. When you sign up with a wireless service, choose a paid text-messaging plan that allows for the sending or receiving of a predetermined number of text messages per month or pay for an unlimited text-messaging plan. If your plan has no text messaging component, you are charged for every text message you send or receive. These days, most shared family plans come with unlimited text messaging, however.

There are different types of text messages. There are text-only messages (SMS, or Short Message Service), as well as text messages that can contain a photo or video clip (MMS or Multimedia Messaging Service). These messages can be sent to one or more people simultaneously.

> **NOTE** The Messages app supports audio and video messages when used to communicate with other iMessage users. Instead of typing a message, use the app's audio recording interface to record a short audio message, and then send it to one or more recipients. Alternatively, it's possible to record and send a short video message using one of the cameras that are built in to your iPhone or iPad. How to do this is explained shortly.

On the iPhone, the process of composing, reading, sending, and receiving text, audio, or video messages is done using the Messages app. The Messages app can be used with your cellular service provider's text messaging service and/or Apple's own iMessage service.

> **NOTE** iMessage is a free text-messaging service operated by Apple that utilizes the Internet. It allows iOS mobile device and Mac users to communicate with other iOS device and Mac users, as long as the devices have access to the Internet. This means you can send a message via iMessage if you are connected to the Internet via Wi-Fi, unlike an SMS or MMS text message, which requires a cellular network connection.

> **TIP** Thanks to the Continuity feature, if someone sends your iPhone a text message, the Messages app running on your iPhone can automatically forward the message to your iPad or Mac. Thus, you can send and receive messages via your iPhone's cellular network from any of your Macs or iOS mobile devices linked to the same iCloud account, as long as your iPhone is within about 33 feet of the iPad and/or Mac and Bluetooth is turned on.

> **TIP** From Settings, it's possible to set up the Messages app to store all of your text messages forever, or save internal storage space in your mobile device by adjusting the Keep Messages option to 30 Days or 1 Year. To do this, launch Settings, tap on the Messages option, and then tap on the Keep Message option.

GET STARTED USING THE MESSAGES APP WITH APPLE'S iMESSAGE SERVICE

When your iPhone or iPad is connected to the Internet via a Wi-Fi or cellular data connection, using iMessage with the Messages app, you can communicate via instant messages with other Mac and iOS mobile device users.

Unlike the text-messaging services available through cellular service providers, Apple's iMessage service is free of charge, and it allows for an unlimited number of text messages to be sent and received.

The service also taps into your iPhone or iPad's other functions and allows for the easy sharing of photos, videos, locations, and contacts; plus, it works seamlessly with Notification Center and Siri.

iMessage enables you to participate in text-based, real-time conversations. When someone is actively typing a message to you during a conversation on iMessage, a bubble with three periods in it appears. You can view and respond to the message a fraction of a second after it is sent. When you use cellular-based text messaging via the Messages app, it is possible to send messages to, or receive messages from, any other cell phone, regardless of a user's wireless service provider.

> **NOTE** In addition to using iMessage, many people who are active on Facebook use Facebook Messenger as a way to communicate in real time using text-based instant messages (which can also include photos, video clips, emoticons, and other content), Internet-based audio calling, or video calling via the free Facebook Messenger app, which is available from the App Store.

SET UP A FREE iMESSAGE ACCOUNT

Because traditional text messaging is tied to a cell phone, which has a unique phone number, there is no need to have a separate username or account name when using the text-messaging feature through your cellular service provider. If you know someone's cell phone number, you can send a text message to that person from your cell phone (and vice versa). However, because iMessage is web-based, before using this service, you must set up a free iMessage account.

The first time you launch the Messages app to use it with the iMessage service, you're instructed to set up a free account using your existing Apple ID. Or, instead of using your Apple ID, tap on the Create New Account option to create an account that's linked to another existing email address.

> **NOTE** iPhone users can associate their cell phone numbers with their iMessage accounts to send and receive text messages using this service. However, an Apple ID or existing email address can be used as well.

To do this, you must complete the information requested from the New Account screen. When the requested New Account information is entered, tap on the Done option. Keep in mind that if you simply enter your existing Apple ID/iCloud account information to set up your iMessage account, and then tap on the Sign In icon, the initial process for establishing an iMessage account is quick.

> **TIP** Just as when you're using FaceTime, the unique Apple ID, email address, and/or iPhone phone number you use to set up your iMessage account is how people find you and are able to communicate with you.
>
> So if you want someone to be able to send you messages via iMessage, that person must know the iPhone phone number, Apple ID, or email address you have set up to work with the iMessage account. Likewise, to send someone a text message via iMessage, you need to know the iPhone phone number, Apple ID, or email address the recipient used to set up his or her iMessage account.

> **NOTE** When you send a text message, it is represented as a blue text bubble if you're using the iMessage service. If you're using your cellular service provider's texting service, your text bubbles are displayed in green.

SOME BENEFITS TO USING iMESSAGE

The biggest benefits to using iMessage over other text-messaging services are that it's free and you can send/receive an unlimited number of messages. The Messages app itself also nicely integrates with other features, functions, and apps on your iPhone or iPad.

Another convenient feature of iMessage is that you can begin a text message–based conversation using your iPhone, for example, and switch to using your iPad or Mac to continue that conversation. This, however, is also now possible with all types of text messaging via the Messages app if you turn on the Continuity/Handoff feature.

TIPS AND TRICKS FOR USING THE MESSAGES APP

The Messages app on the iPhone has two main screens: a summary of conversations labeled Messages, and an actual conversation screen labeled at the top of the screen using the name of the person(s) with whom you're conversing. Both of these screens have a handful of icon-based commands that give you access to the app's features and functions.

On the iPad, the Messages screen is divided into two main sections. On the left is a listing of your previous conversations. When Messages is running, the right side of the iPad screen is the active conversation window. From here, you can initiate a new conversation or respond to incoming messages, one at a time.

CREATE AND SEND A TEXT MESSAGE

The first time you launch Messages on the iPad, the New Message screen is visible, the cursor flashes on the To field, and the virtual keyboard is displayed. If you have contact information stored in the Contacts app, as soon as you start typing in the To field, Messages attempts to match up existing contacts with the name, cell phone number, or email address you're currently typing. When the intended recipient's name appears, tap on it.

> **TIP** To initiate a conversation with someone else, tap on the New Message icon that appears in the upper-right corner of the Messages screen on the iPhone or next to the Messages heading on the upper-left side of the iPad's screen.

To quickly search your Contacts database to find one or more recipients for your text messages, you can also tap on the blue-and-white plus icon in the To field as you're composing a new message. A scrollable list of all contacts stored in Contacts displays, along with a Search field you can use to search your contacts database from within the Messages app.

> **TIP** If you're using an iPhone, to use your cellular service provider's SMS text-messaging service to send a message to another cell phone user, enter the recipient's cell phone number in the To field of a new message. This applies if the person doesn't have an entry in your Contacts database.
>
> If you're using an iPhone or iPad to send a message to another iOS mobile device or Mac user via iMessage, in the To field, enter the recipient's Apple ID or the email address the user has linked with his iMessage account. If the person is using an iPhone, his iMessage account might be associated with his iPhone's phone number, based on how he initially set up the account.
>
> In your Contacts database, you can create a separate field for someone's iMessage username, or when viewing the person's Contacts listing, simply tap on the appropriate contact information based on how you want to send the text message.

After filling in the To field with one or more recipients, if you have the Subject feature turned on in Settings, tap on the optional Subject field to create a subject for your text message, and then tap on the blank field located to the left of the Send icon to begin typing your text message. On the iPhone, a blank field for the body of your text message is available, displayed to the left of the Send icon.

If you're sending only text in your message, enter the text and then tap on the Send icon. Or to attach a photo or video clip to your outgoing text message, tap on the camera icon displayed to the left of the field where you're typing the text message.

> **TIP** When you tap on the camera icon as you're composing a text message, two command options are displayed. Tap on the Take Photo or Video option to launch the Camera app from within Messages, and quickly snap a photo or shoot a video clip using your iPhone or iPad's built-in camera.
>
> If you already have the photo or video clip stored on your phone or tablet that you want to share, tap on the Choose Existing option to launch the Photos app in Messages, and then tap on the thumbnail for the photo or video clip you want to attach to the message.

RECORD AND SEND AN AUDIO MESSAGE

When using iMessage, you can record and send short audio messages via the Messages app. To do this, launch Messages, select the person you want to send the message to, and then press and hold your finger on the microphone icon that's displayed to the right of the compose message field. This begins the recording process. Simply start speaking into your iPhone or iPad (shown in Figure 11.13).

Figure 11.13

Press and hold your finger on the microphone icon in the Messages app to record a short audio message.

When you're finished recording, lift your finger from the microphone icon. You can delete the audio message by now tapping on the "X" icon, or send your audio message to the intended recipient by tapping on the up-arrow icon or swiping your finger upward.

Using the Messages app, it's also possible to receive an incoming audio message. Instead of text being displayed, an audio message icon is displayed. Tap on it to play the message.

> **TIP** From within Settings, you can set up the Messages app to automatically delete audio messages after 2 minutes, or keep them forever (or until you manually delete them). Storing audio messages requires additional internal storage space in your iPhone or iPad. To adjust this setting, launch Settings, tap the Messages option, and then from under the Audio Messages heading, tap on the Expire option.
>
> It's also possible to set up the Messages app with the Raise To Listen feature. When turned on, if you receive an incoming audio message, it automatically plays when you pick up the iPhone and hold it up to your ear.

RECORD AND SEND A VIDEO MESSAGE

In addition to text and audio, the Messages app enables you to record and send short video messages using the camera built in to your iPhone or iPad. Again, this feature only works when utilizing the iMessage service.

To record a video clip from within the Messages app, launch the app, choose a recipient, and then tap on the camera icon that's displayed to the left of the text message composition field.

Select the Take Photo or Video option. When a modified version of the Camera app is displayed (shown in Figure 11.14), select the Video shooting mode and record your video. Alternatively, you can select the Photo shooting mode, snap a photo, and send that image to the intended recipient.

Figure 11.14

Tap on the Camera icon to access a scaled-down version of the Camera app (shown here), or press and hold the camera icon to quickly shoot a video message or snap a photo and send it via the Messages app.

When someone sends you an incoming video message, tap on the message icon to play it. From within Settings, it's possible to set up the Messages app to automatically delete incoming video messages 2 minutes after they've been viewed. This enables you to conserve internal storage space on the device. Alternatively, you can select the Never option to store incoming video messages until you manually delete them.

To do this, launch Settings, tap on the Messages option, and then tap on the Expire option that's found under the Video Messages heading. Tap on either the After 2 Minutes or Never option.

> **NOTE**   Audio and video messages can only be received by iPhone, iPad, and iPod touch users who are using the iOS 8 or iOS 9 version of the Messages app, or by Mac users running the OS X Yosemite or OS X El Capitan version of Messages.

> **(iOS 9) WHAT'S NEW**   Using the iPad's new Split Screen feature, you can keep the Messages app running on one side of the screen (and engage in one or more conversations), while at the same time continue working with another app altogether. There's no longer a need to exit out of the app you were using and then relaunch the Messages app to respond to an incoming message, for example.

PARTICIPATING IN A TEXT-MESSAGE CONVERSATION

As soon as you tap Send to initiate a new message conversation and send an initial text, audio, photo, or video message, the New Message window transforms into a conversation window, with the recipient's name displayed at the top center. Displayed on the right side of the conversation window are the messages you've sent. The responses from the person you're conversing with are left-justified and displayed in a different color on the screen with text bubbles (shown in Figure 11.15).

As the text-message–based conversation continues and eventually scrolls off the screen, use your finger to swipe upward or downward to view what's already been said.

> **TIP**   Whenever there's a pause between the sending of a message and the receipt of a response, the Messages app automatically inserts the date and time in the center of the screen so that you can later easily track the time period during which each conversation took place. This is particularly helpful if there are long gaps and the conversation did not take place in real time.

Figure 11.15
A sample text message conversation via the Messages app.

To delete or forward part of a text message, press and hold down that section of the message. A Copy and More option is displayed. Copy enables you to transfer the selected content to your device's virtual clipboard and then copy it elsewhere. The More option enables you to select more of the text message conversation and then delete or forward it by tapping on the trashcan or Forward icon.

> **TIP**   From the Messages conversation screen on an iPad, tap on the Contact icon displayed in the upper-right corner of the conversation window to view the complete Contacts database entry for the person with whom you're conversing.

To delete entire conversations in the Messages app, press and hold one section of the message conversation, and then tap on the More option. Next, tap on the Delete All option to delete the entire conversation. Or from the Messages screen, which lists the individual conversations you've had or are engaged in, swipe your finger across a listing from right to left, and then tap on the Delete option.

RESPONDING TO AN INCOMING MESSAGE

Depending on how you set up the Messages app in Settings, you can be notified of an incoming message in a number of ways. Notification of a new text message can be set to appear in the Notification Center window. Or, if the Messages app is already running, a new message alert is heard and a new message listing appears on the Messages screen (iPhone) or under the Messages heading on the left side of the iPad screen. If you already have the conversation screen open and a new message from that person you're conversing with is received, that message appears on the conversation screen.

> **TIP** When a new message arrives, a blue dot appears to the left of the new message's listing (under the Messages heading on the iPad or on the Messages screen on the iPhone). The blue dot indicates it's a new, unread message.

To read the incoming message and enter into the conversation window and respond, tap on the incoming message listing. If you're looking at the listing in the Notification Center window, for example, and you tap on it, the Messages app launches and the appropriate conversation window automatically opens.

After reading the incoming text message, use the virtual keyboard to type your response in the blank message field, and then tap the Send icon to send the response message.

RELAUNCH OR REVIEW PAST CONVERSATIONS

From the Messages screen on the iPhone, or from the left side of the screen on the iPad when the Messages app is running, you can view a listing of all saved conversations. Each listing displays the person's name, the date and time of the last message sent or received, and a summary of the last message sent or received. Tap on any of the listings to relaunch that conversation in the Conversation window. You can either reread the entire conversation or continue the conversation by sending a message to that person.

> **TIP** By tapping on one listing at a time, you can participate in multiple conversations at once.
>
> On the iPhone, to exit the conversation screen you're currently viewing, tap on the left-pointing arrow icon that's displayed in the upper-left corner of the screen, labeled Messages.
>
> On the iPad, tap on one of the other listings under the Messages heading on the left side of the screen.

From the Messages screen on the iPhone (or the Messages listing on the iPad that's displayed on the left side of the screen), tap on the Edit icon, and then tap on the red-and-white icon that's displayed next to a conversation to quickly delete the entire conversation.

PARTICIPATING IN A GROUP CONVERSATION

If you participate in a group messaging conversation and it becomes too active and annoying, it's possible to opt out of the discussion.

To do this, from the conversation screen, tap on the Details option, and then turn on the Do Not Disturb feature. Turn off this virtual switch if you want to rejoin the conversation later.

To exit out of the conversation altogether, tap on the Details option and select the Leave This Conversation option.

Also from the Details screen, you can add new people to the group conversation by tapping on the Add Contact option.

SHARE MORE INFORMATION FROM THE DETAILS SCREEN DURING A CONVERSATION VIA THE MESSAGES APP

During the conversation, if you want to share your exact location with the other participant(s), tap on the Details option, and then tap on the Send My Current Location option to send a map that depicts your current location. However, if you move from that location, the information is not updated.

If you want to make your whereabouts known to the conversation's participant(s) on an ongoing basis, tap on the Share My Location option, and then choose the Share for One Hour, Share Until End of Day, or Share Indefinitely option by tapping on it.

Because sending and receiving photos and video clips as part of a Messages conversation has become popular, the Messages app now enables users to quickly see a thumbnail summary of all photos or video clips sent or received during each conversation. This eliminates the need to scroll upward on the screen to "rewind" a conversation to re-view a photo or video clip. To view the thumbnail summary, tap on the Details option and then scroll toward the bottom of the Details screen. Tap on any thumbnail to view a larger version of it. Press and hold your finger on the image to copy it into iOS 8's virtual clipboard to paste it into another app or conversation in the Messages app.

CUSTOMIZE THE MESSAGES APP

From Settings, you can customize several settings related to the Messages app. To do this, launch Settings and then tap on the Messages option.

In the Messages setup window, turn on or off the iMessage service altogether, plus make adjustments that are relevant to sending and receiving messages from your iOS mobile device. For example, by adjusting the virtual switch associated with the Send Read Receipts option to the on position, your contacts are notified when you've read their messages.

You can also set preferences for using text messages (SMS and MMS messages) versus iMessage.

If you turn on the virtual switch associated with the Character Count option, as you're composing a new message, the number of characters it contains is automatically displayed.

MESSAGES APP QUICK TIPS

- It's possible to use Siri to dictate and send text messages using your voice. To do this, activate Siri and say something like, "Send text message to Rusty Rich." When Siri says, "What would you like it to say?," speak your message, and then confirm it. When prompted, tell Siri to send the text message you dictated. Siri can also be used to read your newly received text messages, without your having to look at or touch the iOS device's screen.

- If you want to block someone who has an entry in your Contacts database from being able to send you a message via the Messages app, one way to do this is to launch Settings, tap on the Messages option, tap on the Blocked option, and then tap on the Add New option. Select the Contacts entry for the person or company you want to block. To unblock that person, return to the Blocked submenu screen in Settings and swipe your finger from right to left across the blocked person's name.

- To quickly search for something in any of your Messages app conversations, from the Messages screen that lists the conversations in which you're currently participating, tap on the Search field that's displayed at the top of the screen and enter a name, keyword, or phrase you're looking for. You can also access iOS 9's Spotlight Search feature, which includes the content of the Messages app in searches.

IN THIS CHAPTER

- How to use new features in the iOS 9 version of Safari
- How to create and use offline Reading Lists
- How to use Safari Reader
- How to sync open browser windows with your other Macs and iOS mobile devices

12

SURF THE WEB MORE EFFICIENTLY USING SAFARI

Chances are, if you know how to use a Mac or PC, you already know how to surf the Web using a browser such as Safari, Microsoft Internet Explorer, Firefox, or Google Chrome on your computer.

The Safari web browser on your iPhone (shown in Figure 12.1) or iPad (shown in Figure 12.2) offers the same basic functionality as the web browser for your desktop or laptop computer, but it's designed to maximize the iPhone or iPad's touch-screen and screen size.

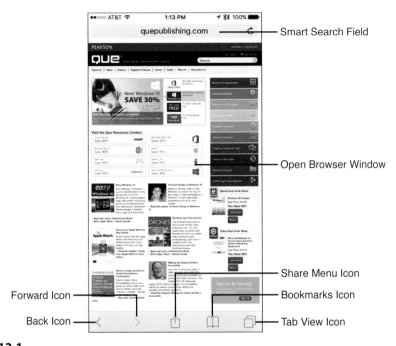

Smart Search Field

Open Browser Window

Share Menu Icon

Forward Icon

Bookmarks Icon

Back Icon

Tab View Icon

Figure 12.1
The main screen of the Safari web browser on the iPhone.

Using the Handoff function, it's possible to begin surfing the Web using Safari on one of your supported Macs or iOS mobile devices and then pick up exactly where you left off on another, as long as all the equipment is linked to the same iCloud account. Only iOS devices with the Lightning connector and 2012 Macs and newer support this feature.

TIP   To turn on the Handoff feature, launch Settings, tap on the General option, and then tap on the Handoff & Suggested Apps option. From the Handoff & Suggested Apps submenu, turn on the virtual switch that's associated with the Handoff option. This must be done on each device. Also turn on your device's Bluetooth feature.

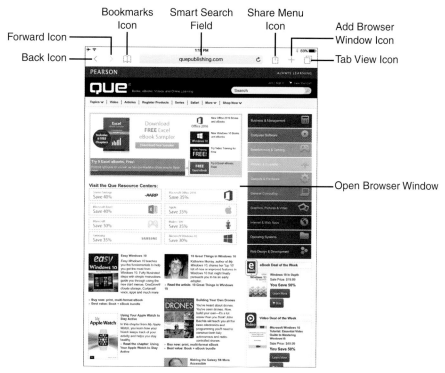

Bookmarks Icon

Smart Search Field

Share Menu Icon

Add Browser Window Icon

Forward Icon

Back Icon

Tab View Icon

Open Browser Window

Figure 12.2

The main screen of the Safari web browser on the iPad.

CUSTOMIZE YOUR WEB SURFING EXPERIENCE

As you'd expect from your iPhone or iPad, surfing the Web is a highly customizable experience. For example, you can hold your device in portrait or landscape mode, and on most websites, also zoom in on or zoom out of specific areas or content. To do this, use the reverse-pinch finger gesture (to zoom in) or the pinch gesture (to zoom out), or double-tap on a specific area of the screen to zoom in or out. Keep in mind that zooming does not work when viewing a mobile optimized website.

To further customize your web surfing experience, launch Settings and tap on the Safari option. The Safari submenu (shown in Figure 12.3) offers a handful of customizable options. Here's a summary of what each is used for:

■ **Search Engine**—The smart Search field is used to enter specific website URLs (addresses) and to find what you're looking for on the Web via a search engine, such as Google, Yahoo!, Bing, or DuckDuckGo. This option enables you to select your default (favorite) Internet search engine. So if you select Google as your default, whenever you perform a search using Safari's Search field, the browser automatically accesses Google to obtain your search results.

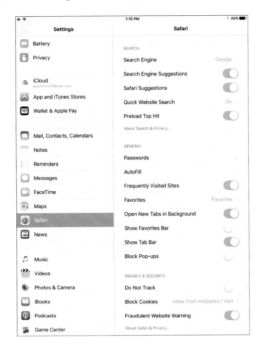

Figure 12.3

Customize your web surfing experience when using Safari from within Settings on your iOS device.

☑ TIP The Safari-related Settings options, labeled Search Engine Suggestions, Spotlight Suggestions, Quick Website Search, and Preload Top Hit can be turned on or off from within Settings.

Search Engine Suggestions, for example, automatically offers additional (related) search term suggestions when you enter a website address or search term in Safari's Search field.

Spotlight Suggestions shows related websites when you perform a search using iOS 9's Spotlight Search feature.

Quick Website Search can be used to search a specific website for a specific term. For example, enter "Wiki New York" into the Search field to access the Wikipedia website and display information related to New York.

Turn on the Preload Top Hit option if you want your favorite and most frequented websites to be displayed first when performing a relevant search.

These options determine when website suggestions are offered when using Safari's Search field, Spotlight Search, or other search-related functions.

> **NOTE** DuckDuckGo.com is a search engine that does not track your web surfing behaviors or activities, so it offers a more private experience. However, you can utilize Safari's enhanced Privacy features to prevent your web surfing activities from being tracked.
>
> To do this, from the Safari menu within Settings, turn on the virtual switch that's associated with the Do Not Track option (refer to Figure 12.3).
>
> It's also possible to open a private browsing session by tapping on the browser window icon and then tapping on the Private option.

■ **Passwords**—Safari can automatically store the passwords you create and use to access various websites. By accessing this feature, you can view the stored database of website-related passwords collected by Safari and edit this database by tapping on the Edit option.

■ **Autofill**—When turned on, this feature helps you fill in online-based forms by remembering your responses and automatically inserting your information into the appropriate fields. It also pulls information from your own Contacts app entry. Autofill is particularly useful when shopping online.

To customize this option and link your personal contact entry to Safari, tap on the AutoFill option, turn on the Use Contact Info option, and then tap on My Info to select your own Contacts entry.

You can also set whether Safari remembers names and passwords for specific websites you visit, as well as credit card information that you use to make online purchases. Tap on the Saved Credit Cards option to add or edit credit card information you have securely stored in Safari for use when making online purchases. This functionality is part of what Apple calls iCloud Keychain.

- **Frequently Visited Websites**—Turn on this feature to display websites you frequent the most often when performing a search, as well as before you enter information into Safari's Search field or into Spotlight Search.

- **Favorites**—This feature serves as a shortcut for accessing websites you frequently visit or that you have favorited. As you begin typing a website address or website name into the Search field, Safari accesses your Favorites list and auto-inserts the appropriate website URL. When you tap on the Search field, a screen with icons representing sites in your Favorites list is displayed. Your Favorites list of websites automatically syncs between your Macs, PCs, and iOS mobile devices that are linked to the same iCloud account. This option now allows you to choose a specific folder where your favorite bookmarks are stored in the device you're using.

> **TIP** If you've created custom Bookmark folders when using Safari on your Mac, you can access and manage them from your iOS mobile device. Plus from the Favorite option within Settings, you can make one of these custom folders your default.

- **Open Links (iPhone only)**—Anytime a new web page opens as a result of you tapping on a link, this feature determines whether the new browser window is opened as the new active browser window or opened in the background as a tabbed browser window.

- **Open New Tabs in Background (iPad only)**—Anytime a new web page opens as a result of you tapping on a link, this feature determines whether the new browser window is opened as the new active browser window or opened in the background as a tabbed browser window. How this option works depends on options you have selected on the Safari submenu of Settings.

- **Show Favorites Bar (iPad)**—When you turn on the virtual switch associated with this feature, your Favorites Bar displays across the top of the Safari screen, just below the row of command icons and the Search field. The default setting for this feature is off because it utilizes some of your onscreen real estate.

- **Show Tab Bar (iPad)**—When turned on, if multiple browser windows are open in Safari, tabs for each window are displayed along the top of the screen, just below the row of command icons and the Search field. The default setting for this feature is on. This makes it faster and easier to quickly switch between open browser windows.

■ **Block Pop-Ups**—When turned on, this feature prevents a website you're visiting from creating and displaying extra windows or opening a bunch of unwanted browser tabs. The default for this option is turned on because this makes for a more enjoyable web surfing experience.

■ **Do Not Track**—By default, when you surf the Web using Safari, the web browser remembers all the websites you visit and creates a detailed History list that you can access to quickly revisit websites. By turning on the Do Not Track feature, Safari does not store details about the websites you visit.

■ **Block Cookies**—Many websites use cookies to remember who you are and your personalized preferences when you're visiting that site. Cookies contain data that gets saved in your iPhone or iPad and is accessible by the websites you revisit. When this option is turned on, Safari does not accept cookies from websites you visit. Thus, you must reenter site-specific preferences and information each time you visit that site. The Block Cookies submenu offers four options: Always Block (meaning all cookies are blocked), Allow from Current Websites Only, Allow from Websites I Visit, and Always Allow (meaning no cookies are blocked).

■ **Fraudulent Website Warning**—Turn on this feature to help prevent you from visiting impostor websites designed to look like real ones, which have been created for the purpose of committing fraud or identity theft. It's not foolproof, but this feature gives you an added level of protection, especially if you use your iOS device for online banking, shopping, and other financial transactions.

■ **Clear History and Website Data**—Use this feature to delete the contents of Safari's History folder in which details about all the websites you have visited are stored. At the same time, cookies (data pertaining to specific websites you've visited) are also deleted.

■ **Use Cellular Data**—This option enables your iPhone or iPad to use the cellular data service (as opposed to a Wi-Fi Internet connection) to download Reading List information to your device from your iCloud account so that it can be read offline. Although this feature is convenient, it also utilizes some of your monthly cellular data allocation, which is why an on/off option is associated with it. The option is available on all iPhones, as well as iPads with Cellular + Wi-Fi capabilities.

■ **Advanced**—From this submenu, view details about website-specific data that Safari has collected. If you choose, you can manually delete this information. You also can enable or disable the JavaScript feature.

HOW TO USE TABBED BROWSING WITH SAFARI

Safari's main screen contains the various command icons used to navigate the Web. On the iPhone, these icons are displayed along the bottom of the Safari screen, while the smart Search field is displayed along the top of the screen.

If you're using Safari on an iPad, the Title bar displays all of Safari's command icons along the top of the screen. Immediately below the Title bar, if you have the option turned on, your personalized Favorites Bar is displayed. Below the Favorites Bar, the Tabs bar becomes visible if you have more than one web page loaded in Safari at any given time (and you have this featured turned on).

SWITCHING BETWEEN WEB PAGES ON AN iPHONE

The iPhone version of tabbed browsing involves Safari opening separate browser windows for each active web page. Tap on the Tab View icon located in the bottom-right corner of the Safari screen to quickly switch between open browser windows (shown in Figure 12.4), because only one at a time can be viewed.

Open Browser Windows

Add Browser Window Icon

Private Surfing Feature ——— Private   +   Done ——— Done Option

Figure 12.4

Safari's Tab view is shown here on the iPhone. To open a new page, tap on the + option near the bottom center of the screen or tap on a web page preview thumbnail to open it.

> **✓ TIP** If you press on the + option for a second or two, a Recently Closed Tabs menu screen appears. You can easily reopen a previously visited but closed browser window by tapping an item listed (which is based on your personal web surfing history).

When you're viewing the Tab View screen, tap on the New Browser Window (+) icon to create a new (empty) browser window and then manually surf to a new website by typing a URL or search term into the Smart Search field, selecting a favorite icon, or selecting a bookmark.

> **✓ TIP** When viewing the Tab View screen in Safari, tap on the Private option to turn on the Private web surfing mode only for the newly open browser windows. This prevents Safari from storing details about the websites you visit and syncing this information with your iCloud account. When you're using this privacy feature, the background color of Safari's toolbar changes to dark gray.

To switch between active (viewable) browser windows that are open, simply tap on one of the web page thumbnails displayed. Scroll through the browser window thumbnails using an upward or downward swipe motion with your finger as needed. To close a window (tab), tap on its "X" icon.

> **✓ TIP** To access browser windows open on your other computers or iOS mobile devices, scroll down to the bottom of the Tab View screen (on the iPhone) to see listings for open browser windows on your Mac(s) and/or other iOS mobile devices linked to the same iCloud account (shown in Figure 12.5). Tap on any of these listings to pick up exactly where you left off on that other device.

Tap the Done option to exit the Tab View screen and return to the main Safari web browser screen. Alternatively, tap on any web page thumbnail displayed in the Tab View screen to open that browser window and continue your web surfing experience at the selected web page.

Figure 12.5

Access browser windows on your iPhone that were left open on any of your Macs or other iOS mobile devices linked to the same iCloud account.

TABBED BROWSING ON THE iPAD

When you tap on a link in a web page that causes a new web page to automatically open, a new tab in Safari is created and displayed. Tabs are shown in Figure 12.6, and each represents a separate open browser window.

Figure 12.6

On the iPad, open browser window tabs are displayed along the top of the screen. Tap on a tab to quickly switch between open browser windows.

> **NOTE** Keep in mind that on the iPad, tabs are not displayed if the Show Tab Bar option is turned off from the Safari submenu of Settings. Turning off the Show Tab Bar and Show Settings Bar enables you to save onscreen real estate that can then be used to display more of the web pages you're visiting. Having these features turned on, however, makes switching between browser windows and reloading frequently visited websites a faster and more convenient process.

As you're viewing a web page, to simultaneously open another web page, tap on the New Browser Window (+) icon displayed near the top-right corner of the Safari screen (between the Share and Tab View icons). When you do this, a new tab is created for an empty browser window. This allows you to visit a different web page without closing the web page(s) you're currently viewing.

The Tab bar can display multiple tabs at once. To instantly switch between web pages, tap on the desired tab. The website name (or web page title) is displayed in the tab for easy reference.

To close a tab, tap on the small x that appears on the left side of that tab.

> **TIP** As you're surfing the Web using your iPad, tap on the Tab View icon located in the top-right corner of the screen to display all the open browser windows on each of your other Macs and/or iOS mobile devices linked to the same iCloud account. Tap on any of these preview windows or listings to open that browser window on your iPad and pick up exactly where you left off when using the other computer or device.
>
> In the example shown in Figure 12.7, the iPad mini 4 is being used, and it's linked to the same iCloud account as an iPhone 6s and iPad Air 2.

> **CAUTION** With the Handoff feature turned on, as you're surfing the Web on your iPhone or iPad, someone can literally follow along and see what web pages you're visiting in real time if they're using Safari on one of your Macs or other iOS mobile devices; that is, if they're signed in using your iCloud account. To prevent this, activate Safari's Private Browsing feature and turn off the Handoff feature.

Open Browser Window Thumbnails
(on the iPad mini 4)

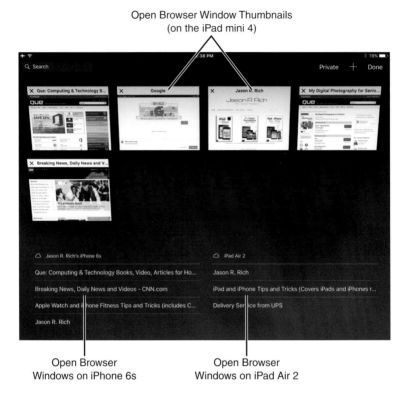

Open Browser
Windows on iPhone 6s

Open Browser
Windows on iPad Air 2

Figure 12.7

Access any browser window that was left open on your Mac(s) or other iOS mobile devices when you tap on the Switch Browser Window icon that's displayed in the top-right corner of the Safari screen when using an iPad.

REMOVE SCREEN CLUTTER WITH SAFARI'S READER OPTION

Not to be confused with Safari's Reading List feature (which is explained shortly), Safari Reader enables you to select a compatible website page; strip out graphic icons, ads, and other unwanted elements that cause onscreen clutter; and then read just the text (and view related photos) from that web page.

The Safari Reader works only with compatible websites, including those published by major daily newspapers and other news organizations. If the feature is available while you're viewing a web page, the Reader icon (as shown in Figure 12.8 and Figure 12.9) is displayed before that web page's URL on the extreme left side of the Smart Search field.

Reader Icon

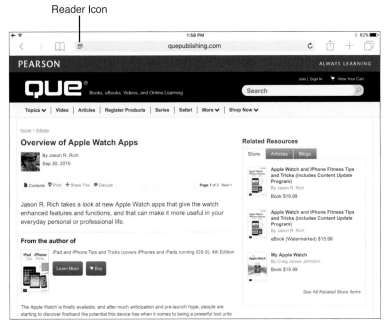

Figure 12.8

An article from QuePublishing.com, without the Reader feature active.

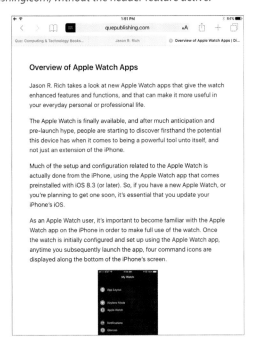

Figure 12.9

The same article from QuePublishing.com but with the Reader feature active.

When you see the Reader icon displayed, tap on it. An uncluttered screen that contains just the article or text from that web page, along with related photos, is displayed. Use your finger to scroll up or down.

iOS 9 WHAT'S NEW When using the Reader feature, tap on the "aA" icon that's displayed on the right side of the Smart Search field within Safari to access a new menu that enables you to change the font used to display the text, as well as decrease or increase the size of the text (shown in Figure 12.10).

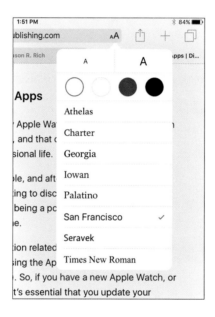

Figure 12.10
From this new menu, it's possible to adjust the font and font size used to display the text when using Safari's Reader feature.

Tap the Reader icon a second time to exit the Reader window and return the web page to its normal appearance.

CREATE AND MANAGE READING LISTS

As you're surfing the Web, you might come across specific web pages, articles, or other information that you want to refer to later. In Safari, it's possible to create a bookmark for that website URL and have it displayed as part of your Bookmarks list or as part of your Favorites Bar. Another option is to add a web page to your Reading List within Safari. In addition to just storing the web page's URL, Reading List stores the actual content of that page for later viewing (including offline viewing).

> **NOTE** The Reading List feature downloads entire web pages for offline viewing, as opposed to simply storing website addresses that you can refer to later. Although this feature downloads text and photos associated with a web page, it does not download animated graphics, video, or audio content associated with that page.

To add a website or web-based article to your personalized Reading List for later review, tap on the Share icon and then tap on the Add to Reading List icon displayed as part of Safari's Share menu.

To later access your Reading List to view any of the stored web pages or articles, tap on the Bookmarks icon and then tap on the Reading List tab. Figure 12.11 shows an example of a Reading List. The Reading List tab looks like eyeglasses.

Reader List Tab

Articles from the Web Stored within Reading List

Figure 12.11

Creating a Reading List is another way to store links related to specific content on the Web that you want to easily be able to find again and access later.

> **✓ TIP**   Like your Bookmarks list and Favorites Bar, the items stored in your Reading List automatically sync with your iCloud account and are almost instantly made available on any other computer or iOS device linked to your iCloud account.

WORKING WITH BOOKMARKS

When you tap on the Bookmarks icon on an iPad, the Bookmarks menu appears along the left side of the screen. It remains visible until you tap the Bookmarks icon again.

On the iPhone, when you tap the Bookmarks icon, the Bookmarks menu is displayed on a new screen in the Safari app.

At the top of the Bookmarks menu are three tabs. The leftmost tab (shaped like a book) is the Bookmarks tab. When you tap on it, your saved list of website bookmarks is displayed. The center tab is the Reading List tab. Tap on it to reveal your reading list (refer to Figure 12.11).

The Shared Links tab (represented by the @ symbol) enables you to see a listing of website links shared with you by your Contacts, as well as subscriptions to RSS feeds or social media accounts (including Twitter). Set this up by tapping on the Subscriptions option that's displayed in the lower-right corner of this menu.

After you tap on the Subscriptions option, add compatible social media accounts (such as Twitter), or if you're visiting a website or blog that has an RSS feed associated with it, visit that site and tap on the Add Current Site option to make it a subscribed feed. From the Subscriptions panel that's displayed, you can then delete a subscribed feed by tapping on its corresponding "-" icon.

> **✎ NOTE**   All of your bookmarks and Safari-related information syncs automatically with your iCloud account and becomes accessible when using any iPhone, iPad, or Mac that's linked to the same iCloud account. This happens when the iCloud-related Safari feature is turned on from within the iCloud submenu of Settings.

OPTIONS FOR SHARING WEB CONTENT IN SAFARI

The iOS 9 version of Safari makes sharing web links and managing web page content extremely easy, thanks to a handful of available options offered by the expanded Share menu.

The Share menu (shown in Figure 12.12), which is accessible by tapping on the Share icon, offers a variety of features for sharing, printing, and managing web page content.

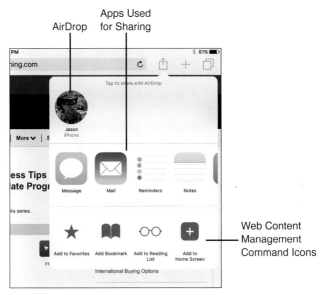

Figure 12.12

Safari's expanded Share menu offers a handful of ways to store, manage, print, and share web page content.

NOTE The options that are available to you from the Share menu vary depending on several factors, including the content you're viewing, as well as whether you have Facebook, Twitter, and other apps set up to work with iOS 9.

TIP If you have the AirDrop feature turned on, when you access the Share menu, the AirDrop option is available. This enables you to wirelessly share content with nearby (compatible) Mac, iPhone, iPad, or iPod touch users. Some older Mac and iOS mobile device models don't support AirDrop.

To turn on AirDrop, open Control Center and tap on the AirDrop button. Next, choose whether you want to communicate wirelessly with Contacts Only or all AirDrop users in your immediate vicinity.

The following options are often available from the Share menu, but vary based on the content you're viewing and how you have integration with some Sharing-related options set up:

- **Message**—Send details about the web page you're currently viewing to one or more other people via text or instant message using the Messages app (without having to leave Safari). Tap on Message, fill in the To field, and then tap the Send button. The website URL is automatically embedded within the text or instant message.

- **Mail**—To share a website URL with others via email, as you're looking at the web page or website you want to share, tap on the Share icon and select the Mail option. In Safari, an outgoing email window appears.

  Fill in the To field with the recipient's email address and tap the Send icon. The website URL automatically is embedded in the body of the email, with the website's heading used as the email's subject. Before sending the email, it's possible to add text to the body of the email message and/or change the Subject.

> **(iOS 9) WHAT'S NEW** The ability to export web page content from Safari and place it directly as a new item into a list in the Reminders app or new page in a notebook in the Notes app is a useful new iOS 9 feature.

- **Reminders**—Create a new item within one of your lists in the Reminders app that contains the web page URL and content that you're currently viewing. Tap on Options to choose which Reminders list the web page content should be added to, add a date/time and/or location-based alert, set a Priority, and add optional text-based notes with the new reminder.

- **Notes**—Use this feature to gather the content from the web page you're viewing and quickly export it into a note in the Notes app. After tapping on the Notes app icon displayed as part of the Share menu, tap on the Choose Note option to select an existing note in the Notes app to add the web page content to, or select the New Note option to create a new Note from scratch. You can also add text-based notes to the web page content by tapping on the Add Text To Your Note option (shown in Figure 12.13).

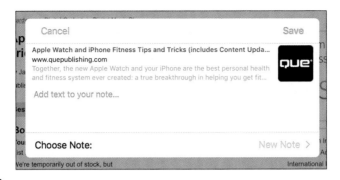

Figure 12.13

Export the contents of a web page (and its URL) directly into the Notes app as a new page, or add the web page content to an existing note page.

- **Twitter**—If you have an active Twitter account enabled in Settings, tap on the Twitter option to create an outgoing tweet that automatically has the website URL attached.

  When the Twitter window appears, enter your tweet message (up to 140 characters, minus the length of the automatically shortened version of the website URL). Tap the Send icon when the message is composed and ready to share with your Twitter followers.

> **✓ TIP** If you're managing multiple Twitter accounts from your iOS mobile device, in the outgoing tweet window, tap on the From field, and then select from which of your Twitter accounts you want to send the tweet you're composing.

- **Facebook**—Thanks to Facebook integration within iOS 9, when you tap on the Facebook option, you can update your Facebook status and include details about the web page you're currently viewing.

- **Other Compatible Third-Party Apps**—A growing number of third-party apps now allow you to export content from Safari to be imported into another app or shared via another app. When you have one or more of these compatible apps installed on your iPhone or iPad, app icons for them are displayed in the Share menu.

■ **More (Top)**—Located to the extreme right of the app icons related to Safari's Share feature is a More icon. Tap on it to customize which app icons appear in Safari's Share menu and to reorder these app icons (by placing your finger on an app icon's Move icon and dragging it up or down in the Activities list). Tap on the Done option to save your changes.

■ **Add To Favorites**—Add a listing for the website you're currently viewing to your Safari Favorites list. This list syncs with iCloud and will be updated on all the Macs, PCs, and iOS mobile devices that you have linked to the same iCloud account.

■ **Add Bookmark**—Tap on this option to add a bookmark to your personal Bookmarks list. When you opt to save a bookmark, an Add Bookmark window appears. Here, you can enter a title for the bookmark and decide whether you want to save it as part of your Bookmarks menu or in your Favorites Bar. It's also possible to create separate subfolders in your Bookmarks menu to organize your saved bookmarks.

> **NOTE** When using Safari on the iPhone, you can maintain a Favorites list; however, to conserve onscreen space, a Favorites Bar is not displayed across the top of the Safari screen like it is on an iPad. Instead, on an iPhone, the Favorites list is displayed as an additional Bookmark folder when you tap on the Bookmarks icon.
>
> When using an iPad, if you turn off the Show Favorites Bar option (found on the Safari submenu within Settings), this is also the case.

■ **Add to Reading List**—Instead of adding a web page URL to your Bookmarks list or Favorites Bar, you can save it in your Reading List for later reference. (It is downloaded to your iPhone or iPad for later viewing, even if no Internet connection is then available.) To access your Reading List, tap on the Bookmarks icon, and then tap on the Reading List tab.

■ **Add to Home Screen**—Save a website URL in the form of a Home screen icon. This feature is explained later in the "Launch Your Favorite Websites Quickly with Home Screen Icons" section.

■ **Copy**—Use this command to copy the URL for the web page you're looking at to the virtual clipboard that's built in to iOS 9. You can then paste that information into another app.

■ **Print**—Wirelessly print a website's contents to any AirPrint-compatible printer that's set up to work with your iOS mobile device. To print a web page, tap on the Print command. From the Printer Options screen, select the printer you want to use, and then choose the number of copies you want printed. Tap the Print icon at the bottom of the Print Options window to send the web page document to your printer.

■ **Find On Page**—This iOS 9 feature enables you to quickly search the open web page for a keyword or search phrase. When you tap on this icon, the iPhone or iPad's virtual keyboard appears, along with a new Search field. Type what you're looking for, and the matching text is highlighted in yellow within the web page you're viewing (shown in Figure 12.14). Use the up and down arrow icons to scroll through the various search results one at a time. Tap the Done option to exit this feature.

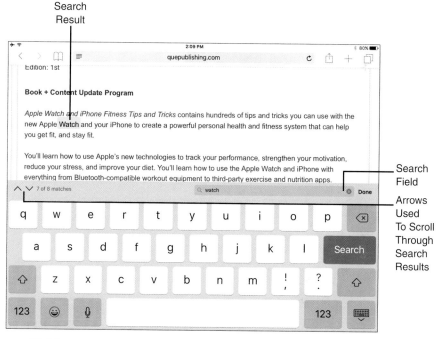

Figure 12.14

Search for occurrences of a specific word or search phrase in the web page you're currently viewing using the new Find On Page feature.

■ **Request Desktop Site**—Anytime you visit a website using the iOS 9 edition of Safari, if a mobile version of the website is offered, that's the version of the website that automatically loads. A mobile website has been custom formatted to accommodate the smaller iPhone or iPad screen size (compared to a full-sized computer monitor). However, if you'd prefer to switch to viewing the Desktop version of the website, tap on the Request Desktop Site icon, and if available, this version of the website loads. You can then use the zoom in and zoom out finger gestures, as well as swipe finger gestures to navigate around the web page.

■ **More (Bottom)**—This More icon is located to the extreme right of the second row of command icons displayed in the Share menu. From the Activities menu, adjust the order in which the command icons are displayed in the Share menu, plus customize some options that relate to third-party apps and your ability to share Safari content with those apps.

CREATE, MANAGE, AND SYNC SAFARI BOOKMARKS

Your iOS device automatically syncs your Bookmarks and related Safari data with your other iOS mobile devices, as well as the compatible web browsers on your primary computer(s).

To activate iCloud sync functionality as it relates to Safari, launch Settings and then tap on the iCloud option. When the iCloud Control Panel appears, make sure your iCloud account is listed at the top of the screen and then turn on the virtual switch associated with the Safari option. This must be done on each of your iOS mobile devices just once.

Once this feature is turned on, your Bookmarks list, Favorites Bar, open browser windows (tabs), Safari Reading List, and Keychain data are automatically and continuously synced with your iCloud account. Thus, when you add a new bookmark while surfing the Web on your iPad, for example, within seconds that same bookmark appears in your Bookmarks list on your iPhone and on Safari that's running on your Mac.

> **TIP**   For Windows PC users, if you download the optional iCloud for Windows software (www.apple.com/icloud/setup/pc.html), your Bookmarks and related web browser data on your PC sync with your iOS mobile device(s) and Mac(s), and vice versa. Simply add a check mark to the Bookmarks option displayed in the iCloud Control Panel. This feature is compatible with the Windows version of the Internet Explorer, Firefox, and Chrome web browsers. When prompted, simply select which web browser you want to sync your Safari bookmarks and data with.

SYNC USERNAMES AND PASSWORDS USING iCLOUD KEYCHAIN

When the iCloud Keychain feature is turned on (on each of your iOS mobile devices and Macs), anytime you enter a username and password for a website you visit, Safari stores that information and syncs it in your personal iCloud account. Then, anytime you revisit that website on any of your Macs or iOS mobile devices that are linked to the same iCloud account, your username and password for that website are remembered and you're automatically logged in.

> **NOTE** iCloud Keychain also remembers credit card information you use when making online purchases from a website. All usernames, passwords, and credit card details are stored using 256-bit AES encryption to maintain security.

To turn on and begin using iCloud Keychain, launch Settings and tap on the iCloud option. Then, from the iCloud Control Panel, turn on the virtual switch that's associated with the Keychain option. Follow the onscreen prompts that walk you through the feature's built-in security precautions.

Next, return to the main Settings menu and tap on the Safari option. Tap on the AutoFill option and turn on the virtual switches associated with the Use Contact Info, Names and Password, and/or Credit Cards options. Also, tap on the My Info option and select your own entry from your Contacts app database.

> **NOTE** For your security, online banking, credit card, and financial websites do not support iCloud Keychain. When you visit these websites, Safari might remember your username, but you must manually enter your password each time.

When using this feature, it's a good strategy to also activate the Passcode Lock feature of your iOS mobile device to prevent unauthorized people from accessing personal information when using your iPhone or iPad to surf the Web.

> **TIP** If you also want iCloud Keychain to store your credit card details for when you shop online, turn on the virtual switch associated with the Credit Cards option. Then, tap on the Saved Credit cards option and enter your credit card details. This needs to be done only once.

Using iCloud Keychain, you no longer need to remember the unique usernames and passwords that you associate with each of the websites you frequently visit. Plus, to make your web surfing experience even more secure, you can use the built-in Password Generator feature to create highly secure passwords for you (which the web browser then remembers).

LAUNCH YOUR FAVORITE WEBSITES QUICKLY WITH HOME SCREEN ICONS

A time-saving alternative to creating bookmarks for your most frequented websites is to create a Home screen icon for each of these websites. When you do this, an icon for that website is displayed on your device's Home screen. When you tap on it, Safari launches and the selected website automatically loads.

To create a Home screen icon, surf to one of your favorite websites. After it loads, tap on the Share icon and then tap on the Add to Home Screen button.

The Add to Home window appears. It displays a thumbnail image of the website you're visiting and enables you to enter the title for the website (which is displayed below the icon on your device's Home screen). Keep the title short. When you've created the title (or if you decide to keep the default title that Safari creates), tap on the Add option in the upper-right corner of the window.

> **NOTE** When you use the Add to Home feature, if you're creating a shortcut for a website designed to be compatible with an iPhone or iPad, a special logo or related icon (as opposed to a web page thumbnail) is displayed.

Safari closes, and you are returned to your device's Home screen. Displayed on the Home screen is what looks like a new app icon; however, it's really a link to your favorite website. Tap on this icon to automatically launch Safari from the Home screen and load your web page.

After you create a Home screen icon for a web page, it can be treated like any other app icon. You can move it around on the Home screen, add the icon to a folder, or delete the icon from the Home screen.

> **TIP** Without manually launching Safari, it's possible to look up and access web content using the Spotlight Search feature built in to iOS 9. Plus, Siri is also fully compatible with Safari. Activate Siri and use verbal commands like, "Launch Safari," "Search the web for [insert topic]," or "Google [insert topic]." It's also possible to ask a question and have Siri search the Web for the answer.

IN THIS CHAPTER

- Get acquainted with the Calendar, Contacts, and Reminders apps
- Rediscover the newly enhanced Notes app
- Stay organized, on time, and productive with your iOS mobile device
- Sync your app data across all your devices and iCloud

13

TIPS FOR USING CALENDAR, CONTACTS, REMINDERS, AND NOTES

Veteran iPhone or iPad users will quickly discover that the Contacts, Calendar, and Reminders apps that come bundled with iOS 9 have the same core functionality as before. However, the Notes app is packed with new features and tools that are useful for note taking, gathering information from a variety of sources, and then organizing and sharing your digital notes.

The Calendar, Contacts, Reminders, and Notes apps continue to be fully compatible with iCloud, which makes synchronizing your app-related data a straightforward process. Plus, from any computer or mobile device that's connected to the Internet, it's possible to access the online versions of these apps, which are automatically populated with all of your most current app-specific data.

Plus, in Notification Center, the Calendar and Reminders apps can easily be set up so alerts, alarms, and notifications related to your schedule and lists are consistently displayed as part of the Today screen.

> **NOTE** The features and functions offered by the Calendar, Contacts, Reminders, and Notes apps are virtually identical on all iOS mobile devices, as well as on the Mac. However, due to varying screen sizes, the location of specific command icons, options, and menus often varies. After you get to know how each app works in general, you can easily switch between the iPhone, iPad, Mac, and/or the iCloud.com online-based versions of these apps without confusion.

SYNC APP-SPECIFIC DATA WITH ONLINE-BASED APPS

To sync your Calendar, Contacts, Reminders, and/or Notes data with Yahoo!, Google, or Microsoft Exchange–compatible software, launch Settings and tap on the Mail, Contacts, Calendars option. Under the Accounts heading, tap on Add Account. Choose which type of account you want to sync data with, such as iCloud, Microsoft Exchange, Google, Yahoo!, AOL, or Outlook.com. Tap on the Other option if you use alternate contact management and/or scheduling software that supports the industry-standard LDAP or CardDAV protocols.

When prompted, enter your name, email address, password, and an account description (as well as any other requested information). After your account is verified, a menu screen in Settings related to that account lists app-specific options, such as Mail, Contacts, Calendars, Reminders, and/or Notes. Turn on the virtual switch associated with any or all of these options. Your iPhone or iPad can automatically and continuously sync your app-specific data on your iOS device with your online-based account. So, if you turn on the virtual switch associated with Calendars, for example, your schedule data is continuously synchronized.

To sync scheduling and/or contact-related data with Facebook, launch Settings and tap on the Facebook option. When prompted, enter your Facebook username and password. Then, near the bottom of the Facebook menu screen in Settings, turn on the virtual switch that's associated with Calendars and/or Contacts.

Periodically tap on the Update All Contacts option as you add new online Facebook friends. Calendar and/or Contacts data is imported from Facebook and incorporated into your Calendar and/or Contacts apps. This includes profile pictures of your online friends who also have an entry in your Contacts database.

SYNC APP-SPECIFIC DATA WITH iCLOUD

The Calendar, Contacts, Reminders, and Notes apps work seamlessly when sync-ing data between your iOS mobile devices, Mac(s), and PC(s) that are linked to the same iCloud account. To set up this feature, launch Settings, tap on the iCloud option, and then turn on the virtual switches associated with Contacts, Calendars, Reminders, and/or Notes. This needs to be done only once, but it must be done separately on each device or computer that's linked to the same iCloud account.

> **NOTE** By setting up app-specific data syncing for Contacts, Calendar, Notes, and Reminders via iCloud, your data automatically gets imported into the online version of these apps that are available via iCloud.com (www.iCloud.com). So, when you sign in to iCloud.com using your Apple ID and password, and then launch the online version of Contacts, Calendar, Notes, or Reminders, all of your current app-specific data is available to you. This can be done from any computer or mobile device that's connected to the Internet, even if that computer or device is not normally linked to your iCloud account.

GET ACQUAINTED WITH THE CALENDAR APP

With its multiple viewing options for keeping track of the scheduling informa-tion stored in it, the Calendar app is a highly customizable scheduling tool. In the Calendar app, any appointment, meeting, activity, or entry that you create and store within the app is referred to as an *event*.

Because the Calendar app can manage and display multiple color-coded calendars at once, when you create a new event, be sure to choose which calendar it gets stored in. For example, you can maintain separate calendars for Work, Personal, Family, Travel, and/or for whatever organization you volunteer for and allocate time to.

From within Calendar, you can also share some or all of your schedule information with colleagues and maintain several separate, color-coded calendars to keep per-sonal and work-related responsibilities, as well as individual projects, listed sepa-rately, while still being able to view them on the same screen.

> **TIP** When you turn on iCloud's Family Sharing feature, a separate color-coded calendar labeled Family is created in the Calendar app. This calendar can be accessed by up to five other family members. Thus, your teens can add details about their after-school activities, sports practices, or drama rehearsals, while weekend family events can be viewed for all to see. Plus, everyone can keep tabs on upcoming vacation dates.

While the Family calendar data is viewable by anyone with Family Sharing access, events stored within other calendars remain private, or viewable only by people you invite to see the information.

More information about setting up iCloud's Family Sharing feature can be found in Chapter 5, "Use iCloud and the iCloud Drive App from Your iPhone or iPad."

CONTROLLING THE CALENDAR VIEW

Launch Calendar from your iOS device's Home screen, and then choose in which viewing perspective you'd like to view your schedule data. Regardless of which view you're using, tap on the Today option to immediately jump to the current date on the calendar. The current date is always highlighted with a red dot.

(iOS 9) **WHAT'S NEW** From the Home screen of the iPhone 6s or iPhone 6s Plus, press and hold your finger on the Calendar app icon to make an Add Event option appear (shown in Figure 13.1). Tap on this to quickly launch the Calendar app and access the New Event screen.

Figure 13.1

Quickly access the New Event screen within the Calendar app by pressing and holding down the Calendar app icon when viewing the Home screen of the iPhone 6s or iPhone 6s Plus.

(iOS 9) **WHAT'S NEW** If event-related information is displayed in an incoming email, such as an upcoming airline flight reservation or restaurant reservation, the Mail app displays an Add Event banner near the top of the email. Tap on this banner (which includes a tiny Calendar app icon) to import the event details from the body of the incoming email directly into the Calendar app as a new event.

On the iPad, switching between Calendar views is as easy as tapping on the Day, Week, Month, or Year tab displayed at the top center of the Calendar app screen.

On the iPhone and iPad, the Calendar app opens on the last view option that you were using previously. However, on the iPhone, you also have access to a detailed Day, Week, Month, or Year view, as well as a Listing view, which works with the Month or Day view.

> **TIP** When the Month calendar view is selected, tap on the Listing icon (which appears near the top-right corner of the screen) to display a list of events for the current day (or the day you select). This information is displayed below the month view of the calendar (shown in Figure 13.2).
>
> When you select the Day view in the Calendar app, the Listing icon shows you all your appointments, hour-by-hour, in a scrollable format that enables you to quickly see your schedule for the previous or upcoming days in addition to the currently selected day.

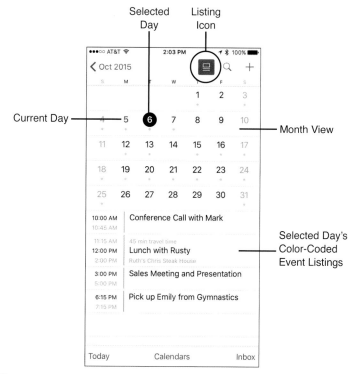

Figure 13.2

The Listing icon in the Calendar app provides an additional way to format and view your schedule on the iPhone's screen.

The Year view shows mini calendars for the entire year. To switch from the Year view to the Month view (shown in Figure 13.3), tap on any month in the Year view.

Figure 13.3

Shown here is the Calendar app's Month view on the iPhone.

From the Month view, switch to the Week view by rotating your iPhone from portrait to landscape mode. In other words, hold your smartphone sideways.

Also from the Month view, to switch to the Day view, tap on a day displayed in the calendar. From the Month view, any day that displays a gray dot in it has event details associated with it.

> ✓ **TIP**   On the iPhone, from the Month or Day view, tap on the Listing icon to view a more detailed and scrollable listing for the selected day's events.

The Year, Month, Week, and Day views in the iPhone version of the Calendar app are switchable in a hierarchical order. If you're in the Day view, for example, you can switch back to the Month view by tapping on the Back icon (a left-pointing arrow), which is displayed in the top-left corner of the screen.

Whether you're using the Calendar app on an iPhone or iPad, your Calendar view options include the following.

THE CALENDAR APP'S DAY VIEW

This view displays your events individually, based on the time each event is scheduled. When using the iPad version of the app, this information is displayed on a split screen. On the left is an hour-by-hour summary of your day, and on the right is a synopsis of the events for that day.

> **NOTE** On the iPhone, the Day view (shown in Figure 13.4) displays a week's worth of calendar dates near the top of the screen. Below that, the selected date is displayed, followed by an hour-by-hour rundown of your events.
>
> On the iPad, the Day display is split into two sections. The selected date, along with a week's worth of calendar dates, is displayed at the top of the screen, followed by a summary listing of appointments and/or events displayed on the left side of the screen. Details about one selected appointment or event are displayed on the right side of the screen by tapping on it.

Figure 13.4

The Day view of the Calendar app lets you see your schedule broken down one day at a time in one-hour increments.

Use the Day view of the Calendar app to see a detailed outline of scheduled events for a single day. Swipe your finger to scroll up or down to see an hour-by-hour summary of that day's schedule.

Swipe right or left along the week's worth of calendar days to see upcoming or past dates, and to view another day's schedule. Tap on a specific day to switch to that date's Day view.

> **TIP**   To quickly find an event, tap on the Search icon, and then enter any relevant text to help you find the item you're looking for that's stored in the Calendar app. This can also be done using Spotlight Search, or a verbal request can be made using Siri. In the Search field, enter a date, time, name, business, meeting location, or other pertinent information. Tap on a search result to view that event listing in detail within the Calendar app.

THE CALENDAR APP'S WEEK VIEW

The view uses a grid format to display the days of the week along the top of the screen and time intervals along the left side of the screen (shown in Figure 13.5 on an iPhone). With it, you're given an overview of all events scheduled during a particular week (Sunday through Saturday).

Scroll along the dates displayed near the top of the screen to quickly view your schedule for past or future weeks.

> **TIP**   To fine-tune this or any other Calendar app view, tap on the Calendars option that's displayed near the bottom center of the screen. A listing of the separate color-coded calendars that the Calendar app is managing is displayed. Tap on a listing to add or remove it from the Calendar view you're looking at.
>
> When you remove a calendar from the calendar view, this does not delete any data; it simply hides the events that are stored in that particular calendar from the display.

THE CALENDAR APP'S MONTH VIEW

This view enables you to see a month's worth of events at a time. On the iPhone, tap any single day to immediately switch to the Day view and review a detailed summary of events slated for that day. From the Month view, use your finger to scroll up or down to look at past or future months. On the iPad, use the Day, Week, Month, or Year tabs, located at the top of the screen, to switch Calendar views.

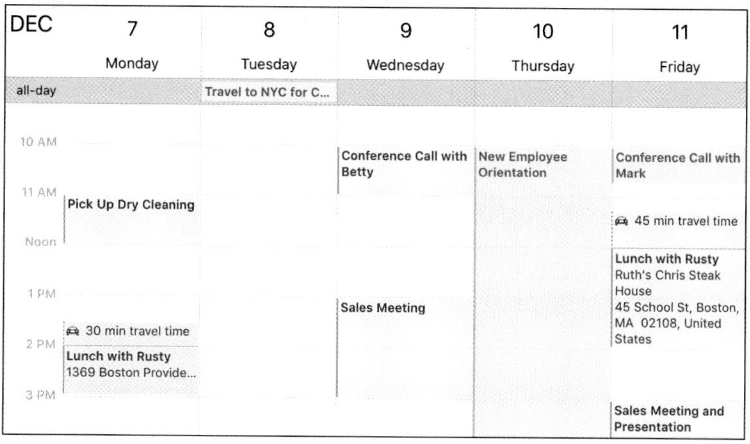

DEC	7	8	9	10	11
	Monday	Tuesday	Wednesday	Thursday	Friday
all-day		Travel to NYC for C...			
10 AM			Conference Call with Betty	New Employee Orientation	Conference Call with Mark
11 AM	Pick Up Dry Cleaning				🚗 45 min travel time
Noon					Lunch with Rusty Ruth's Chris Steak House 45 School St, Boston, MA 02108, United States
1 PM			Sales Meeting		
2 PM	🚗 30 min travel time Lunch with Rusty 1369 Boston Provide...				
3 PM					Sales Meeting and Presentation

Figure 13.5

The Calendar app's Week view.

THE CALENDAR APP'S YEAR VIEW

The Year view enables you to look at 12 mini calendars (with minimal detail displayed).

> ✓ **TIP** Tap on the Inbox option, displayed near the bottom-right corner of the screen, to view invites for events from other people that you might want to import into one of your calendars.

HOW TO ENTER A NEW EVENT INTO THE CALENDAR APP

Regardless of which calendar view you're using, follow these steps to enter a new event:

1. Tap the New Event icon (which looks like a plus sign) in the upper-right corner of the screen. This causes a New Event window to be displayed (shown in Figure 13.6).

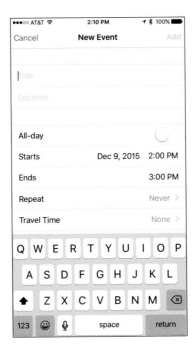

Figure 13.6

Add a new event to the Calendar app from the New Event screen.

2. The first field in the New Event window is labeled Title. Using the virtual keyboard, enter a title for the event.

3. If a location is associated with the event, tap the Location field located below the Title field and enter an address or location. Entering information into the Location field is optional. You can be as detailed as you want when entering information into this field.

> **TIP** By entering a location, your iOS mobile device can calculate travel time to this event from your current location and give you ample warning related to when you need to leave. The Maps app can also use the location information to provide directions to that event.
>
> If you ask Siri a question related to an event's location, such as "Where is my next meeting?" or "How do I get to my next appointment?," the event's location information is used.

> **NOTE** Many of the fields within the New Event screen are optional. In other words, only fill in the fields that are relevant to the new event you're creating. However, the more information you include, the more useful Maps, Siri, and Spotlight Search will be later when you want to refer to event information.

4. If the event lasts for the entire day, turn on the All-Day virtual switch. Otherwise, to set the time and date the event begins and ends, first tap the Starts field. Use the scrolling Date, Hour, Minute, and AM/PM dials to select the start time for your event.

5. After entering the start time, scroll down and tap on the Ends option, and again use the scrolling Date, Hour, Minute, and AM/PM dials to select the end time for your event.

> **NOTE** If the new event you're creating repeats every day, every week, every two weeks, every month, or every year, tap the Repeat option, and choose the appropriate time interval. The default for this option is Never, meaning that it is a nonrepeating, one-time-only event.

6. Turn on the virtual switch associated with the Travel Time option to add between 5 minutes and 2 hours of travel time to that event by tapping on one of the listed options. So, if this event turns out to be one hour away from your previous event scheduled on the same day, one hour's worth of travel time can be added to your schedule. However, if you have a specific location entered in the Location field, your iPhone or iPad can calculate the travel time from wherever you happen to be prior to that event.

7. If you're managing several calendars within the Calendar app, tap on the Calendar option to select in which calendar the new event will be placed. The default calendar is called Home, but you can change this from within Settings.

8. To invite other people to the event, tap on the Invitees option and, when prompted, fill in the To field with the invitees' names or email addresses. Use their name if they already have a contact entry in the Contacts app; otherwise, enter an email address for each person separated by a comma. The people you add as invitees are sent an email allowing them to respond to the invite. The Calendar app keeps track of RSVPs from event attendees and displays this information in the app.

9. To set an audible alarm for the event, tap the Alert option. The Event Alert window temporarily replaces the Add Event screen. In the Event Alert window, tap on the option for how much advance notice you want before the scheduled event. Your options include None, At Time of Event, 5 minutes, 15 minutes, 30 minutes, 1 hour, 2 hours, 1 day, 2 days, or 1 week before the event. Once you tap a selection, you are returned to the Add Event screen.

> **TIP** A Second Alert option is also available from the Add Event screen. If you want to add a secondary alarm to this event, tap the Second Alert option and then set it.

10. Tap on the Show As option to classify how you want an event to appear within your calendar. The default option is Busy. This is information others can see if you opt to share specific calendars with other people.

11. Tap on the URL field to add a website address associated with the event.

12. Tap on the Notes field to add text-based notes you want to associate with the new event. It's also possible to paste content from other apps into the Notes field.

13. Tap the Add option to save the event. Tap the Cancel icon to exit without saving any new information.

> **NOTE** As soon as you create a new event, that information syncs with your iCloud account and all other computers and/or mobile devices that you have linked to that account. If you have the Calendar app set up to sync with another scheduling app or online service, your new data syncs with that app.
>
> This near instant data synchronization also applies if you delete an event.

USE SIRI TO ENTER NEW EVENTS INTO THE CALENDAR APP

Instead of manually entering event information into your iPhone or iPad using the virtual keyboard, or importing/syncing scheduling data from another computer or device, you always have the option to use Siri. Refer to Chapter 2, "Using Siri, Dictation, and CarPlay to Interact with Your Mobile Device," for more information.

> 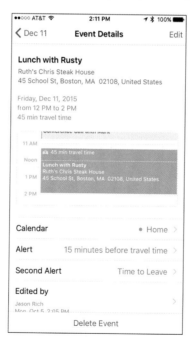 **TIP**   Using Siri, say something like, "When is my next appointment with [name]?" You can also say, "Show me my schedule for Wednesday," or ask, "What's on my calendar for July 7?" to quickly find an event. If you enter information into the Location field as you're creating events, you can later ask Siri, "Where is my next meeting?"

VIEWING INDIVIDUAL APPOINTMENT DETAILS

From any view in the Calendar app, tap an individual event to display the details related to it.

When you tap on a single event listing, a new screen opens (shown in Figure 13.7). Tap the Edit option in the upper-right corner to modify any aspect of the event listing, such as its title, location, start/end time, alert, invitees, or notes.

Figure 13.7

Detailed information about each event stored within the Calendar app can easily be viewed.

At the bottom of an event listing, a map showing the event's location is provided if the Location field has been filled in.

HOW TO DELETE AN EVENT FROM THE CALENDAR APP

To delete an event entry entirely, tap the red-and-white Delete Event option found at the bottom of the Edit window. Or when you're finished making changes to an event entry, tap on the Done option in the upper-right corner of the window.

> **TIP** The Calendar app works with several other apps, including Contacts and Notification Center. For example, in Contacts, you can enter someone's birthday into an entry, and that information can automatically be displayed in the Calendar app.
>
> To display birthday listings in Calendar, tap the Calendars button displayed near the bottom center of the screen in the Calendar app, and then tap on the Birthdays option to add a check mark to that selection. All recurring birthdays stored in Contacts appear in Calendar.
>
> There are also two options related to the Facebook app that enable you to display all the birthdays for your online Facebook friends, and/or all Facebook Events related to your account in the Calendar app. This can be found under the Facebook heading of the Show Calendars screen/window.

QUICKLY FIND APPOINTMENT OR EVENT DETAILS

In addition to viewing the various calendar views offered within the Calendar app, use the in-app Search or Spotlight Search options to find individual events.

CUSTOMIZING THE CALENDAR APP

There are many ways to customize the Calendar app beyond choosing between the various calendar views. For example, you can set audible alerts and/or use onscreen alerts and banners to remind you of events. You can also display Calendar-related information in the Notification Center and/or on the Lock screen.

> **TIP** To customize the audio alert generated by the Calendar app, launch Settings and then select the Sounds option. Tap on the Calendar Alerts option and choose a sound from the menu. Choose the None option from the Calendar Alerts menu to set up Calendar so it never plays audible alerts or alarms.

From the Mail, Contacts, Calendars submenu within Settings, under the Calendars heading, determine how far back in your schedule you want to sync appointment data between your primary computer and your iOS device(s). Your options include Events 2 Weeks Back, Events 1 Month Back, Events 3 Months Back, Events 6 Months Back, and All Events. All Events is the default option.

Tap on the Time Zone Override option and then turn on the virtual switch associated with this feature if you want the Calendar app to always show event dates and times in your home time zone, regardless of which alternate time zone you've traveled to. After you turn on the virtual switch associated with this feature, tap on the Time Zone option to select a home time zone.

USE THE CONTACTS APP TO KEEP TRACK OF PEOPLE YOU KNOW

Contact information related to the people in your life, as well as companies you do business with, can all be stored and easily managed using the Contacts app.

Your personal contacts database might include people you work with, customers, clients, family members, people from your community with whom you interact (doctors, hair stylist, barber, dry cleaners, and so on), your real-world friends, and your online friends from Facebook, for example.

(iOS 9) WHAT'S NEW From the Home screen when using an iPhone 6s or iPhone 6 Plus, press and hold your finger on the Contacts app icon to view a pop-up menu that enables you to quickly create a new contact entry or view your own entry in the Contacts database, which is referred to as My Info (shown in Figure 13.8).

Be sure to create an entry for yourself in your Contacts database and populate it with as much information as possible, because many other apps will access this information in the future for a variety of reasons.

As you receive incoming emails, if the sender includes their details within their email, and this information is not stored within your Contacts app already, you'll have the ability to add it. This is also true if the sender updates their contact information, and it doesn't match what's stored within the Contacts app. Within the Mail app, as you're reading the email, you'll be given the opportunity to create a new contact or update the existing contact's entry within the Contacts app.

For this feature to work, launch Settings, tap on the Mail, Contacts, Calendar option, and then turn on the virtual switch associated with the Contacts Found in Mail option.

Figure 13.8
Use the new Peek function offered by iOS 9 when using the iPhone 6s or iPhone 6s Plus to access this Contacts-related menu directly from the Home screen.

> **NOTE** Contacts is a powerful and customizable contact management database that works with several other apps that also came preinstalled on your iPhone or iPad, including Mail, Calendar, Safari, FaceTime, and Maps, as well as optional apps, like the official Facebook and Twitter apps. It's also fully compatible with Siri and Spotlight Search.

YOU DETERMINE WHAT INFORMATION YOU ADD TO EACH CONTACT ENTRY

Chances are, the same contacts database that you rely on at your office or on your personal computer at home can be synced with your iPhone or iPad and made available to you using the Contacts app.

Of course, Contacts can also be used as a standalone app, enabling you to enter new contact entries as you meet new people and need to keep track of details about them using your iOS mobile device(s).

The information you maintain in your Contacts database is highly customizable, which means you can keep track of only the information you want or need. For example, in each contact entry, it's possible to store a vast amount of information about a person or company, including multiple phone numbers, addresses, and email addresses. Each field is labeled for easy reference. For example, a Contact entry can include someone's home, work, and cell phone numbers.

> **NOTE** To include some fields that aren't provided by default, tap on the Add Field option and select a field type from the submenu.

You can also customize your contacts database to include additional information, such as each contact's photo, as well as detailed and freeform notes related to a contact.

When you're using the Contacts app, your entire contacts database is instantly searchable using data from any field within the database, so even if you have a database containing thousands of entries, you can always find the person or company you're looking for in a matter of seconds, using a wide range of search criteria. This can be done using the Search field in the Contacts app, using the Spotlight Search feature, or with Siri.

THE CONTACTS APP WORKS SEAMLESSLY WITH OTHER APPS

After your contacts database has been populated with entries, Contacts works with many other apps on your iPhone and/or iPad. Here are just a few popular examples:

- When you compose a new email message in Mail, begin typing someone's full name or email address in the To field. If that person's contact information is already stored in Contacts, the relevant email address automatically displays in the email's To field.

- If you're planning a trip to visit a contact, pull up someone's address from your Contacts database and then quickly obtain driving directions to the person's home or work location from the Maps app.

- Activate Siri and request directions to any person or company with an entry stored in your Contacts database. For example, activate Siri and say, "How do I get to John Doe's house from here?"

- If you include each person's birthday in your Contacts database, that information can automatically be displayed in the Calendar app and be set up to remind you (in advance) to send a card or gift.

- As you're creating each Contacts entry, include a photo of that person—by activating the Camera app from the Contacts app to snap a photo, by using a photo stored in the Photos app that you link to the entry, or by acquiring profile photos from social media accounts. For example, to automatically insert profile photos of Facebook friends into the Contacts app, see the section "Add a Photo to a Contacts Entry" later in this chapter.

- When using FaceTime, create a Favorites list of people you often engage in video calls with, compiled from entries in your Contacts database.

- From the Messages app, access your Contacts database when filling in the To field as you compose new text messages to be sent via iMessage, text message, or instant message.

■ If you're active on Facebook or Twitter, you have the option of adding each contact's Facebook and/or Twitter username to their Contacts entry. When you turn on the Facebook feature, the Contacts app automatically downloads each entry's Facebook profile picture and inserts it into your Contacts database.

When you first launch the Contacts app, its related database is empty. However, you can create and build your database in two ways:

1. Sync the Contacts app with your primary contact management application on your computer, network, or online (cloud)-based service, such as iCloud or Microsoft Outlook.

2. Manually enter contact information directly into the Contacts app.

> **NOTE** The Contacts app that comes preinstalled with iOS 9 is 100 percent compatible with and extremely similar to the Contacts app that comes bundled with OS X Yosemite or OS X El Capitan on the Mac. Thus, be sure to set up each version of the app to sync with each other via iCloud, so you always have access to your entire Contacts database.

As you begin using this app and come to rely on it, it's possible to enter new contact information or edit entries either on your iOS mobile device or using your primary contact management application and keep all the information synchronized, regardless of where the entry was created or modified.

HOW TO VIEW YOUR CONTACTS

On the iPhone, the All Contacts screen displays an alphabetical listing of all entries in your Contacts database. Along the right side of the screen are alphabetic tabs, and a Search field is located near the top of the screen.

> **NOTE** If you've used the Contacts app previously, and it has been running in the background, the last contact entry you viewed will be displayed when you relaunch the app.

On the iPad, in the middle of the screen are alphabetic tabs. The All Contacts heading is near the upper-left corner of the screen. Below it is a Search field. After you have added entries in your contacts database, they are listed alphabetically on the left side of the screen below the Search field.

TIP Tap on the Search field to quickly find a particular entry by entering any keyword associated with an entry, such as a first or last name, city, state, job title, or company name. Any content in your Contacts database is searchable from this Search field.

You can also tap a letter tab on the screen to see all entries "filed" under that letter by a contact's last name, first name, or company name, depending on how you set up the Contacts app using the Mail, Contacts, Calendars option in Settings.

On the iPhone, to see the complete listing for a particular entry, tap on its listing from the All Contacts screen. A new screen shows the specific contact's information (shown in Figure 13.9).

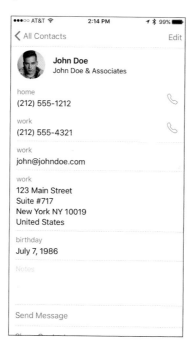

Figure 13.9

A sample contact entry from the Contacts app displayed on an iPhone.

On the iPad, to see the complete listing for a particular entry, tap on it from the All Contacts display on the left side of the screen. That entry's complete contents are then displayed on the right side of the screen.

To quickly find and display any contact in your Contacts database, activate Siri and say, "Find [name] within Contacts." The contact's information will be displayed as a Siri results screen, but the Contacts app will not automatically launch.

HOW TO CREATE A NEW CONTACTS ENTRY

To create a new Contacts entry, tap the New Contact icon (which looks like a plus sign). On the iPhone, it's displayed in the upper-right corner of the All Contacts screen. On the iPad, the New Contact icon can be found near the top center of the Contacts app's screen.

After tapping on the New Contact icon, the New Contact screen appears.

> **NOTE** As you're creating each Contacts entry, fill in whichever fields you want. You can always edit a contact entry later to include additional information. The more information you enter, however, the more data the Contacts app will later be able to share with Siri and other apps running on your mobile device.

In the New Contact screen are several empty fields related to the entry, starting with the First Name field (shown in Figure 13.10).

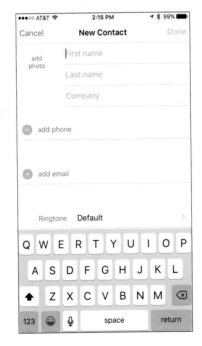

Figure 13.10

From this New Contact screen, create a new contact and include as much information pertaining to that person or company as you want.

Some fields, including Phone, Email, and Mailing Address, enable you to input multiple listings, one at a time. So you can include someone's home phone, work phone, and mobile phone (iPhone) numbers in the entry, for example. Likewise, you can include multiple email addresses, and/or a home address and work address for an individual.

> **TIP** One of the available fields when creating a new Contact entry is labeled Add Related Name. Use this field to add the names of your contact's mother, father, parent, brother, sister, child, friend, spouse, partner, assistant, manager, or other. You can also add your own titles for the Related People field.

> **TIP** It's possible to change the label associated with certain fields (which are displayed in blue) by tapping the field label itself. This reveals a Label menu, offering selectable options for that field. For example, the Label options for the Add Phone field include Home, Work, iPhone, Mobile, Main, Home Fax, Work Fax, Pager, and Other. At the bottom of this Label window, tap the Add Custom Label option to create your own label if none of the listed options applies.
>
> Tap the label title of your choice. A check mark appears next to it, and you are returned to the New Contact screen.

At the bottom of the New Contact screen is the Add Field option. Tap it to reveal a menu containing a handful of additional fields you can add to individual Contacts entries as applicable, such as a middle name, job title, and/or nickname.

> **NOTE** If there's a field displayed that you don't want to utilize or display, simply leave it blank as you're creating or editing a Contacts entry.

Each time you add a new mailing address to a contact's entry from within the New Contact screen, the Address field expands to include a Street, City, State, ZIP, and Country field.

After you have filled in all the fields for a particular entry, tap the Done option, which is displayed in the upper-right corner of the New Contact screen. Your new entry gets saved and added to your contacts database and is then synced with your other computers and/or mobile devices.

HOW TO ADD A PHOTO TO A CONTACTS ENTRY

To the immediate left of the First Name field is a circle that says Add Photo. When you tap this field, a submenu with two options—Take Photo and Choose Photo—is displayed. If the entry already has a photo associated with it, the Edit Photo and Delete Photo options are also displayed.

Tap Take Photo to launch the Camera app from within the Contacts app and snap a photo to be linked to the Contacts entry you're creating. Alternatively, tap on the Choose Photo option. In this case, the Photos app launches so that you can choose any digital image that's currently stored on your iOS mobile device. When you tap the photo of your choice, a Choose a Photo window displays on the Contacts screen, enabling you to move and scale the image.

> **TIP**   As you're previewing the image (shown in Figure 13.11), use a pinch or reverse-pinch finger motion to zoom in or out, and then hold your finger down on the image and reposition it within the frame.

Figure 13.11

Linking a photo with someone's Contacts entry enables you to visually identify the person as you're reviewing your contacts.

After cropping or adjusting the selected photo, tap the Use icon displayed in the upper-right corner of the Choose Photo window to link the photo with that contact's entry.

The photo you link with an entry is displayed by other apps, like Mail, Messages, and FaceTime, that utilize the Contacts app data.

> **TIP** If you use an iPhone, or FaceTime on your iPhone or iPad, from the Ringtone option in the New Contact screen, select the specific ringtone you will hear each time that particular contact calls you. Your iPhone or iPad has many preinstalled ringtones. From the iTunes Store, you can purchase and download thousands of additional ringtones, many of which are clips from popular songs, movies, or TV shows.

EDITING OR DELETING A CONTACT

To edit a contact, tap on its listing from the All Contacts screen to display the contact details, and then tap on the Edit option displayed in the upper-right corner of the screen. Tap any field to modify it. Delete a field by tapping on the red-and-white minus sign icon associated with it, and then tap the Delete button that appears to the right of the entry.

You can also add new fields in an entry by tapping any of the green-and-white plus sign icons and then choosing the type of field you want to add.

When you're finished editing a Contacts entry, again tap the Done option.

> **TIP** To delete an entire entry from your Contacts database, as you're editing a contact entry and looking at the Contact screen for that entry, scroll down to the bottom of it, and tap the Delete Contact option that's displayed in red.
>
> Keep in mind that if you have your Contacts database syncing with iCloud or another contacts database, the contact you delete is removed from all your computers and devices that are connected to the Internet within seconds. There is no "undo" option.

SHARING CONTACT ENTRIES

From the main All Contacts screen, tap on the contact listing you want to share. When the contact's entry is displayed, scroll down toward the bottom of the entry until you see the Share Contact option. Tap it. Then choose to share the contact's details with someone else via AirDrop, text/instant message (via the Message app), or email (via the Mail app).

The entire Contacts entry you selected (stored in .vcf format) will already be embedded in the outgoing email or text/instant message. When you've filled in all the necessary fields, tap the blue-and-white Send icon. Upon doing this, you are returned to the Contacts app.

When the recipient receives your email or message and clicks on the attachment (the contact entry you sent), it automatically is imported into their contact management application as a new entry, such as in the Contacts app running on a Mac, iPhone, or iPad.

CONTACTS APP QUICK TIPS

■ If someone shares a Contacts entry with you via email, when you're viewing the incoming email on your iPhone or iPad, tap the email's attachment. The Contacts entry that was emailed is displayed in a window. At the bottom of this window, as the recipient of the contact's information, tap the Create New Contact or Add to Existing Contact option to incorporate this information into your Contacts database.

■ As you're creating or editing a contact entry, in the Notes field, enter as much information pertaining to that contact as you want using freeform text. It's also possible to paste content from another app into this field using the iOS's Select, Copy, and Paste commands, and using the app switcher to quickly switch between apps.

■ When creating or editing contacts, it's important to associate the correct labels with phone numbers, email addresses, and address data. For each phone number you add to a contact's entry, for example, it can include a Home, Work, Mobile, iPhone, or Other label (among others). For many iOS 9 functions that utilize data from your Contacts database to work correctly (including Siri), it's important that you properly label content you add to each Contacts entry.

CREATE AND MANAGE LISTS WITH THE REMINDERS APP

Use the Reminders app to easily manage multiple lists simultaneously, and if necessary, add alarms and deadlines to individual list items. Plus, it's possible to be reminded of responsibilities, tasks, or objectives exactly when you need this information, based on your geographic location or a predetermined time and date.

The Reminders app works nicely with Siri, Notification Center, and iCloud, which makes synchronizing your app-related data a straightforward process.

(iOS 9) **WHAT'S NEW**   When using the iPhone 6s or iPhone 6s Plus, use iOS 9's Peek feature by pressing and holding your finger on the app icon for the Reminders app when viewing the Home screen. This reveals a pop-up menu that allows you to quickly add items to a specific list you've already created within the app or add items to the app's default list.

On its surface, Reminders is a straightforward list manager. However, it offers a plethora of interesting and useful features.

Using Reminders, create as many separate lists as you need to properly manage your personal and professional life, or various projects for which you're responsible.

TIP   Reminders enables you to color-code lists. Tap on the Edit button displayed to the right of a list's title, and then tap on the Color option. Seven different colors are displayed. Tap on your selection. The list title is displayed in the selected color.

Because your iPhone has Location Services (GPS) capabilities, it always knows exactly where it is. Thus, it's possible to create items within your to-do lists and associate one or more of them with an alarm that alerts you when you arrive at or depart from a particular geographic location, such as your home, office, or a particular store.

For example, have your morning to-do list or call list automatically display on your iPhone's screen when you arrive at work, if you associate just one item on that list with a location-based alarm. Likewise, if you use Reminders to maintain a list of office supplies you need to purchase at Staples or OfficeMax, you can have it pop up on the screen when you arrive at your local office supply superstore.

In addition, you can have a reminder alarm set to warn you of an upcoming deadline. This can be displayed on your device's screen in the Notification Center or as separate alerts or banners, depending on how you have the Reminders app set up to work with the Notifications options offered by your iPhone or iPad (which is adjustable from within Settings).

As you're setting up an alarm, if you want it to repeat every day, every week, every two weeks, every month, or every year, tap on the Repeat option and make your selection. By default, the Never option is selected, meaning the alarm does not repeat.

> **TIP** Just as you do for other apps, to set up Reminders to work with Notification Center and/or display onscreen alerts or banners, launch Settings, tap on the Notifications option, and then tap on the listing for the Reminders app. You can then customize the settings on the Reminders menu screen within Settings.

STAY UP TO DATE WITH REMINDERS

When you launch Reminders for the first time on the iPad, the control center for this app appears on the left side of the screen. On the right side of the screen is a simulated sheet of lined paper.

Tap on the Add List option in the bottom-left corner of the screen to create a new list from scratch. However, if you've already been using the Reminder app on another iOS mobile device or Mac that's linked to the same iCloud account, all of your lists synchronize with the iPhone or iPad you're currently using.

When you create a new list from scratch, it is displayed on the right side of the screen using the temporary heading New List. Enter a title for the new list and then associate a color with it. Tap on the Done option when you're ready to begin populating the list with items (as shown in Figure 13.12 on an iPad), or repeat this process to create another list.

Figure 13.12

Using Reminders, it's possible to create and manage one or more lists. Each list can have as many separate items as you want.

On the iPhone, to create a new list from scratch as you're looking at a list, tap the list name to bring up a master list screen. The New List (+) icon is displayed at the top of this screen (shown in Figure 13.13). Tap on this icon, select the List option, and then type the name of the list and associate a color with it. Tap on the Done option. You can then begin populating the list with items or repeat this process to create another list.

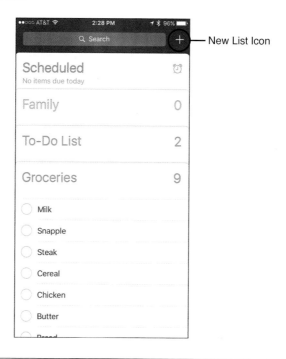

New List Icon

Figure 13.13

To create a new list, tap on the New List (+) option displayed near the top of the Reminders screen on the iPhone. Then name your list and start adding items, one at a time.

When viewing a list, tap on an empty line of the simulated sheet of paper to add an item. The virtual keyboard appears. Enter the item to be added to your to-do list. Next, tap on the Return key on the keyboard to enter another item, or tap on the Info icon (the blue *i* with a circle around it) to the right of the newly added item to associate an alarm, priority, and/or notes with it.

When you're finished adding new list items, tap on the Done option.

To set a date-specific alarm, turn the virtual switch associated with Remind Me On a Day to the on position and then tap on the date and time line that appears below it to set the date and time for the alert.

To set a location-based alarm for that item, enter the Info screen and then turn on the virtual switch associated with the Remind Me At A Location option. Select a location or enter an address and then decide whether you want to be alerted when you arrive or when you leave that destination by tapping on the When I Arrive... or When I Leave... tab.

> **TIP** You have the option to set a priority with each list item. Your priority options include None, Low (!), Medium (!!), and High (!!!).
>
> Although setting a priority for a list item displays that item with one, two, or three exclamation points to signify its importance, adjusting an item's priority does not automatically change its position within the list. You must manually rearrange the order of items on a list.
>
> To do this, while looking at a list, tap on the Edit button. Then place your finger on the Move icon (three horizontal lines) that's associated with the list item you want to move, and drag it up or down to the desired location within the list. Tap the Done button to save your changes.

Different alarms can be associated with each item in each of your lists. You also have the option to create a list item but not associate any type of alert or alarm with it.

When an alarm is generated for a list item, a notification can automatically appear within Notification Center, assuming that you have this feature turned on.

> **TIP** One additional feature of the Reminders app is that you can display a separate list associated with each day on the calendar. When you use the Remind Me On A Day option, a date becomes associated with that item. Then, to review upcoming items related to a particular day using an iPhone, access the Search field from the main menu of lists stored within the app. Displayed to the right is an Alarm Clock icon. Tap on this to display scheduled items for the current day.
>
> On the iPad, tap on the Scheduled option on the left side of the screen.

> **TIP** At the bottom of every to-do list on the iPad is a new Show Completed option. Tap this to display all items originally added to the list you're viewing that have since been moved to the Completed list.

To delete an item from a to-do list, swipe your finger from right to left across the item. A More button and a Delete button are displayed. Tap on Delete to confirm your selection, or tap on the More button to reveal the Info menu options related to that item.

Remember, as soon as you make changes to a list item, if you have iCloud functionality turned on for the Reminders app and have access to the Internet, your additions, edits, or deletions automatically sync with iCloud.

HOW TO DELETE AN ENTIRE TO-DO LIST

If you want to delete an entire list, enter the list and click on the Edit button, and then click on the Delete List option displayed at the bottom of the screen. A warning pops up asking you to confirm the deletion.

On the iPad, you can also locate the list you want to delete from the column on the left, and swipe your finger from right to left across it. When the Delete button appears, tap on it. You also have the option of tapping the Edit button, and then tapping on the negative sign icon that's associated with the list you want to erase. In Edit mode, it's possible to change the order of your lists by placing your finger on the Move icon (three horizontal lines) that's associated with a list and dragging it up or down.

To exit Edit mode, tap on the Done option.

TAKE NOTES OR GATHER INFORMATION USING THE NEWLY REDESIGNED NOTES APP

With the release of iOS 9, Apple has redesigned the Notes app, almost from scratch. It's now much more powerful. In addition to typed notes, it enables you to create, gather, and manage information, including photos, drawings, and handwritten content.

Use the Notes app to keep track of reminders to yourself, brainstorm ideas, take notes in meetings or classes, gather content from other apps that you want to store in one place, or for anything else that you'd use a traditional notebook and writing instrument to document.

(iOS 9) **WHAT'S NEW** When using an iPhone 6s or iPhone 6s Plus, from the Home screen, place and hold your finger on the app icon for Notes to make a pop-up window appear that allows you to create a new note, take a photo and store it in a note, or handwrite/sketch content to be added to a note (shown in Figure 13.14).

Figure 13.14
Use iOS 9's Peek feature to access this menu and quickly start creating specific types of content within Notes, without having to manually launch the Notes app.

WHAT'S NEW When using the Notes app, displayed directly above the virtual keyboard (used for typing note content) are several new command icons (shown in Figure 13.15). In the top-left corner of the keyboard tap on the Undo/Redo icon to reveal additional command icons that allow you to use the Undo, Redo, or Copy/Paste commands.

Tap on the check mark icon to begin creating and formatting an interactive checklist within your note (shown in Figure 13.16).

Tap on the Formatting option to quickly format text that you're typing into the Notes app.

In the top-right corner of the virtual keyboard are the Camera and Draw command icons. Tap on the Camera icon to import an image stored on your mobile device (from the Photo Library), or tap on the Take Photo or Video option to use the device's built-in camera to snap a photo or shoot a video to be imported into the note you're working with.

Tap on the Draw icon to access the Notes app's new drawing/sketch tools, which can also be used for handwriting on your phone or tablet's screen using your finger or a stylus. (If you're using the iPad Pro, this feature works nicely with the optional Apple Pencil stylus.)

Figure 13.15

The Notes app displays special command icons directly above the virtual keyboard.

Figure 13.16

Within a note, it's now possible to create an interactive checklist.

CREATE AND MANAGE NOTES APP FOLDERS

Think of the Notes app as a digital notebook. Each note stored in the app is a separate page that can have its own title and content. Individual notes get stored in folders, which are basically virtual notebooks. Each folder can also be custom named.

Begin by creating one or more virtual notebooks (folders) within the Notes app. This is done from the Folders screen (shown in Figure 13.17) by tapping on the New Folder option, choosing where the content should be stored (in iCloud or only on your mobile device), and then typing a title for that folder.

Figure 13.17

From the Folders screen, create one or more folders (virtual notebooks) within which you store your individual note pages.

To edit folders already created in the Notes app, access the Folders screen and then tap on the Edit option. You can then select and Delete entire folders created using the Notes app.

> **NOTE** Notes created using other apps that were synced with or imported into the Notes app can't be deleted or managed from the Folders screen.

HOW TO CREATE INDIVIDUAL NOTES

From the Folders screen in the Notes app, tap on the folder (notebook) within which you want to create a new note. When the screen for that folder opens, a listing of individual notes stored in it is displayed (shown in Figure 13.18). If the folder is empty, only command icons are displayed on the screen.

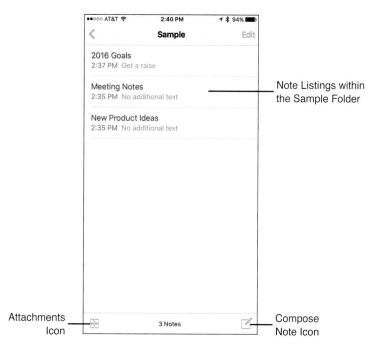

Figure 13.18

From a specific Folder's screen, you can access any notes stored in that folder or create a new note from scratch.

To open and view, edit, or work with an existing note within a folder, access the Folder screen and tap on that note's title/listing.

> **TIP** To view attachments in notes stored in the folder you're viewing, tap on the Attachments icon. The Attachments icon is located in the bottom-left corner of the screen.

To create a new note from scratch, tap on the Compose Note icon. On the iPhone, this icon is located in the bottom-right corner of the screen. On the iPad, it's located in the top-right corner of the screen.

The first line of text in a note becomes its title. Each time a new note is created, the time and date are automatically recorded and displayed.

After typing the Title for the note, tap on the Return key and start typing your note's content. You can type as much content as you want within each virtual note page (shown in Figure 13.19). The note page extends infinitely downward.

Figure 13.19
The note creation screen in the Notes app.

As you're typing content, use the command icons displayed at the top of the virtual keyboard to help you format the text or add checklists, for example.

Tap on the Emoji key on the virtual keyboard to add Emoji characters, or tap on the Dictation key to use iOS 9's Dictation feature to speak into the app and have what you say translated into text and then imported into the note.

If you opt to import a photo into a note, tap on the Camera icon, choose the Photo Library option, for example, and select the photo you want to add. The photo gets imported and embedded into the note.

> **TIP** To delete the note you're currently working with, tap on the Trash icon. Keep in mind, the note will be deleted from the iPhone or iPad you're using, as well as from your iCloud account.

To retrieve an accidentally deleted note, visit the Folders menu screen and tap on the Recently Deleted option. It's then possible to select one or more accidentally deleted notes and move them into a different folder using the Move command that's displayed. Tap on the Move or Move All option, and then choose which folder the notes should be transferred to.

Keep in mind that using iOS 9's Select, Copy, and Paste commands, you can select content from other apps, copy it into the iPhone or iPad's virtual clipboard, and then paste that content into a note in the Notes app. This is easier if you're using an iPad and take advantage of the Split View feature to operate two apps at once on the tablet's screen.

MOVING NOTES BETWEEN FOLDERS

After notes are created and stored within particular folders, you can manually move them between folders. To do this, access the Folders screen and tap on the folder that contains the notes you want to move. Next, tap on the Edit option. Tap on the listing for each note you want to move to select it (shown in Figure 13.20).

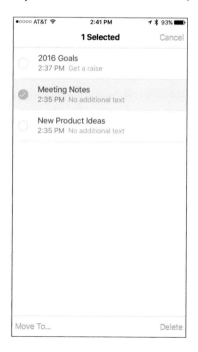

Figure 13.20

From the Folders screen, select the notes you want to move, and then tap on the Move To option.

Once one or more note listings have been selected, tap on the Move To option and select which folder you want to move the notes to.

At this point, the notes are removed from their current folder and moved into the newly selected folder. Instead of tapping on the Move To option, to delete the selected notes, tap on the Delete option.

CREATE INTERACTIVE CHECKLISTS WITHIN NOTES

Using the checklist tool built in to the Notes app, it's easy to add and format inter-active checklists into a note. To do this, place the cursor where you want to insert the list and tap on the Checklist icon. The first empty check mark circle is displayed.

To the right of this icon, type your first list item and then tap the Return key. Now, add a second, third, and fourth item, and keep going until your list is complete (refer to Figure 13.16).

Later, when you tap on one of the check mark circles, a check mark is added to it, indicating that the item has been completed. In a note, add as many separate checklists as you want, and each list can have any number of items. The various lists can be surrounded by other types of content.

USING THE DRAWING TOOLS IN THE NOTES APP

One of the newly added sets of features built in to the iOS 9 edition of the Notes app is the capability to handwrite, draw, or sketch on your iPhone or iPad's screen and store that content in the Notes app.

To do this, tap on the Draw icon displayed in the top-right corner of the virtual keyboard. The Drawing screen is displayed. At the bottom of this screen are three virtual writing/drawing tools, including a pen, highlighter, and pencil.

Tap on the Ruler icon to make a virtual ruler appear on the screen (shown in Figure 13.21), which you can then drag around, reposition, or rotate.

> **TIP** To drag the ruler, place and hold one finger on the ruler and move it around on the screen. To rotate the ruler, place two fingers (separated) on the ruler and rotate your fingers clockwise or counterclockwise.

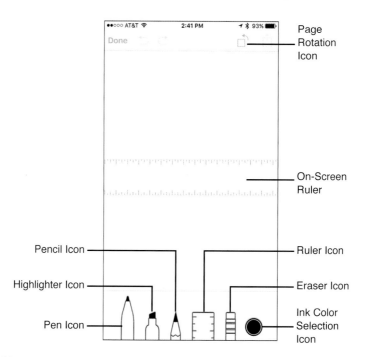

Figure 13.21

Use the Notes app's Drawing tools to draw, sketch, or handwrite content within a note. Use the Ruler tool for added precision.

To erase content that you've drawn on the screen, tap on the Eraser tool and then move your finger on the screen over the areas you want to erase. If you want to delete everything on the screen, however, tap on the Erase All option.

After choosing a virtual writing instrument by tapping on it, tap on an ink color. Swipe your finger across the ink colors to view all the available colors, and then tap on the desired color.

When you're ready, use your finger or an optional stylus to draw or handwrite on the iPhone or iPad's screen. You can switch ink colors or writing instruments as often as you choose (shown in Figure 13.22).

TIP   To undo your last action, tap on the Undo icon, or to Redo that option you just undid, tap on the Redo icon.

If you want to rotate the entire virtual page you're drawing on, tap on the Rotation icon. To share just the drawn content, not the entire note, tap on the Share icon displayed on the Drawing screen.

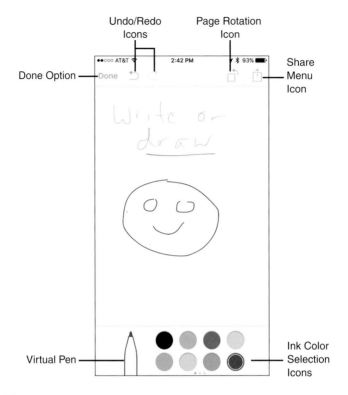

Figure 13.22

Draw, sketch, or handwrite on your phone or tablet's screen and incorporate that content into notes that get stored in the Notes app.

To save your work, tap on the Done option. The content you've drawn is incorporated onto the note page you were previously working on, which can also include typed text and/or photos, for example.

> **NOTE** A single note can contain multiple drawn pages created separately. Tap on the Show Attachments icon to view each separate photo or drawing embedded within your various notes.

SHARING NOTES

As you're viewing a note, tap on the Share icon to access the Share menu (shown in Figure 13.23). From here, you can share the contents of the note via AirDrop, text message, email, Facebook, or Facebook Messenger, for example, or use any listed third-party app that's compatible with the Notes app.

Figure 13.23

The Notes app offers an extensive Share menu.

From the Share menu, it's also possible to Copy content from a note to the device's virtual clipboard and then Paste it into another app. Tap on the Print icon to print the contents of the note using an AirPrint-compatible printer that's wirelessly connected to your iPhone or iPad.

IN THIS CHAPTER

- Play digital music using the redesigned Music app
- Watch music videos, TV shows, and movies with the Videos app
- Acquire new content from the iTunes Store
- Listen to streaming music using Apple Music and iTunes Radio

14

GET ACQUAINTED WITH THE MUSIC, VIDEOS, AND iTUNES STORE APPS

What do eight-track tapes, vinyl records, cassettes, and CDs have in common? These are all outdated methods for storing music that have been replaced by digital music players. The music in your personal library can now be kept in a purely digital format, transferred via the Internet, shared with family members, and listened to on the digital music player included with your iPhone or iPad.

iOS 9 comes with the newly redesigned version of the Music app preinstalled. This app serves as a full-featured digital music player, enabling you to play music. However, before playing your music, you first must load digital music files into your iOS mobile device or choose to stream music from the Internet. There are several ways to do this, including the following:

- Purchase digital music directly from the iTunes Store (using the iTunes Store app) on your iPhone or iPad. An Internet connection is required.

> **NOTE** When you activate the iCloud Family Sharing feature, you're able to share some or all of your iTunes Store digital content purchases with up to five other family members. You decide what content gets shared and have the option of keeping some of your content private, so it's only available through your iCloud account on all of your own iOS mobile devices and Macs. Family Sharing only needs to be set up once. See Chapter 5, "Use iCloud and the iCloud Drive App from Your iPhone or iPad."

- Purchase music using the iTunes software on your primary computer (used to connect to the iTunes Store) and then transfer content purchases and downloads to your iPhone or iPad using the iTunes Sync process or through iCloud.

- "Rip" music from traditional CDs and convert it into a digital format using your primary computer and then transfer the digital music files to your iOS device. For this, the free iTunes software on your computer or other third-party software is required.

- Upgrade your iCloud account by adding the optional iTunes Match service, for $24.99 per year, so you can access your entire digital music library via iCloud, whether that music was purchased from the iTunes Store, ripped from your own CDs, or purchased/downloaded from other sources. To learn more about iTunes Match, visit www.apple.com/itunes/itunes-match.

- Shop for and download music from another source besides the iTunes Store, load that music into your primary computer, convert it to the proper format, and then transfer it to your iPhone or iPad using the iTunes Sync process, or use a specialized app to experience that content.

> **NOTE** The Apple iTunes Store offers the world's largest collection of digital music that's available for purchase and download. This includes more than 30 million songs, such as the latest hits, new music from the biggest bands and recording artists, as well as music from up-and-coming and unsigned artists/bands. You can also find classic songs and oldies from all music genres.
>
> Apple Music subscribers can stream most of the iTunes Store's music collection and listen to it on an on-demand basis.

The Music app is used for playing and managing digital music. If you want to watch videos, TV show episodes, or movies that you've purchased and/or downloaded from the iTunes Store, use the Videos app.

> **TIP** Instead of storing music on your iOS mobile device, you also have the option to stream music via the Internet. One way to do this is using Apple Music or iTunes Radio (an online-based streaming music service that enables you to listen to music via the Music app when your mobile device has Internet access).

To experience the free podcasts available from the iTunes Store, use Apple's own Podcasts app. To access a vast collection of educational and personal enrichment content available from the Apple Store, also for free, take advantage of the under-hyped iTunes U service. To do this, use the free iTunes U app.

Meanwhile, if you want to stream and watch videos from YouTube, this can be done using Safari by visiting www.YouTube.com, but your experience watching this content will be much better if you use the official (free) YouTube app available from the App Store.

> **NOTE** When you stream content from the Internet, it gets transferred from the Internet directly to your iOS device. However, your iPhone or iPad does not save streamed content.
>
> Streaming content from the Internet requires using a specialized app, which is provided by the source of the content. Later in this chapter, you discover which apps are for accessing specific on-demand television programming, movies, videos, radio stations, and other content that gets streamed (not downloaded) to your iPhone or iPad.

GET STARTED USING THE MUSIC APP

In June 2015, Apple released a redesigned version of the Music app, which is chock full of new features and functions, including access to the new Apple Music service. This new version of the Music app now comes preinstalled with iOS 9.

The Music app continues to serve multiple purposes when it comes to experiencing music content. For example, it allows you to play songs or albums that are stored on your iPhone or iPad and that you own. You can also use the app to create, manage, and play back custom song playlists that you create or acquire.

Plus, when your iPhone or iPad has a continuous Internet connection, it's possible to launch the free iTunes Radio feature to stream music from the Internet, listen to the Beats 1 global radio station, and take advantage of the Music app's new Connect feature. Streaming capabilities are also needed to use Apple Music.

DISCOVER THE NEW APPLE MUSIC SERVICE

In June 2015, Apple launched a new music service, called Apple Music. While a free, three-month trial subscription to the service is available, individual users ultimately need to pay $9.99 per month for an ongoing subscription. Apple Music is accessible from the Music app. A $14.99 Family Membership plan (giving up to six people access to the service) is also offered.

Apple Music enables users to stream (not download) any music available from the iTunes Store on an on-demand and unlimited basis. In addition, music from independent bands, artists, and musicians is available.

NOTE Music content you experience via Apple Music is streamed from the Internet, not purchased. One benefit to this on-demand aspect of the listening experience is that songs from Apple Music can be incorporated into your personalized playlists and stored on your mobile device even if you don't own them.

Apple Music also allows users to access precreated playlists compiled by others. In addition, the online-based service allows fans to interact with their favorite artists and music groups in new and innovative ways through a feature built in to the new Music app called Connect.

Another useful feature of Apple Music is that you can quickly select one or more artists, songs, albums, or music genres that you love, and the service recommends similar music based on your personal tastes. This is a great tool for discovering new, up-and-coming artists and bands, or for previewing new music from some of your favorite artists or bands.

 **MORE INFO** You can learn more about Apple Music by visiting www.apple.com/music.

USING THE MUSIC APP: A QUICK TUTORIAL

The Music app is designed to give you total control over your music listening experience when it comes to music stored on your iPhone, as well as when listening to iTunes Radio, Apple Music, and music from the iTunes Store that's streamed from the Internet.

TIP Everything having to do with the Music app, as well as finding and listening to music on your iPhone or iPad, can now be controlled using Siri.

For example, if you're an Apple Music subscriber, at any time an Internet connection is available, activate Siri and say, "Play [insert song title]." Your iPhone or iPad finds and begins streaming that song, on-demand, within a few seconds.

When you launch the Music app from the Home screen on your iPhone or iPad, along the bottom of the screen multiple command icons are displayed: For You, New, Radio, Connect, Playlists (iPad only), and My Music (shown in Figure 14.1). Tap on these icons to manage and experience music via the Music app, iTunes Radio, and Apple Music.

The Music App's New Command Icons

Figure 14.1

The Music app offers a new selection of icons displayed at the bottom of the screen. The Radio icon is selected here.

NOTE With Apple Music disabled in the Music app, the options icons available include My Music, Playlists, Radio and Connect.

Here's a rundown of what each icon is used for:

■ **For You**—Based on past music purchases, your music listening habits using the Music app, and information about your musical tastes that you provide to the app, the Music app recommends music you might be interested in and provides collections of curated playlists. An Internet connection is required.

> **TIP** When viewing the For You section of the Music app, tap on any music selection or listing to begin streaming that music (if you subscribe to Apple Music). Tap on the song's More icon to add the selected (and playing) song to the My Music section of the app, or make it available for offline playing. This feature requires that you turn on the iCloud Music Library feature from within Settings. To do this, launch Settings, tap on the Music option, and then turn on the virtual switch associated with the iCloud Music Library feature.

■ **New**—Discover newly released music from well-known recording artists and bands, as well as music from independent or up-and-coming artists and bands. This includes new singles, new albums, spotlights on new artists, and curated music selections (see Figure 14.2).

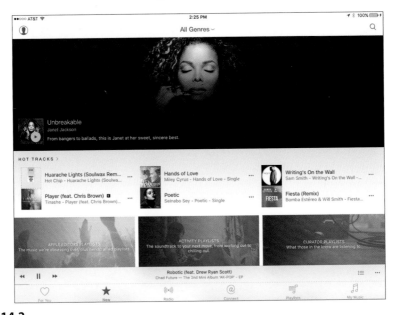

Figure 14.2
Discover new music to listen to that matches your personal taste.

■ **Radio**—In addition to giving you access to the free iTunes Radio service, which allows you to create custom radio stations based on your music preferences or listen to precreated streaming stations, tap on the Listen Now button associated with Beats 1 to tune in to this 24/7 global broadcast. To utilize this feature, a continuous Internet connection is required.

> **☑ TIP** Using iTunes Radio, to listen to a precreated radio station, launch the Music app, tap on the Radio icon, and then scroll down on the screen to the Featured Stations listing. Tap on a listing to play that station, or scroll down further for a more extensive listing of stations based on genre.
>
> Anytime you're listening to any music in the Music app, to quickly create a custom iTunes Radio station based on that music selection, tap on the More icon from the mini-player or Now Playing controls, and then tap on the Start Station menu option.

> **✎ NOTE** Based on the song, album, artist, or music genre you choose, iTunes Radio creates a custom radio station for you. Unless you're a paid Apple Music or iTunes Match subscriber, however, the programming will include commercials.
>
> Keep in mind that iTunes Radio does not allow you to control the song selections or song order. You can, however, skip to the next song at any time, and for songs you like, tap on the heart-shaped "like" button, so iTunes Radio can better learn your music preferences.

■ **Connect**—The Music app offers an interactive online community where any artist or band can communicate directly with fans by publishing music, videos, photos, or other content (shown in Figure 14.3). A growing number of popular, as well as up-and-coming artists and bands, are using this interactive online forum in much the same way as they would use a Facebook page, Instagram feed, Snapchat account, Tumblr page, or Twitter feed, for example, to communicate with their fans. In addition to the content that the artist/band uploads, Connect offers direct access to the selected artist's music.

> **☑ TIP** If you want to see the content uploaded by your favorite artists using the Music app's Connect feature, you first need to Follow that artist. When you begin using the Music app and provide your music preferences, the app automatically follows a handful of relevant artists on your behalf.

To find your own artists/bands to follow, tap on the Connect icon, tap on the Search icon, and then enter the name of the artist/band you're interested in. Tap on a search result related to the artist you want to follow, and then tap on the corresponding Follow button.

To manage your list of followed artists, tap on the Connect icon and then tap on the See Who You're Following option. When the listing of followed artists appears, tap on the Unfollow button for any artists you no longer want to follow, or tap on the Find More Artists and Curators to see additional recommendations for artists and bands you might want to follow. Tap on the Done option to save your changes.

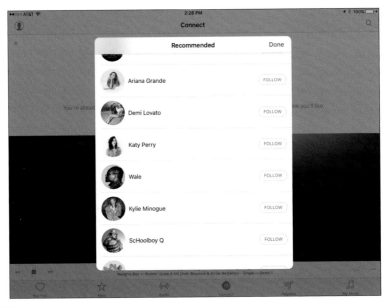

Figure 14.3

Interact with popular and up-and-coming recording artists and bands who you opt to follow by tapping on the Connect icon in the Music app.

■ **Playlists**—On the iPad, tap on the Playlists icon to create, view, and manage your customized music playlists (shown in Figure 14.4). On the iPhone, to work with Playlists, tap on the My Music icon, and then at the top-center of the screen, tap on the Playlists tab. Figure 14.5 shows the Playlist creation and management screen on the iPhone. (Keep in mind, when using an iPhone, if Apple Music is disabled, a Playlists icon is displayed on the toolbar.)

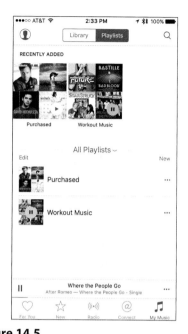

Figure 14.4

Create, listen to, and manage customized playlists using the Playlists feature of the Music app on an iPad.

Figure 14.5

The Playlist management screen is shown here on an iPhone.

- **My Music**—From here you can manage all the music currently stored on your iPhone or iPad. To use the functionality offered in the My Music portion of the app, no Internet connection is required to access music stored in your device. To access music stored in your iCloud account, Internet access is needed.

> **NOTE** On an iPhone, after tapping on the My Music option, tap on the Library tab located in the top center of the screen to find and play individual songs or albums, or tap on the Playlists tab to manage your playlists (shown in Figure 14.6). These tabs are not displayed if you have Apple Music disabled.

> **NOTE** To change how the music is sorted and displayed, tap on the Artists pull-down menu to reveal a pull-down menu that contains options for sorting music by Artists, Albums, Songs, Music Videos, Genres, Composers, or Compilations. To display only music that's stored on your device (as opposed to music stored on your device and available to you via iCloud), turn on the virtual switch associated with the Only Offline Music option displayed at the bottom of this menu.

Figure 14.6

On the iPhone, manage music stored on your smartphone, plus manage playlists by first tapping on the My Music icon. The Library tab is selected here, and the music is sorted alphabetically by artist name.

iOS 9 WHAT'S NEW Anytime music is selected or playing via the Music app, near the bottom of the screen, just above the command icons, a new mini-player is displayed that allows you play/pause the music or quickly access the app's Now Playing screen, which gives you more options than ever before when it comes to controlling the music playing on your iPhone or iPad.

MANAGING YOUR MUSIC VIA THE MUSIC APP

Music stored on your iOS device can be accessed, managed, and enjoyed either one song at a time or by creating and listening to custom playlists.

For example, on the iPhone, when you tap on the Library tab displayed near the top center of the screen (after tapping on the My Music option), or when you tap on the My Music option on the iPad, you see music that's recently been acquired under the Recently Added heading, as well as a listing of all music currently stored on your iOS device. It's possible to organize this music alphabetically by song title, artist, album, genre, or one of several other ways.

To do this, tap on the displayed pull-down menu (shown in Figure 14.7). On the iPad, this pull-down menu is displayed at the top center of the screen, while on the iPhone, it's found below the Recently Added section.

Figure 14.7
Decide how you want to sort and display the music stored on your iPhone or iPad.

On the iPhone, tap on the Playlists tab displayed near the top center of the screen to gain access to the in-app tools for creating, managing, accessing, and playing custom playlists. On the iPad, tap on the Playlists icon.

CONTROLLING YOUR MUSIC USING THE MINI-PLAYER CONTROLS

Whenever music is playing via the Music app, and the app is currently open, the mini-player controls are displayed near the bottom of the screen, just above the five command icons (shown in Figure 14.8).

Figure 14.8
The mini-player controls display the name of the music, a time slider, a Play/Pause icon, as well as a More icon.

To use the mini-player controls, tap on the Play/Pause icon to start or stop the currently selected music or tap on the More icon to display a menu that offers more options.

> **TIP**   From the mini-player, to instantly switch to the Now Playing screen (which is explained in the next section), tap your finger on the mini-player controls.
>
> To then close the Now Playing screen and return to the mini-player controls, and the Music app screen you were previously viewing, tap on the downward-pointing arrow icon displayed in the top-left corner of the Now Playing screen.

CONTROLLING YOUR MUSIC FROM THE NOW PLAYING SCREEN

Whenever music is playing via the Music app, when you access the Now Playing screen, the album/artist artwork is displayed on the screen (shown in Figure 14.9).

Figure 14.9

The Now Playing screen displays information about the currently playing music.

Immediately below the album/artist artwork is the time slider. Move your finger on this slider to fast forward or rewind within the song. To the left of the slider is a clock that displays how much of the song has played. To the right of the slider is a clock that displays how much of the song is remaining.

Below the time slider (on the iPhone) the song's title is displayed, and below that are music control icons, which include

NOTE   On the iPad, the song's title and album info are displayed at the top center of the Now Playing screen.

- **Like**—Tap on this icon to "like" the currently playing song. This helps the Music app better learn your music preferences, which then helps it make more accurate music recommendations and create more personalized programming when using iTunes Radio.

- **Rewind**—Tap this button to switch to the previously played song. Press and hold this button to rewind within the song.

- **Play/Pause**—When the music is playing, press the Pause icon to pause the music. When the music is paused, press the Play icon to restart the music from where you last left off.

- **Fast Forward**—Tap this icon to jump to the next song, or press and hold this icon to fast forward within the song.

- **Up Next**—View a listing of songs stored on your iPhone or iPad, from the current playlist, or from the iTunes Radio programming lineup you're listening to. To switch to a different song, tap on its listing.

NOTE   When playing an album, the Up Next option displays the song that will be played next, whether or not the Shuffle feature is turned on.

Located below the music control icons on the Now Playing screen is the volume slider. Use your finger to move this slider left or right to decrease or increase the volume. Keep in mind that the volume control buttons on the side of your iPhone or iPad and/or the volume control buttons associated with your earphones or headphones can also be used.

TIP   Yet another volume control slider can be found in the Control Center. Place your finger at the bottom of your iOS device's screen and swipe upward to access iOS 9's Control Center.

Displayed along the bottom of the Now Playing screen are four additional icons. On the iPhone, from left to right, these include Share, Shuffle, Repeat, and More. On the iPad, from left to right, these include Shuffle, Repeat, Share, and More.

Here's what each is used for:

- **Share**—Access the Share menu to share with other people details about the song or album you're enjoying, or access the Remove from this Playlist option (if applicable).

- **Shuffle**—Shuffle the order in which the currently selected playlist or music selections are heard.

- **Repeat**—Tap on this icon to continuously repeat the currently selected song.

- **More**—Tap on this icon to reveal a menu that offers the following options: Show in iTunes Store, Share Song, Add to a Playlist, and Remove from My Music.

> **NOTE** When your iPhone or iPad has Internet access, any songs stored in your iCloud account but not currently stored on your iPhone can be streamed from the Internet and listened to on your iPhone or iPad without first download-ing that content. These songs (or albums) display an iCloud icon to the right of their listings.

HOW TO CREATE CUSTOM PLAYLISTS USING THE MUSIC APP

Playlists are used to create a custom selection of songs. If you're an Apple Music subscriber, a playlist can be created from any music that's part of the iTunes Store music collection. However, if you're not an Apple Music subscriber, the music that can be added to playlists is limited to music stored on the mobile device you're using (or within your iCloud account that you own).

> **NOTE** Think of a playlist as being like a custom mix tape. You decide what songs are included, how many songs are included, and the order in which those songs will be played (or they can be played in a random order).
>
> Using the Music app, it's possible to create or access an unlimited number of playlists, so you can have separate playlists for different types of activities or moods, for example.

Thanks to iCloud, when you create a playlist, it almost instantly syncs between your iPhone, iPad, and all other computers linked to your iCloud account. Thus, all your playlists are always accessible when and where you want to experience them.

Furthermore, if you're an Apple Music subscriber, an ever-changing and growing selection of curated playlists are accessible to you via the Music app.

> **TIP** When playing a playlist comprised of music stored on your iPhone or iPad, no Internet connection is required. However, if the music is being streamed from your iCloud account or via the Apple Music service, a continuous Internet connection is required.

CREATE A PLAYLIST USING THE MUSIC APP ON AN iPHONE

Follow these steps to create and save a custom playlist using the Music app on your iPhone:

1. Launch the Music app on your iPhone.

2. Tap on the My Music icon in the bottom-right corner of the screen.

3. Tap on the Playlists tab near the top center of the screen (shown in Figure 14.10). Playlists will appear as an icon on the toolbar if Apple Music is turned off.

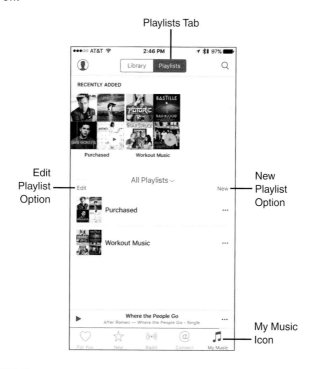

Figure 14.10

Tap on the Playlists tab at the top of the My Music screen to create, manage, or play a playlist stored in the Music app.

4. To the right of the All Playlists option, tap on the New option.

5. Enter a custom title for the playlist (shown in Figure 14.11).

Playlist Photo

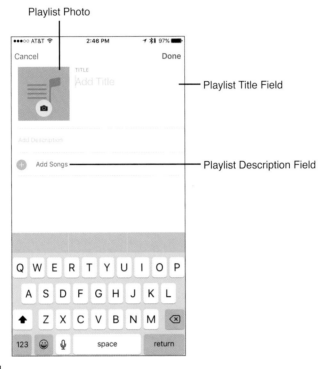

Playlist Title Field

Playlist Description Field

Figure 14.11

Fill in the Add Title and Add Description fields, and select an optional photo/graphic for your playlist.

6. In the Add Description field, type a short description of the playlist. For example, type "Music for Road Trips."

7. Tap on the Photo icon to import any image that you want to associate with that playlist. You can either take a photo using the iPhone or iPad's camera or select a photo already stored on the device.

8. Tap on the Add Songs option.

9. From the Add Music screen, choose an option based on how you want your music selections displayed. Options include Artists, Albums, Songs, and so on (shown in Figure 14.12).

10. If you select Songs, for example, all the songs currently stored on your iPhone or accessible via your iCloud account are displayed in alphabetical order (shown in Figure 14.13). Each song has an Add icon to the right of its listing. Tap on this "+" icon to add the song to your playlist.

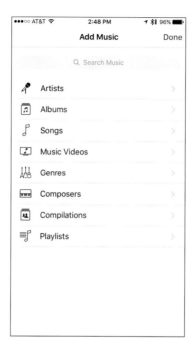

Figure 14.12

Select how you want the music stored on your iPhone to be displayed.

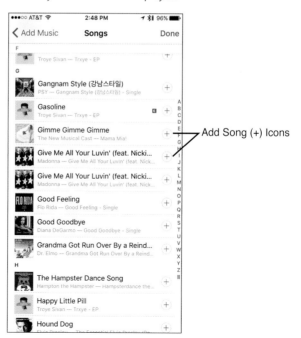

Figure 14.13

Tap on the Add icon associated with each song you want to add to your playlist.

> **NOTE** If you selected Artists or Albums, for example, after tapping on the Add Music option, a list of artists whose music you have stored on your iPhone or iPad, or a list of albums (or partial albums) you have stored on your iOS device is displayed. Tap on a listing to view individual song titles, and then tap on the Add icon associated with each song you want to add. If you select Artists, initially a list of that artist's albums is displayed. Tap on an album to reveal individual songs.

11. Tap on the Done option when you've finished compiling the list of songs to be added to your playlist.

12. A summary screen for your playlist is displayed (shown in Figure 14.14). To the right of each song listing you see a Move icon. Place your finger on any of these icons and then drag it up or down to rearrange the order of the songs.

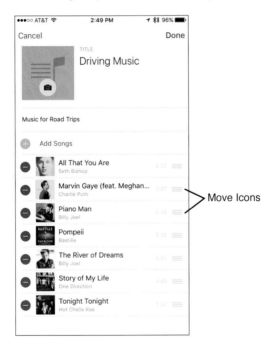

Figure 14.14

Tap on the Move icon and drag to rearrange the order of songs.

13. Tap on the Done option to save your newly created playlist.

14. The new playlist is displayed below the All Playlists heading when you tap on the My Music icon and then the Playlists tab (shown in Figure 14.15).

15. Tap on the playlist listing under the All Playlists heading to access that playlist.

16. Tap on any song listing in the playlist to begin playing it.

Figure 14.15

Access or manage a playlist by tapping on its listing displayed below the All Playlists heading.

Newly Created Playlist

☑ TIP   To edit the contents of a playlist, from the playlist screen while a playlist is being played, tap on the Edit option. Alternatively, while a song from a playlist is playing, access the Now Playing screen, and then tap on the More icon to remove the currently playing song from the currently selected playlist.

To delete a playlist, tap on the My Music icon, followed by the Playlists tab, and then tap on the More icon associated with the playlist title listed below the All Playlists option. From the More menu, tap on the Delete option, and then when prompted, confirm your decision by tapping on the Delete Playlist button.

☑ TIP   Regardless of what you're doing on your iPhone, it's also possible to begin playing a playlist, or any song, by activating Siri and issuing a command like, "Play [insert playlist title] playlist." You can also ask Siri to play a particular song, or music from a specific artist, for example.

CREATE A PLAYLIST USING THE MUSIC APP ON AN iPAD

To create a Playlist using the iPad, begin by launching the Music app on your tablet and then tap on the Playlists icon at the bottom of the screen. Next, tap on the New option near the top-right corner of the screen. Starting at step 5, follow the steps outlined in the previous section.

CONTROL THE MUSIC APP FROM CONTROL CENTER

Once music is playing via the Music app, it's possible to control the playback of that music in several ways. For example, many headphones and earbuds have controller buttons associated with them that replicate the Rewind, Pause/Play, and Fast Forward buttons seen in the Music app.

However, regardless of what you're doing on your iPhone or iPad, it's possible to control music playing using the Music app controls that appear in the Control Center.

To access the Control Center, place your finger near the bottom of the iPhone or iPad's screen and swipe upward. Then, in the Control Center (shown in Figure 14.16), the Music app controls include a time slider; details about the song that's playing; the Rewind, Play/Pause, and Fast Forward icons; and a volume slider. (If you're listening to iTunes Radio, the Rewind icon is replaced by the star-shaped icon for liking the currently playing music.)

Music App Controls

Figure 14.16

The Control Center can be accessed regardless of what app is running. From within Settings, you can also grant permission to access the Control Center directly from the Lock screen.

CUSTOMIZE THE iTUNES STORE AND MUSIC APPS ON YOUR iPHONE

To customize some of the functions and features associated with the iTunes Store and Music apps, launch Settings and tap on the App & iTunes Stores and Music option one at a time.

After tapping on the App and iTunes Stores option, for example, from under the Automatic Downloads option, turn on the virtual switch associated with Music if you want songs you purchase on other computers or mobile devices that are linked to the same iCloud account to automatically be downloaded to the iPhone or iPad you're currently using. If this feature is turned off, you always have the option of manually downloading that music.

> **TIP** If you have a preset cellular data monthly usage allocation, turn off the virtual switch associated with Use Cellular Data. This prevents you from using iTunes Radio or automatically downloading content from the iTunes Store using a cellular (3G/4G/LTE) connection, which will quickly use up your monthly data allocation. These features work fine, however, anytime your iPhone or iPad is connected to the Internet via a Wi-Fi connection.

Upon tapping on the Music option within Settings, one at a time, turn on/off the virtual switches associated with each customizable option, or when applicable, tap on the option to select options from a submenu.

STREAMING MUSIC VIA THE INTERNET

iTunes Radio offers a free music streaming service operated by Apple. This service does not allow you to create custom playlists, but it does allow you to create custom iTunes Radio Stations that play music that the service believes you'll enjoy.

By subscribing to the new Apple Music service, it's possible to create and stream any music you want—either individual songs, entire albums, or custom playlists, pulling from almost any music offered by the iTunes Store.

There are also many other free and subscription-based streaming music services that you can enjoy from your iPhone or iPad. To utilize one of these services, such as Pandora, Last.fm, SoundCloud, Amazon Cloud Player, or Spotify, for example, you need to download and install the app for that service, set up an account, and if applicable, pay for a subscription.

In addition, virtually every radio network and local radio station in the world, as well as Sirius/XM Satellite Radio, now has proprietary apps that allow you to stream live programing from the Internet directly to your iOS device. An AM, FM, or satellite radio receiver is not required, but a continuous Internet connection is needed.

> **☑ TIP**   The free iHeartRadio app, for example, allows you to stream live radio (music) programming from many of the most popular radio stations in the United States. You can also create customized radio stations, based on your favorite music genre, artist, or favorite song(s) using this app.

USE THE VIDEOS APP TO WATCH TV SHOWS, MOVIES, AND MORE

After you purchase and download TV show episodes, movies, or music videos from the iTunes Store, that video-based content can be enjoyed using the Videos app. It can also be viewed on your primary computer using the iTunes software and shared between devices via iCloud. If you have Apple TV, it's possible to stream videos from your iOS device to your home theater system.

After you download or transfer iTunes Store video content to your iPhone or iPad, it is accessible from the Videos app. When you launch the Videos app, you see multiple tabs on the screen, based on the types of video content stored on your device. Figure 14.17 shows the TV show episodes that have been downloaded and are ready to view.

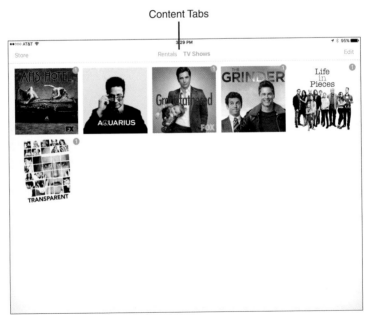

Figure 14.17

Use the Videos app content tabs to view the video content that you have stored on your iPhone or iPad that's downloaded and ready to watch.

> ☑ **TIP**   From within Settings, tap on the Videos option and then turn on the
> virtual switch for the Show iTunes Purchases option to view all compatible content
> you've purchased or acquired from the iTunes Store, including content stored in
> your iCloud account but not downloaded to the iOS device you're using (shown in
> Figure 14.18).
>
> Thumbnails that display a cloud icon represent content stored in iCloud but not
> on the device you're using.

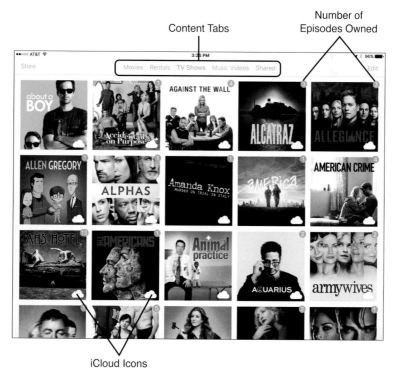

Figure 14.18

After turning on the Show iTunes Purchases option from within Settings, you can see all content you've previously acquired from the iTunes Store, based on which content tab you tap on in the top center of the screen. Shown here are acquired TV shows.

These tabs are labeled TV Shows, Rentals, Movies, and Music Videos. On the
iPhone, they're displayed near the bottom of the screen, whereas on the iPad,
they're displayed near the top center.

> **NOTE** If you have rented movies from the iTunes Store, as opposed to purchasing them, a Rentals tab is displayed in addition to or instead of a Movies tab. Movie rentals can be viewed only on the device on which they were rented and cannot be transferred from one iOS mobile device to another. It is possible, however, to use AirPlay to play rented movies from your iPhone or iPad on an HD TV equipped with Apple TV.

When you tap on the TV Shows, Movies, Rentals, or Music Videos tab, a thumbnail graphic representing each piece of viewable content is displayed. To begin playing a video, tap on its thumbnail graphic.

If an iCloud icon appears in the thumbnail graphic, it means you own that content, but it is not currently stored on your mobile device. Tap on the iCloud icon to download that content from your iCloud account to the device you're using.

> **TIP** When looking at the graphic thumbnails for TV shows you own, the number displayed in a blue circle near the top-right corner indicates how many episodes of that particular TV series you own. Tap on the thumbnail to see a listing of specific episodes and then view them.

To delete video content from your iPhone, access the listing for that particular TV show episode, movie, or music video, and then swipe your finger from right to left across the listing. Tap the Delete button to confirm your decision.

On the iPad, to delete video content, tap on the Edit button near the top-right corner of the screen and then tap on the "X" icon that appears on the movie thumbnail listing(s) you want to delete.

After you delete iTunes Store–purchased content from your iPhone or iPad, it's always possible to redownload it from your iCloud account for free.

To shop for additional video content from the iTunes Store while using the Videos app, tap on the Store.

To play a video, tap on a thumbnail representing the video that you want to watch. If you've downloaded a TV show, for example, a new screen appears listing all episodes from that TV series currently stored on your iOS device (as shown in Figure 14.19). Tap on the episode of your choice to begin playing it, or tap on the Play icon.

For music videos or movies, a similar information screen pertaining to that content is displayed. Tap on the Play icon to begin watching that video content.

Figure 14.19

Multiple episodes of the same TV series are grouped together for easy access and viewing.

TIP   When playing video content, hold your iPhone or iPad in either portrait or landscape mode. However, the video window is significantly larger if you position your iOS mobile device sideways and use landscape mode.

If applicable, based on the video content you're watching, on an iPad, you can instantly switch between full-screen mode and letterbox mode as your onscreen viewing option by tapping the icon displayed in the upper-right corner of the screen.

iOS 9 WHAT'S NEW   If you're using one of the newer iPad models to watch a video using the Videos app, you have the option to use the new Picture-in-Picture feature (shown in Figure 14.20). After you start playing a TV show or movie, for example, tap on the Picture-in-Picture icon in the bottom-right corner of the screen. The video window shrinks and displays Enlarge, Play/Pause, and Close icons. Tap the Play icon to continue playing your video in the smaller screen.

As the video is playing, place and hold your finder on the video window to move it around within the iPad's screen. It's then possible to launch another app and use that app as the video continues playing in its smaller window.

When iOS 9 was first released, only video played using the Videos app supported this feature. However, other popular apps used for streaming video content, like YouTube, HBOGo, Netflix, Amazon Video, and HuluPlus, will no doubt add this feature in the near future (if they haven't already done so).

Video App
Picture-in-Picture   Safari App

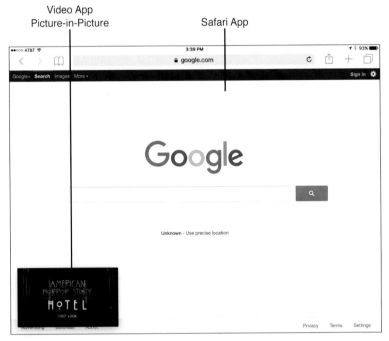

Figure 14.20

Shown here is Safari running on the iPad mini 4, with a video playing in the window located in the bottom-left corner of the screen.

Typically, while video content is playing, it displays in full-screen mode or letterbox mode. Tap anywhere on the screen to reveal the onscreen command icons used for controlling the video as you're watching it (shown in Figure 14.21). When a video is playing, these controls disappear automatically after a few seconds. Tap anywhere on the screen to make them reappear.

NOTE If you're watching a purchased movie acquired from the iTunes Store, below the Play, Rewind, and Fast Forward controls you might discover additional tabs that enable you to access movie-related "extras" that would otherwise be made available as part of the DVD or Blu-ray version of the movie. Tap on any of these tabs to access the bonus content, which is movie-specific.

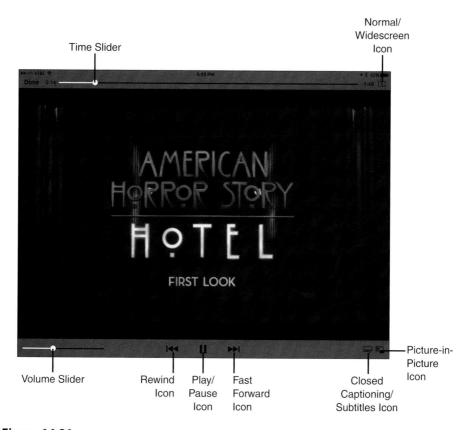

Normal/
Widescreen
Icon

Time Slider

Volume Slider

Rewind
Icon

Play/
Pause
Icon

Fast
Forward
Icon

Closed
Captioning/
Subtitles Icon

Picture-in-
Picture
Icon

Figure 14.21
The onscreen icons for controlling the video you're watching on your iOS device.

Along the top center of the screen is a time slider. On either end of this slider are timers. To the left is a timer that displays how much of the video you've already watched. On the right of the slider is a timer that displays how much time in the video remains. Tap on the Done button in the upper-left corner of the screen to exit the video you're watching.

> **TIP** To manually fast-forward or rewind while watching a video, place your finger on the dot icon that appears on the time slider and drag it left or right.

Near the bottom center of the screen as you're watching video content are the Rewind and Fast Forward icons. Tap on the Rewind icon to move back by scene or chapter, or tap the Fast Forward icon to advance to the next scene or chapter in the video (just as you would while watching a DVD). Press and hold the Rewind or Fast Forward icon to rewind or fast forward while viewing the onscreen content. You can rewind or advance by a few seconds at a time.

Tap the Play icon to play the video. When the video is playing, the Play icon transforms into a Pause icon, used to pause the video.

> **NOTE** If you pause a video and then exit the Videos app, you pick up exactly where you left off watching the video when you relaunch the Videos app. This information is automatically saved.

Use the volume control slider to manually adjust the volume of the audio.

Located near the lower-right corner of the screen while a video is playing (when the controls are visible) are the Captions and AirPlay icons. (On newer iPad models, the Picture-in-Picture icon is also displayed in the lower-right corner of the screen.)

Tap on the Captions icon to adjust captions and/or switch between audio languages, if the video content you're watching supports these features. If not available, the text-bubble icon is not visible.

Tap on the AirPlay option to stream the video from your mobile device to your television set or home theater system via an Apple TV. If you have Bluetooth- or AirPlay-compatible speakers, it's possible to stream just the audio from a TV show or movie, for example, to external speakers or wireless headphones.

> **NOTE** You must use Wi-Fi to stream video from your iOS mobile device to your HD television via Apple TV. Both the iOS mobile device and Apple TV must be linked to the same wireless network.

> **TIP** From the iTunes Store, it's possible to purchase TV show episodes (or entire seasons from your favorite series), as well as full-length movies. In addition, you can rent certain movies.
>
> When you rent a move from the iTunes Store, it remains on your device for 30 days before it automatically deletes itself, whether or not the content has been viewed. However, after you press Play in the Videos app and begin watching rented content, you have access to that video for only 24 hours before it deletes itself. During that 24-hour period, you can watch and rewatch the movie as often as you'd like.

The first time you tap Play to watch a rented movie, you're prompted to confirm your choice. This starts the 24-hour clock and allows the rented movie to begin playing.

Unlike movies you purchase from the iTunes Store (that you can load into all of your computers and/or iOS mobile devices that are linked to the same Apple ID account), rented movies can be stored on only one computer, Apple TV, or iOS mobile device.

USE THE iTUNES STORE APP TO ACQUIRE NEW MUSIC, TV SHOWS, MOVIES, AND MORE

The iTunes Store app comes preinstalled with iOS 9 and is used to acquire music, movies, TV shows, and ringtones.

To utilize this app (shown in Figure 14.22), your iOS mobile device requires Internet access. For smaller-sized files, such as songs, albums, or ringtones, a cellular data connection can be used. However, for larger-sized files, such as TV show episodes and movies, you must use a Wi-Fi Internet connection to download the content.

Figure 14.22

Use the iTunes Store app to purchase music, TV shows, and movie content and acquire free music and video-based content.

NOTE Like the App Store, from the iTunes Store you're able to view detailed descriptions and reviews of content before purchasing (or renting) it.

It's also possible to preview the content or watch a movie's trailer(s). Tap on the Details tab to read a description and access previews (shown in Figure 14.23), or tap on the Reviews tab to see star-based ratings and read reviews.

The process for purchasing content from the iTunes Store is virtually identical to using the App Store, so refer to Chapter 3, "Strategies for Finding, Buying, and Using Third-Party Apps," for more information.

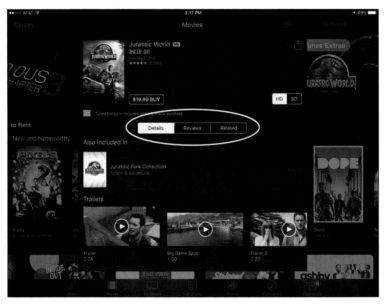

Figure 14.23

Tap on any content's listing to view a detailed Description screen. From here, you can read a description, watch a preview/trailer(s), and access star-based ratings and reviews.

On the iPhone, displayed along the bottom of the iTunes Store screen are five command icons: Music, Movies, TV Shows, Search, and More. Tap on the More icon to access the Ringtones, Genius, Purchased, and Downloads options.

On the iPad, six command icons are displayed along the bottom of the screen, which from left to right are Music, Movies, TV Shows, Top Charts, Genius, and Purchased. The Search field is displayed in the top-right corner of the screen.

To shop for music (or acquire free music), tap on the Music icon. Likewise, to purchase or rent movies, tap on the Movies icon. For TV shows (either individual episodes or entire seasons of a series), tap on the TV Shows icon. Use the Search feature to quickly find audio or video content using keywords.

> **TIP** After you tap on the More icon on the iPhone, tap Purchased to view all past purchases from the iTunes Store. As content is downloading, you can view the progress of that download by tapping on the Purchased icon.

Just like when using the App Store to acquire new apps for your mobile device, when you make a purchase from the iTunes Store, all charges are automatically billed to the credit or debit card you have linked with your Apple ID or offset against any credit your account might have from redeemed gift cards.

> **TIP** You can redeem an iTunes Gift Card and add the credit to the Apple ID account used for making online purchases from the iTunes Store, App Store, or iBook Store. When you select the Redeem option, it's possible to scan a physical gift card using the camera built in to your iOS mobile device so you don't have to manually type the long redemption code.

When you make a purchase from your iPhone or iPad, it immediately gets downloaded to that device and, at the same time, gets stored in your iCloud account. The online storage space required for purchased iTunes Store content is provided free of charge, and does not count against the 5GB of free online storage space your iCloud account comes with.

The same content can then be downloaded and experienced on your other Macs and iOS mobile devices that are linked to the same iCloud account.

> **TIP** The iTunes Store offers a Complete My Season feature for TV show seasons. If you purchase one or more single episodes of a TV series (from a specific season), you can later return to the iTunes Store and purchase the rest of the episodes from that season at a reduced price (based on how many episodes from that season you already own). This feature works just like the Complete My Album feature for your music but relates to TV shows.

WHAT'S NEW If you're interested in purchasing and listening to audiobooks on your iOS mobile device, thousands of titles are available from the iTunes Store. However to acquire and then listen to this content, you now need to use the iBooks app, which is covered in Chapter 15, "Customize Your Reading Experience with iBooks and the News App."

All audiobooks you previously acquired and enjoyed listening to using the Music app have been automatically transferred to the iOS 9 edition of the iBooks app.

Another option is to use the Audible.com service. It too offers a vast and ever-growing audiobook library. Audiobook titles can be purchased online and enjoyed using the free Audible app available from the App Store.

QUICKLY FIND TV EPISODES YOU WANT TO PURCHASE ON iTUNES

When shopping for TV show episodes to purchase and watch using the iTunes Store app, tap on the TV shows button that's displayed near the bottom of the screen. Shows are displayed by series name. The search results display the TV show by season number and by available episodes.

NOTE Purchasing most single TV episodes from the iTunes Store costs $1.99 (standard definition) or $2.99 (high definition). A discount for acquiring a complete season of a TV series is offered.

The price to purchase movies varies, but the rental price is typically $3.99 (standard definition) or $4.99 (high definition).

Most individual songs available from the iTunes Store cost between $0.69 and $1.29, while album prices vary.

In addition to purchasing one episode at a time, the iTunes Store gives you the option of purchasing the entire season at a discounted rate, plus choosing between high definition (HD) or standard definition (SD) video quality. The HD versions of TV shows utilize much larger file sizes and take up much more internal storage space within your device, but they look much better when you watch them.

To save money, purchase an entire season of your favorite show's current season. This is called a Season Pass. Then, when a new episode airs each week and becomes available from the iTunes Store (about 24 hours later), it can be downloaded to your iOS device and made available to you via iCloud using a Wi-Fi Internet connection. You'll also receive a weekly email, plus Notification Center alerts from Apple telling you when each new episode in your Season Pass is available.

When you shop for TV episodes from the iTunes Store (via the iTunes app), they're commercial free and available to watch whenever you want. They're also permanently accessible via your iCloud account to be downloaded to any computer, iOS device, or Apple TV device that's linked to the same iCloud account. Once an episode is download to your iPhone or iPad, an Internet connection is no longer needed to watch it.

> **TIP** Each week, the iTunes Store offers free episodes of featured TV shows. To discover which episodes are being offered, launch the iTunes Store app, tap on the TV Shows icon, scroll down to the bottom of the screen, and under the TV Shows Quick Links heading, tap on Free TV Episodes. Then, from the Free TV Episodes screen, look under the Free Full-Length Episodes heading to see what's currently available.

STREAM VIDEO CONTENT INSTEAD OF PURCHASING AND DOWNLOADING IT

To stream video content from the Internet, you must use a specialized app, based on where the content is originating from on the Internet.

Whenever you're streaming video content, you can pause the video at any time. Depending on the app, you also can exit the app partway through a video and resume watching it from where you left off when you relaunch the app later.

Streamed TV programming and movies may or may not include commercials, based on the service you use to access it. For example, if you use the app from your cable TV service provider or from specific TV networks to stream on-demand programming using your iPhone or iPad, TV commercials are included if the original broadcast programming included commercials. However, if you subscribe to a fee-based service, like Netflix, Amazon Prime, or HuluPlus, streamed content is offered commercial-free.

> **CAUTION** The capability to stream content from the Internet gives you on-demand access to a wide range of programming; however, streaming audio or video content requires a tremendous amount of data to be transferred to your iOS device. Therefore, if you use a cellular data connection, your monthly wireless data allocation will quickly get used up. So, when you're streaming Internet content, it's best to use a Wi-Fi connection.
>
> Not only does a Wi-Fi connection often allow video data to be transferred at faster speeds and at a higher resolution, there's also no limit as to how much data you can send or receive.

Keep in mind that many cable television service providers (such as Xfinity/Comcast and Time Warner), as well as satellite TV service providers, individual television and cable TV networks (ABC, NBC, CBS, FOX, USA Network, Lifetime, SyFy, and so on), and even specific TV shows, often have their own proprietary apps available for streaming content from the Internet directly to your mobile device.

There are also paid streaming services, such as Netflix, Amazon Prime, and HuluPlus, that offer vast libraries of TV shows and movies available for streaming. These services charge a flat monthly fee (starting around $8.00 per month) to stream as much programming as you want to your computer(s) and mobile device(s).

iOS 9 **WHAT'S NEW** If you're not a paid subscriber of the HBO premium cable TV network, it's now possible to subscribe to HBO via the HBO Now app and be able to stream all of HBO's programming using your mobile device. This trend is being adopted by other premium cable TV networks as well. The HBOGo app is used if you're a current HBO subscriber via your cable/satellite service provider.

When you stream TV episodes from the Internet using a specialized app, this programming does not get stored on your iOS device and is available only when your iPhone or iPad has a constant connection to the Internet while you're watching that content. In many cases, a Wi-Fi connection is required.

iOS 9 **WHAT'S NEW** In addition to streaming TV and movie programming using the apps offered by cable TV and satellite providers, some of these apps now allow certain programming to be downloaded and watched offline. A growing number of these apps also now offer access to live programming.

The ability to download and store some TV show and movie content on your iPhone or iPad is also offered by the Amazon Prime streaming service.

IN THIS CHAPTER

- How to use iBooks to access iBook Store and shop for eBooks
- Acquire and listen to audio books using the iBooks app
- Customize your information gathering and reading experience with the new News app

15

CUSTOMIZE YOUR READING EXPERIENCE WITH iBOOKS AND THE NEWS APP

Thanks to Apple's iBooks app, eBooks can easily be acquired and read on any iOS mobile device (or Mac).

If you have a Mac, iPhone, or an iPad, you can use iCloud to sync your eBook library and related bookmarks between computers and iOS mobile devices (that are linked to the same iCloud account). As a result, all your books, even if you've acquired hundreds of them, are available to you regardless of which Mac or iOS device you're using.

Anything having to do with shopping for, downloading, installing, and then reading eBooks on your iPhone or iPad is done using the iBooks app.

iOS 9 WHAT'S NEW The iOS 9 edition of the iBooks app is now also used to acquire audiobooks from the iTunes Store and then listen to them on your iPhone or iPad.

iBooks now has three main purposes. First, it's used to access Apple's online-based iBook Store. From iBook Store, it's possible to browse an ever-growing collection of eBook titles (including traditional book titles from bestselling authors and major publishers that have been adapted into eBook form). Although some eBooks are free, most must be paid for.

> **TIP** As with purchases from the iTunes Store or App Store, eBook purchases made from iBook Store get charged to the credit or debit card associated with your Apple ID. iBook Store purchases can also be paid for using prepaid iTunes gift cards.

Second, the iBooks app is used to transform your smartphone or tablet into an eBook reader, which accurately reproduces the appearance of each page of a printed book on your device's screen, regardless of the device's screen size. So reading an eBook is just like reading a traditional book in terms of the appearance of text, photos, or graphics that would otherwise appear on a printed page.

Third, the iBooks app is now also used to acquire and listen to audiobooks. To find and purchase audiobooks, access iBook Store, tap on the Top Charts icon, and then tap on the Audiobooks tab to see a listing of popular audiobooks. Tap on the Categories option and then choose an audiobook category to narrow your search, or use the Search field to find the title you're looking for.

CUSTOMIZE YOUR EBOOK READING EXPERIENCE

iBooks offers many features that make reading eBooks on your iOS device a pleasure. For example, when you stop reading and exit the iBooks app (by pressing the Home button), the app automatically saves the page you're on using a virtual bookmark, and then later reopens to that page when the iBooks app is restarted.

> **NOTE** Thanks to iCloud, you can begin reading a book on one Mac or iOS mobile device, and then pick up exactly where you left off on another, simply by opening the iBooks app. You are allowed to install copies of your eBooks on all computers and devices that are linked to the same iCloud account, so you do not have to purchase the same eBook multiple times.

CUSTOMIZE iBOOKS SETTINGS

To customize settings related to iBooks, launch Settings and tap on the iBooks option (shown in Figure 15.1). A variety of options are available to you that can be adjusted by turning on or off the virtual switches associated with each feature.

Figure 15.1

From within Settings, it's possible to customize a handful of options related to the iBooks app.

> **TIP** At any time, an eBook's content can be updated by the book's author or publisher. By turning on the Online Content option that's part of the iBooks menu within Settings, your iPhone or iPad will automatically update eBooks you've already acquired when and if new content related to a previously purchased book becomes available.

iBooks enables you to store and manage a vast library of eBooks on your iOS device, the size of which is limited only by the storage capacity of the device itself. Plus, all your iBook Store purchases automatically get saved to your iCloud account. Thus, you can easily download eBook titles you've previously purchased via iCloud when you want to access a particular eBook that is not currently stored on your device.

ORGANIZE YOUR PERSONAL EBOOK LIBRARY

When you launch iBooks, the main Library screen is displayed (shown in Figure 15.2). Thumbnails of the book covers in your digital eBook library are displayed. Tap on the All Books option that's found near the top center of the screen to determine which eBook titles are displayed.

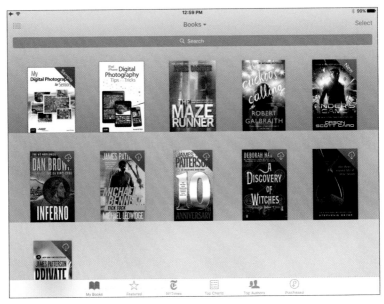

Figure 15.2

Tap on the My Books icon at the bottom of the iBooks screen to see your virtual bookshelf, which displays your eBook titles.

> **NOTE** When you have not yet opened an eBook in iBooks, a blue-and-white New banner appears on its cover thumbnail on the Library screen. If you've only downloaded the free sample for a book, a red-and-white Sample banner is displayed as part of the eBook's cover thumbnail.

Select the All option to display all eBooks you've acquired, including titles stored in your iCloud account but not currently stored on your actual iPhone or iPad. These titles display an iCloud icon in the top-right corner of their thumbnail (refer to Figure 15.2).

To hide the eBooks stored in your iCloud account and display only eBooks currently stored on your iPhone or iPad, turn on the virtual switch near the bottom
of the Collections window, which appears when you tap on the All Books option
(shown in Figure 15.3).

Figure 15.3

*From the Collections menu, create new Collection folders, each of which can have a custom title,
like Summer Reading or Blurb Photos Books.*

From this Collections menu, it's also possible to manually sort your eBook library
into separate Collections, each of which can have a custom name. To do this, tap
on the Edit option that's displayed to the right of the Collections heading, or tap
on the "+ New Collection" option that's listed as part of the Collections menu.

Once you've created additional Collections, you can easily move eBooks into a
specific Collection to organize them. To do this, return to the main Library screen,
and tap on the Select option. Next, tap on one or more eBook thumbnails that you
want to transfer from the default All Books Collection into a specific Collection. As
each eBook title is selected, a blue-and-white checkmark icon appears in the lower-
right corner of its thumbnail.

Tap on the Move icon, and when the Collections menu appears, tap on the name
of the Collection you want to move the selected eBooks into.

> **TIP** In addition to eBooks that have been formatted to be read using the iBooks app, this same app can also be used to view PDF files. When PDF files are transferred into the iBooks app, they automatically get placed in a separate Collection, called PDFs.

To delete eBooks stored on your iPhone or iPad (but keep them in your iCloud account), from the Library screen, tap on the Select option, tap on the eBook(s) you want to delete, and then tap on the Delete option that's displayed near the top-left corner of the Library screen.

> **TIP** A cellular or Wi-Fi Internet connection is needed to load eBooks into the iBooks app from iBook Store. However, after an eBook is loaded into the app, an Internet connection is no longer needed.

NAVIGATING AROUND THE iBOOKS APP

Displayed along the bottom of the Library screen in the iBooks app running on an iPhone are five command icons (shown in Figure 15.4). Here's how to use several of these options to find the eBook(s) you're looking for from Apple's online-based iBook Store:

- **My Books**—Tap on this icon to access the Library screen and view your personal eBook collection.

> **TIP** On the iPhone, after tapping on the My Books option, choose how you want to sort your eBook titles by tapping on one of the tabs displayed along the top of the screen (refer to Figure 15.4).
>
> Tap on the icon in the top-left corner of the screen to toggle between a list view and bookshelf view of the eBooks stored within the app (and/or available to you via iCloud).

- **Featured**—Access iBook Store and browse through books that Apple considers to be "featured" titles (shown in Figure 15.5).

Figure 15.4

These five command icons are displayed at the bottom of the screen when using an iPhone.

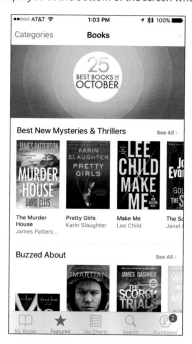

Figure 15.5

The Featured screen in iBook Store showcases eBooks that Apple chooses to highlight.

> **☑ TIP**   After tapping on the Featured button, scroll to the bottom of the screen to access the Apple ID [Your Username] button, the Redeem button, and the Send Gift button. Tap on the Apple ID button to manage your Apple ID account. Tap on the Redeem button to redeem iTunes Gift Cards and add credit to your Apple ID account. Tap Send Gift to send someone you know an eBook as a gift. You must know the recipient's email address to do this.

- **Top Charts**—Tap on this option to display the charts listing the bestselling eBooks within iBook Store (and also seek out audiobooks). Near the top of the screen, three tabs are displayed. Tap on the Books tab to discover multiple charts, including a chart for Paid eBooks and Free eBooks. Tap on the Audiobooks tab to search for audiobooks. Tap on the Top Authors tab to view an alphabetical listing of popular authors who have books available from iBook Store.

- **Search**—Tap on the Search option to reveal a Search field, within which you can type any book title, author name, keyword, or search phrase that helps you locate a specific book. Tap on any listing to view the Description for that book.

- **Purchased**—Tap on this option to quickly find and reload any eBook you've previously purchased.

> **☑ TIP**   When viewing the Purchased screen, tap on the Sort option to organize the book listing based on Most Recent or Name.

When using the iBooks app on an iPad, displayed along the bottom of the screen are six command icons (shown in Figure 15.6).

> **☑ TIP**   Displayed in the top-right corner of the iPad screen is the Search field. Tap on it anytime if you know the title of a specific book you're looking for. In this field, you can also search for eBooks based on an author's name, keyword, genre, or any search phrase. Tap on any listing to display that book's Description. If you already know what you're looking for, using the Search field is typically the fastest way to find it.

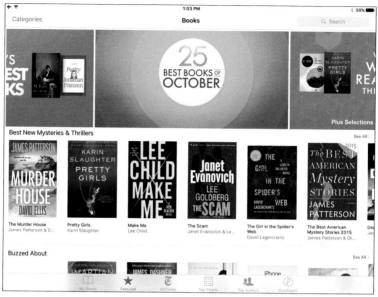

Figure 15.6

*As you'd expect, the Featured screen when viewed on the iPad reveals a lot more information
than what you see when viewing the same screen on an iPhone.*

The My Books, Features, Top Charts, Top Authors, and Purchased command icons
at the bottom of the iPad screen serve the same purpose as they do when using
the iPhone version of iBooks. On the iPad, however, there's also the NYTimes icon.

Tap on this NYTimes icon to display the *New York Times* Bestsellers list for both fic-
tion and nonfiction books. Only titles from this bestsellers list that are available in
eBook form from iBook Store are listed.

> **TIP** The Top Charts list can be customized to show titles from a spe-
> cific category or genre. To choose a specialized Top Chart listing, first tap on the
> Categories option and select a specific Category.

> **NOTE** It is possible to download and read eBooks acquired from sources
> other than iBook Store using iBooks; however, the eBooks must be a compatible
> file format. The iBooks app works with PDF files (or eBooks in PDF format), as well
> as eBooks created in the industry-standard ePub format.

LEARN MORE ABOUT SPECIFIC EBOOKS WHILE VISITING iBOOK STORE

As you add books to your eBook library, the cover art for each title is displayed in the Library screen. Tap on the My Books icon displayed near the bottom of this screen to view the Library screen.

To see an alternative listing view of the Library screen, tap on the Listing icon. The icon is comprised of three horizontal lines (shown in Figure 15.7). To return to the default Thumbnail view, tap the icon showing six squares.

Listing
Icon

Figure 15.7
Sort and then view your eBook collection using the virtual bookshelf format, as opposed to viewing a listing of eBooks.

> ✔ **TIP**   From the Library screen's Listing view screen, tap on the Most Recent, Titles, Authors, or Categories tab to sort your eBook collection. To search this listing on an iPhone, tap on the Search field that's displayed below the tabs. On the iPad, to make the Search field appear, place your finger near the center of the screen and swipe downward.

HOW TO FIND A SPECIFIC EBOOK—FAST

Use the Search field to enter the eBook title, author's name, subject, or keyword that's associated with what you're looking for. Entering a specific book title reveals very specific search results. However, entering a keyword relating to a topic or subject matter reveals a selection of eBook suggestions that somehow relate to that keyword.

Tap on any listing to reveal a more detailed description relating to a particular eBook. As you review a description for an eBook, look carefully at its ratings and its written reviews, especially if it's a paid eBook.

LEARN ABOUT AN EBOOK FROM ITS DESCRIPTION

A typical eBook listing includes the eBook's cover artwork, its title, and author. An eBook's description, however, is divided into several sections. Tap on the Details, Reviews, and Related tabs to view all information pertaining to a specific eBook.

> **NOTE** Using iBook Store to shop for eBooks is similar to using the App Store to acquire apps or using the iTunes Store to acquire TV shows, music, or movies. Each title has a detailed description screen, ratings and reviews associated with it, and a sample of the book can be downloaded for free into the iBooks app.
>
> Figure 15.8 shows a typical eBook description screen. The title, book cover, and price are displayed near the top, and the Details, Reviews, and Related tabs are displayed below this information.

Figure 15.8

Read a detailed description of an eBook before making your purchase and downloading it. The book's Price button and Sample button are also displayed near the top of the description.

A Share icon appears at the upper-right corner of an eBook description. Tap on it to share details about the eBook description with others. In the Share menu, there is also a Gift button. Tap on this to purchase and send the eBook as a gift for someone else. To do this, you need to know her email address.

> ☑ **TIP** You can preview an eBook before paying for it. As you're looking at a book's description, tap on the Sample button to download a free sample of that eBook. The length of the sample varies and is determined by the eBook's publisher. It is usually between a few pages and a full chapter.

Tap on the Reviews option to access the iBook Store Ratings chart, which showcases the book's average star-based rating and how many ratings the book has received. You can also see this average star-based rating broken up to see exactly how many stars (from one to five) the book has received from your fellow iBook Store customers. Below the star-based ratings are more detailed, text-based reviews written by other iBook Store customers.

PURCHASING AN EBOOK

To quickly purchase and download an eBook, tap on the Price button. When you tap on a price button, it changes to a Buy Book button. Tap this button to confirm your purchase decision. You then need to enter your Apple ID password to begin the download process. If your iOS mobile device is equipped with a Touch ID sensor, you can approve your acquisition using a fingerprint.

If you're downloading a free eBook, tap on the Free button displayed instead of a Price button. Then tap on the Get Book button.

It typically takes about 30 seconds to download a full-length eBook to your iPhone or iPad, depending on the speed of your Internet connection and the size of the eBook's digital file. As soon as it's downloaded and ready to read, the book's front cover artwork is displayed as part of the Library screen in the iBooks app.

CUSTOMIZE YOUR EBOOK READING EXPERIENCE USING iBOOKS

To begin reading an eBook that's stored in your iPhone or iPad, from the Library screen, tap on a book cover thumbnail to open the eBook.

While reading eBooks, you can hold the iPhone or iPad in portrait or landscape mode. Then, as you're reading, tap anywhere on the screen to make the various command icons and buttons appear (shown in Figure 15.9).

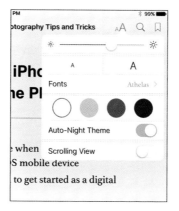

Figure 15.9

Tap on the "AA" icon to customize the appearance of the text in the eBook you're reading.

> ✅ **TIP** Tap on the Library button to automatically bookmark your location in an eBook and return to iBooks' Library (My Books) screen.

Tap on the Table of Contents icon to display an interactive table of contents for the eBook you're reading. Then tap on any chapter number or chapter title to immediately jump to that location in the book. Or, near the top center of the Table of Contents screen, tap on the Bookmarks option to see a list of manually saved bookmarks you have previously set as you were reading that eBook. Tap on the Notes tab to review the notes you've manually added to pages as you were reading.

> ✅ **TIP** Whenever you tap on the Library option while reading an eBook, or press the Home button to return to the device's Home screen, your current location in the book is automatically bookmarked and saved.
>
> At any time, however, you have the option to manually add a virtual bookmark to as many pages in the eBook as you want. Then, by tapping the Table of Contents icon, and then the Bookmarks tab, you can see a complete list of manually placed virtual bookmarks in the eBook, and return to any of those pages quickly.

To exit the Table of Contents screen and return to reading your eBook, tap on the Resume option.

Three command icons appear to the right of the eBook title. Tap on the "AA" icon to reveal a pop-up window (refer to Figure 15.9). It offers a screen brightness slider and a small and large "A" button, which are used to instantly decrease or increase the font size in the book you're reading.

Tap on the Fonts button to change the text font, or tap on one of the Themes buttons to change the theme used to display the text (and the background color) for the eBook you're reading.

Choose the theme that is best suited for the lighting available and is also visually pleasing to you.

> **TIP** If you turn on the virtual switch associated with Auto-Night Theme, your iPhone or iPad measures the ambient light in the area where you're reading, and then automatically turns on the Night theme if you're reading in a dark or dimly lit area.

> **TIP** The normal book viewing mode shows each page of the book you're reading, as well as icons on the top of the page, and page number information on the bottom. The Scroll mode, which has a virtual switch to turn it on or off, enables you to scroll up or down continuously within an eBook, as opposed to turning pages.

Tap on the Search icon (which is shaped like a magnifying glass) to display a Search field. Use this feature to locate any keyword or search phrase that appears in the eBook you're currently reading.

As you're reading, to turn the page, swipe your finger from right to left (horizontally) across the screen to move one page forward, or swipe your finger from left to right to back up one page at a time.

> **TIP** To turn the page, you can also tap on the right side of the screen to advance or the left side of the screen to go back. However, if you have the Both Margins Advance option activated (which can be done in Settings), tapping either margin advances to the next page.

Displayed at the bottom of the screen is the page number in the eBook you're currently reading, as well as the total number of pages in the eBook. The number of pages remaining in the current chapter is displayed to the right of the page number.

TOOLS YOU CAN USE WHILE READING

As you're reading an eBook, hold your finger on a single word. A group of command tabs appears above that word labeled Copy, Define, Highlight, Note, Search, and Share.

Use your finger to move the blue dots that appear to the left and right of the word to expand the selected text to a phrase, sentence, paragraph, or entire page, for example.

Tap on the Define tab to look up the definition of a selected word. (Internet access is required to use this feature.)

Tap on the Highlight tab to highlight the selected text. It's possible to choose the color of your highlights, or underline the selected text by tapping on the yellow circle icon displayed above the word. Tap on the white circle (with a red line through it) to remove highlights, or tap on the Note icon to create a new note.

When you tap on the Highlight option, you're given the option to choose a highlight color (shown in Figure 15.10). The last highlight color you selected determines the color of the sticky note that appears when you tap on the Note option. This enables you to easily color-code your highlights and/or notes.

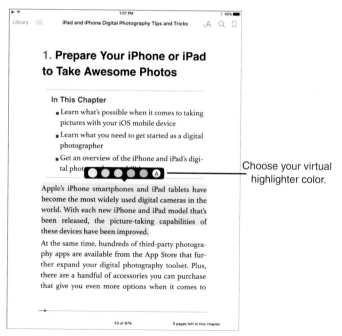

Choose your virtual
highlighter color.

Figure 15.10

It's possible to highlight text as you're reading or add a virtual sticky note to the margin of a page that contains your typed notes.

If you tap on the Note tab, a virtual sticky note appears on your device's screen, along with the virtual keyboard. Type notes to yourself about what you're reading. When you're finished typing, tap anywhere on the screen outside the sticky note box. A sticky note icon appears in the margin of the eBook. You can later tap on this icon to read your notes or annotations.

Tap on the Search tab to enter any word or phrase and find it in the eBook. A search window appears below the Search field. References to each occurrence of your keyword or search phrase are displayed by chapter and page number. Tap on a reference to jump to that point in the book.

ALTERNATIVE METHODS FOR READING YOUR EBOOKS

Although Apple has worked out distribution deals with many major publishers and authors, the iBook Store does not offer an eBook edition of every book in publication.

> **TIP** In some cases, eBook titles are available from Amazon.com or Barnes & Noble (BN.com) but not from iBook Store. Or if Amazon.com, BN.com, and iBook Store offer the same eBook title, the price for that eBook might be lower from one of these other online-based booksellers.
>
> So, if you're a price-conscious reader, it pays to shop around for the lowest eBook prices. Just because you're using an iPhone or iPad does not mean you must shop for eBooks exclusively from iBook Store.

Perhaps you previously owned a Kindle, Nook, or Kobo eBook reader before purchasing your iPhone or iPad and have already acquired a personal library of eBooks formatted for that device. If you want to access your Kindle, Nook, or Kobo eBook library from your iPhone or iPad, download the free Kindle, Nook, or Kobo Reading apps from the App Store.

These apps prompt you for your Amazon, Barnes & Noble, or Kobo account information to sync your purchased content to the app. To purchase new Kindle- or Nook-formatted eBook titles, you must visit Amazon.com or BN.com using Safari or your primary computer. After you make your purchase, your eBooks can be automatically synced to the Kindle or Nook app on your device.

DISCOVER THE NEW NEWS APP

The News app that comes preinstalled with iOS 9 is a powerful yet easy-to-use information gathering tool.

Apple has teamed up with some of the world's leading newspapers, magazines, and news organizations, as well as bloggers, website operators, online publications, and content providers, to offer a single app that gathers articles together and formats this content into a highly personalized, nicely formatted, digital publication that provides only articles, information, and news that covers exactly the topics you're interested in.

Best of all, this personalized digital news feed is updated and available 24/7, and it is completely free. The app takes a few minutes to initially set up, but after this process is completed, the News app gathers content on your behalf from potentially a wide range of sources and presents it to you on your iPhone or iPad's screen.

The News app works in several ways to customize your news feed. First, you can "subscribe" to specific publications and read articles published by those sources. Second, it's possible to select topics of interest to you and have the News app gather information related to those topics from many different sources. Third, you have the option to choose keywords or phrases and have the app gather articles and news stories that contain those specific search terms.

WHAT'S NEW An update to the News app made with iOS 9.0.2 introduces Daily Briefings, which are published by specific publications, such as *The New York Times*, on a daily basis, to summarize important news events of the day. Daily Briefings are updated once per day for each publication. For example, Daily Briefings associated with *The New York Times* is published daily at 6am (EST). It's possible to subscribe, for free, to any available Daily Briefings, from publications or news sources supporting this feature.

The News app works with iCloud, so after you set up the app once to personalize your news feed, the content the app collects syncs across all your iOS mobile devices automatically.

TIP The News app requires Internet access to collect articles and content. However, manually selected articles can be saved for offline viewing at your convenience.

To save an article, tap on the Save (bookmark shaped) icon in the top-right corner of the screen as you're reading an article (shown in Figure 15.11).

When you want to access your saved articles, launch the News app and tap on the Saved icon. A listing of your saved articles is displayed. Tap on an article's listing to read it, or swipe from right to left across the listing and then tap on the Delete button to delete it.

Save
Icon

Figure 15.11

Tap on the Save icon associated with specific articles you want to store on your iPhone or iPad for later review. Then tap on the Saved icon to access those articles.

GET STARTED BY CUSTOMIZING THE NEWS APP

Launch the News app from the Home screen, and then invest a few minutes initially customizing the app. From the Welcome to News screen, tap the Get Started option.

From the Pick Your Favorites screen, scroll through the displayed list of news organizations, newspapers, magazines, websites, and content providers and choose those you're interested in by tapping on their respective thumbnails.

Choose at least one of the displayed options, which include CNN, ESPN, *The New York Times*, and *The Wall Street Journal* (shown in Figure 15.12).

Tap on the Continue option. Based on your initial selections, the For You screen is formatted with content of interest to you. However, using the Favorites, Explore, and Search tools built in to the app, it's possible to further customize the content you are presented with on an ongoing basis.

NAVIGATING AROUND THE NEWS APP

Along the bottom of the News app screen on both the iPhone and iPad are five command icons (shown in Figure 15.13). Here's a summary of what each tool is used for:

- **For You**—Tap on this icon to read your personalized digital publication (news feed) that's continuously updated with content of direct interest to you. Articles are collected in real time from a wide range of online-based sources and content providers.

- **Favorites**—View and edit the collection of sources and content providers that you selected for the News app to follow on your behalf.

- **Explore**—Based on specific topics and content categories, discover new sources and content providers that you're interested in having the News app follow for you. New sources and content providers are continuously being added, as are specific topics available within each main content category.

- **Search**—In the Search field, enter a topic, subject matter, keyword, name, company name, industry, hobby, area of interest, or anything else you want the News app to gather articles about on your behalf.

- **Saved**—As you read specific articles in the For You news feed, if there's an article you want to save for later reference, tap on the bookmark-shaped Save icon associated with it to save that article for offline viewing.

> **NOTE** Using your iPhone or iPad's Internet connection, the News app gathers content on a continuous basis and displays only the most current information. As newer content becomes available, older content disappears from your news feed, unless you manually save specific articles.

Figure 15.12

Begin the News app's customization process by selecting at least one source or content provider from the Pick Your Favorites screen.

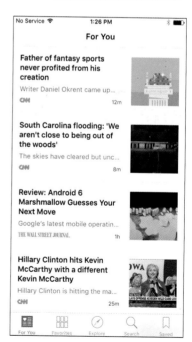

Figure 15.13

Use these command icons to navigate around the News app.

> **TIP** To further customize the News app, launch Settings, tap on the News option, and then manually adjust options related to Notifications, the app's capability to refresh content in the background, and determine whether the app uses a cellular data connection (when available) to access the Internet (as opposed to using a Wi-Fi Internet connection).

READ ARTICLES THAT CATER TO YOUR INTERESTS

After setting up the News app, launch it whenever you have time to browse or read the collected articles in your news feed. To do this, tap on the For You icon. All the articles collected for you by the app are displayed on a single screen, using a digital newspaper-style format.

Each article listing in your feed includes a headline, cover photo (when applicable), the first sentence or two from each article, the source of each article, and when it was published (shown in Figure 15.14).

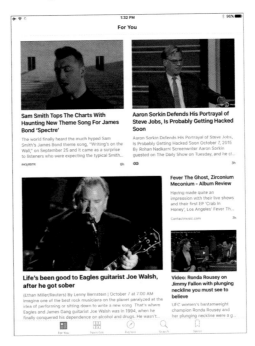

Figure 15.14

Your news feed (shown here on the iPad) is populated with article listings that the News app collects for you. Tap on any article listing to read it.

To read an article in its entirety, simply tap on its preview listing. Otherwise, keep scrolling downward to view all the articles in your current news feed. Keep in mind, your news feed gets updated continuously as new content is published. The articles toward the top of your news feed are the most current.

> **☑ TIP** To view, add to, or modify your collection of Favorite topics and content sources, tap on the Favorites icon.
>
> If you want to delete a source (so the News app stops following it for you), tap on the Edit option, and then tap on the "X" displayed in the thumbnail for the source you want to remove (shown in Figure 15.15).

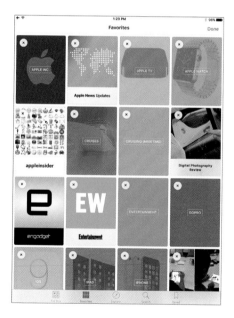

Figure 15.15

Your personal list of sources that the News app collects content from can be viewed and edited at any time by tapping on the Favorites icon.

HOW TO EXPAND YOUR PERSONALIZED COLLECTION OF SOURCES AND CONTENT PROVIDERS

At any time, to discover new sources and content providers that the News app can follow on your behalf or to add new topics of interest, tap on the Explore icon and then scroll through the list of publications, topics, and content providers.

When you come across one or more sources that you want the News app to begin following, tap on the "+" icon associated with its listing.

Sources and content providers are sorted by category, which include News, Business, Politics, Travel, Technology, Sports, Science, Entertainment, Food, Style, Home, and Arts. Upon tapping on one of these categories, dozens, and in some cases hundreds, of sources and content providers are listed that you can choose from.

> **TIP** To find articles, content, or news stories based on a specific keyword or phrase, tap on the Search icon and in the Search field type the word or phrase that relates to what you're looking for.
>
> From the listing of search results (shown in Figure 15.16), tap on the Add ("+") icons associated with the ones of interest. Search results are sorted into sections labeled Top Hit, Topics, and Channels.
>
> After selecting any of the search results for the News app to follow, tap on the Done option. Now, when you tap on the For You icon, your news feed is updated with content from the added sources.

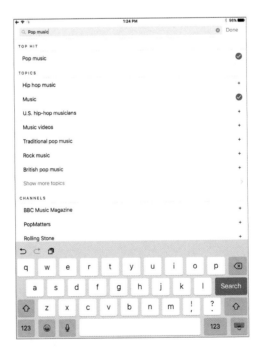

Figure 15.16
Using the Search tool is one way to pinpoint sources and content providers that you want the News app to follow on your behalf.

By using the tools offered by the News app and investing a few minutes per day to read the articles and content it collects, you can easily stay informed on general news, company or industry-related news, or any topics whatsoever you're interested in.

The News app focuses only on topics you deem relevant to your personal or professional life and presents the information in a format that makes it efficient to go through quickly, using one centralized app that's available when and where you need it.

> **NOTE** Unlike when you subscribe to the digital edition of most newspapers or magazines, the content collected by the News app is free of charge and can come from many different sources from around the world.

SOME FINAL THOUGHTS

In the past few years, the technology built in to the various iPhone and iPad models has progressed incredibly fast and has introduced us to entirely new ways to communicate, stay informed, collect and utilize information, better organize our lives, and become more productive.

By combining this technology with the powerful iOS operating system, which integrates with the collection of apps that come preinstalled with all iPhone and iPad models, we can do amazing things with these iOS mobile devices as soon as they're turned on for the very first time.

Yet, when you start installing third-party apps to your smartphone and/or tablet and simultaneously use it to access to the Internet, what's now possible can literally be life changing.

This, however, is only the beginning! Your iPhone or iPad is also capable of connecting to or remotely controlling other technologies and devices in ways that can dramatically improve your life, save you money, and change the way you handle many tasks.

For example, from anywhere in the world, you can now remotely control your home theater system (DVR and television set) or home security system, open/close your garage door, adjust the lighting, control the thermostat, answer your doorbell (and unlock the door), and turn on/off major appliances in your home.

The same iPhone or iPad can link with your vehicle to help you navigate, safely communicate with others, or stay entertained while you're driving, while also alerting you of maintenance or repair issues that need to be dealt with.

In addition, you now can use your iPhone or iPad to help monitor and improve your health and well-being. For example, you can sync an iOS device with specialized medical, health, and/or fitness-related equipment so you can better manage personal medical conditions, your fitness and daily activity, your diet and nutrition, and even monitor and improve your sleeping patterns.

☑ TIP   The power and capabilities of your iPhone can be expanded upon even more when you use it with the Apple Watch.

Now that you understand how to use your iPhone and/or iPad, as well as the majority of the apps that come preinstalled with iOS 9, begin exploring some of the cutting-edge ways you can use this technology to improve your everyday personal and professional life.

Focus on how you can best utilize third-party apps, based on your needs, lifestyle, and work habits, and discover how optional technologies can be used with your iPhone and/or iPad to greatly expand their capabilities.

And, just when you think you've mastered your current iPhone and iPad running iOS 9, you can be sure that Apple will introduce new and more advanced iPhone and iPad models, as well as updated versions of the iOS, that will make today's technology soon seem antiquated.

🄸🄾🅂🄰 WHAT'S NEW   The iPad has changed the way people interact with tablet-based computing devices, but the new iPad Pro takes a major leap forward. Its larger screen, faster processor, optional keyboard, and Apple Pencil stylus further bridge the ever-shrinking gap between what's possible using a tablet versus what can be handled on a desktop or notebook computer.

Index

Numbers

3D Touch feature, using on iPhone 6s, 7

A

About option, 49

Access on Lock Screen option, 47

Activity app, using with Apple Watch, 251

Add Call option, 232, 234

AirDrop tool

accessing content, 115

and AirPlay, 61

availability, 114–115

enabling and disabling, 113

security precaution, 115

sending content from Share menu, 114

sending images wirelessly, 213

sending photos with, 188

Airplane mode, 19, 37–38, 60

AirPlay tool

accessing from Control Center, 116–117

showing images on TV, 217

speakers, 116

streaming content, 116–117

AirPrint feature, 117–118. *See also* printing

Alarm Clock app, 61

alarms
  entering for events, 338
  setting in Reminders app, 351, 353–354
  setting with Siri, 82
albums, moving images between, 219
Alert Tones, finding, 95
App and iTunes Stores, 58
app icons, reorganizing, 64–65
App Store app, 92, 98
  accessing, 101
  account management, 103–104
  app listings, 104
  browsing, 103
  description screen, 105–106
  Details tab, 106
  Featured icon, 103
  redeeming iTunes gift cards, 103–104
  Related tab, 106
  Reviews tab, 106
  searching for apps, 102
  Top Charts icon, 103
  Updates command icon, 107
app switcher
  accessing, 11, 23
  shutting down apps in, 23
Apple ID account, 98, 136
Apple Music service, 24, 83, 370
Apple Pay, 3, 25–26. See also Wallet app
  debit and credit cards, 58
  initiating for payments, 259

managing with Wallet app, 252–253
  requirements for iPhone, 253
  security, 255
  setting up and using, 253–255
Apple Watch, 89
  Activity app, 251
  navigation information, 158
  using Health app with, 250–251
Apple website, 17
AppleCare support, 267
appointment details, viewing in Calendar app, 339–340
apps. See also Background App Refresh; third-party apps; universal apps
  exiting and returning to Home screen, 11
  launching with Siri, 76
  Made By Apple, 111
  managing children's acquisitions, 110–111
  organizing in folders, 63–64
  removing from folders, 64
  reviewing in Notification Style heading, 44
  searching by relevancy, 108–109
  updating, 109–110
  user-installed, 60
apps installed, listing, 43
articles
  finding, 422
  reading with News app, 420–421
Ask To Join Networks option, 39
aspect ratio, choosing for images, 208

attachments

dealing with, 286–287

inserting into email, 278–279

audio, 55–56

audio messages, sending with iMessage, 294–295

audiobooks

finding, 94

purchasing and listening to, 398

Auto-Lock, 51. *See also* Lock screen

B

B&W tools, using with images, 211–212

Background App Refresh, 51. *See also* apps

backing up with iCloud, 136–138

backups

deleting, 123

maintaining, 29–30

Badge app, 45–46

Battery options, 37, 57

Bluetooth

accessing from Control Center, 60

wireless headsets, 37, 40, 227, 245

bookmarks. *See* Safari bookmarks

books. *See* ebooks; iBooks app

brightness slider, 61

Brookstone website, 17

browser windows, accessing, 311

browsers. *See* Safari web browser

built-in flash (iPhone)

vs. HDR, 199

using, 195–196

C

Calculator app, 61

Calendar app, 59. *See also* events; meetings

calculating travel time, 336

customizing, 340–341

deleting events, 340

entering events, 335–338

Family Sharing feature, 329–330

features, 329

finding appointments, 340

finding events, 340

launching, 330

Listing icon, 331

New Event screen, 330

sharing with family, 138

syncing with online-based apps, 328

viewing appointment details, 339

Calendar views

choosing, 330

Day, 331–333

Month, 331–332, 334

switching, 331

Week, 332, 334–335

Year, 332, 335

call forwarding, setting up, 226

Call in Progress screen, 230–232

Call Over Wi-Fi feature, 236–237

call waiting signal, responding to, 233–234

calls. *See also* missed calls; Recents call log

  Accept and Decline buttons, 225

  accepting, 224–225

  adding, 232, 234

  allocation for talk minutes, 242

  answering on iPads and Macs, 227–228

  answering on iPhones, 223–227

  blocking, 231

  Continuity activation, 227

  ending, 232

  initiating, 228

  initiating with Siri, 77–78

  making from iPhones, 234–235

  Message option, 225

  numeric keypad, 231–232

  Remind Me option, 225

  returning to, 232

  sending to voicemail, 223

  tracking usage, 242

  vibration patterns, 244

Camera app, 20, 61. *See also* photos; selfies

  Autofocus Sensor, 197

  availability, 186

  built-in flash (iPhone), 195–196

  Exposure Control options, 197–198

  features, 186–187

  HDR shooting feature, 194–196

  HDR vs. built-in flash, 199

  launching, 189–190

  launching from Lock screen, 66

  Live Photo, 191

  Pano shooting mode, 194, 200–201

  Photo shooting mode, 193

  shooting HD video, 201–203

  Shooting Mode menu, 192–194

  shooting photos, 190–192

  shooting video, 190–192

  Slo-Mo option, 193

  Square shooting mode, 193

  taking photos, 192

  Time-Lapse feature, 192–193

  Timer option, 194

  Video shooting mode, 193

  viewing photos, 192

  zoom feature, 199

Camera Connection Kit, 189

caps lock (virtual keyboard), 13

CarPlay feature, 89, 227

cellular and cellular data, 40–41

cellular data usage, reducing, 270

cellular service providers, 222–223

chats. *See* Facebook Messenger app

checklists

  creating in notes, 362

  using in Notes app, 356

"childproofing" devices, 51

children, managing apps obtained by, 110–111

Clipboard icon, 280

Clock app, controlling with Siri, 82

Color tools, using with images, 210–211

composing email messages, 273–277

conference calls
    engaging in, 234
    initiating, 232
Contacts app, 59
    Add Field option, 342
    adding images to, 217–218
    adding information to, 342–343
    pop-up menu, 341
    syncing with online-based apps, 328
    tips, 350
    using Siri with, 72–73, 77
    using with other apps, 343–344
Contacts database
    accessing during calls, 232
    searching, 343
Contacts entries
    adding photos to, 348–349
    creating, 346–347
    deleting, 349
    dialing calls from, 236
    editing, 349
    finding and displaying, 345–346
    sharing, 349–350
    viewing, 344–346
Continuity and Handoff functions, 41, 119–120
Control Center
    accessing AirPlay from, 116–117
    AirDrop and AirPlay, 61
    Airplane mode, 60
    Bluetooth, 60
    Calculator, 61
    closing, 62
    Do Not Disturb mode, 60
    flash (iPhone), 61
    Music controls, 62
    Playlists, 61
    Rotation Lock, 60–61
    screen brightness slider, 61
    Timer icon, 61
    Wi-Fi, 60
conversations. See calls; Messages app
cookies, blocking, 309
Copy command, 279–280
copying
    content from notes, 365
    images between albums, 219
    images to apps, 217
    phone numbers, 235
    URLs for web pages, 322
credit card
    adding details to Wallet app, 255–259
    choosing for Apple Pay, 58
    storing in Wallet app, 253
Crop tool, 208–209
currency conversions, using Siri for, 87
Cut command, 279–280

D

Data Roaming option, 41
debit card
    adding details to Wallet app, 255–259
    choosing for Apple Pay, 58
    storing in Wallet app, 253

deleting
backups, 123
cards from Wallet app, 261
Contacts entries, 349
conversations in Messages app, 298
to-do items and lists, 355
ebooks, 406
events from Calendar app, 340
incoming messages, 284–285
notes, 360
playlists, 385
stored photos, 218
videos, 390
Dictation mode
using with Siri, 75, 84
versus virtual keyboard, 88
digital images. *See* images; photos
digital music, loading on devices, 367–368. *See also* music
digital publications, finding, 94
directions. *See also* Maps app
getting from Siri, 82–83
reversing in Maps app, 164
turn-by-turn in Maps app, 155–159
disabling features, 36
Discover credit card, support for, 3
Display & Brightness settings, 52
Do Not Disturb mode, 19–20, 48
accessing from Control Center, 60
enabling, 228–230
documents
syncing iCloud with, 128–130
transferring automatically with iCloud, 134

double touch gesture, 11
drawing tools, using in Notes app, 362–364
driving with headsets, 227
DuckDuckGo.com search engine, 307

E

ebook library
display options, 410
organizing, 404–406
ebooks. *See also* iBooks app
bookmarking, 413
command tabs, 415
Define tab, 415
deleting, 406
displaying selectively, 405
finding, 94, 410–411
Fonts button, 414
Highlight option, 415
learning about, 411–412
Library option, 413
Note tab, 416
page numbers, 414
purchasing, 412
reading, 412–416
screen brightness slider, 414
Search field, 414
Search tab, 416
sharing details about, 412
Table of Contents, 413
text appearance, 413
themes, 414
turning pages, 414
viewing mode, 414

editing
  Contacts entries, 349
  folders in Notes app, 358
  photos, 208
  videos, 206–208
email accounts
  adding to Mail app, 264–267
  customizing, 268
email messages. *See also* Mail app
  composing, 273–277
  formatting text in, 276–277
  forwarding, 288
  importing photos into, 277
  inserting attachments, 278–279
  inserting photos and videos, 278
  moving, 287
  organizing in folders, 287
  printing, 288
  QuickType feature, 276
  reading, 11, 281–282
  replying to, 288
  saving unsent drafts, 280–281
  sending and accessing with Siri, 82
  viewing, 272
Emoji/Symbols keyboards, 14
enabling features, 36
Enhance feature, editing photos
  with, 208
entertainment info, getting from
  Siri, 84–86
events. *See also* Calendar app; meetings
  deleting from Calendar app, 340
  entering in Calendar app, 335–338

entering using Siri, 338–339
finding in Calendar app, 340
scheduling with Siri, 81
external keyboards, 17. *See also* keyboard
  shortcuts; virtual keyboard

F

Facebook. *See also* social networking
  services
  account integration, 169–171
  Privacy Settings, 168
Facebook, publishing photos on, 215
Facebook app
  accessing features, 172
  Check In option, 174
  friend requests, 173
  friends list, 174
  main menu, 173
  Nearby Friends, 174
  News Feed, 173–174, 177
  Notifications, 174
  People You May Know, 173
  Photo option, 174
  Privacy settings, 173
  profile, 173
  Search field, 174
  Settings option, 173
  Status icon, 174
  updates, 172
Facebook Messenger app, 172–173
  emojis, 176
  instant messaging, 175
  launching, 175

muting and unmuting c onversations, 176

real-time chats, 176

Facebook option, sharing web content, 321

Facebook page, accessing, 173

FaceTime app, 60, 232

Family calendar, viewing, 140

Family Sharing feature, 138–140

Favorites list

creating and using, 240–241

dialing phone numbers in, 241

editing contacts in, 240

Fetch feature, 268

file transfers. See AirDrop tool

files. See also AirDrop tool; folders

accessing with iCloud Drive app, 140–144

syncing iCloud with, 128–130

filters, using in Photos app, 209

Find My iPhone/iPad feature, 28–29

five-finger pinch (iPad), 9

flash (iPhone), 61, 195–196. See also True Tone flash

flashlight, using iPhone as, 61

Flickr

account integration, 169–171

uploading images to, 216

folders, 63–64. See also AirDrop tool; files

accessing with iCloud Drive app, 140–144

organizing email messages in, 287

forwarding email messages, 288

free apps, 98–99

full-screen mode, viewing images in, 204–206

G

Game Center app, 60

games, onscreen tapping, 48

gestures

double touch, 11

five-finger pinch (iPad), 9

hold, 8

multi-finger horizontal swipe (iPad), 11

pinch, 8

pull-down, 8–9

swipe, 8

swipe up, 9

tap, 8

two-finger (iPad), 9

GPS devices, using, 147, 158

H

Handoff feature, 50, 118–120, 227–228, 304

Handset and Speaker mode, using for calls, 232

handyPrint website, 118

HBO Now app, 400

HD video, shooting, 201–203. See also videos

HDR shooting feature, 194–196

HDR vs. built-in flash, 199

headsets, driving with, 227. See also Bluetooth

Health app (iPhone)
  features, 248
  Medical ID feature, 251–252
  using, 249–250
help, getting from Siri, 74–76
"Hey Siri" app, 22. *See also* Siri
hold gesture, 8
Home button tips, 11–12
Home screen
  accessing, 65
  icons, 326
  reorganizing apps on, 64–65
  returning to, 10–12
hotspots, choosing for Wi-Fi, 37–39. *See also* Personal Hotspot feature; private wireless hotspot

I

iBook Store, 410–412
iBooks app, 60. *See also* ebooks
  command icons, 406–407
  customizing settings, 403
  Featured option, 406–409
  features, 401–402
  My Books option, 406
  NYTimes icon, 409
  organizing ebook library, 404–406
  Purchased option, 408
  Search option, 408
  Top Charts option, 408
iCloud
  automatic document transfer, 134
  customizing for apps, 130–131

  Photo Library, 134–135
  sharing photos, 130
  syncing with data, documents, and files, 128–130
  unique Apple ID, 136
iCloud account, upgrading, 126
iCloud Backup
  setting up, 29–30
  using, 136–138
iCloud content
  Automatic Downloads settings, 126
  availability, 124–125
  deleting and reinstalling, 125
  Family Sharing feature, 125
iCloud Drive app, 22
  file summary, 143
  previewing files, 141–143
  transferring files, 141
  using on mobile devices, 140–144
iCloud for Windows, downloading and installing, 134, 324
iCloud functions, customizing, 35. *See also* Storage & iCloud Usage
iCloud integration, 25
iCloud Keychain, 129, 324–325
iCloud online storage space
  conserving, 123
  displaying and managing, 122–123
  fees, 122
  free email account, 124
  freeing up, 123–124
iCloud Photo Library, launching, 134–135, 188, 219

iCloud support, enabling and disabling, 128–129

iCloud.com

    accessing app-specific data from, 132–133

    Drive screen, 133

    logging off from, 133

iHeartRadio app, 388

image size, choosing before sending, 215

images. *See also* photos

    adding to Contacts app, 217–218

    adding to Favorites, 205

    copying to apps, 217

    cropping, 208–209

    emailing, 214–215

    moving between albums, 219

    ordering prints from, 213

    sending via text/instant message, 214

    sending wirelessly via AirDrop, 213

    showing on TV via AirPlay, 217

    uploading to Flickr, 216

    viewing in full-screen mode, 204–206

IMAP email account, 266

iMessage account, setting up, 291–292

iMessage app

    audio messages, 294–295

    benefits of, 292–293

    conversation screens, 293

    video messages, 296–297

iMovie app website, 203

in-app purchases, 100

inbox, refreshing, 288

Instagram app, 182–183

installed apps, listing, 43

instant messaging, 289–291

investments, checking with Siri, 79–80

iOS 9 features

    Apple Music, 24

    Camera app, 20

    "Hey Siri" app, 22

    iCloud Drive app, 22, 121

    iCloud integration, 25

    Maps app, 21

    multitasking, 23

    Music app, 24

    News app, 20, 100

    Notes app, 21

    Notification Center, 22–23

    QuickType Keyboards, 24

    Spotlight Search, 22

    third-party apps, 25

    Wallet app, 22, 26

iOS 9 operating system

    compatibility, 2

    features, 3–4

    terminology, 3

    upgrading to, 4–5

iPad, 4–5

    Airplane mode, 19

    cellular data, 40–41

    Control Center, 61–62

    creating playlists on, 385

    cursor movement, 277

    five-finger pinch gesture, 9

making discoverable, 61

multi-finger horizontal swipe, 11

Multitasking option, 50

Notification Center in landscape mode, 43

rebooting, 12

running multiple apps, 24

Split Screen feature, 279

Tab view, 313

tabbed browsing, 312–314

text formatting icon, 277

turning off, 18–20

two-finger gesture, 9

waking up, 12

iPad display options

Picture in Picture, 15–17

Slide Over, 14–15

Split View, 15–16

iPad Pro

Pencil stylus, 17

stylus device, 6

iPhone, 4–5

3D Touch feature on 6s, 7

Airplane mode, 19

answering calls, 223–227

cellular, 40–41

Control Center, 61–62

customizing playlists on, 381–385

linking to car, 89

making calls from, 234–235

making discoverable, 61

Peek gesture, 7

Pop gesture, 7

rebooting, 12

switching between web pages, 310–312

turning off, 18–20

turning on flash, 61

unlocking to receive calls, 225–226

using as flashlight, 61

waking up, 12

Wallet & Apple Pay, 58–59

iPhone Health app

features, 248

Medical ID feature, 251–252

using, 249–250

iPhone Upgrade Program, 223

iTunes

gift cards, 103–104

purchases, 389

ITunes Radio, cellular data monthly usage, 387

iTunes Store app, 58, 98, 390, 392, 394–399. See also Music app; playlists

accessing purchased content, 126–128

audiobooks, 398

TV episodes, 398–399

iTunes Sync process, 30–31, 125

iTunes U content, finding, 95

K

keyboard shortcuts, creating with virtual keyboard, 14. See also external keyboards; virtual keyboard

Keychain feature. *See* iCloud Keychain

keypad, displaying for calls, 231–232

L

Language option, selecting for Siri, 72

Light tools, using with images, 210

list management. *See* Reminders app

Live Photo option, using Siri with, 191. *See also* photos

Location Services

    disabling to take pictures, 57

    icon, 37

    using with Spotlight Search, 50

Lock screen, 47. *See also* Auto-Lock

    features, 65

    launching Camera app from, 66

    unlocking, 65

Logitech website, 17

lost devices, finding, 28–29

M

Made By Apple apps, 111

Mail app, 59. *See also* email messages

    adding email accounts to, 264–267

    customizing mailboxes, 287

    customizing options, 267–271

    formatting email messages, 276

    increasing text size, 288–289

    Notify Me feature, 289

    Pop menu, 289

    Quote Level option, 280

    scrolling up and down, 289

    zooming in and out, 289

Mail app options

    Always Bcc Myself, 271

    Ask Before Deleting, 270

    Default Account, 271

    Flag Style, 270

    Increase Quote Level, 271

    Load Remote Images, 270

    Mark Addresses, 271

    Organize by Thread, 270–271

    preview, 268

    Show To/Cc Label, 269

    Signature, 271

    Swipe, 269–270

Mail app's Inbox

    deleting incoming messages, 284–285

    Edit button, 284

    features, 283

    forwarding messages, 288

    incoming attachments, 286–287

    organizing messages in folders, 287

    printing messages, 288

    refreshing, 288

    replying to messages, 288

    viewing emails, 285–286

    VIP List feature, 286

Mail option, sharing web content, 320

mailbox, customizing, 287

Maps app, 21, 60. *See also* directions

    2D and 3D views, 154

    3D Flyover feature, 149

    businesses and services, 160

    compass, 149

    contacts, 162

Directions option, 149

Drive tab, 157

Drop A Pin option, 153

enhancements, 146

Favorites menu, 151–152

Flyover map, 163–164

impact on battery, 164

Info screen, 152

interactive location screens, 161–162

Location Information screen, 161–162

My Location icon, 148, 150–151

Popular Apps Nearby, 162

public transportation, 163–164

reversing directions, 164

rotating maps, 152

route overview, 157

Satellite view, 153–154

Search field, 149–150, 152

search results, 150

Share menu, 151

Show Traffic option, 150, 158

Show/Hide Traffic option, 153

Standard view, 153–154

Start and End locations, 155–156, 159

tips, 164–165

Transit feature, 153–155, 157, 163–164

turn-by-turn directions, 155–159, 161, 165

using, 147

using Siri with, 82–83, 148

using voice commands with, 148

using with iCloud, 165

using with other apps, 148

Walk tab, 157

Yelp! information screens, 147–148, 162–163

zooming in and out, 152

math calculations, using Siri for, 86

Medical ID feature, using in Health app (iPhone), 251–252

meetings, scheduling with Siri, 81. *See also* Calendar app; events

messages. *See* email messages

Messages app, 60

audio messages, 294–295

blocking messages, 301

Continuity feature, 290

customizing, 301

deleting conversations in, 298

features, 289–291

group conversations, 300

relaunching conversations, 299–300

responding to messages, 299

reviewing conversations, 299–300

searching conversations, 301

sharing from Details screen, 300

sharing web content, 321

text messages, 293–294

text-message conversations, 297–298

using with iMessage service, 291

video messages, 296–297

mini-player controls, controlling music with, 377–378

missed calls, displaying, 241. *See also* calls

movie info, getting from Siri, 84–86

movies. *See also* videos
acquiring from iTunes Store, 395–399
finding, 94
renting vs. purchasing, 390, 392, 394–395
watching with Videos app, 388–395
moving apps on Home screen, 64–65
multi-finger horizontal swipe (iPad), 11
multitasking, 23, 50. *See also* tasks
music. *See also* digital music
acquiring from iTunes Store, 395–399
controlling from Now Playing screen, 378–380
Fast Forward icon, 379
Finding, 94
organizing alphabetically, 377
playing and pausing, 376
Play/Pause icon, 379
streaming, 369–370
streaming via Internet, 387
Up Next icon, 379
volume slider, 379
Music app, 24, 60. *See also* iTunes Store app; playlists
Add Music screen, 382, 384
Connect icon, 373–374
controlling from Control Center, 385–387
controlling with Siri, 83–84
customizing playlists, 380–385
features, 368–370
launching, 371
mini-player controls, 376–378
New icon, 372
Playlists, 374–375, 377
Radio icon, 373
For You icon, 372
Music controls, displaying in Control Center, 62
music videos, watching with Videos app, 388–395
muting calls in progress, 231

N

News app, 20, 60, 100
command icons, 419
customizing, 418–420
Favorites icon, 421
features, 417–418
navigating, 418–419
The New York Times, 417
reading articles, 420–421
sources and content providers, 421–423
notes
copying content from, 365
creating, 359–361
deleting, 360
interactive checklists, 362
moving between folders, 361–362
sharing, 320, 365
undeleting, 361
Notes app, 21, 60
Camera icon, 356–357
command icons, 357
drawing tools, 362–364

drawing/sketch tools, 356–357

features, 355

formatting text, 356–357

interactive checklist, 356

managing folders, 357–358

Peek feature, 355–356

pop-up window, 355

syncing with online-based apps, 328

Undo/Redo icon, 356–357, 363

using Siri with, 84

virtual writing instrument, 363

Notification Center, 22–23

Alerts option, 45

Allow Notifications, 43

Badge app, 45–46

customizing content, 42

iPad in landscape mode, 43

managing customizations, 66–67

Show in Notification, 43

Sounds, 43

tips, 46–47

widgets, 43

notifications, viewing, 44

Now Playing screen

features, 378

More icon, 380

music control icons, 379

Repeat icon, 380

Share icon, 380

Shuffle icon, 380

numeric keypad, using with calls, 231–232

nutritional intake data, tracking, 250

O

online storage space. See iCloud online storage space

Open Table app, making meal reservations with, 163

organizing apps in folders, 63–64

outgoing voicemail message, recording, 237

P

page, returning to top of, 11

panoramic photos, shooting, 194, 200–201

Passcode Lock feature, 27, 325. See also Touch ID & Passcode options

passwords, syncing with iCloud Keychain, 324–325

Paste command, 279–280

payments. See Apple Pay

PDF files, finding, 95

Peek feature, 7, 355–356

Pencil stylus (iPad Pro), 17

Personal Hotspot feature, 120. See also hotspots

Phone app, dialing from Contacts entries, 236

phone conversations. See calls

phone numbers

copying, 235

dialing manually, 235

Photo Library. See iCloud Photo Library

Photo shooting mode, 193

photos. *See also* Camera app; images; Live Photo option; selfies

adding to Contacts entries, 348–349

deleting, 218

disabling Location Services for, 57

editing, 208

importing into email, 277

inserting into email, 278

loading into devices, 187–189

printing, 212–213

publishing on Facebook, 215

saving, 188

sending via AirDrop, 188

sharing, 130, 216

shooting with Camera app, 190–192

snapping with Camera app, 197–200

storage, 200

taking with Camera app, 192

tweeting, 215

using as wallpaper, 53–54, 218

Photos & Camera app, 60

Photos app, 186–187, 204

Adjust feature, 209

editing tools, 209

filters, 209

support for iCloud's Family Sharing, 219

Picture in Picture display (iPad), 15–17

pictures. *See* photos

pinch gesture, 8

playlists. *See also* iTunes Store app; Music app

customizing with Music app, 380–385

deleting, 385

editing contents of, 385

managing, 375–376

playing, 61

podcasts, finding, 60, 94, 369

POP3 email account, 266

printing. *See also* AirPrint feature

email messages, 288

files, 117–118

photos, 212–213

website contents, 322–323

prints, ordering from images, 213

Privacy option, 57–58

private wireless hotspot, establishing, 41. *See also* hotspots

public transportation, using Maps app for, 163–164

pull-down gesture, 8–9

purchased content, sharing, 138–140

Push feature, disabling, 268

Q

QuickType Keyboards, 24

R

reading ebooks. *See* ebooks; iBooks app

reading emails, 11

reading lists, creating and managing, 316–318

rebooting devices, 12

Recents call log, accessing, 241–242. *See also* calls

redeeming iTunes gift cards, 103–104

Redo icon, 280

reminders, using Siri for, 78

Reminders app, 60. *See also* to-do items

    Add List option, 352–355

    alarms, 351, 353–354

    deleting items from to-do lists, 355

    displaying lists on calendar, 354

    Family list in, 140

    prioritizing list items, 354

    sharing web content, 320

    Show Completed option, 354

    syncing with online-based apps, 328

    using, 350–352

    viewing lists, 353

Reset feature, 51–52

restaurant info, getting from Siri, 84–86

restaurant reservations, making with Open Table app, 163

restoring backed-up data, 29–30

Restrictions, 51

ringer

    adjusting volume, 56, 223

    silencing, 223–224

ringtones

    customizing, 56, 243–244

    finding, 95

roaming, 41

Rotation Lock, accessing from Control Center, 60–61

route overview map, 157

S

Safari app, 60

Safari bookmarks, managing, 318, 324

Safari web browser. *See also* sharing web content

    Advanced options, 309

    Autofill option, 307

    Block Cookies, 309

    Block Pop-Ups, 309

    Bookmark folders, 308

    bookmarks, 318

    Clear History and Website Data, 309

    Do Not Track, 309

    favorite websites, 307

    Favorites, 308

    Fraudulent Website Warning, 309

    Frequently Visited Websites, 308

    Handoff feature, 304

    main screen on iPad, 305

    main screen on iPhone, 304

    Open Links (iPhone), 308

    Open New Tabs in Background (iPad), 308

    Passwords option, 307

    private Browsing feature, 313

    Reader option, 314–316

    Reading Lists, 316–318

    Recently Closed Tabs menu, 311

    removing screen clutter, 314–316

    Search Engine option, 305–306

    sharing web content, 318–324

Show Favorites Bar (iPad), 308

Show Tab Bar (iPad), 308

switching between web pages, 310–312

switching browser windows, 311

syncing usernames and passwords, 324–325

Tab view, 310–311

Use Cellular Data, 309

saving

photos, 188

text messages, 291

unsent drafts of email messages, 280–281

scheduling meetings and events, 81

screen, returning to top of, 11

search engine, choosing for Safari, 305–306

Search field, 35

searching with Siri, 80–81

Select All command, 279–280

Select command, 279–280

selfies, displaying with Siri, 87. *See also* Camera app; photos

Settings app

About option, 49

accessing, 34

accessing from Control Center, 47–48

Airplane mode, 37–38, 40

App and iTunes Stores, 58

Auto-Lock, 51

Background App Refresh, 51

Battery options, 57

Calendar app, 59

Contacts app, 59

Display & Brightness, 52

Do Not Disturb mode, 48

enabling and disabling features, 36

FaceTime, 60

Game Center, 60

General options, 49–52

Handoff & Suggested Apps, 50

iBooks, 60

iPad, 35

Keyboard, 51

Mail app, 59

Maps, 60

Messages, 60

Multitasking (iPad), 50

Music, 60

News, 60

Notes, 60

Notification Center, 42–47

Photos & Camera, 60

Podcasts, 60

Privacy option, 57–58

Reminders, 60

Reset, 51–52

Restrictions, 51

Safari, 60

Siri, 49

Software Update, 49

Sounds option, 55–56

Spotlight Search, 49–50

Storage & iCloud Usage, 50

Touch ID & Passcode, 56

Vibrate mode, 55

Videos, 60

Virtual Switch, 36

Wallpaper, 52–55

Share menu

sending content from, 114–115

using with photos, 216

sharing

app-specific information, 168

notes, 365

purchased content, 138–140

sharing web content. *See also* Safari web browser

Add Bookmark, 322

Add To Favorites, 322

Add to Home Screen, 322

Add to Reading List, 322

Copy option, 322

Facebook option, 321

Find On Page option, 323

Mail option, 320

Messages option, 320

More option, 322, 324

Notes option, 320

Print option, 322–323

Reminders option, 320

Request Desktop Site option, 323

third-party apps, 321

Twitter option, 321

Shutter button, locating, 203

Siri. *See also* "Hey Siri"

activating, 11, 70, 73–74

activating calls with, 77–78

alarms, 82

answering questions, 80–81

benefits, 87

checking investments, 79–80

checking weather, 79–80

control of Clock app, 82

customizing, 71–73

Dictation mode, 75

to-do items, 78

enabling and disabling, 49

entering events into Calendar app, 338–339

entertainment info, 84–86

getting directions, 82–83

getting help from, 74–76

improved capabilities, 6

issuing commands to, 77

Language option, 72

launching apps with, 76

male and female voices, 49

mathematical calculation, 86

movie info, 84–86

Music app, 83–84

Notes app, 84

practicing with, 87

proofreading messages, 87

receiving greeting from, 72

reminders, 78

requirements, 70–71

restaurant info, 84–86

scheduling meetings and events, 81

sending email, 82

sports info, 84–86

text messaging, 79, 301

timers, 82

tips, 75–76, 86–87

Tweets, 86–87

using Location Services with, 70

using with Contacts, 72–73, 76–77

Voice Feedback option, 72

web searches, 80–81

Skype, 221–222

Sleep mode

activating, 18–19

waking up from, 12, 18–19

Slide Over display (iPad), 14–15

slideshows, creating, 217

Slo-Mo option, 193

Smart Keyboard, 17

social networking services

Facebook app, 171–174

Facebook Messenger app, 175–176

Flickr, 169–171

Instagram app, 182–183

Location Services, 168

News Feeds in Facebook app, 177

signing up for, 168

Twitter app, 178–180

Vimeo, 169–171

YouTube app, 180–182

Software Update, 49

songs

adding to playlists, 382–383

"liking," 379

rearranging order of, 384

rewinding, 379

Sounds option, 55–56

speaker volume, adjusting, 56

speakerphone feature, using, 226–227

special effect filters, using in Photos app, 209

spell-checking (virtual keyboard), 13

Split View display (iPad), 15–16

sports info, getting from Siri, 84–86

Spotlight Search feature, 9–10, 22, 49–50, 236

Square shooting mode, 193

Stopwatch app, 61

storage. See iCloud online storage space

Storage & iCloud Usage, 50. See also iCloud functions

streaming

content, 116–117

music, 369–370

music via Internet, 388

video content, 399–400

stylus device

using with iPad Pro, 6

versus virtual keyboard, 17

surfing the Web. See Safari web browser

Swipe gesture, 8

Swipe Up gesture, 9

syncing app-specific data
  with iCloud, 329
  with online-based apps, 328
syncing with iTunes. *See* iTunes Sync process

T

tabbed browsing
  on iPad, 312–314
  with Safari, 310–312
tap gesture, 8
tasks, continuing, 50, 118–120. *See also* multitasking
text messages
  creating and sending, 293–294
  dictating and sending with Siri, 301
  participating in conversations, 297–298
  reading and sending with Siri, 79
  saving, 291
  sending, 289–291
third-party apps, 25. *See also* apps; universal apps
  in-app purchases, 100
  availability through iCloud account, 93
  compatibility with devices, 95–97
  confirming purchases, 92
  downloading and installing, 92–94
  finding, 94–95
  free, 98–99
  getting details about, 96
  getting prices of, 92

paid, 99
restoring and reinstalling, 93
scalability, 92
sharing web content, 321
shopping for, 92, 97
subscription-based, 100
Touch ID sensor, 92
universal type, 93, 96
viewing purchases, 93
thumb, swiping with, 11
Time-Lapse feature, 192–193
Timer feature, 61
timers, setting with Siri, 82
to-do items. *See also* Reminders app
  deleting, 355
  using Siri for, 78
top of screen, returning to, 11
Touch ID & Passcode options, 56. *See also* Passcode Lock feature
Touch ID sensor, 27, 92
transferring files. *See* AirDrop tool
Transit feature, 163–164
True Tone flash, 196. *See also* flash (iPhone)
turn-by-turn directions, 155–159, 161, 165
turning off devices, 18
TV episodes, finding with iTunes Store app, 398–399
TV shows
  acquiring from iTunes Store, 395–399
  finding, 94
  watching with Videos app, 388–395

tweeting photos, 215

tweets

composing, 179

sending via Siri, 86–87

Twitter, account integration, 169–171

Twitter app, 178–180

Twitter option, sharing web content, 321

two-finger gesture (iPad), 10

U

Undo icon, 280

universal apps, 93, 96. *See also* apps;
third-party apps

unlocking Lock screen, 65

unlocking phones, 225–226

Updates command icon, 107

upgrading to iOS 9, 4–5

URLs for web pages, copying, 322

usernames, syncing with iCloud
Keychain, 324–325

V

Vibrate mode, turning on, 55

vibration patterns, customizing, 56, 244

video content, streaming, 399–400

video messages, recording and
sending, 296–297

Video shooting mode, 193

videos. *See also* HD video; movies;
YouTube

editing, 206–208

inserting into email, 278

playing, 390

shooting with Camera app, 190–192

streaming and watching, 369

streaming from mobile devices, 394

watching, 15–17

Videos app, 60

AirPlay option, 394

Captions icon, 394

deleting content from iPhone, 390

exiting, 394

Fast Forward icon, 393–394

launching, 388

onscreen controls, 393

pausing, 394

Rewind icon, 393–394

timers, 393

volume control, 394

Vimeo, account integration, 169–171

VIP List feature, 272, 286

virtual keyboard. *See also* external keyboards; keyboard shortcuts

alternative keys, 13

auto-capitalization, 13

autocorrection, 13

caps lock, 13

creating shortcuts, 14

customizing, 51

versus Dictation mode, 88

displaying and hiding, 13

dividing in half, 12–13

Emoji/Symbols keyboards, 14

enlarging keys, 13

keyboard shortcuts, 13

predictive, 13

spell-checking, 13

splitting (iPad), 13

toggling click sound, 13

unlocking and moving, 13

Virtual Switch, turning on and off, 36

voice recognition. *See* Dictation mode

voicemail

blue dot next to messages, 238

exiting, 239

Greeting screen, 238

listening to, 238

message length, 238

recording outgoing messages, 237

sending calls to, 223

Voice-over-IP phone calls, 221–222

volume, adjusting, 56, 223

volume slider, using with music, 379

W

waking up devices, 12

Wallet app, 22, 26. *See also* Apple Pay

acceptance of, 260

and Apple Pay (iPhone), 58–59

Card Details screen, 257

changing Billing Address, 259

deleting cards from, 259, 261

launching, 259

managing Apple Pay with, 252–253

membership cards, 260–261

reward cards, 260–261

setting default card, 257–258

storing credit and debit cards, 253, 255–259

using, 252–253

Wallpaper

availability, 52

changing, 53

using photos as, 53–54

weather, checking with Siri, 79–80

Web browser. *See* Safari web browser

web content, exporting, 320–322

web pages, switching between (iPhone), 310–312

web searches, using Siri for, 80–81

websites. *See also* Safari web browser

AirPlay speakers, 116

AirPrint printers, 117–118

Apple, 17

Apple ID accounts, 136

Apple Pay, 261

Brookstone, 17

external keyboards, 17

handyPrint, 118

iMovie app, 203

launching favorites quickly, 326

Logitech, 17

Wallet app, 261

Zagg, 17

widgets, in Notification Center, 43

Wi-Fi, 37–39, 60

wireless service providers, 222–223

World Clock app, 61

Y

Yelp! information screens, 147–148, 162–163

YouTube, streaming and watching videos from, 180–182, 369. *See also* videos

Z

Zagg website, 17

zooming in and out, 8

More Best-Selling **My** Books!

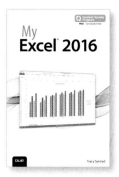

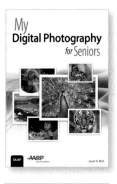

Learning to use your smartphone, tablet, camera, game, or software has never been easier with the full-color My Series. You'll find simple, step-by-step instructions from our team of experienced authors. The organized, task-based format allows you to quickly and easily find exactly what you want to achieve.

Visit quepublishing.com/mybooks to learn more.

REGISTER THIS PRODUCT
SAVE 35%*
ON YOUR NEXT PURCHASE!

How to Register Your Product

- Go to quepublishing.com/register
- Sign in or create an account
- Enter ISBN: 10- or 13-digit ISBN that appears on the back cover of your product

Benefits of Registering

- Ability to download product updates
- Access to bonus chapters and workshop files
- A 35% coupon to be used on your next purchase – valid for 30 days

    To obtain your coupon, click on "Manage Codes" in the right column of your Account page

- Receive special offers on new editions and related Que products

Please note that the benefits for registering may vary by product. Benefits will be listed on your Account page under Registered Products.

We value and respect your privacy. Your email address will not be sold to any third party company.

* 35% discount code presented after product registration is valid on most print books, eBooks, and full-course videos sold on QuePublishing.com. Discount may not be combined with any other offer and is not redeemable for cash. Discount code expires after 30 days from the time of product registration. Offer subject to change.

quepublishing.com